A God's Own Tale

SUNY Series in Chinese Philosophy and Culture
David L. Hall and Roger T. Ames, editors

A God's Own Tale

The *Book of Transformations*
of Wenchang,
the Divine Lord of Zitong

TERRY F. KLEEMAN

State University of New York Press

Published by
State University of New York Press, Albany

© 1994 State University of New York

For information, address State University of New York Press,
State University Plaza, Albany, N.Y. 12246

Production by Cathleen Collins
Marketing by Dana Yanulavich

Library of Congress Cataloging in Publication Data

Kleeman, Terry F., 1955–
    A god's own tale : the Book of transformations of Wenchang, the
Divine Lord of Zitong / Terry F. Kleeman.
        p.   cm. — (SUNY series in Chinese philosophy and culture)
    Contents: Includes bibliographical references and index.
    ISBN 0-7914-2001-9. — ISBN 0-7914-2002-7 (pbk.)
    1. Tzu-t'ung-ti-chün hua shu. 2. Wen-ch'ang (Taoist deity)
    I. Tzu-t'ung-ti-chün hua shu. English. II. Title. III Series.
BL1942.85.W45K56   1994
299'.51482—dc20   93–34016
                                                                         CIP

10 9 8 7 6 5 4 3 2 1

Contents

Illustrations

矯詔軀虎圖

Figure 1. As King of Swordridge Mountain the Divine Lord slays a marauding tiger.

Preface

Wenchang is a god known throughout the Chinese world. Always portrayed as a stern mandarin in formal dress, he sits in judgment on mortal men and writes his verdicts in the Cinnamon Record, a constantly updated ledger of men and their fates as ordained by Heaven and modified by their own moral behavior. He is the patron deity of the literary arts, granting inspiration to poets through the ages but also aiding the lowliest callow student as he prepares for his examinations. He is the personification of Confucianism, often substituting for Confucius on altars, always finding his niche in the Confucian Temple and in the schools, preaching and practicing the cardinal values of filial piety and loyalty. He is a constellation of six stars near the Big Dipper that have received the worship of Chinese emperors for two millennia. But he is so much more.

Wenchang is also the Divine Lord of Zitong, a fearsome protector deity who can summon hordes of fell troops from the netherworld to protect the Chinese state and the Sichuan region. He is Master Zhang of the Northern Ramparts who sends progeny to the devoted and the deserving to carry on their line. He is Master of Enlightening Transformation of the Nine Heavens (*jiutian kaihua zhuzai* 九天開化主宰), a messianic savior who instructs his flock through spirit writing, dreams, and possessed mediums, leading them to virtue in the face of impending apocalyptic disasters.

But long before he received any of these exalted titles, he was the Viper. From his solitary cave atop Sevenfold Mountain, this giant poisonous serpent summoned thunder and storm to do his bidding. The people of Zitong, the town at the foot of his mountain, fearing his thunderous might but needing the life-giving moisture it brought, propitiated him with sacrifice so that his anger might be directed against invaders and other interlopers.

The cult to this multifaceted god is both typical of Chinese deity cults in its re-creation of traditional modes of interaction with the divine and exceptional in the degree to which it brings together all of the major Chinese conceptions of the divine in one figure. Wenchang unites local and national cults, diffuse and institutionalized religion, zoomorphic and anthropomorphic conceptions of deity, and the "Three Teachings" of Daoism, Buddhism, and Confucianism into one faith in a multi-vocal deity who both represents and enforces basic values like filial piety, service to the state, veneration of learning, charity to the less fortunate, and personal transcendence. The origins of this comprehensive, syncretic god are found in the late twelfth century with the appearance of the *Book of Transformations* (*Huashu* 化書).

The introduction to this book will present an overview of the development of the Zitong cult and detail the circumstances of composition of the cult's scriptures. This is the story of how a local cult grew to claim the allegiance of the Chengdu Plain, then all of China; of how a nature spirit developed progressively more complex personae; and how the power of revelation redefined the god and his cult. I have set forth the Song period expansion of the cult in greater detail elsewhere (Kleeman 1993); here I focus on the *Book of Transformations*, attempting to demonstrate how the text took form and how it facilitated this expansion.

In the translation section of this book the god of Zitong presents his own story of how he reached his ultimate position in the divine hierarchy. The *Book of Transformations* is a revealed autobiography of the god, chronicling his origins, his repeated incarnations in human form, the divine offices he held, and his failings and successes along the way. The text is important as the first scripture explicitly revealed through spirit writing, as an early example of autobiography, as a stage in the development of Chinese fiction, and as a unique, early example of the genre of "morality books" (*shanshu* 善書). But more than any of these, the *Book of Transformations* was the defining blueprint for the Wenchang cult, a major force in the religious world of late imperial China.

I present here an integral translation of the seventy-three "transformations" or chapters revealed in 1181. These chapters present a unitary picture of the god that traces his progress through many lives and 1,400 years of Chinese history, culminating in the god's final apotheosis in the fourth century A.D. and assumption of the divine post for which he is best known, head of the Wenchang Palace. The spirit writing group responsible for these seventy-three chapters produced a number of other documents from the hand of the god and together this body of material redefined the god in a number of startling and innovative ways. Modern editions of the *Book of Transformations* include twenty-one chapters revealed to another medium in 1194 and three dating from the mid-thirteenth century. I have omitted this material in the present work because of considerations of space, but also because a focus on the related scriptural products of one medium provides a more detailed and consistent view of the cult. Moreover, the later chapters, which bring the god's career into the Song, raise many difficult historiographic questions and have survived in two significantly different recensions.

The translation is based upon the edition of the *Book of Transformations* reprinted in the *Collected Essentials of the Daoist Canon* (*Daozang jiyao*, hereafter referred to as DZJY) because it is readily available in major research libraries the world over and because it reflects the Song recension of the text. Bibliographic details for this and other editions are provided in the Appendix, "Extant Editions of the *Book of Transformations*." The version in the Ming *Daoist Canon* (*170 Zitong dijun huashu*, hereafter referred to as DZ), while accessible, is a Yuan recension that underwent considerable editing in 1316. On the whole, variants within the first seventy-three "synoptic" chapters that I translate here are minor and seldom yield significantly different translations but the DZ versions of chapters 74 on are quite different, as detailed below (pp. 75–77). All extracanonical editions of the *Book of Transformations*, which survive only as rare books in a handful of collections in London, Paris, Munich, Tokyo, and Boston, are of the Song recension. The earliest, dating to the end of the Ming dynasty (1645), preserves many early readings that were subsequently "corrected" by Qing editors. Another important witness is a lengthy paraphrase of the text by Cao Xuequan 曹學全 (1574–1647) in his *Extensive Record of Sichuan* (*Shuzhong guangji* 蜀中廣記, hereafter referred to as SG).

Translation is always a struggle to maintain fidelity to the original while making the text comprehensible to a modern, nonspecialist audience, and this is particlarly the case in translating from medieval Chinese. In translating the *Book of Transformations* I have tried to keep the translation itself as close as possible to the original without doing harm to English syntax. I have largely resisted the temptation to rewrite the short, parallel sentences of the original into long, flowing English phrases and convert metaphors into Western near-equivalents. To maintain comprehensibility I have adapted a mode of translation first developed by Edward Schafer for the translation of poetry. After the exacting translation of each chapter I append a "Commentary," which paraphrases the original text, filling in gaps in the narrative and explicating imagery while at the same time trying to situate the practices and beliefs described within the context of Chinese religious and social history. I have also adopted from Schafer several of the distinctive translations for which he is famous, particularly for terms whose other translations seem inaccurate. Thus I regularly translate *di* 帝 as "thearch," except when it seems too unwieldly, as in the title *dijun* 帝君, which I translate "Divine Lord," and translate *xian* 仙 as "transcendent" rather than the imprecise "immortal" or Schafer's own overly recondite "sylph."

Many scholars have contributed their insights and corrected my mistakes in this manuscript. First mention must go to Michel Strickmann, now of the University of Bordeau, and Kristofer Schipper of the École Pratique des Hautes Études who guided me in the dissertation of which this translation originally constituted a part. David Keightley and Jeffrey Riegel were also astute readers of the dissertation and saved me from many errors. Other scholars who graciously offered comments on this work include Nathan Sivin, Victor Mair, Susan Naquin, Judith Boltz, Stephen Bokenkamp, Kenneth Dean, Richard von Glahn, Franciscus Verellen, Li Fengmao, Fukui Shigemasa, Yamada Toshiaki, Yusa Noboru, Maruyama Hiroshi, and Romeyn Taylor. Special thanks are due my colleagues at the University of Pennsylvania, who in addition to contributing their wisdom also covered courses and wrote letters that permitted me the leave time and funding to complete this project. All remaining errors are mine and mine alone.

I was supported through the course of this endeavor by a dissertation fellowship from the American Council of Learned Societies and by a grant from the Research Foundation of the University of Pennsylvania. I was fortunate to be granted access to many important libraries around the world. The staffs of the East Asiatic Library of the University of California at Berkeley, the library of the Institut d'Asie of the École Française d'Extrême-Orient, the Institute of Oriental Culture of the University of Tokyo, and the East Asia collection of the University of Pennsylvania were immensely helpful.

Finally none of this would have been possible without the constant support and frequent sacrifice of Faye Yuan Kleeman (Ruan Feinuo) and Alexandra Grace Kleeman.

Abbreviations

Because of the simplified style of reference adopted in this book, there are very few abbreviations. They are:

DZ   *Zitong dijun huashu* 梓潼帝君化書. In the Zhengtong reign period Daozang, Harvard-Yenching Index no. 170, Schipper (1975), no. 170.

DZJY   *Wendi huashu* 文帝化書. Under the character *xing* 星 in the Daozang jiyao 道藏輯要. Printed at Erxian'an 二仙庵 in Cheng-du, 1906.

SG   Extended excerpts and paraphrase of the *Book of Transformations* in *Shuzhong guangji* 蜀中廣記, by Cao Xuequan 曹學全 (1574–1647), (Shanghai: Commercial Press, 1935): 79/28b–50a.

Unless otherwise noted, references to the dynastic histories are to the modern, punctuated editions first published by Zhonghua shuju and since reprinted by numerous publishers, and references to the classics are to the texts in the Harvard-Yenching Index series. Texts from the Daozang are cited in the format adopted by the Projet Tao-tsang, i.e., the serial number of the text in Schipper (1975) followed by the title in romanization (omitting hyphens within semantic units).

圖 攴 化 易 誅

Figure 2. *The God of Thunder Fire prepares to strike down an unfilial daughter-in-law. As the Viper, the god of Zitong may have been pictured similarly, though with serpentine rather than avian features, and may have been equally at the beck and call of the divine administration.*

INTRODUCTION

Early History of the Cult

The cult to the god later known as Wenchang began in a small town in northern Sichuan called Zitong 梓潼 for the catalpa trees (*zi*) that dot its hills and the Tong river that winds sinuously through its valley. Nestled in the foothills of the Swordridge Mountains that separate the Wei River Valley and the Chengdu Plain, Zitong was subject to terrible storms in which thunder and lightning seemed to crash down from the surrounding hills and peaks. There was one mountain in particular, a few miles north of town, that the people of Zitong thought to be the source of the terrifying thunder, and of the much-needed rain that accompanied it. It came to be called Sevenfold Mountain for the seven turns in the road leading up its ridge, curves cut by a giant venomous snake called the Viper who lived in a cave high atop the mountain and spoke through the thunderclap. The people of the town may have worshiped the snake from Neolithic times but the historical record begins with the fourth-century *Record of the Land of Huayang* (*Huayangguo zhi* 華陽國志) of Chang Qu 常璩, the earliest surviving history of the Sichuan area and one of the first works of regional history in China.[1] The entry for the county of Zitong reads as follows:[2]

---

1. *Huayangguo zhi jiaozhu*, 1. The text was written sometime after 347.
2. Huayangguo zhi, 3/22; Huayangguo zhi jiaozhu, Liu Lin ed., 3/145. Later citations will refer to these two editions.

Zitong county. Seat of the commandery government. Established in the first year of the Yuanding reign period of Emperor Wu of Han (116 B.C.). There is located Five Wives Mountain (*Wufu shan* 五婦 山),[3] the place where of old the Five Stalwarts of Shu dragged out the snake, causing the mountain to collapse. There is the Shrine of the Good Board (*Shanban ci* 善板祠),[4] also called Ezi 蚕子 ("the viper").[5] Every year the people offer up ten "thunder shuttles" (*leizhu* 雷杼); by the end of the year they are nowhere to be seen. They say that the thunder has taken them away.

Eight hundred years later, when the god himself, having undergone numerous transformations, was able to reveal his life story, his primary terrestrial home was still atop the mountain and he was still striking down evildoers by casting the magical "thunder shuttles." These potent projectiles found near places where lightning has struck were either slivers of lightning-shattered rock or clumps of vitrified sand formed by the force of the lightning bolt.[6] Elsewhere in China they were called "thunder stones" (*leishi* 雷石), "thunderclap axes" (*pilifu* 霹靂斧), or "thunderclap wedges" (*piliqi* 楔).[7] Through the ritualized return of these numinous objects the people of Zitong simultaneously reproduced and regulated the magical power of their deity.

In this fourth century account the cult has already claimed for its god a role in a key Sichuanese myth cycle, that of the Five Stalwarts (*wuding* 五 丁).[8] These five he-men performed feats of strength and valor for King Kaiming 開明王 (ca. fourth century B.C.), the last king of the independent state of Shu, but with their aid the king pursued frivolous and wanton pro-

---

3. Five Wives Mountain is north of modern Zitong. See Zang Lihe 1936: 118.1.

4. The meaning of this name is unclear and I have found no other example of its use. Maspero (n.d.: 311) apparently takes it to refer to the shrine itself, for he says that the temple on Sevenfold Mountain is made of wooden boards. It is much more likely that the characters *shanban* constitute an echoic binome, perhaps of local Sichuan origin, referring to snakes in general or one specific variety of snake. Another possibility is that Shan Ban was the personal name of the god. The god of the nearby Western Marchmount (i.e., Mount Hua 華山) is surnamed Shan. See *Wuyue zhenxing tu* 五嶽眞形圖, quoted in *Gujin tushu jicheng*, "Shenyidian" 神異典 24, 491/2a2.

5. This character *e* 蚕, "viper," is very rare and all later sources, with the exception of the *Beimeng suoyan* (quoted, *Taiping guangji* 458: 11), have adopted the more common homophone *e* 惡, "evil," or have further modified it to *ya* 亞, "secondary." See Ding Fubao 1959: 10/914, p. 8846, for a detailed discussion of the original character.

6. I owe the latter suggestion to Robert Chard of Oxford University.

7. Feng Yan discusses these objects in *Fengshi wenjian ji jiaozheng*, 21–24. This topic is explored in greater depth in Kleeman 1988: 10–12.

8. This myth cycle is described in detail in the Commentary to chapters 44–48.

jects that led to the loss of his throne and the first colonization of Sichuan. The five are said, for example, to have erected a giant tumulus for the king's dead favorite and hauled huge stone oxen reputed to defecate gold across the mountains and into the capital. Steven F. Sage (1992: 111) characterizes the King Kaiming of these stories as "tragically fated to fail . . . the victim of his own unrestrained passions" and the Stalwarts are even more ambiguous in character, seemingly heroic figures who are ultimately responsible for the destruction and subjugation of their native land. The Stalwarts' final mision was to escort to Shu five maidens, gifts from the King of Qin, who hoped thereby to distract the king of Shu while Qin planned its invasion. The serpent-god of Zitong thwarted these plans by bringing his mountain down upon the heads of both Stalwarts and maidens.

The cult's early development was due, in part, to the location of this mountain. It lies on what was the main road connecting Sichuan and its capital Chengdu with the national capital Chang'an (modern Xian, Shaan-xi) and the North China Plain. The temple complex, from at least Song times on, actually straddled the road with buildings and pavilions on either side. The mountain's god was therefore the first divine representative of the Sichuan region that any foreign traveler or invading army encountered and its first line of defense against invasion. This protective function is evident in the story of the Five Stalwarts and crucial, as well, to the next element of cult lore, the tale of Yao Chang.

Yao Chang 姚萇 (330–393) was a fourth-century Qiang military leader who briefly ruled his own state but is best known for killing the Former Qin ruler Fu Jian 苻堅 (338–385), who had once threatened to conquer all of China.[9] The earliest version of Yao's encounter with the god is probably the following passage from the *Spring and Autumn Annals of the Sixteen Kingdoms* (*Shiliu guo chunqiu* 十六國春秋):[10]

When (Yao) Chang followed Yang An in invading the Shu region, he once took a nap during the daytime by a stream. Above him there was a divine radiance shining brightly, and those about him all remarked on this. Advancing to the Zitong ridge, (Yao) saw a man, who said to him, "You, sir, should quickly return to Qin. Qin has no ruler. It will fall upon you (to become ruler)." Chang asked him his name. He replied, "Zhang Ezi." After he had finished speaking, he disappeared.

---

9. Yao Chang's biography is found in *Jinshu* 106/2964–73. It is interesting to note that Yao's wife's maiden name was She 蛇 ("snake"). On Fu Jian, see Rogers 1966.

10. *Shiliu guo chunqiu jibu* 50/379.

When Yao had occupied Jin territory and proclaimed himself emperor, he established a temple to His Excellency Zhang at that place to offer sacrifices to him.[11]

In this tale the god has a human form and identity, and has been given the Chinese surname Zhang 張, a choice that was to have great significance as the cult progressed. In later versions of the encounter, dating to no later than the ninth century, the god bestows upon Yao Chang a *ruyi* scepter that gives Yao control over otherworldly troops.[12] Whatever the exact origins of this tale (one suspects that Yao Chang or his supporters had a hand in its formulation), the anthropomorphization of the god to which it attests was a major step in cult development. The god was now human in form and implicitly a "human god" (*renshen* 人神) or divinized dead human.[13] This was an important consideration for elite promoters of the cult who desired that it conform to traditional standards of orthodoxy.

Canonical expositions of religion insisted that worship of "gods of mountains and streams" be restricted to the highest levels of the administration, that is, in the feudal system that prevailed when they were formulated, to the feudal lords who owed nominal fealty to the Zhou king but were the effective rulers.[14] In such codes the ruled were limited to worshiping their ancestors and tutelary deities. Provision was made, however, for sacrifice to local figures who had in some way contributed to the community, as in the following passage from the *Record of Rites* (*Liji*), a Han compilation of Warring States (403–221 B.C.) ritual codes:[15]

When the sage kings established the sacrifices, if a man had promul-

---

11. This passage is, according to Tang Qiu, found only in the Ming reconstructed edition of Tu Qiaosun 屠喬孫. Tang Qiu accuses Tu of including too much material in his reconstruction, but Tang bases himself on an admittedly abridged version. In short, there is no way to determine if this passage is an authentic portion of the *Shiliu guo chunqiu* that was deleted from the Sui abridged edition but preserved in some other source, or an extraneous addition by Tu. It does, as I argue below, present a simpler image of the god that suggests it is relatively early. If this passage ultimately derives from some work other than the *Shiliuguo chunqiu*, it is unclear what that work would be. Rogers characterizes Tu's work as a combination of the "chronicle" (*zaiji* 載記) accounts of the *Jinshu* and relevant portions of the *Zizhi tongjian*, but neither source contains this passage, and it is quite different from all other versions of the tale that I have seen. Cf. Rogers 1966: 19–22.

12. This aspect of the tale is first alluded to by Li Shangyin (813–858), *Quan Tang shi* 539/6171. In his *Jinshu* (106/2972) biography Yao has a prophetic dream in which the deceased Fu Jian attacks with just such "demon troops" (*guibing* 鬼兵).

13. For the term *renshen*, see *Hou Hanshu* 13/514.

14. *Liji zhengyi*, "Wangzhi," 12/16a–b. Cf. *Liji zhushu*, "Quli," 5/17a.

15. *Liji zhengyi*, "Jifa," 46/14b.

gated a legal code for the masses, then they sacrificed to him; if a man had died in performance of his duties, then they sacrificed to him; if a man had through his efforts brought stability to the state, then they sacrificed to him; if a man had been able to fend off great calamities, then they sacrificed to him; if he could forestall major problems, then they sacrificed to him.

Throughout imperial times this passage was used as justification for incorporating new gods with important local followings into the canon of acceptable objects of worship. To apply this passage, however, required that the god in question have been a historical figure with significant accomplishments to his credit. Fearsome zoomorphic figures like the Viper did not qualify.

One important route through which dead humans came to receive sacrifice and eventually enter the pantheon was to die in battle. Although worship of such figures might actually originate in attempts to placate a disturbed and potentially harmful soul after a violent death, a dead warrior could be considered to have "died in performance of his duties" and perhaps even to have "brought stability to the state" and "fend[ed] off great calamities." We do not know when this standard was first applied to the Viper, but by the tenth century the god of Zitong was identified as a fallen war hero[16] and poets sung his praises.[17]

Confirmation for the anthropomorphization of the god by the mideighth century is found in official titles granted the god by two Tang emperors. In China, temporal rulers often sought an accommodation with local divinities by bestowing upon them imperial titles and ennoblements. The deity was given a fixed position within the hierarchy of the Sacrificial Canon, and the local representative of the central government was charged with the supervision of his worship. To the local cult, such honors constituted a marked increase in prestige, and conferred certain perquisites commensurate with the rank of the title bestowed.[18]

Both these examples of canonization of the Divine Lord of Zitong came

---

16. *Taiping huanyu ji* 84/7a.

17. See Song Qi's "Zhang Ezi miao" 張蜑子廟 in *Jingwen ji* 8/91, and the poem by Li Shangyin and Wang Duo cited in notes 12 and 22.

18. The best study to date of the canonization process is Hansen (1990: 79–104), though her assertion (p. 79) that it became common only in the eleventh century is open to question. The two examples discussed below, which have their origin in direct imperial attention, do not fit Hansen's model well, but the god's later titles were probably acquired in a way very similar to those cited in her examples.

when internal rebellion had threatened the throne and led the embattled emperor to seek aid in any quarter. When Emperor Xuanzong 玄宗 (r. 712–756) fled to Sichuan following the rebellion of An Lushan, Zhang Ezi is said to have appeared to him, and Xuanzong conferred upon him the title Chancellor of the Left (*zuo cheng* 左丞).[19] A century later Emperor Xizong 僖宗 (r. 874–888) again fled to Sichuan in the face of a mounting rebellion. In 881, as he was entering Sichuan, the god Zhang Ezi manifested himself before the emperor at Jiebo Ting 桔柏亭 in Li 利 province.[20] As a result Zhang was ennobled as the King Rescuing the Obedient (*Jishun Wang* 濟順王). The emperor personally visited his temple and, unbuckling his sword, bestowed it upon Zhang Ezi.[21] Wang Duo 王鐸 (?–884), Lesser Tutor to the Heir Apparent, accompanied the emperor and was eyewitness to the event. He composed the following poem, entitled "Visiting the Zhang Ezi Temple at Zitong," to commemorate it:[22]

> The sage emperor of thriving Tang unbelts his "Green Reed,"[23]
> To establish the fame of the newly enfeoffed Rescuer of the Obedient.
> In the rain at night the dragon discards the three foot scabbard,
> Amidst spring clouds the phoenix enters the Nine-storied Fortress[24]
> At Sword Gate the auspicious ethers move in response to the thunder,
> The clear brightness of Jade Rampart Mountain awaits the
>   suppression of the bandits.[25]
> Report to the various generals and ministers east of the barrier only
> That achievements that will reach to Heaven depend on otherworldly
>   troops.

---

19. This event is recorded in many sources, but I have been unable to find any record of it in the dynastic histories of the Tang. It is perhaps not surprising that official record keeping should break down in this time of disorder. See *Song huiyao jigao*, "Li" 20/55b, where we are told that the god came out to welcome Xuanzong at Wanli Qiao 萬里橋 (south of modern Huayang county, see Zang 1936: 1051.2). This tale was part of the lore surrounding the Divine Lord of Zitong that was incorporated into the *Book of Transformations*. Cf. chapter 78 of the translation below.

20. Probably to be identified with Jiebo Ford, northeast of Zhaohua county, Sichuan. Zang 1936: 716.1.

21. See *Taiping huanyu ji* 84/7a; *Tang shi jishi* 65/983.

22. This poem is found in *Quan Tang shi* 557/6461; *Tang shi jishi* 65/983; and *Sichuan tongzhi* 37/43b.

23. Green Reed was a famous sword of antiquity. See *Baopuzi* 38/167.

24. The term Nine-storied Fortress can have more exalted referents in the Taoist heavens, but here it refers to the capital. The *Tang shi jishi*, 65/983, notes that at the time both the popular sentiment, confirmed by the diviners, was that the emperor would be able to return to the capital in spring.

25. Jade Rampart Mountain (Yulei shan 玉壘山) is southeast of modern Lifan, Sichuan. See Zang 1936: 237.2.

In this poem the god of Zitong, responding to Xizong's earnest entreaty, takes dragon form to smite the evildoers himself with the newly acquired imperial blade, but also dispatches supernatural soldiers to aid in suppressing the rebels and restoring Xizong to his throne. This military power, already foreshadowed in later versions of the Yao Chang tale, accords well with his identity as a fallen warrior.

In 1004 the god was further honored for aid in suppressing a local Sichuanese rebellion with the title King of Heroic Prominence (*yingxian wang* 英顯王), the first of a series of Song (960–1289) ennoblements.[26] In 1132 his title was increased by the addition of the two characters "martially valorous" (*wulie* 武烈) for bringing to an end a popular rebellion that had claimed the life of the Commandant of Lu Prefecture 瀘州帥 (Sichuan).[27] In these tales the cult clearly allies with the central government against all local and refractory forces, thus paving the way for the god's acceptance as a national figure transcending his local origins.

The god of Zitong was a powerful protector deity, but what truly set him apart from other gods of the day was the facility he developed for communication. Chinese gods communicate with their followers in a number of ways: through direct spirit possession, through dreams, and through divinatory techniques like oracle slips, moonblocks, and the like, responding to inquiries concerning health, longevity, worldly success, and eschatological fate. Although the god of Zitong must have responded to questions in a variety of ways from very early on, early references to cult activity mention spirit possession and physical manifestation in human form. In sources from the Northern Song, the god expresses his approval of aspiring examination candidates through great storms, but also speaks directly, if sometimes enigmatically, to the candidates in dreams. This marked the beginning of a conversation between Wenchang and his adherents that continues to this day, a conversation in which the god both answers specific questions and gives long, rambling lectures on correct moral behavior.

These two trends—anthropomorphization and communication—culminate in the late twelfth century in a series of revelations from the god. These revelations, which depended on a comparatively new oracular technique, spirit writing, dramatically redefined the cult and its god. Among these revealed texts was the *Book of Transformations*. The next section will provide some background concerning this new mantic technology.

---

26. *Song huiyao gao*, "Li" 20/55a–b.

27. *Tingshi* 3/1a–b. The Divine Lord is said to have materialized in the midst of the rebel leaders to pronounce his doom upon any who did not surrender immediately.

Spirit Writing

The *Book of Transformations* was created through an oracular technique called *fuji* 扶乩 ("wielding the stylus") or *fuluan* 扶鸞 ("wielding the phoenix"), usually translated in English as "spirit writing" or "planchette." A god is thought to descend into the brush or other writing implement held by one or more spirit mediums and through it predict the future, diagnose illness, write magical charms, and issue moral exhortations. Spirit writing has been an important means by which man and god communicated in China for the last millennium.[28]

The origins of spirit writing in China are not well documented. Some have claimed that the fourth-century Maoshan revelations were in fact effected in this manner, but evidence is inconclusive and descriptions in the *Declarations of the Perfected* 眞誥 suggest rather a waking vision that the recipient later transcribed.[29] If the Maoshan revelations were revealed through spirit writing, they would be the earliest direct antecedent to the *Book of Transformations*. Other early scriptures were found hidden in caves or revealed in dreams and recorded upon waking.[30]

The earliest indisputable references to the practice of spirit writing date from the tenth century. A good description of a divination performed in an informal setting is found in the *Record of Investigations of the Divine* (*Jishen lu* 稽神錄) of Xu Xuan 徐鉉 (917–992):[31]

> In Jiangzuo (the area south of the Yangzi River) there was a certain Zhi Jian支戩, who hailed from Yugan 餘干 (Jiangxi). For generations his family had been minor clerks. In his generation, Jian was unique

---

28. The primary source for the study of early spirit writing is the accounts collected by Xu Dishan in his *Study of the Spirit Writing Superstition* (*Fuji mixin de yanjiu*, 1941) which in turn draws upon the section on spirit writing in *Collected Ancient and Modern Books* (*Gujin tushu jicheng*, "Shenyidian," ch. 310). Earlier studies like Zhao Weibang 1942 have been largely superseded by Jordan and Overmyer 1986. The following discussion draws heavily upon Xu and Jordan and Overmyer (especially the historical overview in 3/36–63). Citations below will refer to Xu's work in the format "Xu #", the # being the serial number applied to each account. All sources have been traced back to original editions wherever possible, but these sources will be cited only when the text is translated or when a significant discrepancy has been found between Xu and the original.

29. This claim was made most recently by Hu Fuchen (1989: 58). The relevant passage is *1016 Zhengao* 眞誥 19/9b, where we read, "Lady Wei transmitted them to her disciple . . . Mr. Yang, causing him to write them out in clerk script."

30. Bokenkamp (1986) relates the discovery of the *Preface to the Five Talismans of the Numinous Jewel* (*Lingbao wufu xu* 靈寶五符序) in a cave. Li Shi 李石, a twelfth-century devotee of the Wenchang cult, received the text of the *Tract on Retribution of the Most High* through a dream. See Yoshioka 1952: 74; Brokaw 1991: 41.

31. *Jishen lu* 6/14b. Cf. Jordan and Overmyer 1986: 43.

in his fondness for learning and composition and ventured to style himself "Flowering Talent."[32] It was the night of the full moon of the first month, when the common people of the day divined by dressing up the grain winnowing basket in clothing, sticking a chopstick in its mouth, and having it draw in a pan of flour. Jin observed members of his household doing this and playfully intoned, "I beg to divine what office Flowering Talent Zhi will one day attain." It then drew the characters *sikong* 司空 (Minister of Works) in the flour.

The god invoked in this séance was undoubtedly the Purple Lady 紫姑, goddess of the privy. Her role in divination is ancient. In the earliest surviving record of her worship, the fifth-century *Garden of Marvels* (*Yiyüan* 異苑) of Liu Jingshu 劉敬叔 (d. ca. 468), she is already associated with this night of the first full moon of the New Year:[33]

> There is a Purple Lady god abroad in the world. A tradition handed down from antiquity states that she was the concubine of a man whose primary wife was jealous of her. The wife would always assign her the dirty jobs. On the fifteenth day of the first month she died of anxiety. For this reason people today make an effigy of her on this day. At night in the privy or beside the pigpen they summon her, chanting, "Zixu 子胥 [the husband] is not here; Lady Cao 曹姑 [the primary wife] has also gone home. The little lady can come out and play." When the one holding the image feels it become heavy, then the god has arrived. They set out wine and fruits and as soon as they notice the face shining and taking on color, it begins to jump about ceaselessly. It can divine all sorts of things, predict the future of the silk crop, and is also adept at guessing riddles. When the answer is good, then it dances exaggeratedly; when the answer is bad, it sleeps facing up.

Although we have no direct evidence for this, it seems safe to assume that the Purple Lady began to communicate through the more expressive means of spirit writing sometime during the Tang. It would have been easy to see in the goddess's ecstatic dancing the outlines of a character, then conclude that the goddess was trying to communicate.

---

32. This term originally referred to individuals recommended for government service. By Song times it became an alternate term for examination candidates in the Metropolitan Examination. See Hucker 1985: 2633.

33. Xu #2, p. 11. On the *Garden of Marvels*, see Wang Guoliang 1984: 322–23.

The Purple Lady was approached on a variety of topics and often responded in poetry that won the praise of literati. It seems that the medium,
particularly in these early examples, was often a low-status female within a
gentry household. In such cases the elegance of the revealed poetry was held
up as evidence for the authenticity of the revelatory event. Zhou Mi 周密
(1232–1308) tells of a retainer skilled in spirit writing whom he tested by
demanding a heptasyllable regulated verse on a set topic. Zhou concludes
that even assuming the retainer could have written the verse, he could not
have done so as rapidly as the god had.[34]

A variety of other gods and transcendents manifest through the planchette. Perhaps because many of the mediums were female, female transcendents and lower-level female divinities (serving maids to the Jade Thearch,
etc.) are common. These minor deities on the margins of the sacred world
aroused some suspicion in the minds of literati. Many goddesses speak out
in defense of their honor, as did Transcendent Lady He 何仙姑 and the
Divine Woman of Mount Shamanka 巫山神女, who denied rumored affairs
with Lü Dongbin and King Xiang of Chu 楚襄王 respectively (Xu 23, 24).
The Purple Lady herself, as one might expect from her impure associations,
was neither entirely respectable nor always reliable. We see this view
reflected in a story from the renowned poet Su Shi's *Dongpo's Forest of
Intentions* (*Dongpo zhilin* 東坡志林):[35]

> In the ninth month of the first year of Shaosheng (1094), I visited
> Guangzhou and paid a call on the Great Master Exalting the Way
> (Chongdao dashi 崇道大師) He Deshun 何德順. A divine being de-
> scended into his room, saying she was a female transcendent. Rhapso-
> dies and poems were immediately produced that were exceptional and
> free of mundane words. Some had doubts because they had been
> transmitted through the winnowing basket, a device used by the god-
> dess the Purple Lady. But if you savor the words, you will find they
> are not something the Purple Lady could have created.

While not openly hostile, the tone of this passage is deprecatory, suggesting that the Purple Lady was not possessed of exceptional literary skill. But
the Purple Lady was far from the worst spirit who might manifest through
the planchette. In the same passage, Su goes on to note that the appearance

---

34. See "The great transcendent writes poetry" (*Daxian bi shi* 大仙筆詩), dated 1291, in Zhou Mi,
Guixin zazhi, bieji, shang, 259.

35. *Dongpo zhilin* 3/96.

of ghosts from the hells, birds, and animals is not to be remarked upon, since "curious hedonistic dilettantes" always followed the worthy ministers and great officials who were the intended respondents. Xu Dishan has collected tales recording communications by a woman who had hanged herself and another who had committed suicide rather than be raped and who lay still in a common grave (Xu 26, 27). These revealing deities are restless spirits and potential malefactors.

The preferred respondent to the diviner's supernatural summons was a more respectable figure. But even a concerted attempt to invoke a respectable divinity could go awry when confronted with an impish sprite, as in this late Qing story by Wu Chichang 吳熾昌 (b. 1870):[36]

> A group of students had gathered at a phoenix [spirit writing] altar to ask their fortunes. The phoenix wrote, "Drunkard Zhao 趙酒鬼 has arrived." They all cursed him, saying, "We invited Transcendent Lü. How dare a savage ghost interfere! We are going to request that the great transcendent's sword behead you!" The phoenix halted, then began again, writing, "The Daoist Dongbin happened to be passing by. What do you want to ask?" The students solemnly bowed twice, then asked about their fates in the examination. The phoenix wrote, "Rub more ink." Thereupon each person prepared ink on his inkstone and in a moment they had filled a bowl. Kneeling, they asked how they should use it. The phoenix said, "You students divide it up and drink it, then hear my pronouncement." They all divided the ink and drank it. When they had finished, the phoenix wrote in large characters, "Normally you do not study; now you drink ink at the last moment. I am not Patriarch Lü; I am still Drunkard Zhao!" The students were mortified and destroyed the altar.

The god invoked in this story is Lü Dongbin 呂洞賓, one of the Eight Transcendents and a special object of devotion by Complete Perfection Daoists, alchemists, pharmacists, and many others. In tales of his manifestations he is an enigmatic, trickster-like figure who speaks in riddles and is usually recognized only after he has disappeared.[37] Perhaps because this aspect of his character accords well with an oracular role in which not all information can or should be revealed to the supplicant, he has long been one of the most popular of the gods speaking through spirit writing.

---

36. *Kechuang xianhua* 1/14a; Xu 54.
37. On Lü Dongbin, see Baldrian-Hussein 1986.

Although early accounts of spirit writing tend to center on simple divination, another use for this oracular technique soon developed. Mao Xianglin 毛祥麟 (fl. 1870) distinguishes two types of planchette writing groups:[38]

> There are those who transmit talismans and registers. Always late at night when the populace has settled in for the night they burn talismans and chant spells. The god then descends into the planchette and they ask it about the lucky and unlucky. Often these prove to be correct. Nowadays everyone establishes cults worshiping the gods. They make no use of talismans and spells. They only establish an altar, chant scriptures, and heal the sick. They do not talk about good and bad fortune. Most of their statements encourage one to do good and they use them to collect donations, saying that they will do all kinds of good works.

Mao, influenced by the more topical, pragmatic divinations recorded in literati notebooks, clearly saw this latter type of spirit writing-centered religious group as a recent development, but this was not the case. The *Book of Transformations* is the product of just such a devotional group; hence they must date from no later than the twelfth century. Modern spirit writing groups are direct descendants of this tradition and continue to produce voluminous amounts of ethical tracts. Most of these groups, like the Zitong cult in the Song, also practice divinatory spirit writing, responding to the questions of believers on a variety of topics both mundane and spiritual.

One might imagine that literati members of such a group would take a directing but somewhat removed position, avoiding trance and possession in order to preserve their dignity and status. There is evidence, however, that the line between scholar-official and trance medium was narrower than this, and that there was social mobility between the two groups. Hong Mai tells of a certain Chen Wenshu who "had studied to be a scholar when young" (*xiao xi ruye* 小習儒業). Chen learns spirit writing skills and soon is producing "a thousand words every time his pen touched paper." In the end Chen is abandoned by his possessing spirit and returns to the life of a scholar.[39]

Direct communication with the divine is empowering, and power represents a threat to the established order. Officials like Mao Xianglin were concerned with the political implications of spirit writing groups, but suspicion of such bands with their nocturnal planchette sessions and secret rites was

---

38. *Moyu lu* 6/92.
39. *Yijian zhi, Sanzhi, xin* 10/1463; Xu 15.

not limited to traditional literati. The thirteenth-century *Dialogic Treatise of the Perfected Bai Haiqiong* (*Haiqiong Bai Zhenren yulu* 海瓊白眞人語錄) records the following comment from the Daoist ritual specialist Bai Yuchan (fl. 1209–24):[40]

> Some take the secret spells of exorcists and mediums and mix them up with the true Law. Some take the spirit writings of divine beings and call them secret transmissions. When you ask them about this, they say it accords with ritual regulations (*ke* 科). If you distinguish them [from other scriptures], they maintain they are true oral transmissions. Alas, this is an error of the heretical adept, not a fault of the common people.

Spirit writing was a potent force promoting religious innovation in traditional China. Because the gods communicated directly rather than through churchly intermediaries, their pronouncements were to some degree self-legitimizing. Bai is concerned that new scriptures created through spirit writing will be accepted even though they never passed through an orthodox line of transmission. As we shall see, the Zitong cult is a prime example of a religious tradition founded on just such newly revealed material.

Spirit Writing in the Zitong Cult

The cult to the Divine Lord of Zitong supplies us with unique information concerning the role of spirit writing in religious contexts during the Sung. But first, let us review briefly the other means by which the god of Zitong communicated with his worshipers.

In the earliest tales the god manifests physically to interact with the temporal world. This was the case in the earliest myth of the god in human form, the tale of his encounter with the fourth-century warlord Yao Chang. It was still the case in 1004, when the god appeared on the city walls of Chengdu to aid in the suppression of a rebellion. An inscription from 1207 records the god's continuing practice of appearing in human form throughout the Sichuan area. These avatars were, however, rare and, if tales of the transcendent Lü Dongbin are any measure, the faithful could not be assured of identifying the god until it was too late and he had returned to the sacred realm.

From at least the eleventh and twelfth centuries the god became known for his accuracy in predicting and determining the results of the civil service examination. A number of tales from twelfth-century sources describe ex-

---

40. *1307 Haiqiong Bai Zhenren yulu* 2/15a–b. On this scripture, see Boltz 1987: 177.

amination candidates who pass by the Zitong temple, pay obeisance to the god, and are rewarded with information concerning the examination or with successful performance on the exam. Cai Tao 蔡絛 (?–1126) tells how the god used the forces of nature to make manifest his prediction.[41]

> Leaving Chang'an toward the west, on the road to Shu, there is the shrine to the God of Zitong, which has long been acclaimed most extraordinary. When an official passes by it, if he can obtain a send-off of wind and rain, he will certainly reach the office of Prime Minister. If a Jinshi-degree candidate passes by and gets wind and rain, then he will certainly place first on the Palace Examination. It is said that since antiquity this has never proved false. There once was a Wang Tixing 王提刑 who, when passing by the temple, encountered a great wind. Wang grew proud of heart because of this, but only in his case was the prognostication not realized. At the time Prime Minister Jiefu 介甫 (i.e., Wang Anshi 王安石, 1021–86), eight or nine years of age, was traveling in attendance upon his father. Only later was it realized that the send-off of wind and rain was for Jiefu.
>
> While the Duke of Lu (i.e., Yan Zhenqing 顏眞卿, 709–85) was in command of Chengdu, one day he was summoned back to the capital. He encountered a great storm, and nearly twenty inches of water covered level places. Subsequently he rose to the highest office.
>
> The Prime Minister He Wenzhen[42] also had a dream which said, "You will indeed be first in the Palace Examination. The topic of the emperor's question will be the Dao. When Wenzhen reached the capital he happened to get a copy of the Scripture of the Way and its Virtue annotated by the emperor, and day and night he studied it exhaustively. When it came time for the examination the topic of the exam question was in fact the Dao and he placed first in the Palace Examination.

The expression of the god's will through storm is no doubt a carryover from his original identity as a thunder god. The opening passage implies that the location of the temple on the road from Chengdu to the capital at

---

41. See *Tieweishan congtan* 4/11b–12a. Other examination tales are found in *Yijian zhi, ding,* 8/606; *Yijian zhi, jia* 18/158. Cf. Kleeman 1988: 43–48, where these accounts are examined in detail.

42. I.e., He Li 何桌 (1089–1127). He placed first on the examinations of 1115 and held a variety of offices, including Vice Director of the Esotericariat, which Hucker (1985: 395, entry 4826) characterizes "as de facto head of the government." It is said that after the fall of the capital in 1127 he starved himself to death. See *Songshi* 353: 11135–36; *Zhongguo lishi dacidian: Songshi*: 215.

Chang'an was a key factor in the development of the god's reputation as a patron of the examinations. Such tales demonstrate both the god's growing oracular reputation and his increasing popularity among the educated elite.

In the final tale related by Cai Tao the god revealed himself in a dream; other stories set in the eleventh century also record dreams in which the god appears to answer (or hint at the answer to) inquiries.[43] This type of somnambulent communication occurs in the *Book of Transformations* (ch. 53) and remains an important means by which the god communicates with supplicants throughout cult history. A specialized structure for those seeking incubatory dreams, the Terrace of Answering Dreams (Yingmengtai 應夢臺), was part of the Zitong temple complex from at least the late Song (it is said that Tang Emperor Xuanzong made use of this facility when visiting the temple in the eighth century) and remains a popular tourist site today. There is even a late comment to the effect that a version of the *Scripture of the Great Grotto* was transmitted by the god in a dream.[44]

Another means by which the faithful might make inquiry of the god was oracle slips (*qian* 籤). Oracle slips are strips of bamboo or other wood on which is printed or engraved either a short oracular statement or a reference to a specific entry in a list of such statements.[45] The Zitong cult developed its own set of oracle slips after demands for this type of divination grew too great and priests were forced to resort to slip sets revealed by other gods. This set of slips, now preserved in the Daoist canon (*1299 Xuanzhen lingying baoqian*), is of uncertain date, but probably derives from the Yuan period.[46]

---

43. Cf. *Yijian zhi, ding* 丁, 8/606, and *jia* 甲, 18/158.

44. This comment comes in an annotation to the *Original Biography of Thearch Wen* (*Wendi benzhuan* 文帝本傳) in DZJY, sub *xing* 星, 8/2b. Although the *Original Biography* and its comment may be quite old, it might also be as late as 1908, the date of printing of DZJY. This passage may refer to the new collation of the *Scripture of the Great Grotto* revealed in 1302, but the language used in describing this revelation (*jiangshu* 降書) suggests spirit writing as the means of revelation. See 5 *Taishang wuji zongzhen Wenchang dadong xianjing* 1/5a.

45. A number of sets of oracle slips have been published by Banck (1976) and by Sakai, Imai, and Yoshimoto (1992). The best study of these texts and their use remains Strickmann's unpublished paper (1983).

46. A reference in the preface (1b) to the "ninety-eight transformations" of the Divine Lord indicates that the text cannot antedate the revelation of 1267. Other elements of the preface, including mention of the *Esoteric Biography of Qinghe* but not the *Book of Transformations* and mention of dream divination but no spirit writing as predecessor to the oracle slips, suggest an early date. The text can be no later than 1367 for it is mentioned in a stele of that date. See the "Record on the Traveling Shrine to Wenchang" ("Wenchang xingci ji" 文昌行祠記) in *Shanyou shike congbian* 40/29a–32a.

Despite these diverse modes of communicating with the god of Zitong, the cult adopted spirit writing as its primary means of revelation. We have seen that spirit writing had been in wide use for at least two centuries by the time of the revelations of Liu Ansheng, but there is no earlier record of its use in formal religious settings.[47] This is probably more an accident of the historical record than an accurate reflection of the religious practice of the time. Still, it is significant that the texts revealed to Liu Ansheng are the earliest surviving scriptures explicitly acknowledged to have been effected through spirit writing. If the Zitong cult had been the first to use this method for revealing scripture we should expect some attack upon the cult for this innovation, or at least an attempt within the revealed material to defend the practice, and these are wholly lacking, but the Zitong cult must have been one of the first to use it so effectively.

Spirit writing has certain advantages over other methods of revelation. McCreery (1973: 34–40), describing contemporary religious practice on Taiwan, makes some interesting points concerning the privileged position of spirit writing revelation vis-à-vis oral revelation. He notes that spirit writing revelation usually originates with celestial gods rather than the lower-level gods of the terrestrial administration that communicate through oral revelation, that it occurs at fixed times within institutionalized settings, and that it is analogous to "access by way of proper bureaucratic channels." Although some of these characteristics may have arisen because of spirit writing performed within highly ritualized settings by organized religious groups, the literate character of this mantic technology was surely one element in its adoption by the Zitong cult.

The next section will introduce a series of spirit writing-generated texts that were to change forever the nature and fate of the Zitong cult.

The Revelation to Liu Ansheng

By at least the latter half of the twelfth century the Divine Lord of Zitong had begun to communicate through the planchette as well. It is possible to reveal a message or text in a dream that the recipient records on waking, as in the case of the *Ledger of Merit and Demerit of the Transcendent*

---

47. Li Fengmao (1990: 379) argues that *570 Lingjianzi*, a meditation manual attributed to Xu Xun, was composed by planchette sometime in the middle of the Northern Song and it would thus antedate the *Book of Transformations* by a century, but the only evidence he offers for this dating is that the form of the Xu legend contained therein is earlier than the early thirteenth century Bai Yuchan version.

Lord of Supreme Tenuity.[48] But this form of transmission is susceptible to errors of memory, particularly in the case of a lengthy work, and because the revelatory experience is private, questions arise about its authenticity. The adoption of spirit writing as a primary means of communication represented, therefore, a significant advance for the cult. It led to the production of a series of texts and scriptures that then formed the basis for later cult expansion and consolidation.

We are fortunate to have a detailed description of the way spirit writing was practiced at the cult site on Sevenfold Mountain:

> In his hall there is a Descending Brush Pavilion (*jiangbi ting* 降筆亭). Within the pavilion a five-colored flying phoenix is hung by a golden rope. In the mouth of the phoenix there is a brush. Golden Flower paper is used, and there are always several hundred sheets left under the brush.[49] The local prefecture (*fu* 府) headquarters dispatches an official to seal the door to the pavilion very securely, so as to avoid any deception. When the communication has been completed a bronze bell within the pavilion will ring of itself. The temple clerk announces this to the prefecture. The [representative of the] prefecture opens the locks and takes the writing to examine the response. Most of the communications sent down through the brush basically encourage people to be loyal and filial. Books are produced and registers transmitted in order to set a model for educated scholars and make manifest the commands of the Dao.[50]

The supervisory role played by representatives of the central government is particularly noteworthy. The state realized the disruptive potential of divine pronouncements in a cult setting and kept a close watch on the literary products of the cult.[51]

---

48. *186 Taiwei xianjun gongguo ge.* The preface to this work records its revelation in a dream in 1171. Cf. Brokaw 1991: 46.

49. Golden Flower paper was a specialty of the Sichuan paper industry. Made by dripping gold paint on plain paper, it was used during the Tang and Song dynasties to record the signatures of successful examination candidates. Several hundred sheets of this must have represented a considerable expense. See *Rongzhai suibi, xu,* 13/4b–5b.

50. "Circumstances of the Book of Transformations of the Great Thearch of Numinous Response" ("Lingying dadi huashu shishi" 靈應大帝化書事實). This text is preserved in the *Wendi quanshu,* ch. 14, and the 1771 illustrated edition of the *Wenchang huashu.*

51. The messages as described seem innocuous enough, centering on precisely the virtues the state wished to promote. But in the nineteenth century the cult site was producing portent-based warnings to the government to reform its ways (Gray 1878: 145). Such pronouncements have a long history in China, and if they were already part of the literary production of the cult during the Sung, it is easy to

It is curious, in view of the well-established facilities there and the obvious authority that a text from the cult center would have, that most of the cult texts that survive from the Song do not derive from Zitong. Instead, the most productive center seems to have been on Jeweled Screen Mountain (*Baopingshan* 寶屏山) near Chengdu.[52] There, before the Altar of the Mysterious Union in Jade Vacuity (*Xuanhui yuxu tan* 玄會玉虛壇) in the Pavilion of Central Harmony and Sincere Response (*Zhonghe chengying lou* 中和誠應樓), the Divine Lord of Zitong revealed the *Book of Transformations* as the culmination of a series of revelations spanning thirteen years. The primary recipient of this divine outpouring was a man named Liu Ansheng 劉安勝, who is referred to as Attendant Transcendent of the Phoenix Ministry (*luanfu shixian* 鸞府侍仙) and a Perfected (*zhenren* 眞人). Judging from the content and style of his writings he was an educated man, trained in the classics and their commentaries, probably a failed examination candidate, perhaps a schoolteacher. He shared his religious enterprise with several relatives and had patrons in the community who could finance the publication of his revelations in deluxe illustrated editions.

The first text to be revealed to Liu was the *Transcendent Scripture of the Great Grotto* 大洞仙經, in the autumn of 1168.[53] The scripture is said to have been revealed together with a *Register* (*lu* 籙) and a *Rite* (*fa* 法). In the *Book of Transformations* the god receives all of these documents, and puts them to efficacious use.[54]

Next to appear was the *Esoteric Biography of Qinghe* (*Qinghe neizhuan* 清河內傳), a short account of the many incarnations of the god.[55] We cannot be sure of the date, except that it was between 1168 and 1177, when the text was carved on a stele in a temple in Hangzhou.[56] Chapter 90 of the *Book of Transformations* tells us that at the same time a *Register* was ex-

---

see how such literature, blaming present and future natural disasters on the moral failings of the people in power, could have inspired governmental oversight. Further, there is an inherent distrust throughout Chinese history of any group that can command the primary loyalties of its adherents, and a forum for the continuing personal revelations of a god must have seemed particularly dangerous.

52. The exact location of this mountain is unknown.

53. *1214 Gaoshang dadong Wenchang silu ziyang baolu* 1/5a.

54. The scripture first appears in chapter 6. The Primordial Heavenly Worthy presents the Rite and Register in chapter 12. It is unclear what is intended by this Rite and Register. Robinet (1983: 403) suggests that a ritual preceding the core of the original *Scripture of the Great Grotto* in the Wenchang recension is to be identified with this Rite.

55. This text is to be found on pages 1a–3a of the like-named *169 Qinghe neizhuan*. The genre of secret or esoteric biography (*neizhuan*) has a long history. The most famous example is the *Esoteric Biography of Han Wudi* studied by Schipper (1965).

56. *Liang-Zhe jinshi zhi* 9/55b–57a.

pounded.[57] It is unclear whether this refers to some now lost work, perhaps the *Register* that accompanied the *Transcendent Scripture of the Great Grotto*, or to an earlier version of the *Precious Register* discussed below. If, however, it is the *Register of the Great Grotto* to which reference is made, the date of the *Esoteric Biography* could be earlier. The medium was again Liu Ansheng.

The next date that we can definitely associate with these revelations is 1181. In that year the *Precious Register of Purple Sunlight of Wenchang, the Director of Emoluments of the Exalted Great Grotto* was revealed.[58] This scripture lists numerous officials of the Wenchang Palace, including a considerable number of figures mentioned in the *Book of Transformations*.[59]

The major revelation of 1181, however, was the *Book of Transformations*. The first seventy-three chapters of the modern work were revealed at this time. Liu Ansheng was again the medium, but the work was too long for him to transcribe alone. He was aided by his two sons, Liu Dangcheng 劉當程 and Liu Yunqia 劉允洽, and an elder cousin (*zuxiong* 族兄), Liu Jianshan 劉兼善, the four alternating as the medium.

The Altar of the Mysterious Union in Jade Vacuity, the site of the revelation, was constructed in this year or shortly before at the behest of the Divine Lord of Zitong, who commanded Liu, his sons, and his cousin as well as several other local men, Ji Fu 計府, He Dunxin 何敦信, Wei Dan 衛丹, and Li Mao 李茂, to establish an altar in the Pavilion of Sincere Response.[60]

Below I would like to take a brief look at each of these revealed texts and their significance for the development of the cult and Chinese religion in general before focusing in on the process of composition of the *Book of Transformations*.

The Transcendent Scripture of the Great Grotto

The *Great Grotto* scripture was the foundation of the Shangqing movement and central to the original fourth-century revelation. By the twelfth century it had become the keystone of one of the two great Daoist scriptural traditions, the other being the Lingbao scriptures, which had as their foremost

---

57. DZJY chapter 90.

58. *1214 Gaoshang dadong Wenchang silu ziyang baolu* 1/2b.

59. E.g., Bai Hui (appearing in ch. 30, below), Gong Yuanchang (ch. 31), Wu Jian (= Wu Yijian of ch. 32), Yi Min (ch. 35), etc. This list is found at 1/11b–12b of the *Precious Register*.

60. The preceding discussion is based upon the preface to DZJY and DZJY chapter 90.

exemplar the *Scripture of Salvation* (*Duren jing* 度人經).[61] As Robinet points out in her study of the various editions of the *Great Grotto* scripture, the Wenchang recension, presumably deriving from the planchette of Liu Ansheng in 1168, tries to bridge the gap between these two traditions by attributing the *Great Grotto* scripture to the Primordial Heavenly King (an alternate name for the Primordial Heavenly Worthy who reveals the *Scripture of Salvation*), and by stressing the devotional recitation of the text rather than its use as a focus for the internal meditation practiced by the Shangqing school.[62] The intended purpose of this recitation is nicely set forth in the following passage from the Divine Lord of Zitong's preface to one edition of *Transcendent Scripture of the Great Grotto of Wenchang*:[63]

> My accumulated mysterious merit and marvelous actions were in each case due to possessing and reciting this *Transcendent Scripture of the Great Grotto*. I further obtained the *Rite* and *Register* of the Great Grotto and therefore was able to fully receive the divine efficacy of the scripture, establishing good and exorcising evil, rescuing the living and saving the dead, dispelling disasters and prolonging life. Later, amidst the shades of the dead, powerful gods and spirits of altars and temples came to ask that I recite the scripture and all then thanked me saying, "The power of your scripture, Perfected Official, enhanced my awe-inspiring power and transferred my spirit to the record of the good."

Thus the scripture, in addition to gaining merit for its possessor, has a much more exalted role to play in the cosmic battle between good and evil. Through his invocation of this scripture the Divine Lord places himself on the transcendent plane of the gods of orthodox Daoism, and there he accepts the worship and hears the entreaties of all the minor local deities

---

61. On this scripture and its expansion during the reign of Song Huizong, see Strickmann 1978.

62. Robinet 1983. Note that this god is called the Primordial Heavenly Worthy in the *Book of Transformations* (e.g., ch. 6). I am grateful to an anonymous reader for SUNY Press for pointing out that the earliest Daoist use of scripture was for ritual recitation rather than meditation. This practice, then, represents a return to an earlier mode of religious praxis rather than a new innovation.

63. 5 *Taishang wuji zongzhen Wenchang dadong xianjing* 1/3b. The last date in this preface is 1302, but portions of it may be as early as 1168. The preface begins with an account of the encounter between the epidemic demons and the Divine Lord. This resembles strongly the version in the *Book of Transformations* (ch. 12) but the *Scripture of the Great Grotto* is featured more prominently and care is taken to identify the three revealing deities. It is difficult to determine whether this was originally part of the 1168 revelation of the scripture later adapted for use in the *Book of Transformations*, or whether this part of the preface is a later work selecting and embellishing appropriate portions of the *Book of Transformations* to tell the story of the scripture.

worshiped in temples across China. Although the above quote may be as late as the beginning of the fourteenth century, this reidentification of the god as a Daoist cosmic savior belonging to a totally different order of being from the local gods worshiped in other temples was implicit in the decision to make him revealing deity of the *Perfected Scripture of the Great Grotto*, and is maintained, as we shall see below, in the *Book of Transformations*.

The Precious Register

As noted, we cannot be certain but it seems likely that the Precious Register of Purple Sunlight of Wenchang, the Director of Emoluments of the Exalted Great Grotto is to be identified with the Register of the Transcendent Scripture of the Great Grotto mentioned in the Book of Transformations; in any case, the Precious Register must have been a document of great importance to cult members. The primary function of a register is to list the names and often the images of gods.[64] The Precious Register lists the various identities of the Divine Lord and a number of local gods associated with him and his transformations, as well as the gods manning the Wenchang Palace over which he presides. It also includes a number of representations of the gods. Originally registers like this functioned as manuals for meditation, and the illustrations aided the practitioner in visualization. As we have seen above, by this time the focus of practice, at least within this variety of Daoism, had shifted from meditation to ritual practice, and it was the recitation of the names of the gods and the reproduction of their depictions rather than their internal visualization that invoked and moved them to action on one's behalf. Registers served a related function in investing the practitioner with numerous divisions of supernatural soldiers who protected the devotee and did his bidding. It was the control of such troops afforded by this scripture that permitted the Divine Lord to seize and subdue the epidemic demons.[65]

The *Precious Register* distinguishes itself from other Daoist registers by its relentless emphasis on official position as the goal of religious endeavor. The work opens with a small rite in which the new possessor officially accepts the scripture and vows to "revere and worship the true teaching, regulate and cultivate myself, increase my talents, sharpen my judgment, purge myself of demonic obstructions, chase forth evil monstrosities, achieve

---

64. On registers and their use, see Schipper 1980, 1985b.
65. Chapter 12.

prominence on the examination, and be promoted in rank and emolument."[66] The functions of the Wenchang Palace are laid out in a three-dimensional schema. The Palace administers emoluments, determines status, and promotes the worthy. Each function is carried out in three spheres. Emoluments are bestowed in the Heavenly, temporal, and Subterranean worlds. Status is classed into superior (in recognition of filial behavior, chastity, or hidden merit), average (for compassion, integrity, and virtuous conduct), and inferior (for knowledge, ancestral merit, and literary talent) categories. It is interesting to note the relatively low ranking given the talents most often thought to lead to success on the examinations. Worthiness is also classified into superior (for being filial, loyal, or benevolent), average (for integrity, etiquette, wisdom), and inferior (for perseverance, talent, and decisiveness).

The focus on success in an official career is also evident in a section concerning responsive dreams (*yingmeng* 應夢).[67] Eight images that the Divine Lord sends to petitioners in dreams as marks of favor are depicted: a jade cat, a white horse, a white deer, a brown cow, a large demon, a black dog, the ritual beheading of five tigers, and the angry slaying of three men. Ten anecdotes relate how individuals received one of these signs in a dream and went on to great success on the examinations and in their subsequent careers. All these anecdotes involve the *Precious Register*. The text explains that ideally one first has a dream including one of these images then receives the *Precious Register*, but it is also possible to receive the *Precious Register* and then have the portentous dream. An interesting feature is the role of the 30th Celestial Master, Zhang Jixian 張紀先 (1092–1126), as a transmitter of the scripture in one anecdote.[68] The eight images are no doubt the images of responsive dreams depicted on the eight inner walls of the Terrace of Responsive Dreams in the temple complex on Sevenfold Mountain.[69]

---

66. *1214 Gaoshang dadong Wenchang Silu ziyang baolu* 1/1b.

67. 3/11a–14b.

68. There is other evidence of links between the cult and the Celestial Master church on Longhu Mountain. Three Celestial Masters are listed as transmitters of the scripture: the 42nd, Zhang Zhengchang 張正常 (1335–77); the 43rd Zhang Yuchu 張宇初 (1361–1410); and the 44th, Zhang Yuqing 張宇清 (1364–1427, *Precious Register* C18a). Further, in the Yuan recension of the *Book of Transformations* the penultimate chapter relates the incarnation (manifestation?) of the Divine Lord as the 36th Celestial Master, Zhang Zongyan 張宗演 (1244–91), his choice of his successor and the revival of the Celestial Master movement. See DZ 4/32a–b.

69. This terrace is described in the Song dynasty "Circumstances of the Book of Transformations of the Great Thearch of Numinous Response" ("Lingying dadi Huashu shishi"). See above, note 50.

The Book of Transformations

The revelation of the *Book of Transformations* in 1181 was the culmination of this series of pronouncements from the god. It is a complex document, incorporating much early cult lore and treating a diverse range of religious and ethical problems. The god portrayed therein is also a complex figure, combining the roles of savior, teacher, moral exemplar, and divine protector. Still, the primary goal was to portray the god as a god that transcended regional limitations, and above all else, a god of the scholar-official elite.

This was conveyed in a number of ways. First and foremost was through the incarnations and divine postings of the god himself. The first two incarnations are particularly important in this regard. Both have as their primary setting the imperial court during the Western Zhou, a time of special significance as the "golden age" of Chinese antiquity. During the first incarnation the Divine Lord is summoned to the court to attend the young King Cheng (r. 1042–1005 B.C.),[70] and thus becomes a colleague and ally of the Duke of Zhou, the prototypical good minister and sage regent so highly revered by Confucius.[71] In his second incarnation the god is born as the son of a former high court official, and eventually takes up his father's former position in the court of King Xuan (827–781).[72] The attribution of two poems in the *Shijing* to the god, and the assertion that he is the Zhang Xiaoyou mentioned in yet another poem from that revered collection, further bolstered the god's claims to an important role in this formative period of Chinese civilization.[73] There is one further incarnation as a temporal official, during the Latter Han dynasty.[74]

In the course of these incarnations as officials the Divine Lord provides a model of proper conduct in office. Prompted by considerations of loyalty to the ruler and the state (*zhong*), a cardinal Chinese virtue, he travels tremendous distances to serve the state at considerable personal peril. In both incarnations he is opposed by unscrupulous colleagues and in the second incarnation his loyal remonstrances eventually result in his death. The god also demonstrates unselfish concern for the state by recommending a talented subordinate for his own position and by placing the state's need for

---

70. Dates for the Western Zhou follow the reconstructed chronology of David Nivison (1983: 47).
71. Confucius considered it evidence of his own moral decline that he had not dreamed of the Duke of Zhou. Cf. *Lunyu* 7/5; Lau 1979: 86.
72. Chapters 21–30.
73. Chapters 23–25.
74. Chapter 67.

able officers above his own familial obligations in recommending the son of the man who had caused his father's death.[75]

The Latter Han incarnation provides a model for local administration rather than court service. His virtuous and compassionate rule, stressing the suasive power of exemplar and ritual over the coercive power of law, results in peace, social harmony, and divine approbation expressed through favorable natural conditions.

The temporal administration of China was paralleled by a divine administration staffed by the gods, and so close was the relationship between these two systems that the actions of the Divine Lord in executing his divine offices could also serve as models for proper conduct in temporal positions. Official service in the sacred realm, as in this realm, presented a variety of moral dilemmas concerning how to properly interact with one's superior, fellow officials and subordinates, and the governed, both elite and mean, while maintaining ethical principles like loyalty and filial piety that were themselves often in conflict. The *Book of Transformations* sanctions appropriate intervention into the jurisdictions of other officials, as when the neighboring dragon-god of Qingli Pool indicts and the Divine Lord as Mountain King cashiers a mountain god for kidnapping and defiling a new bride on her wedding night or when he memorializes to temper the doom pronounced upon a town by a god in a neighboring district.[76]

The debate about when and how to serve new rulers once the old ones have lost the mandate and the country is as old as the beginning of the Zhou but must have had special relevance to officials confronted with the shifting fortunes of the Song state during the twelfth century. The Divine Lord was confronted with such a problem when a rapidly expanding state of Qin seized control of first the Shu state, then the empire as a whole. He opposes the Qin takeover of Shu until Heaven speaks forth, making clear that the Mandate over the Sichuan region has shifted to Qin, and then he dutifully accepts this new situation.[77] When other local gods, agitated by these changes, fall to quarreling, endangering the inhabitants of their regions, he acts as mediator to resolve their differences.[78]

There are also several anecdotes concerning the conduct of officials in office. Chapter 62 tells of two local magistrates, one cruel, the other corrupt. Both receive reprimands from the god and reform. This contrasts

---

75. Chapters 15 and 26.
76. Chapters 32 and 33.
77. Chapter 47.
78. Chapter 51.

sharply with two tales of pairs of good and evil clerks, in both of which the evil clerks die.[79] Members of the official class seem to have enjoyed special dispensation in the divine world of the *Book of Transformations* just as they did in the temporal court system of China. Entry into the ranks of official-dom is shown in the *Book of Transformations* to depend upon filial behavior, as in the case of the man who was recommended for an official post for his virtuous conduct in accepting a bastard offspring of his grandfather as his own uncle or the man who was granted a divine post for copying a scripture out in his own blood to aid his ailing father.[80]

In anecdotes not directly concerning officials it still seems that members of the educated gentry dominate. Three protagonists are specifically said to be wealthy, another is a descendant of the old royal house of the state of Shu, a third is a rich landowner.[81] The slanderer in chapter 54, who goes about fomenting lawsuits and disparaging virtuous men for their humble origins, also belongs to this gentry class. Even some who the text implies are not well-off financially seem to be respected community leaders from old, established families.[82] The Divine Lord himself, in his first incarnation, expresses the interests of the elite through his creation of charitable institutions for the benefit of less fortunate members of his lineage.[83]

Although the interests of the educated elite are at the fore in the *Book of Transformations* there is still a message for the common man. Everyone benefited from the type of honest, compassionate, and dedicated official that the *Book of Transformations* promotes. Beyond this, we find tales centering on craftsmen, poor peasants, widows, and orphans.[84] One man is criticized for rejecting his destitute natural father in favor of his wealthy adopted father.[85] Further, the provision of progeny is a frequent theme in the work, and although the individuals seeking progeny in the *Book of Transformations* are often well-off, this aspect of the god must have appealed to all segments of Chinese society.[86]

If the primary intended audience of the *Book of Transformations* was the scholar-official and would-be scholar-official, its primary purpose was reli-

---

79. Chapters 56 and 58.
80. Chapters 58 and 32.
81. Chapters 41, 52, and 60; chapter 61; chapter 36.
82. Chapter 38.
83. Chapter 18.
84. Chapters 55, 33, 57, and 40.
85. Chapter 50.
86. Chapters dealing with progeny are 2, 21, 41, 50, and 65. Of these, the protagonists of chapters 41 and 50 are said to be rich.

gious in nature. This purpose was twofold: to portray the god of Zitong as a celestial Daoist deity within the unitary pantheon of the Chinese religious world, and to disseminate his message of salvation through moral renewal to a troubled world.

The Daoist identity claimed for the deity at the time of the revelation of the *Transcendent Scripture of the Great Grotto* and adumbrated in the *Precious Register* is further supported by the *Book of Transformations*. Daoist gods are star gods and the celestial character of the Divine Lord is manifest in both his origins and his apotheosis. The god is born amidst primeval chaos and resides for eons in the constellation Zhang before descending into this world.[87] The culmination of his sojourn in this world is his assumption of control over the Wenchang Palace.[88] His stewardship of the Cinnamon Record there is a Taoist office, bestowed upon the Divine Lord by the Thearch. In the course of his transformations he presides over a Daoist grotto-heaven and meets Laozi, who praises him and bestows upon him his magic elixir.[89]

At the same time, a strong Buddhist influence is evident. When condemned by the Thearch to unending torment for his actions in inundating a city, the Buddha releases him and grants him supernatural powers. At the close of his first incarnation he goes in search of an Ancient August Master dwelling in the Western Region, who advocates Buddhist teachings like "extinction" (*mie* 滅, a common translation for nirvana). But closer inspection reveals that this figure also propounds the quietist teachings of philosophical Daoism and that extinction means only an end to the "dusty bonds" of this life. The teachings of this Ancient August Master in fact represent the ancient conception of Buddhism as a variety of Daoism, a conception associated with the "conversion of the barbarians" theory.[90] Thus in the *Book of Transformations* Buddhist figures are not rejected or denied, though their position or rank within the divine hierarchy is unclear, but they do function within a Daoist universe.

The net effect of the revelation of the *Book of Transformations* was to fashion an image of the god that would appeal to a wide range of society, but would have a special appeal to the scholar-official class. Hymes has interpreted both officially sponsored Daoist movements of the Northern Song and literati shrines established to Neo-Confucian teachers during the South-

---

87. See chapters 1 and 2 of the translation.
88. Chapter 73.
89. Chapters 20 and 48.
90. On this topic, see the Commentary to chapter 19.

ern Song as attempts to achieve a national integration through religion.[91] In dealing with cults like that to the Divine Lord of Zitong it is difficult to distinguish motives of self-interest from larger concerns about the well-being of society, but the ecumenical approach to diverse religious traditions and the unitary sacred realm portrayed in the scriptural products of the cult would have furthered such a goal.

---

91. Hymes 1986: 192–99.

The *Book of Transformations*

The *Book of Transformations* is a revealed scripture, transcribed through spirit writing over a limited period of time, probably no more than a few days. There were four mediums involved in the project, though Liu Ansheng seems to have been the primary recipient of the message. We know relatively little about the process of spirit writing revelation in premodern China, even less about the intertextual relations between such revealed material and its antecedents or models. Some of the material that found its way into the *Book of Transformations* was already part of cult lore, since it occurs in earlier sources, but may have undergone substantial revision in the process of revelation. Other elements may have been wholly new, "original" creations of the mediums and their controlling deity. This section will discuss the composition and structure of the *Book of Transformations*, primarily on the basis of internal evidence.

The *Book of Transformations* seems to divide naturally into several discrete sections. Some relate continuous narratives that span as many as twenty chapters; others seem to be collections of independent, chapter-length stories with only relatively abstract unifying themes. Since we know that four mediums took part in the revelation, it is tempting to see in these changes the alternation of different mediums, each with a distinctive message and mode of presentation. I have, however, been unable to discern consistent variations in diction or vocabulary that would confirm such a thesis. Moreover, there seems to be an overarching, unifying theme to the work: the spiritual development of the god. Perhaps this unifying structure was the result of a group of mediums accustomed to working together and sharing a mature, well thought-out conception of the god. Liu Ansheng had been the instrument of the Divine Lord's revelations for at least thirteen years when the *Book of Transformations* was produced, and the sons and cousin who shared in the revelation were probably not neophytes . But it may also be the result of intentional manipulation. The revelatory process itself permits a certain amount of editorial supervision. Spirit writing requires, in addition to the medium, an interpreter who writes out the oracular script in more understandable, fixed form, and can thus shape the message to a certain extent.

One must also admit the possibility of considerable editing and "correcting" after the fact; such emendation is common among modern spirit writing groups.[92] The mature development of this editorial process is visible in a newly annotated edition of Wenchang's *Scripture of the Great Grotto* dating to 1936.[93] The postface lists the editorial board, which includes, in addition to the two actual mediums, styled Controllers of the Phoenix, two men in charge of promoting and disseminating the scripture, an "inner" and "outer" recorder, an editorial chief and a chief of scribes, as well as sixteen individuals assigned to collate, check, copy, and recollate the text. With a staff like this, a manuscript came out well polished indeed. We will never be certain how much of an editorial apparatus Liu Ansheng had, but the result was an extended prosimetric narrative with a coherent message tailored to a specific audience.

The first twenty chapters constitute one continuous narrative, the longest in the *Book of Transformations*. It is a tale of considerable dramatic power, centering on the god's incarnation as a man named Zhang Shanxun 張善勳. The narrative is a well-integrated whole, tracing the god from celestial origins through birth, childhood, education, religious ordeals, a successful career, return home in old age, religious enlightenment, and final apotheosis with the attainment of a divine position. If this does not represent the incorporation of a pre-existent tale, and I have found no antecedent, direct or indirect, this narrative alone must be judged a significant literary achievement.

There are several striking features of this story. One is its regional character. The god is born into an as-yet un-Sinified (at the time of the tale, ca. 1000 B.C.) region of Southeast China. Local culture is described in some detail, as is the incarnated god's first encounter with Chinese civilization and his subsequent efforts to promote this high culture in his native land. The location of the all-important first incarnation of this Sichuanese deity in the distant Southeast is curious. Perhaps it reflects a conscious attempt to appeal to the people of this region, to which the cult was in the process of expanding. In the late twelfth century the Southeast was the center of both political power and literati culture.

A second singular feature of this tale is the prominent role played by the Zhang clan. In chapter 2 the god is born to a man surnamed Zhang in part

---

92. Gary Seaman, personal communication, March 1993. Seaman described a case in which the god himself directed the insertion of a passage from another work into the record of his own communication.

93. *Dadong xianjing zhushi*, ch. 2, Lu 1b, in *Zangwai daoshu* 4:412a.

because the constellation Zhang was ascendant. Chapter 3 relates the origin myth of the Zhangs, linking this clan specifically to the Wu region. In chapter 18, after retiring from an illustrious career, Zhang Shanxun returns to his native land and devotes himself to charitable works centering on the less fortunate members of his clan. Now the god of Zitong had long been associated with the surname Zhang and the Song was a time when lineage ties were becoming more and more important. Still, it seems that there was more to this connection than a simple concurrence of cult lore with historical trends. The predecessor to the *Book of Transformations* was a much shorter version of this work known as the *Esoteric Biography of Qinghe* (*Qinghe neizhuan* 清河內傳) and Qinghe was the choronym of one of the most prominent Zhang clans.[94] Moreover, we know that members of this Qinghe Zhang clan held hereditary posts controlling the main temple outside Zitong.[95] If the medium revealing these scriptures were himself a Zhang, our conclusion would be simple, but, in fact, of the individuals named as participants in the revelation not a single one is surnamed Zhang, nor does the revelation take place at the main temple itself. This does not preclude the possibility that some of these men had affinal ties to the clan, or that they were in some sense sponsored by the clan, but it also raises the possibility that the Zhang clan had already created and circulated in some form legends of the god's incarnations that featured the clan prominently.

A third feature of this first narrative is a decidedly Daoist slant. Most of the god's actions, whether assuming a divine or human identity, through the course of the *Book of Transformations* are free of sectarian character. They reflect beliefs about right and wrong, the composition of the universe, and the role of the divine world that are part and parcel of the diffuse, "popular" religion that was common to all Chinese of the day. The chapters concerning Zhang Shanxun also partake of this common worldview, but Daoist deities and scriptures play a more prominent role. For example, elsewhere in the *Book of Transformations* the high god is referred to simply as Di 帝, "the Thearch," or Shangdi 上帝, "the Supreme Thearch," both of these

---

94. On choronyms and their significance, see Johnson 1977.

95. This is one conclusion that can safely be drawn from the intriguing but badly damaged "Cliff Record of the Late Zhang Zihou of the Song Dynasty" ("Song gu Zhang Zihou yanji" 宋故張子厚巖記) preserved in the *Zitong County Gazetteer* (*Zitongxian zhi* 梓潼縣志: 4/24b–26b). The subject of the inscription, Zhang Guang 張光 (1062–1131), was at least the third generation of this clan to control the temple. Although Zhang Guang must have been a prominent figure in Zitong (he is the only figure from the Song commemorated with an inscription), he seems to have left no trace in historical records. The Zhang Zihou mentioned in *Songshi* 69/11476 as a son of Zhang Jun 張俊 (1086–1154) is too young.

being common references to the Jade August Supreme Thearch 玉皇上帝 who rules over the popular pantheon. But in this narrative Zhang Shanxun finds, worships, and is aided by a statue of the Primordial Heavenly Worthy 元始天尊, a distinctively Daoist analog of the high god and one of the three pure emanations of primordial vapor who constitute the highest Daoist trinity.[96] Moreover, Zhang Shanxun comes into possession of the *Transcendent Scripture of the Great Grotto* 大洞仙經, one of the holiest of Daoist scriptures and the centerpiece of the fourth-century Maoshan revelations.[97] Ultimately he receives as well a *Rite* and a *Register of the Great Grotto*, secretly transmitted texts that are used to activate the *Transcendent Scripture*, and through them gains command over the fell troops of the other world that Daoists used to such advantage in eliminating the malefic demons and sprites worshiped in popular cults. Finally, this tale concludes with Zhang Shanxun's encounter with the Ancient August Master 古皇先生, a mysterious figure preaching a doctrine similar to that found in the "Laozi converting the barbarians" literature.

The primary medium Liu Ansheng styles himself "Phoenix Transcendent," a title reflecting his role as a spirit writing medium, but he was probably an ordained Daoist as well. As discussed above, among the scriptures revealed through him prior to the *Book of Transformations* was a new recension of this same *Transcendent Scripture of the Great Grotto* and a *Precious Register* that is meant to accompany it. Thus whatever role preexisting legends created by or for the Zhang clan had on the formation of this Zhang Shanxun tale, its final form must owe much to the training and creative efforts of Liu Ansheng.

The second narrative, consisting of chapters 21 through 30, tells the tale of Zhang Zhongsi 張忠嗣, better known by his cognomen, Zhang Zhong 寂仲. The distinguishing feature of this series of chapters is the identification of the god with the formative period of Chinese classical antiquity. In the Zhang Shanxun incarnation the god had already assisted and collaborated with the fabled Duke of Zhou 周公 and his nephew King Cheng 成王. Here we see the god coming to the aid of the besieged King Xuan 宣王 (r. 827–782 B.C.) and assisting in the imperial restoration. In the course of his official career Zhang Zhong composes two poems that become part of the normative *Scripture of Poetry* (*Shijing*) and is praised by name in a third.

This sort of classical foundation for a cult was of great importance. Clas-

---

96. On these highest figures of the pantheon and their relationship, see Kubo 1986: 126–32.
97. Wenchang is still worshiped through the recitation of this scripture in Yunnan province. See below, pp. 82-83.

sical canons like the *Record of Rites* largely proscribed popular worship, but left loopholes for the worship of figures who had contributed to the well-being of the state or their native region.[98] Conservative critics could always dismiss the claims made for a god in a work like the *Book of Transformations* and argue for the banning of the cult as "licentious sacrifice" (*yinsi* 淫祀). But the material presented in the *Book of Transformations* at least provided his supporters with ammunition with which to argue that the god was indeed worthy of worship. Moreover, faced with a popular god of proven numinous efficacy and a specialization in affairs of the most acute concern to the literati (childbirth, the examinations, and the official career), many were no doubt delighted to have this way of rationalizing their devotion.

The first two narratives, concerning Zhang Shanxun and Zhang Zhongsi, share several features. Most prominent of these is a focus on the concerns of the gentry class from which most officials were drawn. The Chinese dress that Zhang Shanxun adopts is that of the gentry, not Chinese peasant garb. The strict mourning practices he observes upon the death of his parents could only be pursued by individuals of sufficient means and leisure to remove themselves from worldly affairs for years at a time. The roles of spiritual healer and medical physician adopted by Shanxun were professional positions requiring literacy and training (Hymes 1987). They were open to members of the lower intelligentsia but were also often pursued by younger sons of high gentry lineages. Shanxun's actions at court, recommending worthy individuals and remonstrating with the ruler at his own peril, are exemplars of proper conduct directed at aspiring officials.

The Zhang Zhongsi incarnation displays a similar intent. The father in this incarnation had been a high official in the Zhou court and Zhongsi inherits this position. He composes one poem now found in the *Shijing* to counter the slanders of scurrilous officials and another to exhort the ruler to use talented men (chs. 24 and 25). Placing the interests of the state above his own honor, he recommends for office the worthy son of a family enemy (ch. 26) and then intercedes to assist the marriage plans of a dead colleague. He dies, in the end, because of his opposition to the enthronement of an unworthy heir apparent. These themes are all common in the standard historical sources used to indoctrinate young members of the gentry.

In connection with the first incarnation, I mentioned the prominent role of Daoism in Zhang Shanxun's life. This element is not absent in the life of Zhang Zhongsi. Zhongsi's mother instructs him in the teachings of a Dao-

---

98. See above, pp. 4–5 and n.15.

ist scripture, the *Scripture of Inner Meditation,* and recommends to him a number of Daoist practices. The presence of this Daoist material in sections specifically devoted to creating an acceptable gentry image for the god reflects the degree to which Daoist faith and doctrine had penetrated gentry circles of the day.

The first incarnation had ended with Zhang Shanxun passing quietly into oblivion in accord with the teachings of the Ancient August Master, and the interim before his second incarnation was filled with his administration of Monarch Mountain. The second incarnation ends quite differently. Compelled to commit suicide by the new king, the wrathful spirit of Zhong Zhongsi appears as a wraith, haunting the palace for three days. But after this enmity is vented, a similar transition occurs, with the disembodied god proceeding to Snow Mountain and an appointment as Great Transcendent. It is interesting to note that even in the case of divine beings, the ancient Chinese belief in mountains as the primary destination of dead souls still exercises its influence.[99]

Thus the first thirty chapters comprise two long narratives of similar structure and theme. The next thirty-two chapters (31–62) are independent tales focusing on the god's actions as a divine official. Although all these chapters share a certain similarity, they can be divided into two groups, the first (31–40) centering on the god as King of Swordridge Mountain 劍嶺山王, and the second (41–62) in which the god is usually referred to as Master Zhang of the Northern Ramparts 北郭張生.

The first series, which I will call the King of Swordridge Mountain incarnation, is the first to link the god with the Sichuan region. The cult to the god of Zitong had originated on Sevenfold Mountain outside of Zitong, one of the foothills of the Swordridge mountain chain that separates the Sichuan basin from the Han River Valley of southern Shensi province. We may assume, then, that a primary function of these chapters is to legitimize the power of the god in his native place. The first chapter of this series performs this task admirably. First an official rescript transfers the god to this new position, assuring the reader that he is the duly appointed representative of the divine administration for that region. Next the god exercises this authority by summoning together all of the divine beings within his

---

99. This belief is already evident in Han dynasty tomb contracts, where we find formulations like "The living to Chang'an, the dead to Mount Tai!" and survives in the position of the Lord of Mount Tai as the first of the otherwise Buddhist Ten Kings of Hell. See Sakai 1937; Seidel 1987: 30; Teiser 1988: 170. The belief is also common in Japan, although a Chinese origin for the Japanese formulation of this doctrine has yet to be demonstrated. See Yamaori Tetsuo 1989: 6.

territory and leading them on a mission to rid the region of a predatory tiger of great age and power.

The rest of the chapters in this incarnation record how the god used his power to aid the people of his region. We see him controlling natural forces by quelling a flood (ch. 37), distributing food in a famine (ch. 38), and relieving a drought (ch. 39). He also intervenes directly in human affairs, protecting a filial son and a virtuous widow from those who would harm them (chs. 40 and 34), solving a complicated murder case in which an innocent man was implicated (ch. 35), and punishing a landlord who required his tenant farmers to murder their children (ch. 36). Perhaps most interesting, however, are cases in which he interacts with other members of the divine administration. In one case he punishes a mountain god under his jurisdiction who had ravished a new bride (ch. 32); in another, he succeeds in staying the hand of a superior, the White Thearch, who is about to annihilate a whole town because of the misconduct of one of its members (ch. 33). These demonstrate the extent to which the bureaucratic model was applied to the divine realm in the twelfth century.

The next series of twenty-two chapters follows with no transition. The first chapter of this series, "Northern Ramparts" (ch. 41), introduces the new identity of the god. He is Master Zhang of the Northern Ramparts, also known as Zhang Zhongzi. The setting for these tales shifts to Chengdu, the traditional capital of the Sichuan region. There are two themes that run through these twenty-two chapters: the role of the god in early Sichuan history and his role as a provider of progeny.

The setting for the historical material is the state of Shu during the Warring States period, the latter half of the first millennium B.C. Two chapters center on a dispute between the Shu king Yufu 魚鳧 and his younger brother (chs. 42 and 43). But the primary focus of this material is the legendary King Kaiming 開明王 and his strongmen, the Five Stalwarts 五丁. They seem to have an ambiguous status in Shu legend-history, local heroes who end up bringing about the downfall of the state. Master Zhang repeatedly manifests in human form to warn the king about employing them, but he is consistently ignored (chs. 44–46). Finally the Five Stalwarts are sent to escort five jezebels, presents from the King of Qin who hopes to invade and conquer the distracted King Kaiming. Master Zhang resorts to desperate measures, taking the form of a giant snake to do battle with and kill the Five Stalwarts (ch. 47).

This final confrontation between snake and strongmen had been a part of the earliest strata of cult lore. The god of Zitong had been a snake and the single act he is credited with in our earliest source is the death of the Stalwarts and their charges. To the authors of the *Book of Transformations* this was a climactic event, and it is followed by a retreat to a mountain, in this case the fabled Kongdong where the god meets Laozi and receives his blessing. It is tempting, then, to take this as the end of a series, paralleling the denouements of the first and second incarnations. But this same Zhang of the Northern Ramparts occurs again in chapters 59 and 60, and I believe it best to treat all the chapters from 41 to 62 as one unit.

The second theme running through these chapters is birth and protection of children. The initial chapter, which first introduces Master Zhang of the Northern Ramparts, has him giving an extended lecture on conduct that will aid in the production of children. Related material is found in chapter 50, where the god reconciles an adopted son and his true father; chapter 52, where he reunites a mother and son; chapter 53, where he returns an abducted daughter to her father; and chapter 58, where he punishes a man who mistreats his younger brother and rewards a man who recognizes a bastard son.

In addition there are a number of chapters treating rather standard themes such as the punishment of slanderers (ch. 54), corrupt officials (chs. 49, 56, 62), butchers (ch. 61), dishonest craftsmen (ch. 55), and the like. These chapters would seem to fit equally well in the preceding King of Swordridge Mountain series.

The disparate themes found in the Master Zhang of the Northern Ramparts series are united by a single figure better known as Transcendent Zhang. Today Transcendent Zhang is a bow-wielding patron of dramatic performers, but also a sender of progeny and protector of children. His image in the Song was similar. Su Xun 蘇洵, the father of the illustrious Su Shi and Su Che, is said to have prayed to the god before their birth. Su says, "As to Transcendent Zhang, this god was originally the constellation Zhang and often illuminated [i.e., was born into?] the Zhang clan. Entering Shu, he was called Master Zhang of the Northern Ramparts."[100] The reference to the Northern Ramparts clearly indicates the god's ties to Chengdu.

It appears, then, that two bodies of legendary material have been conflated. There was originally a serpentine thunder deity surnamed Zhang from northern Sichuan, who had vanquished the Five Stalwarts. There was

---

100. Guo Zizhang, "Wenchangci ji," Guo goes on to explain: "He wields a bow and carries arrows because the god was originally a scion of the Zhang clan and was the first to make bows and bowstrings for the Yellow Thearch. He does not forget his beginnings." Guo cites several passages from the *Record of Rites* indicating a connection between the birth of male progeny and bows.

another god surnamed Zhang from Chengdu who provided progeny and was linked to the culture hero Hui, offspring of the Yellow Thearch and inventor of the bow. It seems likely that legends also connected this Chengdu Zhang to the Kaiming–Five Stalwarts cycle, but these legends do not survive independently or as part of Transcendent Zhang cult lore. When the Zitong cult expanded to Chengdu, probably in the Tang, the two gods were identified. The link must have seemed self-evident given their common connection to the Five Stalwarts cycle and to the Zhang surname. Eventually Transcendent Zhang tales became part and parcel of the Divine Lord's group of miracles. The earliest surviving tale still attributed to Transcendent Zhang dates from the opening years of the Song. The only surviving scripture dedicated to Transcendent Zhang, the *Perfected Scripture of Wondrous Response for the Injection of Life and Leading-in of Progeny Expounded by Transcendent Zhang, the Great Perfected, Responsive Transformation of Wenchang* (*Wenchang yinghua Zhang Xian dazhenren shuo zhusheng yansi miaoying zhenjing* 文昌應化張仙大眞人說注生延嗣妙應眞經), clearly indicates both in the title and in the body of the scripture that the god is to be identified with Wenchang.[101] The subsuming of one cult within another is not unprecedented, but it is curious that the Transcendent Zhang cult should survive as an independent entity.

The next set of four chapters (63–66) documents the incorporation of another local Sichuan cult into the body of Zitong lore. There was an ancient tale of a magical snake/dragon who caused the inundation of an entire city. One version of this tale localized the event in Qiong Pool 邛池, near modern Xichang, Sichuan. By the early tenth century the snake in this legend had been identified as Zhang Ezi, reflecting the appropriation of this legend by the Zitong cult.

In the original tale the serpent had been adopted and raised by an old woman. It grew and its appetites grew with it, until the beast happened to eat the local magistrate's prize horse. When the magistrate retaliated by killing the old woman, the snake caused forty days of rain that flooded the entire town, killing all its inhabitants. The tenth-century tale had changed little, substituting an old couple for the old woman and having the snake save them before the magistrate could effect their deaths.

---

101. This scripture is found in DZJY, sub *xing*, and the *Wendi quanshu*, chapter 12; an independent edition from the nineteenth century is preserved in the Cambridge University Library. The text is preceded by a preface dated 1734 and attributed to Heavenly Deaf (Tianlong 天聾), an attendant of the Divine Lord since the Song. The text focuses on ten moral injunctions, the observance of which will result in progeny, and each injunction is illustrated by a tale from the *Book of Transformations*.

This tale of a filial but violent nature spirit was acceptable to the cult in the tenth century but was inappropriate for the literati persona of the god being fashioned in the twelfth. The god's actions were rationalized by demonizing the victims. One of the great villains in Chinese history has been the Empress Lü, wife of the founder of the Han dynasty and nearly its usurper. In the *Book of Transformations* the god is said to have been incarnated as the favorite distaff son of the emperor, Ruyi. When the emperor dies, the empress has both the son and his mother, the Lady Qi, killed. The prefect and many of the residents of the town that was to become Qiong Pool were reincarnations of the Lüs, and the old woman who nurtures the snake is Lady Qi. The god's actions are thus understandable, if not wholly defensible, as growing out of filial piety and a sense of injustice. The tale is bracketed by authority figures, further reducing the god's culpability. First the Thearch orders him to be born, against the god's better judgment, as Ruyi (ch. 63); after the incident, the god is punished for his actions, but in the end granted absolution by no less than the Buddha.

The final seven chapters depict the god's apotheosis and ultimate position within the divine hierarchy. Three transitional chapters (67–69) detail three incarnations working off the karma of Qiong Pool. First the god is born as Zhang Xun 張勳 in the first century A.D.. He becomes Prefect of Qinghe, the ancestral home of an important branch of the Zhang clan, and lives a model life of the ideal benevolent local official. Next he is born circa 140 as Zhang Xiaozhong 張孝忠 ("filial and loyal") and lives a rather ordinary temporal life, all the while functioning as a divine judge in his sleep. But some remnant of the karmic disturbance engendered by his inundation of thousands of living souls still remains. Before final apotheosis, he must himself die a violent death. This happens in chapter 69 where, incarnated as an anonymous advisor to Deng Ai (197–264), he meets his death in battle.

Chapter 70 records a triumphal meeting with the Thearch, who praises him for his good works and presents him with a *ruyi* ("as you like it") scepter. This "as-you-like-it" scepter is a feature of one of the cult's earliest myths, wherein the god presents it to a fourth-century military figure, Yao Chang. This chapter is the first surviving reference to the divine origin of this scepter. The incident with Yao Chang is not mentioned at all in the original revelation, but was part of the revelation of 1194. It is possible that the place of the scepter in cult lore influenced the choice of the historical Ruyi, son of Han Gaozu, as the incarnation leading up to the inundation of Qiong Pool (ch. 63).

Chapter 71 begins the god's final incarnation (in this revelation). The god is again born into the world, and takes as his parents the man and woman who had been his father and mother in so many incarnations; here again he belongs to the Zhang clan. The year of his birth is given as A.D. 287, conforming to accounts placing his historical life in the Jin dynasty. The date of his birth is fixed on the third day of the second lunar month, the date on which festivals to the god are still held.

The next chapter recalls the god to his divine status. The process begins with the god reasserting his power over the element of water. This sign of awakening leads to the arrival of an emissary of Heaven, who informs the god of his previous transformations and leads him back up to the Heavens, where he is reunited with his divine family. The authority over all aspects of the Shu region, including the affairs of living and deceased mortals, is put into his hands. In the final chapter the god is given another, higher responsibility. He is appointed keeper of the Cinnamon Record, a ledger recording the good and evil actions of men and their consequent reward or punishment. This Cinnamon Record was of particular importance because it determined who would succeed on the civil service examinations and what sort of a career he would have.

The final two chapters, then, make powerful claims for the god. First the god is identified as a special protector and judge for the Sichuan region, justifying the widespread devotion the god received there. Then the final chapter boldly makes a further claim to authority over the fates of all officials, living and dead, in all parts of the empire. Whereas the god's special role within Shu was a well accepted fact, the second assertion was a direct, evangelical challenge to a host of local and regional cults specializing in examination aid or prognostication. Whatever the personal histories and meritorious achievements of these examination gods might be, all were now required to acknowledge their subordination to an obscure figure from a remote mountain in Sichuan as the single supreme arbiter of the fates of officials. By setting himself up as the patron deity of the literati, the god claimed a wealthy, socially mobile segment of society that would, by its very nature, protect the god from most claims of heterodoxy and social disruptiveness.

The *Book of Transformations* is composed of disparate parts deriving from different hands. Some are no doubt fresh innovations that presented to the faithful unsuspected episodes in their god's past. Others present age-old features of the cult that would have been familiar to all its adherents. But even these traditional features have been molded to present the god in the best light and to provide the god with a consistent persona.

The image of the Divine Lord depicted in the *Book of Transformations* was definitive on the translocal level. Within the Zitong community the god continued to be the omnifunctional local deity responding to the immediate needs of the populace that we see throughout traditional China. This is why rebels like Zhang Xianzhong 張獻忠, at the end of the Ming, were able to claim the god's support in their battle against legitimate authority and win over the local populace to this interpretation. But on the national level, although the god continued to respond to a variety of requests and function in a variety of ways, all of these aspects are rooted in the complex deity portrayed in the *Book of Transformations*. In this sense the book was a great success and Liu Ansheng can be considered the founder of the modern cult.

The Teachings of the *Book of Transformations*

The *Book of Transformations* is not merely a hagiography, it is a didactic work, intended to instruct its readers and induce a change in their lives. This purpose is stated explicitly in the Divine Lord's preface to the 1181 revelation:

> There are two processes of transformation. There is the transformation of physical transformation (*bianhua* 變化); there is the transformation of moral transformation (*jiaohua* 教化). Entering Being from Non-being, the past becoming the present, the young and vital becoming old and dying, the old and dying becoming young infants, this is the transformation of physical transformation. The Three Mainstays, the Five Constants,[102] right and wrong, deviant and correct, the ruler using mores to influence his subordinates, this is the transformation of moral transformation.

The previous section traced the physical transformations of the god as he evolved from age to age, from incarnation to incarnation. Here we will examine the moral transformation that is the explicit purpose of the *Book of Transformations* by considering the ethical content of the tales therein and the world view that the text embodies.

Perhaps the most obvious message of the *Book of Transformations* is that personal cultivation through appropriate conduct will result in progress toward a transcendent goal, that divinity can be attained through personal

---

102. The Three Mainstays are the relationships of ruler and subject, father and son, and husband and wife; the Five Constants are benevolence, righteousness, propriety, knowledge, and credibility. On these seminal ethical terms, see Hsü Dau-lin 1970–71.

隸　掌　挂　籍　圖

Figure 3. The Divine Lord peruses the Cinnamon Record

effort. This is an old theme in Daoism, recalling Ge Hong's famous proclamation, "I at this very moment know that transcendence (*xian* 仙) can be
attained."[103] The Divine Lord of Zitong has a celestial origin in primeval
chaos, but he elects to descend to this world and undergo a process of personal refinement spanning two millennia that culminates in his reintegration into the Heavens at the upper reaches of the pantheon. The *Book of
Transformations* is a record of his path of cultivation but also a map revealing how an aspiring immortal could pursue his goal through ethical endeavor,
service to the state, and religious praxis. We will first examine the sacred
realm and its interactions with the temporal world as portrayed in the *Book
of Transformations*, then present the fundamental principles that inform that
work's ethical worldview.

The Sacred Realm of the Book of Transformations

In comparing the sacred realm of Chinese religion in general and the *Book
of Transformations* in particular to that of other cultures, one is immediately
struck by the many parallels in the Chinese case between the sacred and profane worlds. Humans move from one realm to the other without dramatic
shifts in identity, lifestyle, or social relations. For the most part, officials
upon death become divine officials and incarnating divine officials become
temporal officials; personal names and lineage membership survive the great
transition and actions of dead and living members of a lineage continue to
influence each other; moral culpability and merit earned while alive continue to influence the fate of the individual and his family. Parallels in
structure and organization are particularly striking.

Atop the sacred realm of the *Book of Transformations* sits an autocratic
ruler, the Jade Thearch, often simply called the Thearch. He rules through
a vast bureaucracy of divine officials that extends down to every village and
household of this world and encompasses all the realms of the dead, the
divine, and the demonic. The system is simpler than that of Daoist doctrine
in that there is no mention in the *Book of Transformations* of the many
homologous superimposed heavens that we find in Daoist sources as early
as the fifth-century *Chart of the Ranks and Responsibilities of the Perfected
Spirits*.[104] There is a similar dearth of reference to the many celestial

---

103. *Baopuzi* 3/10/9.
104. *167 Dongxuan lingbao zhenling weiye tu.* See the summary of this pantheon in Kubo 1986:
111–12.

officers who populate these heavens; only those offices occupied by the Divine Lord at the beginning and end of his journey of transformation are mentioned.

There is, by contrast, considerable detail concerning the terrestrial component of the divine administration. These gods, often referred to as "earth spirits" (*diqi* 地祇), are the direct counterparts of mortal officials and like them still require the sustenance of human food in the form of "bloody victuals" (*xieshi* 血食).[105] The upper echelons of this bureaucracy are occupied by figures associated with natural features, primarily mountains and rivers. The gods of the five marchmounts (*wuyue* 五嶽) arrayed in the five cardinal directions (including the center) have general authority over all the gods of their region much as they were thought to have ruled regional feudal lords in Warring States times.[106] Mountain kings (*shanwang* 山王) supervise smaller regions but are near enough to the marchmounts in authority to challenge their actions when necessary (ch. 33). River gods are dragons, subordinate to the Sovereign of the Seas (*hairuo* 海若).[107] No mention is made in the *Book of Transformations* of city gods (*chenghuang shen* 城隍神), but there are village gods (*yishen* 邑神) and hamlet gods (*lishen* 里神, chs. 36–38, 40) as well as tutelary deities (*tudi* 土地) of individual households (ch. 40). These chthonic spirits are aided in their tasks by the family ancestors, who also watch over their descendants and report to the bureaucracy any threat posed to them by mortal or divine malefactors (ch. 60). Terrestrial spirits were once conceived of as semi-zoomorphic divine beings far removed from human experience like the Viper, but in the *Book of Transformations* they are portrayed as dead humans selected to fill bureaucratic posts on the basis of merit, though river dragons still seem to be of a different order.

Demons also retain their monstrous, nonhuman identities in the *Book of Transformations*, but even they are portrayed in a somewhat positive light. Demons have always had an ambiguous role in Daoism. Given free rein, they are vicious, blood-thirsty malefactors who wander about killing, stealing, and sowing disease. But these demons can also be tamed and organized

---

105. On this topic, see Kleeman 1994; and my article "Licentious Cults and Bloody Victuals: Standards of Religious Orthodoxy in Traditional China," forthcoming in *Asia Major* (1995).

106. Kleeman 1994. See, in particular, the subcommentary to *Shangshu zhengyi* 2/19a.

107. Although these water gods seem to occupy a hierarchy parallel to that of earth gods, they are not completely independent; in chapter 33 a river god is summoned and commanded by the god of Western Marchmount and in chapter 32 a dragon indicts a neighboring mountain god for rape.

under demonic generals and kings into armies that can subjugate unruly ghosts, fend off supernatural attacks, and aid the state in the maintenance of order and the suppression of rebellion. Daoist priests and laymen receive a series of registers giving them control over progressively larger groups of these fell troops.[108] The *Book of Transformations* reflects this ambiguous attitude toward demons. In chapter 12 the Divine Lord first awakens to his divine identity when combatting a group of epidemic demons that had already claimed his parents as victims. After his divine troops have rounded up five half-animal demons, they plead for mercy, explaining that they attack only individuals with "a heavy accumulation of otherworldly offenses" or "those whose heavenly lifespan is at an end." Thus demons are seen to have their proper place in the world acting as Heaven's instruments in collecting the evil and ill-fated, but still subject to the commands of protecting deities like the Divine Lord. In fact, one of the transformational identities of the Divine Lord worshiped in the main temple in Zitong is that of Wenzu 瘟祖, Patriarch of Epidemic Demons.

Buddhist deities have a similarly ambiguous role in the *Book of Transformations*. The tremendous appeal of Buddhism during the Song is evident in the rise of Neo-Confucianism, which rejected Buddhism as foreign while assimilating much of its doctrine and practice into Confucianism. Other Song religious movements, like the Complete Perfection school of Daoism that arose in North China in the twelfth and thirteenth centuries, treated Buddhism more straightforwardly as one of three Chinese religious traditions all sharing common goals and ethical standards. The uncertain status of Buddhism in such arrangements is evident in the thirteenth-century polemical debates that pitted representatives of the Complete Perfection school against Buddhists.[109] In the *Book of Transformations* the Buddha is a mighty figure replete with salvific power and the Divine Lord receives from him a Buddhist title, but the Buddha seems to stand outside the Chinese pantheon, neither superior nor subordinate to the Thearch, and no specifically Buddhist role (mendicant world-renouncer, begging monk, master of a paradaisical realm, or fully enlightened Buddha) is ever adopted or even promoted as a serious goal by the Divine Lord.

---

108. Many Yao tribes still organize their social structure on the basis of such registers. See Strickmann 1982; Lemoine 1982. Lowell Skar is currently investigating the role of Daoism in the Yao society of northern Thailand.

109. For the relations between the Complete Perfection school and Buddhism, see the essays reprinted in Kubo 1992.

The sacred realm of the *Book of Transformations* is an amalgam of the Daoist and popular pantheons. This is evident in the Divine Lord's course of development. One would normally expect him to move through various offices of the terrestrial administration, perhaps paralleling his real world rise in official titles, or if he is to be considered a Daoist deity, to begin with a relatively low-level transcendent position before transferring to progressively more exalted stellar ranks. Instead he seems to jump back and forth between the two pantheons. He becomes sovereign of one of the most famous Daoist grotto-heavens, populated entirely by transcendents (ch. 20), then is named Great Transcendent of secluded Snow Mountain (ch. 21) before being appointed a Mountain King with sovereignty over a collection of unruly mountain gods and spirits who still subsist on blood sacrifice (ch. 31). Daoism since its inception had wavered between rejecting the popular pantheon as profane and evil and accepting this pantheon as a debased, clearly subordinate counterpart of the pure Daoist heavens. During the Song this process of accommodation accelerated as Daoist priests increasingly came to incorporate rites to popular deities within the framework of their Offerings (*jiao* 醮) and Fasts (*zhai* 齋) to the celestial pantheon of the Daoist heavens. The Zitong cult, however, seems to promote a more radical amalgam of the two pantheons, one that sees transcendents and gods as essentially similar and of comparable rank.

The unifying feature of this syncretic cosmology that I call the unitary sacred realm is an extensive system of recordkeeping and merit-based reward and punishment. Everyone from the lowest tutelary household god to the Thearch himself has a role in compiling, reviewing, and enforcing the dictates of these cosmic records. Just as the Divine Lord in one incarnation is called upon to sit in judgment on the quick and the dead (ch. 68), these records record the good and evil acts of living and dead humans, and all manner of supernatural beings. The actions recorded therein, in turn, determine one's disposition after death, official positions within the divine hierarchy, and eventual rebirth. Judgments based on these records have an independent legitimacy that transcends the barriers of death and rebirth, as we see in the case of the woman who was fated to die by lightning for unfilial behavior toward her mother-in-law but died before the sentence could be executed; thirty years later in a new physical form the punishment still hung over her head (ch. 57).

The god of Zitong has a key role in this scheme as the master of the most important set of records, the Cinnamon Record. A story in the 1194 continuation of the *Book of Transformations* gives us insight into the nature of this record. A man named Li Deng 李登 has consulted a Daoist priest because in spite of great talent he has been unsuccessful in four attempts at obtaining the *jinshi* degree. The priest consults the Divine Lord, who quotes the following entry in the Cinnamon Record:[110]

When Li Deng was first born he was bestowed a jade seal and was fated to place first on the district examinations at eighteen and be valdedictorian at the palace examinations at nineteen. At thirty-three he should have reached the rank of Chancellor of the Right (*youxiang* 右相). After being selected he spied on a neighbor woman, Zhang Yanniang. Although the affair had not been resolved, he had her father, Zhang Cheng, bound and thrown into jail. For this crime his success was postponed ten years and he was demoted to the second group of successful examinees. After being selected at the age of twenty-eight he encroached upon and seized the dwelling of his elder brother, Li Feng, and this resulted in litigation. For this his success was postponed another ten years and he was demoted to the third group of graduates. After being selected at the age of thirty-eight, he violated Madame née Zheng, the wife of a freeman in his room in Chang'an, then framed her husband, Bai Yuan, for a crime. For this his success was postponed a further ten years and his standing was demoted to the fourth group. After being selected at the age of forty-eight, he stole Qingniang, the maiden daughter of his neighbor Wang Ji. As an unrepentant evil-doer, he has already been erased from the records. He will never pass.

Although clearly subordinate to a figure like the Thearch, the Divine Lord is positioned at the confluence of the myriad streams of reports issuing from officials at all levels of the divine bureaucracy. On the basis of the merits and demerits recorded in the Cinnamon Record the Divine Lord determines two essential aspects of human fate, birth and occupational achievement, functions reflected in his titles as "injector of life" (*zhusheng* 注生) and "director of emoluments" (*silu* 司祿). Since both of these roles are related to the god's new association with the constellation Wenchang, I will first discuss the historical background of this asterism and its worship before considering the ethical significance of the *Book of Transformations*.

---

110. DZ 79, 4/18b–19a; DZJY 80, 80a–b.

The Constellation Wenchang and Its Worship

The personification of Wenchang as an astral deity is of great antiquity. The earliest reference is found in the "Distant Wandering" ("Yuanyou" 遠遊) poem of the *Elegies of Chu* (*Chuci* 楚辭). There we read:

> I made Wen Chang follow, too, to marshal the procession,
> Disposing the gods in their places in my retinue.[111]

Already Wenchang seems to be in a commanding position, directing other gods and able to keep them in order. The reason for this image of Wenchang lies in the identities of its constituent stars.

The constellation Wenchang consists of six stars in Ursa Major (ϑ, Φ, Θ, f, e, and another Ursae Majoris).[112] They are arrayed in a crescent above the ladle of the Big Dipper. The "Monograph on the Heavenly Offices" ("Tianguan shu" 天官書) of the *Shiji* (ca. 100 B.C.) describes the constellation in the following terms:

> The ladle (*kui* 魁) of the Dipper wears a basket as a cap. The six stars are called the Palace of Wenchang. The first is called the Superior General (*Shangjiang* 上將); the second is called the Subordinate General (*Cijiang* 次將); the third is called Noble Minister (*Guixiang* 貴相); the fourth is called Director of Fates (*Siming* 司命); the fifth is called Director of the Interior (*Sizhong* 司中); the sixth is called the Director of Emoluments (*Silu* 司祿). The stars in the middle of the ladle of the Dipper are the prison of noble personages.[113]

Later sources give a slightly different enumeration of the stars composing Wenchang. In the *Hanshu* the fifth star is the Director of Emoluments and the sixth star is the Director of Disasters (*Sizai* 司災). Astrological treatises in the dynastic histories from the *Jinshu* on give the fourth star as the

---

111. Hawkes 1985: 197. In his notes to this line (p. 202) Hawkes explains Wenchang's role by saying that he was a patron of officials, "well qualified to see that the attendant deities were arranged in correct order of precedence," but this is anachronistic. He is more a representative of high officials than a patron.

112. Ho 1966: 74. Yi Shitong (1981: 19) lists six primary and eight "supplemental" (*zeng* 增) stars associated with Wenchang (items 233–46), one of which does not have a Western name (p. 167).

113. *Shiji* 27/1293; *Shiki kōchū kōshō* 27/9. The last sentence of this passage probably refers to only four of the six, a group sometimes called the Heavenly Administrators (*Tianli* 天理). The *Jijie* commentary to this passage quotes a *Tradition* ("Zhuan") identifying four stars within the ladle as the *Tianli*. Wang Yuanqi 王元啓 (1714–86) speculates that the characters *sixing* 四星, "four stars," have dropped out of the text.

Director of Emoluments, the fifth star as the Director of Fates, and the sixth star as the Director of Bandits (*Sikou* 司寇).[114]

The identifications made in the *Shiji* seem to have been the most widely accepted during the Han. The *Chunqiu yuanming bao* 春秋元命包, one of the "apocrypha" texts of the Han dynasty, explains the function of each star as follows:

> The Superior General establishes awesome martial (might); the Subordinate General rectifies the attendants; the Noble Minister administers written affairs; the Director of Emoluments rewards achievement and promotes scholars; the Director of Fates is in charge of disasters and divine punishment; the Director of the Interior is in charge of aiding and administering.[115]

In the "Treatise on Astrology" ("Tianwen zhi") of the *Jinshu* we are told that these six stars are the Six Offices (*liufu* 六府) of Heaven, and that they are in charge of "assembling and calculating the Way of Heaven" (*jiji tiandao* 集計天道).[116] In traditional portent astrology they had special relevance for high officials of state, and stellar irregularities (comets, novae, etc.) occurring in this constellation were thought to foretell a threat to or from one of these officers.[117]

Some of the constituent stars of Wenchang have a history of worship even longer than that of the constellation as a whole.[118] There are poems dedicated to the Greater and Lesser Directors of Fates among the Nine Songs of the *Elegies of Chu*. In the *Zhouli* we read of burnt offerings made to the Director of Fates and the Director of the Interior at the Southern

---

114. *Hanshu* 6/1275 and *Jinshu* 11/291.

115. Quoted in the "Suoyin" commentary to the *Shiji* 27/1293; *Shiki kōchū kōshō* 27/9.

116. *Jinshu* 11/291; Ho 1966: 74; cf. *Suishu* 19/532. Ho identifies these six offices with six similarly named heads of tax offices, a group Hucker (1985: 3789, p. 317) calls the Six Tax Supervisors. If this identification is correct, the unifying element must have been their common function in "keeping the books," with the stellar counterparts maintaining ledgers of constantly increasing and decreasing personal balances of life and fortune much as the tax supervisors kept track of governmental income and outlays for their departments. But the functions attributed to the six constituent stars in various sources seem far removed from tax collection, and it may be that the Six Offices are unrelated positions within the divine hierarchy. It is uncertain exactly what the phrase concerning calculating the Way of Heaven originally referred to, but it could certainly have been interpreted as a reference to his stewardship of the official registers.

117. Schafer 1977: 91, 121.

118. Yamada (1975: 148) goes so far as to suggest that the focus of popular worship had already in Warring States times shifted to the Director of Fates.

Tumulus.[119] The three Directors came to be a regular object of sacrifice at the imperial suburban sacrifices, and this practice continued into late imperial times. Wenchang as a constellation was sometimes included among the astral deities worshiped at the time of these sacrifices; such was the case during the Jin dynasty and the Liang.[120] The Director of Fates was also the worshiped by the common people. In the *Fengsu tongyi*, after noting the Director of Fate's connection with Wenchang, Ying Shao 應劭 (?–ca. 204) describes images of this god painted on a board and either carried by travelers or worshiped in a separate room within the home.[121]

The name Wenchang originally must have referred to the appearance of the cap that was thought to cover the ladle of the Dipper (mentioned in the *Shiji* quote above), and hence should be understood as "patterned (or perhaps variegated) brilliance." By Tang times another interpretation prevailed. "*Wen*" was taken to refer to literature, and "*chang*" was interpreted as "flourishing, resplendent," hence Schafer's translation, "Literary Glory." Wenchang came to be the patron star of all literati, not only the six high officials specifically correlated with its constituent stars, and was often simply called *wenxing* 文星, "literary asterism."[122] Still, within the conservative occult traditions there was dispute concerning this wider interpretation of the significance of Wenchang as late as the seventeenth century.[123]

Wenchang appears frequently in Tang poetry, although usually under the name Literary Asterism, and was the symbol par excellence of the poet. Thus a group of imbibing poets is called a "gathering of Literary Asterisms," a poet's death is betokened by the asterism plunging from the sky, and another poet feels the need to assert that his writer's block is not the result of an occlusion of the constellation. It was also a representative of the civil

---

119. *Zhou li zhushu* 18/2a, Yamada 1975: 148. In his commentary to this passage, Zheng Zhong 鄭眾 (*zi* Sinong 司農, ca. 5 B.C. –A.D. 83) identifies the Director of Fates as Wenchang, and the Director of the Interior as the Three Terraces (*Santai* 三台). Zheng Xuan 鄭玄 (127–200) gives the more familiar identification of these two stars as the fourth and fifth stars of the Wenchang constellation. He also quotes a work linking the Director of Fates, Director of Interior, and Director of Emoluments with the upper, middle, and lower of the Three Terraces respectively.

120. *Jinshu* 19/584; *Suishu* 6/108.

121. *Fengsu tongyi tongjian* 8/65.

122. Schafer 1977: 121.

123. Xu Yingqiu 徐應秋 (1616 *jinshi*) records an incident at the end of the Chenghua reign period (1465–87). A comet passed through Wenchang, and the traditional interpretation was that this foretold an event influencing a member of the cabinet; in the event, however, a scholar at the Imperial University was demoted, revealing that Wenchang represents all literati, not merely high officials of state. Note that this story was recorded only because the traditional interpretation was still thought authoritative. See *Yuzhi tang tanhui* 20/37b.

virtues, and was often contrasted with asterisms symbolizing war and the military.[124]

At some point Wenchang came to have a special association with the civil sevice examination. This was in many ways a natural development from his earlier roles as the astrological analogue of high officials, and the patron saint of literati, and his association in particular with the Director of Emoluments, who, as we have seen above, already in the Han was thought responsible for the advancement of worthy individuals in office. Explicit attribution of this function to Wenchang, however, comes rather late. The earliest example I have found is by Wu Ceng 吳曾 (fl. 1170), who records the story of a man who won the first position on the examination in ritual, yet is not made Valedictorian (*zhuangyuan* 狀元). A prophecy has revealed that a Valedictorian will not appear until a gap in a bridge called the Wenchang Wier is sealed.[125] The earliest cult document linking Wenchang and the Divine Lord of Zitong dates to 1168, or roughly contemporaneous with this story. No doubt it was because of Wenchang's previous association with the examinations and the fate of the literati that it was chosen as the celestial alter-ego of the Divine Lord. This identification was first granted official recognition under the Yuan in 1316.[126]

The constellation also occurs in Taoist scriptures prior to the rise of the Zitong cult. The image of the asterism in these sources is at times quite different from that eventually adopted by the cult to the Divine Lord. The *Summoning Rite of the Ten Registers* (*1210 Zhengyi fawen shilu zhaoyi*), which Kobayashi dates to the late fifth century, invokes the Divine Lord as Director of Fates in Charge of Records of the Three Heavens.[127] Penetration into more popular levels of Daoism is evidenced by a "land contract" (actually a sepulchral document giving title to the grave in sacred space) from 485 invoking the Supreme Lord Lao and a host of traditional gods. At the bottom of the ceramic contract is a charm (*fu* 符) depicting the Dipper, Wenchang, and other circumpolar constellations. Wang Yucheng concludes that this charm is "an expression of worship of the Wenchang stars."[128] In the *Scripture of the Mysterious Gate and Sea of Jewels* (*Xuanmen baohai jing* 玄門寶海經, a pre-Tang work preserved in *1032 Yunji qiqian* 24/4a), the

---

124. Schafer 1977: 121–22.

125. *Nenggaizhai manlu* 18/14a.

126. See below, p. 74.

127. See *1210 Zhengyi fawen shilu zhaoyi* 4a; Kobayashi Masayoshi, personal communication, December 1991.

128. Wang Yucheng 1991: 87. On land contracts, see Kleeman 1984 and Seidel 1987.

"spirit-lord of the asterism Wenchang" is said to correspond to the Son of
Heaven and the Director of Fates. He can summon forth the fruits of the
mountains, and has a zoomorphic form, appearing as a gibbon in the morning, a monkey at noon, and a dead stone at dusk. To the Sichuanese ritual
specialist Du Guangting 杜廣庭 (850–933), Wenchang is a stellar abode
for a number of gods. He speaks of the "many saints of Wenchang in the
Six Palaces of the southern sky" who are in charge of the record of life, and
to whom one prays for life and fortune.[129] Wenchang occurs as a single
personified god again in *220 Wuchang xuanyuan santian yutang dafa*, a text
compiled in 1158 that Boltz characterizes as a "synthesis of Tianxin thera-
peutics and Shenxiao *liandu* rites."[130] There (5/8b–9a) the Dao Lord Wenchang, Exalted Perfected of the Supreme Bourne, ascends Mount Emei and,
seeing the people being oppressed by demons, creates a ritual to kill and
suppress them. This reference brings us close to the origins of the Zitong
cult, both temporally and geographically. But a more purely astronomical
understanding of the term was still common in certain Taoist circles. *770
Hunyuan shengji*, compiled in 1191, still speaks of Wenchang as a constellation from which the divinized Laozi emerges.[131]

Several features of the god Wenchang made him an appealing figure to
assimilate into the Zitong cult. Of primary importance was the association
of the constellation with literary inspiration and a successful career; this dove-
tailed perfectly with the Divine Lord's growing reputation as an examination oracle. The great antiquity of the Wenchang image, its appearance in
canonical works like the *Elegies of Chu*, and its role in the most solemn and
sacred of state rituals meant that the god possessed tremendous legitimacy, a
legitimacy badly needed by the expanding Zitong cult as it sought believers
in areas outside Sichuan and among the upper echelons of the scholar-
official elite. Finally, the presence of the god Wenchang in formal Daoist
scripture, albeit in a bewildering variety of guises, held a similar import for
China's indigenous religious professionals; the Divine Lord's revelation of a
major recension of a core text like the *Transcendent Scripture of the Great
Grotto* was much more acceptable now that he could be located within their

---

129. *616 Guangchengji* 7/8a. *1225 Daomen kefan daquanji*, usually attributed to Du, contains a full
ritual to the Divine Lord of Zitong as the "Master of the Director of Emoluments of Sevenfold
Mountain." But if portions of this work were in fact edited by Du, this ritual was certainly not one of
them. It cites the god's official eight-character title, which was awarded in 1154. On Du Guangting,
and his works see Verellen (1989).

130. Boltz 1987: 36–37. I have converted the romanization in this quote into pinyin.

131. *770 Hunyuan shengji* 7/35b.

own pantheon, and it was easier to justify granting him a subsidiary shrine within Daoist abbeys. Cults like the Way of Pure Brightness dedicated to Xu Xun were at this time also forging links to stellar deities like the Transcendent Lord of Grand Tenuity who was the revealing deity of their *Ledger of Merits and Demerits* (*186 Taiwei xianjun gongguo ge*). The Zitong cult was fortunate that a star god with such apt specializations and well-documented history was still available for assimilation, but their success was in part a result of their own boldness in claiming not merely the support of this stellar deity but his identity with their own object of worship.

Ethical Principles of the Book of Transformations

Ethics has always been central to Chinese thought. The earliest surviving historical documents, the speeches and pronouncements of the *Book of Documents*, justify political actions like usurpation in ethical terms. The rites (*li* 禮) so central to the Confucian tradition are not empty ritual forms but concrete expressions of ethical principles that both define and reproduce the proper order of society. Even the seemingly Machiavellian teachings of the legalists are rather heavy-handed attempts to maintain a cosmically sanctioned social hierarchy. With the rise of institutionalized religion in the second century A.D. more explicit codes of conduct were formulated as sets of precepts (*jie* 戒) tailored to laypeople and religious professionals. Seekers of transcendent immortality like Ge Hong affirm that moral conduct is a prerequisite for their arcane alchemical practices and biographies of antinomian figures like Ruan Ji (210–63) stress that their breaches of etiquette are rooted in an excess of cardinal virtues like filial piety rather than their absence.[132]

The ethical principles expressed in the *Book of Transformations* are well within the mainstream of Chinese ethical thought. They center on two values that glue the Chinese social order together, filial piety (*xiao* 孝) and its political correlate, loyalty (*zhong* 忠). The ethical positions propounded by the *Book of Transformations* can be surveyed under four rubrics, involving the individual's responsibilities toward the family, the community, the state, and the gods.

The family is important in all Chinese ethical systems but it had a special significance for the Zitong cult that was manifest in the tales of the *Book of*

---

132. See, for example, the story of Ruan Ji's unconventional but heartfelt mourning for his mother in *Jinshu* 49/1361; Mather 1976: 374.

Transformations, in temple architecture, and in state recognition. In the *Book of Transformations* the god of Zitong repeatedly encounters members of his divine family; they form a karmic group working toward a common goal through many incarnations, adopting new identities while maintaining the same gender and generational relationships. The cult site in Zitong since Song times has had a Family Blessings Tower (*jiaqinglou* 家慶樓) where statues of his extended family surround the god and this was copied at many Zitong temples. During the Song the god was already famous for the large number of his relatives who had received official titles.[133] Twice in the *Book of Transformations* the god in human form regrets his separation from his temporal family and looks forward to being reunited with them.[134] Moreover, he was worshiped as a fertility god who sent sons, especially sons fated to achieve great success on the examinations and in their official careers, sons who might even be avatars of the god. Finally, the role of the god as patron and representative of the Zhang clan also suggests a special significance placed on the traditional family.

The primary injunction of filial piety was concern and physical care for the parents, both while alive and after death. When a parent is ill, the child must be prepared to make any sacrifice to restore health. In his first incarnation the Divine Lord sucked the pus out of his mother's suppurating abscess, then sliced off the flesh of his own thigh to feed her (ch. 7). He recommended for divine office a son who had copied a scripture in his own blood in order to heal his father (ch. 32) and protected a son who had offended a violent knight by denying him meat intended for an ailing mother (ch. 34). Responsibilities for one's birth parents do not end even when formally adopted into another family (ch. 50). While the son of a low-born concubine might have to obey his classificatory mother (i.e., father's primary wife) while alive, after her death he should search out his birth mother and try to make amends for the hardships she has suffered (ch. 52).

Continuing to serve one's parents after their death is equally important. In his first incarnation the Divine Lord makes an elaborate show of observing the demanding classical funerary rituals due his dead parents and carefully guards their tomb long after the end of the prescribed three-year mourning period (chs. 10–11). Revenge for the death of a parent is sanc-

---

133. *Mengliang lu* 14/6a.

134. In chapter 17 the god, after a long period of service at court and feeling like "a bird with tired wings," conceives a "desire to return home"; in the *Esoteric Biography of Qinghe*, as the divine emissary is about to lead him off to his new position in the Heavens, his only doubt about leaving this mortal coil is revealed when he asks, "What about the members of my family?"

tioned; the Divine Lord confronts even fearsome demons responsible for his parents' death (ch. 12) and, another time, pursues the murderers across centuries and changes in identity (ch. 64–65). The importance of maintaining family traditions is evident when the god journeys to the capital to assume the hereditary post from which his father had been banished to his death for outspoken criticism of the king (ch. 22).

Although the parents are the center of filial devotion, the *Book of Transformations* advocates concern for the extended family. On the broadest level, the god looks after his entire clan, which "all come from the same root," by establishing a charitable estate to support poor members and by aiding in the education, marriage, medical treatment, and burial of his kinsmen (ch. 18). The importance of sibling bonds is revealed when the god gives up his own son in order to continue his dead brother's line (ch. 23) and when he punishes an abusive elder brother (ch. 58). Infanticide, a problem then as it is now, is strongly condemned (ch. 35), as are customs that give precedence to sons and slight daughters (ch. 53). Distaff offspring of concubines and serving girls are to be accorded the same treatment as sons of the primary wife (ch. 58). On the whole, though, sons are viewed primarily as extensions of the father and instruments through which he can perform good works. Thus when one son is given over to a dead brother's family to continue his line, the matter of the child's desires is not raised, and both sons in the first incarnation are married off to the orphaned daughters of a colleague even though a match with the destitute offspring of an official who had died out of royal favor was surely not the most advantageous coupling that could have been arranged (ch. 27).[135]

If women as mothers received their sons' devotion and, whenever circumstances permitted, loving care, as wives the women in the *Book of Transformations* live lives bounded by duty to their spouses and their spouses' lineages. Nowhere is this as succinctly expressed as in the prayer intoned by the widowed mother-to-be of the god's second incarnation, which ends, "Send down on [her in-laws'] behalf your supernatural aid and permit me to bear a male child to carry on the Zhang clan. Then though I may forfeit my own life, I would have no regrets" (ch. 21). A woman facing imminent execution for mistreating her mother-in-law in a previous life expresses a similar mind-set. She regrets only that her death will leave her husband and mother-in-law with no one to serve them and will humiliate her birth

---

135. In the 1194 revelation the sons of the Divine Lord are employed more actively, incarnating in this world to battle evil and save the empire. See DZJY chapters 76, 79, and 86.

parents, and prays only that her sentence be postponed until she can give birth to a son who can carry on the line (ch. 57). The case of the Divine Lord's first wife, who, having become enamored of the god, dies rather than accept as husband the unworthy young man chosen by her family then revives three years later to marry the Divine Lord, suggests a certain amount of justification for females deciding their own fate, but in fact the young woman is merely recognizing a karmically ordained relationship and her very limited purpose in life is revealed when she dies as soon as their son loses his baby teeth (chs. 8–9). The importance of this admittedly limited role is, however, made clear in the second incarnation, when the god's widowed mother instructs him in ettiquette, history, and the classics, stands in for the father at his capping ceremony, and finally guides the god in meditative practice and metaphysical principles (chs. 22 and 28). In the *Book of Transformations* a woman is not merely a bearer of children and servant to her in-laws, but also a source of wisdom and unselfish love.

Although secondary to the family, the community is the object of considerable concern in the *Book of Transformations*. This is clearly reflected in the god's first incarnation, during which the god promoted the adoption of Han Chinese dress and customs among his non-Chinese countrymen, taught them to read the classical Chinese canons, and sacrificed a numinous statue of the Primordial Heavenly Worthy to quell a threatening typhoon (chs. 4–6). In this same incarnation the god devotes himself to allaying the ravages of disease, mastering first the exorcistic medicine of the priest, then the physiological cures of the physician, assiduously refining these arts until "anyone whose Heavenly lifespan was not exhausted did not die before their time" (chs. 12–13).[136] In divine office the god worked equally diligently to further the interests of the community, punishing not only robbers, kidnappers, and murderers, but also slanderers and fabricators of fraudulent weights and measures (chs. 60, 53, 49, 54, 55). He walks a fine line in protecting the oppressed while preserving the social order, as when he reprimands the landowner who imposed infanticide on his tenant farmers by demonstrating the evil consequences of this policy without ever challenging the landowner's right to pursue it (ch. 36).

Service to the state is central to the ethos of the *Book of Transformations*. The Divine Lord of Zitong incarnates repeatedly as a temporal official and

---

136. In the 1194 continuation of the *Book of Transformations* the god also manifests in human form to save drowning men and women in a flood and to bury festering, untended corpses. See DZJY chapters 83 and 92.

functions as a divine official when not so engaged. His conduct in both types of office was intended to serve as a model for officials and future officials among his readers just as the temporal and divine officials he punishes through these lives were intended as warnings. Although he does occasionally enjoy the fruits of his high offices, particularly in the chapter "Returning Home in Glory" (ch. 17), the focus is clearly on the duties of his office. His devotion to these responsibilities is so great that, as he remarks when he has attained high office in his first incarnation, "my love for my lord and concern for my country never allowed me a moment's peace of mind" (ch. 16).

The official values promoted in the *Book of Transformations* are quite traditional. The official is to put the good of the state above his personal welfare, expressing resolute opposition to improper courses of action through remonstrances that are, however, often couched in the indirect language of the *Book of Poetry*.[137] Worthy colleagues whose counsel is ignored or who have fallen victim to unjustified slander are to be defended at court (chs. 16, 24) and should righteous protest lead to their death, their family should be aided (ch. 27). Subordinates are to be treated kindly but carefully supervised—not given free rein to plunder the populace (chs. 56, 62, 67). The common people are to be governed with justice tempered by compassion, emphasizing rehabilitation rather than punishment (ch. 67). In addition to his civic duties, the Divine Lord sometimes must take up arms in defense of his homeland, but this is a minor theme.[138]

The area of government service presented certain ethical dilemmas. Prime among them was how to reconcile the conflicting imperatives of unswerving loyalty to one's lord and acceptance of the shifting Mandate of Heaven amidst the tumult of dynastic change. The Divine Lord responds to the Qin conquest of Sichuan by withdrawing from the world, but resumes his duties when he is informed of an injustice needing rectification, and counsels a pair of agitated dragons to accept the changed political situation (chs. 48, 50, 51). A similar problem is posed in the second incarnation when the son of a blood-enemy responsible for the death of the incarnated god's father turns out to be an exemplary young man and promising official; the Divine Lord places duty to the state above personal revenge in recommending him for high office (ch. 26). The *Book of Transformations* also provides examples of appropriate interference in the affairs of other officials (ch. 33)

---

137. Chapters 24, 25, and 29. As a divine official with nothing to fear from the ruler's anger, the Divine Lord's protests became more bold (chapter 44–46).

138. Chapter 69. In the 1194 revelation, however, this role of martial protector is far more prominent. Cf. DZJY chapter 75, 76, 87, DZ chapter 84, 85.

and of times when independent action without prior approval from the
central government is justified (ch. 31). As to the delicate question of official corruption in a society in which bribery was widespread, a son is not
condemned for trying to obtain the freedom of his unjustly imprisoned
father through bribery, but the official who takes his gift and then executes
the father is severely punished (ch. 49). Two stories raise questions about
the reliability of forced confessions, but in both cases only the intervention
of a divine being can right the injustice (chs. 35, 49).

Not surprisingly, the *Book of Transformations* provides a good deal of information about the normative relations between man and god. The will of
the gods should be consulted through traditional divinatory means like
scapulimancy and *Yijing* divination (ch. 50) and their warnings embodied
in natural disasters and other anomalies should be heeded (ch. 33). Men
owe the gods reverence expressed through worship of their statues, but the
Divine Lord derides those who worship false gods whose images are mere
earth and wood, devoid of true numinous power (ch. 72). Scriptures, both
Daoist and Buddhist, are to be copied, recited, and worshiped; such acts
bring both supernatural aid in this life and merit in the next one (chs. 11–
12, 28, 32). Pilgrimage in search of a divine teacher and/or enlightenment
is a worthy goal (chs. 19, 30), but it is also possible to encounter the gods
on one's home turf as they travel through the land in magnificent proces-
sions and attend local religious ceremonies (chs. 48, 66, 56). The gods, like
men, are subject to moral codes and when a god acts unethically he can suffer reprimand, demotion, "corporal" punishment, or imprisonment (chs.
32, 33, 66).

The *Book of Transformations* fulfills many functions, introducing the
Divine Lord, legitimizing his power, and locating him within China's great
intellectual and religious traditions, but its role as a model of principled
conduct in a confusing world was certainly one of its most important and
probably its most enduring, a primary reason for its continuing popularity
and frequent reprinting many centuries after its composition. The next section will discuss the role of the *Book of Transformations* within the Chinese
literary tradition, including its place among the earliest examples of the
genre of "morality books."

The *Book of Transformations* as Literature

The *Book of Transformations* is unique in Chinese literary history; there seems
to be no other example of a revealed, prosimetric autobiography of a god.

But all literary works, no matter how innovative, are given birth within traditions of literary expression and narrative structure, and this is particularly true of scripture. By the twelfth century China possessed a long, diverse literary history and the author(s)[139] of the *Book of Transformations* drew, consciously or unconsciously, from earlier Chinese historic, hagiographic, and scriptural traditions. Similarly, although no book exactly like the *Book of Transformations* was produced for other deities, the *Book of Transformations* did have a profound effect on subsequent hagiographic compositions and perhaps on the development of Chinese fiction. This section will examine the antecedents for the *Book of Transformations* and its influence on later Chinese literature, both sacred and secular.

Traditional Antecedents

One important source of the *Book of Transformations* lies in historical writing. Much of Chinese history is recorded in anecdotes of limited length focusing on specific incidents and meant to convey a single message. This is true of the fourth-century B.C. *Traditions of Zuo* (*Zuozhuan* 左傳), which presents an annalistic account of history as specific, discrete events, and of the biographies and treatises of standard histories, which string together incident after incident with little attempt to show how one event influenced subsequent actions (Egan 1977). Hagiographic collections like the *Traditions of Arrayed Transcendents* (*Liexian zhuan* 列仙傳, tr. Kaltenmark 1953) follow this model as well. Another subgenre of historical writing, often mistakenly treated as a nascent fictional prose, is the "accounts of anomalies" (*zhiguai* 志怪), which also takes the form of one or more disparate anecdotes concerning a specific place or person.[140]

The *Book of Transformations* draws from this tradition its basic style and narrative technique. The earliest elements of cult lore (the Viper's encounter with the Five Stalwarts, the inundation of Qiong Pool, the encounter with Yao Chang) are recorded in anecdotes found in official histories and

---

139. As noted above (pp. 28–29), the "author" of a text like the *Book of Transformations* is a complex concept, including the implied author (the Divine Lord himself), the actual mediums who wielded the brush, and the editors, a group that may include the mediums as well. Henceforth I will use the term "author" to refer to this composite entity.

140. On the *zhiguai* genre as a whole, see DeWoskin 1983. On the fundamentally historical character of these materials, see the recent articles by Yu (1987) and Hammond (1990). See also Kleeman 1992–93, where I argue that the primary standard by which literati in late imperial China judged the orthodoxy of cult lore was whether it derived from explicitly fictional sources (like novels) or from the type of historical source discussed here.

early regional gazetteers like the *Account of the Land of Huayang* (*Huayang-guo zhi* 華陽國志). Moreover, the tales of the Divine Lord's interactions with the temporal realm while in divine office, which make up a substantial portion of the work (chs. 31–62), are also, taken individually, anecdotes. Some no doubt circulated orally, perhaps even in written collections that do not survive, as independent tales. Finally, in terms of style, the language of the *Book of Transformations* is a simple literary Chinese very similar in diction and vocabulary to that of historical works and anecdotal collections.

The autobiographical viewpoint in the *Book of Transformations* is distinctive. Wu Pei-yi (1990) has shown that China possesses a long and distinguished history of autobiographical writings. Prominent early examples are chapters in the *Records of the Historian* (*Shiji* 史記) of Sima Qian 司馬遷 (145–86 B.C.), the *Discourses Weighed in the Balance* (*Lunheng* 論衡) of Wang Chong 王充 (27–?), and the *Master Embracing Simplicity* (*Baopuzi* 抱朴子) of Ge Hong 葛洪 (283–343).[141] The *Book of Transformations* differs from these works in several ways. First, while these works append a one-chapter autobiography to a lengthy book on unrelated topics as a way of introducing the author and explaining his motivations, the *Book of Transformations* is an integral work wholly concerned with the life of the god who eventually becomes the Divine Lord of Zitong. The god, his maturation, spiritual growth, good deeds and sins are the sole focus of the book.

Second, these early examples, in spite of their autobiographical character, are written in the third person, giving the author a certain emotional remove and seeming objectivity.[142] In the *Book of Transformations* the first-person pronoun is prominent. The reader is never in doubt that he is being directly addressed by the individual who experienced the narrated events. The resulting sense of immediacy and direct communication greatly increases the emotive power of the text. We hear the god squirm and rationalize as he deals with his own guilt, and exult as he receives exculpation and honors from the most powerful forces of the universe. In a text designed to change the behavior of its readers, this direct, personal communication was no doubt very effective.

Finally, the *Book of Transformations* is explicitly didactic in purpose. Earlier autobiographies were intended to introduce and explain the background of

---

141. Sima Qian's autobiography is found in *Shiji* 130/ 3285–3322. For Wang Chong, see *Lunheng jiaoshi*, v. 4, 30/1179–99; Forke 1911: I/64–82. Ge Hong's autobiography is found in *Baopuzi* 50/199–204; Ware 1966: 6–21.

142. Wu comments (p. 9), "Prior to 1560 very few Chinese autobiographers could bring themselves to abandon the posture of the historian and thus to depart from third-person narration."

a larger work that carried a moral message. Here the autobiography itself is the message. Through his many transformations the Divine Lord presents models of appropriate behavior for the filial son, devoted husband, caring father, and compassionate official. In this sense, the work is much closer to the biographies (*zhuan* 傳) of a standard history like Sima Qian's *Records of the Historian* than his "Personal Preface" or even the accounts in hagiographic collections, which teach a lesson about the nature of the unattainable sacred rather than a prototype for personal transcendence.

Autobiography inevitably raises questions about the conception of the "self." The "self" of the *Book of Transformations* transcends the individual human being; the Divine Lord possesses many identities and many names. Still there is a constant core that constitutes the god's subjectivity and that informs the first-person narrator of the text. This transcendent identity is linked to the surname Zhang, which the Divine Lord assumes in every incarnation except when he was commanded to assume the identity of son of the Han emperor Liu Bang (ch. 64),[143] but is ultimately defined by the god's role in a transcendent family group that share many of his incarnations. Through this family we see that the Divine Lord's subjectivity has social ties and emotions of love and concern for these family members that surpass the bonds of any one lifetime or human identity. Thus the self in the *Book of Transformations* is a reincarnating, transforming individual who experiences multiple human identities as he or she progresses along a path of spiritual development. By defining personal growth in terms of moral cultivation, the *Book of Transformations* sets the stage for the interiority and self-examination of the late Ming autobiographical works discussed by Wu.

Buddhist Antecedents

Buddhism had a profound influence on all aspects of Chinese literature, especially hagiography.[144] The relevant category of Indic literature is the records of "noteworthy deeds," known in Sanskrit as *avadāna*, and its subgenre, the *jātaka*.[145] *Avadāna* are illustrative tales relating a significant action, usually good, and its subsequent karmic result; in *jātaka* the agent in the story is a

---

143. This connection to the Zhang clan is considerably atttenuated in the revelation of 1194.

144. On Buddhist influence on Chinese fiction, see Mair 1983, 1989. On its relevance to the Chinese poetic tradition, see the startling revelations in Mair and Mei 1991.

145. The literature on *avadāna* is extensive. Nakamura (1980: 137–40) gives a good overview of important Western and Japanese scholarship. Many of these tales have been translated by Chavannes (1934), Feer (1891), Speyer (1909), and, most recently, Strong (1983). See also Winternitz 1927: 2/277–94.

previous incarnation of a bodhisattva or buddha. A distinguishing feature of these stories is a diachronic narrative structure consisting of the time of narration by the Buddha and the time the actions in the story occur (Winternitz 1927: 2/278, Teiser 1988: 116n8). The *Book of Transformations*, and native Chinese compositions in general, do not imitate this structure, which was intended to ascribe scriptural authority for the tales by putting them in the mouth of the Buddha. Still, especially in the case of the *jātaka*, the *Book of Transformations* must have been, directly or indirectly, inspired by these examples of good deeds in a former life leading to an ultimate spiritual realization and apotheosis. Further, the moralistic anecdotes of the *Book of Transformations* are similar to Buddhist didactic tales found in collections like the *Records of Clear Retribution* (*Mingbao ji* 明報記).[146]

Stylistically the *Book of Transformations* shows both influences from and dissimilarities with Chinese Buddhist literature. The basic prosimetric format of the *Book of Transformations*, a format common in later Chinese vernacular fiction, derives ultimately from Buddhist scripture.[147] The most direct antecedent of the *Book of Transformations* in this regard may be Tang transformation texts (*bianwen*), which display the typical Indic alternation between poetic and prose portions. It should be noted, however, that the poetry in the *Book of Transformations* is rhymed and follows traditional Chinese prosodic rules. Further, the prosimetric form of Buddhist scripture was adopted into Daoist scripture early on, thus providing a native model for the author(s) of the *Book of Transformations*.[148]

In terms of diction, the *Book of Transformations* does not closely resemble Buddhist literature. Buddhist scripture tends to prolixity, with extended series of parallel descriptive phrases and frequent repetition of long passages of text. The *Book of Transformations*, by contrast, is typically Chinese in style, favoring the conciseness and avoidance of repetition that characterizes Chinese historical writing. Buddhist technical terminology occurs only very rarely and foreign-sounding transliterations of Sanskrit terms are wholly lacking.

Daoist Antecedents

What of possible Daoist antecedents to the *Book of Transformations*? Boltz (1987: 131) discusses a genre of "chronicles of the prophetic epiphanies of

---

146. On the history of these Buddhist tale collections in China, see Gjertson 1981, 1989.

147. Mair (1989: 88–98) has convincingly refuted a variety of arguments seeking a native origin for the prosimetric format.

148. For a revealing assessment of Buddhist influences on early religious Taoism, see Zürcher 1980.

Lao-tzu." The first of these is the *Scripture on the Transformations of Laozi* (*Laozi bianhua jing*), which Seidel (1969: 59–82) concludes was composed in Sichuan sometime shortly after A.D. 155. This text expounds upon the primordial origins of Laozi and the cosmological significance of his body, then goes on to recount a series of manifestations in this temporal world as instructor to a variety of historical figures from the beginning of the Zhou dynasty up through the second century A.D.

The intriguing similarities between this work and the *Book of Transformations* are tempered by the following considerations. First, the Divine Lord of Zitong's tale does include a primordial origin but this origin does not possess the cosmological significance of Laozi's. Laozi is coeval with primordial chaos and seems to be instrumental in the creation of the cosmos; the Divine Lord also originates in a time before this world took form and derives from these origins his special relationship with the Zhang clan and Southwestern China, but there is nothing of the demiurge in him. Second, although the Divine Lord does sometimes take on human form temporarily, both in the *Book of Transformations* (e.g., in the Five Stalwarts series found in chs. 44–47) and, if we are to believe the "Record of the Grotto of Flying Aurorae of the Purple Prefecture," in Song period Sichuan as well, his primary mode of appearance is full incarnation in human form, following the course of life from birth to death, all the while oblivious to his true identity. Finally, because Laozi begins as a fully realized deity, he does not follow the pattern of descent into the temporal realm, trial through temporal hardship, and reintegration into the stellar realm through ultimate apotheosis. There is also a question as to how widely diffused and well-known the *Scripture on the Transformations of Laozi* was in the Song. The only surviving copy is a nearly illegible sixth-century manuscript unearthed at Dunhuang at the beginning of this century. The text is, however, quoted by the tenth-century Sichuanese liturgicist and mythographer Du Guangting; hence it is not inconceivable that a copy was available in the Chengdu region at the time of the composition of the *Book of Transformations*.[149]

In any case, there were a number of works concerning the divine career of Laozi in circulation during the Song. These included an *Esoteric Biography of Laozi* (*Laozi neizhuan* 老子內傳) in three chapters, the title of which strongly recalls the *Esoteric Biography of Qinghe*, a *Poems on the Twenty-four Transformations of Lord Lao* (*Laojun ershisi hua shi* 老子二十四化詩) in one chapter attributed to Du Guangting, and a *Record of the Beginning and*

---

149. *725 Daode zhenjing guangsheng yi* 2/6b. Cf. Seidel 1969: 62.

End of Lord Lao (*Laojun shizhong ji* 老君始終記), also in one chapter. All
of these are no longer preserved, but they did survive through at least part
of the Song and, judging from their titles, they may have provided a model
for the author(s) of the *Book of Transformations*.[150]

Better known works on Laozi that might have influenced the composition
of the *Book of Transformations* are the *Scripture of Laozi's Conversion of the
Barbarians* (*Laozi huahu jing* 老子化胡經) and the *Scripture of Western
Ascension* (666 *Xisheng jing* 西昇經). The *Scripture of Laozi's Conversion of
the Barbarians* is an ancient text dating from the earliest Buddho-Daoist contacts.[151] Because it tried to link the two faiths by claiming the Buddha was
an incarnation of Laozi, it became a favorite topic of later polemical debates, including those held before the Mongol emperor in the thirteenth
century.[152] The *Scripture of Western Ascension* has recently been translated
by Livia Kohn. It also contains an account of Laozi's departure for the Western Regions, but the focus of the work is on instructions for meditational
practice.

Divine biographies of Laozi were still being produced in the Song. The
Dragon-Resembler Biography (773 *Youlong zhuan* 猶龍傳) of Jia Shanxiang
賈善翔 (fl. 1086) portrays the god as cosmic demiurge, transmitter of sacred
texts, and preceptor to generation after generation of political leaders. The
Sacred Record of the Amorphous Origin (769 *Hunyuan shengji* 混元聖記), a
mammoth compilation of lore concerning Laozi, his avatars, and government
patronage of his cult, was completed only ten years after the revelation of
the *Book of Transformations*.[153] These texts, filled with abstract theological
speculation and court rescripts, bore little resemblance to the *Book of Transformations*, but did provide a current precedent for large-scale sacred biography.

A more interesting parallel to the *Book of Transformations* within the
Laozi corpus is the *Explications on Illustrations of the Eighty-one Transforma-*

---

150. See van der Loon 1984: 102–7. The *Laojun neizhuan*, attributed to an otherwise unknown
Zhang Linting, was in existence in 1042 but was reported missing in 1144. The *Laojun shizhong ji* was
also reported missing in 1145. The *Laojun ershisi hua shi*, the most intriguing because it uses the term
"transformation" (*hua*) and included poetry, was also reported missing in 1145, but if it was indeed
from the hand of Du Guangting it would not be surprising if it survived in the Sichuan of 1181. Cf.
Verellen 1989: 209.

151. On the origins and early history of this scripture, see Zürcher 1959: 288–320. Seidel (1984)
has studied and translated a Dunhuang manuscript verion of the scripture deriving from the Lingbao
school.

152. These debates are discussed in Kubo 1992. Cf. Ren Jiyu 1990: 527–33.

153. The contents of these two works are summarized in Boltz 1987: 131–36. Cf. *Daozang tiyao*
0764, 0768.

tions of the Supreme Lord Lao (*Taishang Laojun bashiyi hua tushuo* 太上老君八十一化圖說), which traces the manifestations of Laozi up to the 1090s. Li Fengmao has argued that this text's composition can be assumed to date from shortly after this last incarnation. If so, it would be a significant predecessor to the *Book of Transformations*, but Yoshioka, after a detailed, chapter-by-chapter comparison with other biographies of Laozi, dated the text to 1232.[154] In any case, the elaborate illustrations of surviving editions of this work can give some idea what the original illustrated 1181 edition of the *Book of Transformations* must have looked like.

These biographies of Laozi differ markedly from the *Book of Transformations* in their attitude toward Buddhism. As far as we know, all these biographies of Laozi highlight the "transforming the barbarians" doctrine that the historical Buddha had been a later, degraded manifestation of Laozi after his departure for the Western Regions. All were no doubt used in the polemics of Buddho-Daoist debate and the *Scripture of Western Ascension*, in particular, was banned during the Yuan dynasty for precisely this reason.[155] The *Book of Transformations*, on the other hand, seems deeply committed to the "unity of the three religions" position, although it never explicitly uses this term. During the course of the god's development he meets both Laozi and the Buddha and is praised and rewarded by both. A certain disdain is expressed for the profane idol worship of the masses, but Daoism, Buddhism, and Confucianism are all treated as worthy of respect. This is particularly remarkable considering the decidedly Daoist nature of other scriptures revealed to this same medium, such as the *Transcendent Scripture of the Great Grotto* and Wenchang's companion *Precious Register*.

The Song boom in extended hagiography was not confined to Laozi; many cults compiled lengthy accounts of the avatars and celestial actions of the figures at the center of their worship. Two prominent examples with significant parallels to the Zitong cult are those directed toward the third-century exorcist Xu Xun 許遜 and that to the Thearch of the North Xuanwu 玄武. Li Fengmao identifies three Northern Song (960–1127) hagiographies of Xu Xun that are predecessors to the account by Bai Yuchan 白玉蟾.[156] As we shall see in the next section, a prosimetric version of Bai's account published in 1250 shows definite influence from the *Book of Transformations*.

---

154. Li Fengmao 1990: 368; Yoshioka 1959: 172–246.
155. An Pingqiu and Zhang Peiheng 1990: 258–60.
156. Li Fengmao 1990. Cf. Boltz 1987: 70–78.

The cult to the Thearch of the North shows remarkable similarities to and interactions with the Zitong cult. As in the case of Wenchang, worship of Xuanwu or the "Mysterious Warrior" as the cosmic ruler of the North goes back to Zhou times but first enfeoffments of the god occur in the Tang and the cult site on Wudang Mountain in Hubei achieves national prominence only in the Song.[157] The primary cult chronicle is the *Record of the Revealed Sacred of the Supreme Thearch of the Mysterious Heaven* (*958 Xuantian shangdi qisheng lu*), a prose account of the god's miracles and resulting imperial honors. Lagerwey (1992: 326–27, nn. 3, 6) argues that although the present text is no earlier than late Yuan or early Ming (i.e., fourteenth century), the text "reflects, basically, the state of the cult as of the mid-eleventh century." A considerable portion of the text may in fact date from this period, but the text also records a major new recension revealed by a Perfected named Dong Suhuang in 1184.[158] The Divine Lord of Zitong produced a preface to this new edition through the invoker (*zhu*) at his temple on Sevenfold Mountain. It was not uncommon for one deity to write a preface for another—the Sichuanese god Li Bing wrote one for the 1194 revelation of the *Book of Transformations*—but the revelation of such a preface at the Zitong cult center suggests that a type of imprimatur is being given the book by the Zitong cult, and further implies close ties between the two cults and a certain overlap in their memberships. The record in a Yuan period annotated edition of a key Xuanwu scripture of a proclamation (*die* 牒) issued by the Divine Lord in 1197 also testifies to the interaction between the two cults at this time.[159]

A new genre of religious writing known as "morality books" was taking form in the twelfth century. The *Tract on Retribution of the Most High* (*1167 Taishang ganying pian*) is a collection of ethical rules and injunctions that probably had been developing over a period of several centuries, but it reached its final form and was published with an extensive commentary in

---

157. Lagerwey 1992 is the most detailed record of cult history and scripture. Seaman 1987 translates an important scripture of the cult produced by spirit writing in the Ming. Grootaers 1952 compares this scripture with popular traditions in modern China, supplying invaluable information on the popular iconography and hagiography of the god.

158. *958 Xuantian shangdi qisheng lu* 1/21a. That Dong Suhuang is a revealing deity rather than a medium, as implied by Lagerwey, is clear from *775 Taishang shuo Xuantian da sheng Zhenwu benzhuan shenzhou miaojing* 1/4b.

159. *775 Taishang shuo Xuantian da sheng Zhenwu benzhuan shenzhou miaojing* 5/13a–15a. The proclamation to all local and tutelary gods across China warning of the fate of the evildoers in the approaching kalpic disasters shares a common theme with Xuanwu's teachings but it is unclear whether this passage is meant to imply a role for Xuanwu in the promulgation of this document.

1164. The editor and commentator was Li Shi 李石 (d. ca. 1182), a Sichuanese literatus with long-standing ties to the Zitong cult.[160] The *Ledger of Merit and Demerit of the Transcendent Lord of Supreme Tenuity* (*186 Taiwei xianjun gongguoge* 太微仙君功功過格), which first quantified the merit or demerit resulting from various actions, was revealed to a member of the Perfected Lord Xu (i.e., Xu Xun 許遜) cult in Sichuan in 1171.[161] The *Book of Transformations*, coming some ten years later in the same region of China, was undoubtedly influenced by these works. The *Book of Transformations* itself can be considered a morality book, and is so classified in Sakai's study of this genre (1960), but if so, it is unique in its presentation of ethical rules within the context of historically sited anecdotes rather than in explicit lists. The Zitong cult did go on to produce numerous morality books, including the famous *Writing on the Hidden Administration* (*Yinzhiwen*).[162]

Influences on Later Literature

Finally, we must consider the influence of the *Book of Transformations* on Chinese literature. Perhaps the most important aspect of this work is its central position in the Wenchang cult and its role in the vanguard of a whole body of cult scriptures. The *Book of Transformations* was reprinted many times in Ming and Qing China, both independently and as a major element in large collections of Wenchang scriptures or morality books. But the other works in these collections generally have a different format, being collections of ethical exhortations similar to the *Tract on Retribution of the Most High*. There is a sort of summary of the *Book of Transformations* from the Qing dynasty often printed within such collections called the "Annals of Wenchang" ("Wenchang benzhuan" 文昌本傳).[163]

A more direct influence is to be found in the Xu Xun 許遜 (239–92)

160. On *Taishang ganying pian*, see Brokaw 1991: 36–43, Yoshioka 1952: 70–104, An Pingqiu and Zhang Peiheng 1990: 261–63. Liu Ts'un-yan comes to a very different conclusion about the authorship of this work, although it is unclear upon what basis, in Hervouet 1978: 370–71. The *Taishang ganying pian* survives in the Daoist canon (HY 1167), as well as in many printed editions, and remains one of the most common texts supplied free in Chinese temples.

161. For an account of this revelation, see the preface to the Daozang edition, *186 Taiwei xianjun gongguoge*, Preface, 1b. Cf. Brokaw 1991: 43–52; Akizuki Kan'ei 1978: 217–46.

162. The *Yinzhiwen* was translated long ago by D. T. Suzuki and Paul Carus (1906) and more recently in Kleeman (forthcoming). Sakai (1957) takes the text to the late Ming, but Chinese scholars regularly attribute it (apparently on internal grounds) to the Southern Song. Hu Ying (1375–1463) apparently knew the work. See below, page 77.

163. It is this "Annals" that is paraphrased by Doré (1920: 44–56) rather than the *Book of Transformations* itself, which he misidentifies with a like-named work by Tan Qiao 譚峭 (fl. 922).

cult, which, we have seen, was active in Sichuan at the time of the *Book of Transformations*.[164] The Xu cult, known as the Way of Pure Brightness (Jingmingdao 淨明道), produced a number of biographies of Xu Xun and his mentor Wu Meng 吳猛. One by the famous Southern Lineage Daoist Bai Yuchan (fl. 1209–24) must have been written within fifty years of the *Book of Transformations*, yet still shows no influence in its presentation of Xu cult lore. The *Record of the Eighty-Five Transformations of the Perfected Lord Xu of West Mountain* (*448 Xishan Xu Zhenjun bashiwu hua lu* 許眞君八十五化錄) of 1246, however, reflects much greater influence. This work makes very few changes to information collected by Bai Yuchan but adopts wholesale the format of the *Book of Transformations*.[165] The entire work is divided into eighty-five *hua* or "transformations" and an eight-line, hepta-syllabic poem is interposed at the beginning of each new transformation. Schipper (1981: 108, n. 3) is no doubt correct in his assumption that these poems were revealed through spirit writing. Thus sixty-five years after the appearance of the *Book of Transformations* its reputation and level of popular support were sufficient to make leaders of an important sect, that to Xu Xun, reshape the central scripture of their movement.

Finally, there is the question of the influence of the *Book of Transformations* on later Chinese fiction. Here we are in the realm of speculation. Still, at this formative stage of Chinese prose fiction, the appearance of a lengthy prosimetric work in the first person like the *Book of Transformations* must have been both startling and inspiring. Moreover, the unstinting literati orientation of the text and the role of the god as patron of literary endeavors must have made it far more influential among authors than the semipopular colloquial stories of *bianwen*. A detailed exposition of the influence of the *Book of Transformations* on Chinese fiction must, however, await further research.

---

164. Much of the following discussion is based upon Boltz 1987: 70–78.

165. In an otherwise perceptive study of Xu Xun cult lore, Li Fengmao (1990) misconstrues the relationship between these two works by assuming as date of composition for the *Book of Transformations* the date of the Yuan recension found in the Daozang (*170 Zitong dijun huashu*).

神兵執崇圖

Figure 4. *The Divine Lord masters and drives forth the pestilence demons (ch. 12).*

The Cult in Late Imperial China

After the redefinition of the cult through the revelations to Liu Ansheng, the worship of the Divine Lord of Zitong continued to spread until he became one of a handful of truly national deities, each with his specific specialty but responding to prayers on a variety of topics. The *Book of Transformations* also went through a series of expansions, revisions, and reprintings. This section will trace these changes over the last six centuries.

The Revelation of 1194

In 1194 an additional twenty-one episodes of the epic tale of the incarnations of the Divine Lord of Zitong were revealed. The 1194 preface, from the pen of the god Li Erlang 李二郎, says of this second revelation:

> The Layman of Completion Chapel Yang Xing 了庵居士楊興 is Dong Chang, the former retainer of the [King of] Heroic Prominence. . . . He brought along Feng Ruyi, Cleric of Central Harmony 中和道人馮如意, who made of himself an incense candle (i.e., burnt incense on his head) and, bearing the phoenix, inquired of the god.[166]

No record remains of Feng Ruyi, but we do know a bit about Yang Xing, who claimed to be a reincarnation of Dong Chang 董常, the retainer of the Divine Lord when he was incarnated as the seventh-century philosopher Wang Tong 王通 (584–617).[167] Yang hailed from Zizhong and was once Prefect of Langzhou.[168] In 1206 he was demoted after being charged with avarice and cruelty.[169] Wei Liaoweng 魏了翁 (1178–1237) wrote him a sympathetic letter lamenting the difficulty of disproving slander.[170]

---

166. DZJY 17b.
167. This incarnation is detailed in DZJY chapter 78, DZ chapter 77.
168. The administrative seat of Langzhou was southeast of modern Cangxi county, Sichuan, during the Song. Zang 1936: 1204.2–3.
169. *Songhuiyao jigao,* "Zhiguan," 74:20b.
170. *Heshan xiansheng da quanji* 61/4a–5a.

In the 1645 edition of the *Wenchang huashu* a postface (*ba* 跋) attributed to Yang Xing is preserved.[171]

The purpose of the new episodes was to bring the account of the incarnations of the Divine Lord up into current times, as is expressed in the preface:

> The transformations revealed on Jeweled Peak were only seventy-three in number. The account was abbreviated and not detailed. The tale of the people's reliance upon the god's protection from the inception of the state up until today must not fail to be recorded.[172]

The 1181 revelation, which ended with the apotheosis of the god in the fourth century, had not included any of the historical or quasi-historical incidents from the fourth century on that had become part of cult lore. These accounts gave important legitimacy to the cult and were included in this new revelation. Thus we find tales of the historical encounters between the god and Tang emperors Xuanzong and Xizong (chs. 79 and 81) as well as an account of the conversion of the late Tang scholar and Han Yu disciple Sun Qiao 孫樵 (ch. 82). Here also we find a version of the legendary encounter between the god and Yao Chang (chs. 74 and 75). And finally, we read of the god's role in the suppression of the Wang Jun 王均 rebellion of 1000, for which he was ennobled King of Heroic Prominence 英顯王 (ch. 85).

The 1194 revelation also added much material about the god that does not survive in any other source. It is unclear whether this was part of oral literature surrounding the god or was made up whole cloth by Yang Xing and Feng Ruyi. In at least two cases the tale survives in another source, and in that source there is no mention of the Divine Lord of Zitong.[173] In any case it became part of cult lore from this time on.

The 1181 revelation, ending as it did with the apotheosis of the god and his assumption of heavenly office, implied an end to the god's human incarnations. The 1194 revelation rejected this, and claimed two subsequent incarnations for the god, the Sui philosopher Wang Tong and Sichuanese general Zhang Jun 張浚 (1097–1164). The family of the Divine Lord had also received titles during the course of the twelfth century, but, except for his mother and father, played no active role in the text of the 1181 revel-

---

171. This rare edition is preserved in the Harvard-Yenching Library, and is identical to that in the Naikaku Bunko Library in Japan. See the appendix listing editions of the *Book of Transformations*.

172. DZJY 17b.

173. DZJY chapters 77 and 91; DZ chapters 76 and 89.

ation. The 1194 revelation assigned to the divine family a much more active part in the Divine Lord's plans. His sons, in particular, repeatedly incarnate to do his bidding, first as the son and nephew of Xie An 謝安 (320–85, ch. 76), then as Zhang Qixian 張齊賢 (943–1014, ch. 84), then as Sima Guang 司馬光 (1019–1086, ch. 86). In one case five sons and a retainer all incarnate to aid in repelling Liao forces (ch. 87).

This brings us to one distinguishing feature of this second revelation: a concern with external invasion and a sort of Sinocentrism that sought to rally support for traditional Chinese values and cultural norms. Zhang Jun was a local hero in Sichuan who earlier in the twelfth century had successfully defended the region against the incursions of Jin forces. He must have been very popular among the inhabitants, and this would have been a sufficient reason to include him in the new, expanded *Book of Transformations*. But this theme of defending China from the barbarians occurs again and again, in Xie An's defeat of Fu Jian, in the actions of the god's incarnated sons in repelling Jurchen Liao invaders, and in Zhang Jun's defense against the Jin (ch. 76, 87, and 88). This Sinocentrism involves a commitment not merely to the Song dynasty, as evidenced by the Divine Lord's aid at the time of its founding (chapter 84), but also to traditional Chinese culture, as reflected in his promotion of the teachings of Confucius during his life as Wang Tong at the time of the reunification of China under Chinese rule (ch. 78).

A second distinguishing characteristic of the 1194 revelation is a more narrowly religious tone. This is evident in chapter 83, wherein the god saves people from a natural disaster and is rewarded by the Ancient Buddha with the title of Tathāgatā ("thus come one") and in chapter 92, when he is promoted to the rank of Heavenly Thearch (*tiandi* 天帝) for his good works in burying the dead. There is also a strong emphasis on the approaching kalpic apocalypse and the need for salvation from the ensuing disasters (chs. 92 and 94). This millenarian aspect of the cult is much less evident in the first seventy-three chapters of the *Book of Transformations*.

Finally, I would like to mention a somewhat subjective consideration. The chapters deriving from the revelation of 1194 are less learned and more popular in character than those from 1181. The language itself is more pedestrian; the poems, though difficult in both cases, tend to be merely obscure rather than recondite; and the anecdotal material is rather more derivative.[174]

---

174. Of the eighteen chapters of anecdotes within the *Book of Transformations* I have found only

These three features indicate a difference both in the authors and in the intended audience of these two revelations. The first revelation was directed toward scholars and would-be scholars. The author, to the degree that one can speak of the author of a revealed text, was learned in the classical commentarial tradition that every aspiring official mastered. The first two incarnations, in particular, present extended narratives of considerable dramatic interest. The culmination of the text is the appointment of the god to a post in charge of the fate of would-be officials and their subsequent careers.

The second revelation was directed toward a wider audience of the more overtly pious. Both of the figures associated with the 1194 revelation have Buddhistic-sounding religious epithets. The religious emphasis of this material, the millenarian tendencies, and the claims that prominent figures of recent history were in fact divine incarnations all would have been distasteful to some literati. There is also considerable looseness with regard to historical fact, such that contradictory claims are made as to the god's identity at a given time,[175] and later scholars who attacked the *Book of Transformations* on this count regularly refer to incidents in the 1194 revelation.[176] Further, the second revelation boldly claims very prominent figures of recent history as incarnations of the god, whereas the first stuck to mysterious men who had received no more than passing mention in historical sources. The Sinocentric tendency in the material from the second revelation reflects both a diminution of Sichuanese parochialism and an attempt to appeal to xenophobic Chinese of all classes. Finally, the ultimate chapter of the revelation records a number of fresh manifestations of the god that portray the cult as dynamically expanding at a rapid rate.

We should not, however, overemphasize these differences. The second revelation seeks a broader selection of worshipers from diverse segments of society, but these potential worshipers are all of necessity literate and the great majority of the literati class must have found the entire combined work acceptable, since it was preserved, transmitted and repeatedly republished by members of this class.

---

two containing anecdotes found in another source, both from among the four chapters of anecdotes originating in the 1194 revelation. The second tale in DZJY chapter 77 shares a common source with a tale in *Yijian zhi,* "jia," 17/147, and this is also true of chapter 91 and *Yijian zhi,* "jia," 7/58.

175. Chapters 74, 75 and 76, for example, associate the god with three different figures in the latter half of the fourth century.

176. E.g., Wang Shihan (1707–?) in *Hanmen zhuixue xubian* 30a–31a.

The Revelation of 1267

At the time of the revelation of the *Book of Transformations* the cult to the Divine Lord of Zitong already blanketed the area of modern Sichuan and had expanded at least to the capital in the Southeast.[177] A network of traveling merchants, itinerant religious professionals, and often-transferred officials disseminated new cult developments to communities of Sichuanese emigrés and new converts all along the Yangzi River basin, such that by 1177 the *Esoteric Biography of Qinghe*, revealed at most eleven years before in Sichuan, was already carved in stone and displayed in the god's temple in the capital. After the fall of portions of Sichuan to Mongol forces in the 1230s and the subsequent large-scale immigration of elite families to the Southeast there was a new spate of temple building, enfeoffments, and other religious activity directed toward the Divine Lord of Zitong.

In 1267 the final three chapters of the Song recension of the *Book of Transformations* were revealed. These three chapters are wholly occupied with the precarious state of the Song empire. Chapter 95 discusses the Divine Lord's successful efforts to suppress the rebellion of Wu Xi 吳曦 in 1206–7 and his unsuccessful battles against Yuan invaders in 1231 and 1255. Chapter 96 tells how he allied with two other Sichuanese gods to preserve Song rule in a portion of southern Sichuan. In chapter 97 the god has been forced to flee from his ritual center on Sevenfold Mountain and has taken up residence in a cavern in Guizhou. There he gathers together a number of prominent literati of the past, including Li Bo and Su Shi to compose seventeen books that will revive traditional Chinese culture. At this same site a new redaction of the *Transcendent Scripture of the Great Grotto* is revealed and a ritual (*yi* 儀) is dictated and inscribed in stone.[178] These chapters were not immediately incorporated into all editions of the *Book of Transformations*, for Zhao Wen (1239–1315), writing in Jiangxi sometime around 1300, knows of only ninety-four transformations.[179]

We see in these chapters an intensification of the Sinocentrism of the 1194 revelation. As Smith (1992: 668) has noted, "[f]rom 1231 to 1280,

---

177. This expansion is discussed in detail in Kleeman 1993.

178. See 5 *Taishang wuji zongzhen Wenchang dadong xianjing* 1/5a.

179. See "Record of the Wenchang Pavilion" ("Wenchang ge ji" 文昌閣記) in *Qingshan ji* 29a–31b. This piece is undated and the date of 1300 is only conjecture based on the fact that Zhao treats the establishment of a temple in 1263 as being so far removed from memory that its date must be treated as hearsay. The Yuan editors writing in 1314 (see below), however, must have been familiar with these chapters, since they included ninety-seven chapters in their edition (while replacing these specific chapters).

Mongol shock troops systematically laid waste to Sichuan," and it would be half a millennium before Sichuan's population regained Song levels. As the patron deity of Sichuan and a strong upholder of the Chinese tradition, the Divine Lord of Zitong formed a focus for popular opposition to the Yuan invaders, and it was no doubt this tendency that led the Mongols to shut down the temple on Sevenfold Mountain.

Official Recognition during the Yuan

Patronage of the cult did not end immediately with the victory of the Yuan forces in 1279. In 1281 the government awarded the temple in Ningbo a new plaque reading "Martial Virtue and Literary Glory (Wenchang)" 武德 文昌.[180] But the cult had been a rallying point for the opposition to the northern invaders and there does seem to be a hiatus of activity in the cult. A decline in patronage of the best-known examination god was a predictable result of the Yuan suspension of the examination system and the widespread rejection of service under an alien conquest dynasty. The cult's fortunes through this period are described in the following passage from a stele by Yu Ji 虞集 (1272–1348), which also notes the god's special appeal to the scholar-official class:[181]

> The Palace of Wenchang is a shrine to the God-lord 神君 of Seven-fold Mountain in Zitong county, Shu. Of old, when Shu was at the height of its prosperity, the common people were fond of praying and sacrificing, and the palaces of the gods stood door to door (xiangwang 相望). But for the most part they were worshiped and believed in only by common merchants, local men and women, exorcists, and mediums (shiwu 師巫). Only the so-called God-lord of Sevenfold [Mountain] received the offerings of scholars and great officials, who believed that he was the god who had charge of emoluments, presided over the realm of literature, and supervised the examinations. When the Song perished, Shu was ravaged and not one of the inhabitants survived. The offerings to the gods were suspended. After the exam-

---

180. *Yanyou Siming zhi* 18/30b.

181. *Xuegulu* 46/8b, cited in Morita 1984: 417, n. 64. This stele commemorates the construction of a Wenchang Spirit Palace in Xiangru county (modern Peng'an county, Sichuan). This decline in open support was felt throughout the empire, as shown by the shrine to the Divine Lord in Shanxian, Zhejiang, which was destroyed in 1296 and not rebuilt until 1344. See "Wenchangci zhitian ji" ("Record of Purchase of Land for the Wenchang Shrine") in *Yuezhong jinshi ji* 9.

inations had been abolished for more than forty years we heard of no
supernatural feats from Wenchang. In the first year of Yanyou (1314),
when the Son of Heaven made an especially sagacious decision and,
clearly summoning all within the empire, selected officials through the
examinations, the people of Shu gradually began to offer sacrifice to
Wenchang again.

The cult received a major boost from the reinstitution of the civil service
examinations. In 1316, at the culmination of the three-year examination
process, a new recension of the *Book of Transformations* was revealed, ex-
cising passages that portrayed non-Chinese peoples unfavorably and might
have offended the Mongol rulers of the Yuan dynasty or inspired popular
opposition.[182] In the spring of that year the Commission for Ritual Observances, noting that the god already possessed the highest possible title of
"king" and the most exalted epithet, "Divinely civil, sagely martial, filially
virtuous, loyal and benevolent," awarded the god the temple plaque "Aid to
civilization and completer of transformation" (*Youwen chenghua* 佑文成
化).[183] In the seventh month of the same year Emperor Renzong 仁宗
(Ayurbarwada, r. 1311–20) found a way to surpass these titles by bestowing
upon the god the title "Divine Lord of Vast Benevolence, the Supporter of
the Primordial and Initiator of Transformation, Wenchang, the Director of
Emoluments" (*Fuyuan kaihua Wenchang Silu hongren dijun* 輔元開化文昌
司錄宏仁帝君).[184]

The honors bestowed upon the god at this time were directly related to
the need on the part of the Mongol rulers for educated Chinese administrators. The emperor expresses this in his rescript:[185]

---

182. This is discussed in greater depth in the following section.

183. The conferral of this plaque is recorded in the *Esoteric Biography of Qinghe* (*169 Qinghe neizhuan* 6b–7a). The documents in this text are generally arranged in chronological order, but this plaque
must have been awarded before the conferral of the title of Divine Lord in the seventh month (see
following note) and it is the conferral of this plaque that is referred to by the obscure notation in the
preface to the 1316 recension of the *Book of Transformations*, "In spring of the third year of Yanyou
(1316) the Sectretariat followed the proposal of the Court of Imperial Sacrifices" (DZJY, "preface" 3a).
This is confirmed in the 1341 "Traveling Shrine Record" of Zhao Yanzhi (*169 Qinghe neizhuan* 9b).
On the Commission for Ritual Observances, a variant term during the Yuan for the Court of Imperial
Sacrifices that was responsible for the conduct of state sacrifices, see Hucker 1985: 476, entry 6140.

184. The text of the imperial rescript conferring this new title is recorded in the *Esoteric Biography
of Qinghe* (*169 Qinghe neizhuan* 6a–b). The "Traveling Shrine Record" of 1341 quotes parts of this
rescript, including one line not in the *Qinghe neizhuan* text of the rescript, which must therefore be
abridged (*169 Qinghe neizhuan* 9b).

185. *169 Qinghe neizhuan* 6b.

Oh, I want talented men to appear generation after generation. . . . I want civil administration to shine forth.

This rescript was the first formal recognition by the state of the connection between the Divine Lord of Zitong and the constellation Wenchang. This connection was vital in claiming an orthodox position within the state pantheon.

The Yuan Recension of the Book of Transformations

As part of the reinstitution of the examinations and the rehabilitation of the Divine Lord of Zitong, a new recension of the *Book of Transformations* was published. This recension is preserved in the Daoist canon under the title *Book of Transformations of the Divine Lord of Zitong* (*170 Zitong dijun huashu* 梓潼帝君化書). It was created specifically for presentation to the throne at the time of the ennoblement of the Divine Lord of Zitong as Wenchang in 1316. The individuals involved in this editing are unknown, but something of the procedure followed is related in the revealed preface to the work:[186]

> My *Book of Transformations* in ninety-seven fascicles (*zhi* 帙) has been in circulation among the people for a long time. From the hands of dissolute scholars have sprung numerous errors like writing *lu* 魯 for *yu* 魚, *yin* 銀 for *gen* 根, or confusing the "jade" 玉 and "stone" 石 radicals in the compound *wufu* 碔砆.[187] If the book is shown to others without these mistakes being clearly corrected, they will say that it is merely an assemblage of foolish fables by dilettantes fond of tales about the gods. In the midst of all these doubts I found these upright and virtuous gentlemen who repeatedly collated and corrected the northern and southern texts. They then inquired of the gods and I charged them, saying, "Recently the southern text really has many obscure and slanted passages. The northern text has received my personal collation, and the events recorded are clear. In the section up to the chapter 'Dingwei' (ch. 71) errors have been corrected. In the section after the chapter 'Cinnamon Record' (ch. 73) superfluous and

---

186. DZ, Preface, 4b–5a.

187. In fact, use of either radical in this compound seems acceptable, and there are some examples where they are mixed. See Morohashi 7–20990, p. 7828; 8–24295, p. 8512. These are formulaic examples of easily confused characters, not actual examples of textual problems in the *Book of Transformations*.

confused passages have been deleted and revised. I have further added two new chapters, 'The Revived People' (*Sumin* 甦民) and 'The Examination System' (*Keju* 科舉) for a total of ninety-nine. I have temporarily left these chapters blank to accommodate my future intentions. The collators may prepare carved blocks and publish the text in order to show future sages. I hope there will be no further doubts."

From this passage we see that during the Yuan there were already two major lineages of texts, one current in North China and one in South China, and various editions of the text were widely diffused throughout China. The comments about graphic errors suggest manuscript transmission, but the seventy-three chapter and the ninety-four chapter recensions were printed soon after their revelation. Both manuscript and printed editions were in circulation.

The Yuan preface indicates that only minor revisions were made on the first seventy-three chapters. This accords well with the state of the text as we know it. The first seventy-three chapters of the DZ and DZJY texts are substantially identical except for occasional variant characters. There is considerably more variation in the following twenty-four chapters, reflecting the "deletions and revisions" mentioned above.

Comparing the DZ and DZJY texts we can discern several motivations for the revision. DZJY chapter 92, "Deliverance from Suffering," contains references to impending kalpa disasters, and hence is at least implicitly millenarian. The corresponding chapter 91 in DZ tells the same story much more briefly, and deletes all references to the apocalypse. But the overriding concern seems to have been to delete passages that disparage non-Chinese peoples, in order to avoid offending the Yuan emperor to whom this scripture was to be presented. The first indication of this is the complete deletion of DZJY chapter 76. In this chapter relatives of the Divine Lord incarnate as members of the Xie family during the Eastern Jin and defeat the invading army of Fu Jian at the famous battle of the Fei River, thus preserving Chinese rule in South China. In chapter 84, also deleted, the second son of the Divine Lord and a retainer are incarnated to aid the Song house. In chapter 87 the five sons of the Divine Lord all incarnate to ward off the invasion of the Jurchen barbarians; it does not appear in the DZ text. Finally, chapters 95, 96, and 97 are all missing from the Yuan text. In these chapters the Divine Lord tries unsuccessfully to forestall the Yuan invasion, then is forced to flee before it, yet plans to restore the supremacy of Chinese culture.

Much of the revision is designed to cover up the wholesale deletions mentioned above. Chapter 91, for example, is split into three separate chapters of the DZ text (87, 88, 89). But there are also other concerns that led to the creation of new material. The Southern Song recension of the *Book of Transformations* already contained a condemnation of the killing of sentient beings, found in chapter 61 of both DZ and DZJY. The editors of the Yuan edition were extremely concerned about this question, and added two new chapters, DZ 95 and 97, detailing the terrible punishments visited on those who killed to eat. There is also a second story centering on the necessity to bury the dead (DZ ch. 94; cf. DZJY ch. 92, DZ chapter 91). Finally, DZ chapter 96, in which the Divine Lord incarnates as one of the hereditary Celestial Masters, indicates that the Yuan editors were linked to the reinvigorated Zhengyi lineage based at Longhushan.

Post-Yuan Developments

With the Yuan ennoblement the Divine Lord of Zitong was officially identified with the examination system and the scholar-official elite. The penetration of the cult to the Divine Lord of Zitong into the official school system was of signal importance for its development. Future officials were indoctrinated into the worship of the god at the same time that basic Confucian values were instilled. Unfortunately, the cult's spread to the schools is largely undocumented. A Yuan inscription mentions the introduction of a shrine to the Divine Lord into the school in Fuzhou in 1349.[188] By the fifteenth century the god was worshiped in schools throughout the empire.

The Divine Lord inspired devout worship from some at the highest levels of Chinese society. A prominent example is Hu Ying 胡濴 (1375–1463), Minister of Rites (*libu shangshu* 禮部尙書) during the early Ming, who left behind two prayers to the god.[189] Hu's special ties to Wenchang may derive from his service as an examiner for more than ten metropolitan examinations. He was also an active proponent of morality books and the earliest figure to mention the Divine Lord's best known literary product, the *Writing on the Hidden Administration* (*Yinzhiwen*).[190] Hu's multifaceted

---

188. Gong Shitai, "Wenchangci ji," in *Wanzhai ji* 7/17a, cited in Morita 1984: 418, n. 74.

189. The prayers (*jiwen* 祭文) are preserved in *Gujin tushu jicheng*, "Shenyidian" 490/21a–b. On Hu Ying, see the *Dictionary of Ming Biography* (Goodrich and Fang 1976: 643–44), and his biography in *Mingshi* 169.

190. Hu mentions "the Divine Lord's tract on the hidden administration" in the second prayer cited above. He is also said to have distributed a text printed by the government in 1419 and titled *The Hidden Administration of Good Works* (*Weishan yinzhi* 爲善陰騭). See Goodrich and Fang 1976: 643–4.

understanding of the god is reflected in the text of one of his prayers, offered on the god's birthday:

> In my humble opinion, the Divine Lord is the god of loyalty and filial piety, Director of Emoluments, charged with recruitment and promotion. He saves men from kalpic disasters, and manifests his transformations in many regions. He helps scholars achieve fame in the examination and responds [to prayer] by letting his blessings flow.

Not everyone was willing to accept all aspects of the new, combined Divine Lord of Zitong. Ye Mengding, a high official and renowned scholar of the mid- to late thirteenth century, was called upon to compose a text commemorating the establishment of the Traveling Shrine to the Perfected Lord of Zitong in Yanzhou (modern Jiande, Zhejiang) in 1261. Ye, who did not hail from Sichuan and had made a name for himself by destroying so-called "licentious shrines,"[191] expresses certain doubts about the god but is reassured by the cult's emphasis on loyalty and filial piety. He laments, however, that no one has yet distinguished this ethical core from the "theories of ninety-four transformations, concoctions of mediums that denigrate and calumniate the gods and spirits."[192] In this seeming reference to the *Book of Transformations* (in a recension without the last three chapters added around 1267), Ye expresses delight with the Divine Lord's program of moral transformation but rejects accounts of his physical transformations as too Buddhist. During the Ming there were still conservatives who objected to the scope and level of the Divine Lord's worship. One was Cao Duan 曹端 (1376–1434), who condemned the worship of Wenchang, and many other deities as "licentious cults" (*yinsi* 淫祀).[193] His objections seem to have fallen on deaf ears (the god's temple in the capital was renovated and official sacrifice made on his birthday in 1454), but the call was taken up some half a century later by Zhang Jiugong 張九功 and resulted in a memorial by Zhou Hongmo 周洪謨 (1419–91) that proposed a major

---

191. Ye's biography in *Songshi* 414/12433 records that he destroyed the licentious shrine(s) of a village in Wanzai, Jiangsu, and sealed the "demon-infested well" (*yaojing* 妖井) around which the cult had grown.

192. *Jingding Yanzhou xuzhi* 4/5a. Ma Tingluan (1222–89) also seems to have some reservations about the *Book of Transformations*. In a dedication of a shrine to the Divine Lord of Zitong he remarks, "as for the *Book of Transformations* that is transmitted in the world today, I do not know what to say about it" (*wu buneng zhi qi shuo* 吾不能知其說). See *Biwu wanfang ji* 17/3a.

193. See Ching 1987: 211–13 for a translation of Huang Zongxi's comments on Cao. I am indebted to Daniel Overmyer for this reference.

reform of the state cult based on classical injunctions.[194] As for the Divine Lord of Zitong, Zhou recommended:

> Now the god of Zitong manifested his numinous power in Shu, so it is proper that he be worshiped in temples of that region, but why should he be offered cult in the capital? . . . I beg that . . . sacrifices to him be abolished. All [shrines to] Zitong in schools throughout the empire should be ordered destroyed, in the hope that this will be sufficient to dispel the delusions in the people's minds.

This memorial was approved by the emperor with certain exceptions, the god of Zitong not among them, but it is unclear whether Zhou's proposed reforms were ever effected. The same year this memorial was submitted, Zhou was impeached for personal and familial breaches of official ethics and forced into retirement.

Whatever the real result of the protests of Zhang Jiugong, belief in the god of Zitong cult does not seem to have been seriously diminished thereby. The Wenchang Palace in the capital was renovated in 1454[195] and again at imperial command in 1477.[196] Lu Can 陸粲 (1494–1551) tells of how the god had incarnated as the son of virtuous parents and attained high court rank. Xu Yikui 徐一夔 (1318–ca. 1400) had credited the god with the increasing success of Hangzhou area examination candidates[197] and Xu Yingqiu 徐應秋 (Wanli [1573–1619] period *jinshi*) affirms that his astral home, the constellation Wenchang, "represents all the literati of the empire" (*tianxia siwen zhi ying* 天下斯文之應).[198] Guo Zizhang 郭子章 (1543–1618), writing around 1587, distinguished three types of devotees of the god: warriors who worshiped him as a dead hero and supernatural opponent of rebels, aspiring officials who believed he controlled their fates and careers on the basis of the Cinnamon Record, and those who prayed to him as Transcendent Zhang, a supplier of progeny.[199]

---

194. The memorial is recorded in *Libu zhigao* 84/19a–28b. On Zhou Hongmo, see *Mingshi* 184/4873–74. Ray Huang's biography in Goodrich and Fang (1976: 269–71) characterizes Zhou as "pedantic and authoritarian."

195. *Ming yitongzhi* 1/26a.

196. The imperial rescript ordering this second renovation dated 1477 and another commending the god dated 1479 are reprinted at the beginning of the 1645 ed. of the *Book of Transformations*.

197. *Xihu youlan zhi* 12/165.

198. *Yuzhi tang tanhui* 20/37a–39a.

199. "Wenchangci ji" 文昌祠記 in *Guo Zizhang ji* 1/9a–b, *Wendi quanshu* 14/32b. Guo had a long and distinguished official career culminating in the position of Minister of War (*bingbu shangshu* 兵部尚書) and was posthumously awarded the title Junior Guardian of the Heir-Apparent (*taizi shao-*

Cult history took an unexpected turn at the end of the Ming when the rebel Zhang Xianzhong 張獻忠 passed through Zitong on his way to conquer Sichuan. He happened to quarter his troops in the temple on Sevenfold Mountain. It is said that the inhabitants of Zitong were spared when the god appeared to Zhang in a dream,[200] or that Zhang noticed his own name on one of the temple plaques.[201] For whatever reason, Zhang established a special relationship with the god and his temple, formally acknowledging the god as his clansman (*tongzong* 同宗). A century later it was discovered that Zhang Xianzhong was still being worshiped in the temple as an incarnation of the Divine Lord and it is likely that he did in fact make this claim in an attempt to win the support of the locals.[202]

The national cult during the Qing was not influenced by the heterodox affiliations of the original cult center in Zitong. The god continued to be worshiped throughout the land in a variety of guises. The *Book of Transformations* was repeatedly reprinted as were many ethical tracts attributed to the god, some in large collections like the *Cinnabar Cinnamon Collection* (*Dangui ji* 丹桂集) and the *Complete Works of the Thearch Wen* (*Wendi quanshu* 文帝全書). Wenchang pavilions came to be incorporated into almost all Confucian temples. The god received his ultimate official honor in 1857 when he was promoted to the rank of Middle Sacrifice (*zhongsi* 中祀), a rank he shared with Confucius and Thearch Guan 關帝.

Besides individual worship at his temples throughout the country and in the homes of believers, there were diverse groups and social organizations dedicated to the god. They transmitted his teachings through the planchette, edited and published his scriptures, celebrated his birthday with festivals, built and repaired his temples. One term for such groups was Wenchang Congregation (*Wenchang hui* 文昌會). At the opening to a Wenchang scripture called the *Supreme Grotto-Mystery Numinous Jewel Per-*

---

bao 太子太保). Guo's administration while still in regional positions was so exemplary that there were shrines dedicated to him while he was still alive (*shengci* 生祠) in three different provinces. Zhang was also a prodigious author, with twenty-five books credited to him in the *Mingshi* on topics ranging from poetry to local history, temple gazetteers and folklore, and mountain gazetteers. See the detailed account of his works in Goodrich and Fang 1976: 775–77. On the multiple identities of the god of Zitong, see Kleeman 1993. For more information on Transcendent Zhang, see the discussion above, pp. 34–36.

200. *Shu bi* 3/47. Cf. Wang Daisheng 1985.

201. One of the incarnations claimed for the Divine Lord in the revelation of 1194 was as Zhang Jun 張浚, whose style was Zhongxian 忠獻.

202. A stele reproduced in *Mianyangxian zhi* 6/313 records the discovery of Zhang's statue and its destruction. A similar stele was on display in the Sichuan Provincial Museum, Chengdu, when I visited in 1985.

fected Scripture of the Original Vow of Wenchang, the Divine Lord of Zitong, there is a song the celebrant intones before silently praying for admittance into this congregation and into the salvific grace of the Divine Lord:[203]

> Those wishing to enter the Congregation of Wenchang, Director of Emoluments,
> Must each produce this thought with supreme, utmost sincerity:
> I Believe in and worship the Three Treasures: the Dao, its scriptures, and its masters.
> Believe in and worship the transcendents and sages of the ten directions,
> Believe in and worship the many perfected spirits of Sevenfold [Mountain],
> Only desire that your mercy will reach down to me.

The Congregation spoken of here is an abstract grouping of the faithful rather like the "Christian church," but the term was also applied to more concrete gatherings. In Gu Lu's record of 1820s Suzhou seasonal observances, a description of both official and private worship of the god is followed by an account of the Wenchang Congregation on the occasion of the god's birthday:[204]

> The third day [of the second lunar month] is the birthday of the Divine Lord Wenchang. A senior official (of Suzhou?, *dali* 大吏) offers sacrifice at the temple beside Zhutangsi (Bamboo hall monastery). The temple is on the border with Changzhou 長洲 and for this reason the administrator of Chang city also offers sacrifice there. In other towns that have a temple to him the administrator conducts sacrifices on his behalf. Elsewhere, in Daoist temples, dharma institutes, guilds (*huiguan*) and morality halls (*shantang* 善堂), where they worship and make offerings to images of the god, all possess a *Record for Performing the*

---

203. The text is printed in a compendium of works dedicated to Wenchang and Thearch Guan, *Wen Wu sheng zhenjing baochan hece* [Combined volume of perfected scriptures and precious penances] (Taibei: Miantiantan, 1984), "Benyuan zhen jing," first chapter, 2. The piece is titled "Hymn of worship and request" ("Liqing ji" 禮請偈) and is followed by the notation, "After worshiping and silently setting forth your own intentions, rise and chant the [following] spell." This liturgy setting the stage for the ritual reading of the *Scripture of the Original Vow* is not found in the canonical version of the scripture, *29 Yuanshi tianzun shuo Zitong dijun benyuan jing.* It is of uncertain date, certainly not new with the 1984 printing, but not as old as the Yuan-Ming scripture itself, perhaps from the Qing and certainly from a professional rather than scholarly milieu. There is every reason to think that the compilers of the 1984 compendium still perform the ritual as recorded and take this vow to join the congregation.

204. *Qingjia lu* 2/2b–3b.

Exalted Offering.[205] They say that the Divine Lord is in charge of the affairs of the Wenchang Office and controls the record of emoluments for mortals. The gentry (*shidafu*)[206] respond to him with special reverence. Even though they are poor, they still prepare their portion of incense and throng to his halls, calling this the Wenchang Congregation.

Such public celebrations to Wenchang seem to have died out except at the main temple in Zitong (see below), but Suzuki Seiichirō, writing in 1934, tells how degree holders, teachers, and literati would gather at the Wenchang temple on his birthday to offer an ox and fruit.[207]

Despite dire predictions to the contrary, the worship of Wenchang has survived into the twentieth century in a variety of contexts.[208] A prime example is the Grotto Scripture Congregations (*Dongjing hui* 洞經會) still active throughout large parts of Yunnan province.[209] Thought to date back to at least the late Ming or early Qing, these groups assemble local notables and merchants to sing the text of the *Transcendent Scripture of the Great Grotto* with elaborate musical accompaniment. The performances occur on auspicious occasions like Wenchang's birthday in a ritual arena, most often a Wenchang Palace, before an altar with statues of Wenchang and his two attendants (in one case a bronze statue brought back from the temple in Zitong), surrounded by banners displaying the titles of Wenchang's divine family.[210] The groups are not led by Daoist priests; the nominal head of the congregation is normally the highest ranking local official and the congregation directors are all educated members of local elite families.[211] Modern reports make no mention of the *Book of Transformations* in this con-

205. This phrase, *ju xiu chong jiao lu* 俱修崇醮錄, is difficult to construe. Here I follow the punctuation of Wang Mai 王邁 in treating the last four characters as a book title, though I have no record of a book of this name. See the 1986 ed. of *Qingjia lu*, 2/48–49.

206. For a definition of this important term, see Ebrey 1984: 3–5.

207. Suzuki (1934, tr. by Gao Xianzhi and Feng Zuomin 1984: 338).

208. Hodous (1929: 77) reported of the god that, "His images are crumbling and the god . . . is disappearing from the memories of man."

209. The following discussion is based upon Song Enchang 1985; Yang Cenglie 1990; and Rees 1993. I am indebted to Kenneth Dean, Judith Magee Boltz, and Victor Mair for supplying me with information on these groups.

210. Yang Cenglie 1990: 124, 126–27.

211. There are also August Scripture Congregations, thought to be somewhat earlier, which focus on the recitation of the *Scripture of the Original Actions of the Jade August* (*Dongxuan lingbao gaoshang Yuhuang benxing jijing*, presumably the same text as *10 Gaoshang Yuhuang benxing jijing* and *11 Gaoshang Yuhuang benxing jijing*). The members of these groups are younger, more numerous, and relatively lower in status than the Grotto Scripture Congregation members. See Yang Cenglie 1990: 116.

text but there are among the other texts recited a text called the *Complete Eight Trigrams* (*Quan bagua* 全八卦) said to relate Wenchang's avatars and miracles and morality texts originating in the Wenchang cult like the *Ten Principles of the Banana Window* (*Jiaochuang shize* 蕉窗十則). These congregations are said to have entered Yunnan from the Jiangxi-Zhejiang area and this type of devotional group may have been quite widespread in Ming-Qing China.[212]

The god still communicates on a regular basis with spirit writing groups in Taiwan.[213] His altars at major Taiwanese temples like Longshansi 龍山寺 and Zhinangong 指南宮 are well supplied with offerings and craftsmen still carve his statues for anxious parents of students facing the college entrance examination. In Hong Kong the Monmo Temple (Wenwu miao 文武廟), dedicated to Wenchang and Thearch Guan, is among the city's most popular. Religion in China itself will never be what it was before the KMT raids of the 1930s and the depredations of the Cultural Revolution, but the Yunnan devotional societies mentioned above still meet and a statue of the god is still worshiped in a side building of the administrative center of state-regulated Daoism, the Baiyunguan 白雲觀 in Beijing. The temple on Sevenfold Mountain is no longer controlled by Daoist priests and the locals are not always sure of the god's identity, but he is worshiped all the same, especially in a temple festival held each year during the first two weeks of the second lunar month.[214] In all these places men and women offer incense to the Divine Lord of Zitong in the hope that he will respond to their prayers and bestow his blessings.

---

212. Song Enchang 1985: 120. It is remarkable that this typically Chinese worship should survive among the Naxi and Bai tribesmen of the southwest frontier but disappear from the Chinese heartland.

213. Jordan and Overmyer 1986: 66, 113, 121, 152.

214. I was able to visit this festival in 1989, and Stephen Bokenkamp visited the temple shortly after the celebration in 1986. Because of the antiquity of the wooden structures (I was told) sacrifice and the lighting of candles and incense were not permitted within the temple compound itself. Instead, the faithful slaughtered their chickens outside and brought blood and feathers in to smear on temple altars and stele as a token of their devotion.

TRANSLATION

Traces of the Transformations 化跡總詩

Fated events will come to pass, truly there is a timing.
How can one still doubt that a man can bring glory to the Dao!
Do not for the sake of a hundred-story tower's completion
Contest, leaving traces that hang down through history.
Canonical and solid, let them criticize[1] and boast.
Cause and effect can perhaps be perceived in word and deed.
Now again he takes on the habit of this human world,
To transmit a hundred poems from Qinghe.

COMMENTARY

In this opening poem the stage is set for the tale to come. The reader is urged to look beyond the transient attractions of fortune and fame to see a moral message embodied in the Divine Lord of Zitong's series of experiences. Over the following seventy-three transformations (the "hundred" is a standard literary trope for "many") the god will indeed experience tremendous success, both temporal and divine, but

---

1. Following DZ in reading *ji* 譏, "to criticize," for *ji* 機, "pivot, opportunity." The DZJY reading is difficult to construe.

also devastating failure and punishment. The purpose is to propagate and glorify the Way (*hongdao* 弘道).

I have translated this poem in the third person, as if the medium or some lower-level possessing spirit is introducing the god, but it would not be impossible to read it in the first person. I am uncertain whether this poem was an original part of the 1181 revelation or a later addition. It is found in all editions of the *Book of Transformations*, but in DZ it is part of the Preface, rather than the main text.

I.　*Primordial Mandate*　　　　元命[2]

When Hundun first divided into opaque and clear,
In the astral quarter of the Southeast the phosphors shone sharp and bright.[3]
In its midst was contained the billowing energies of the Great Monad.[4]
I was already in secret correspondence with the quintessence of Creation.
Alone I occupied the stellar palace above the Twin Maidens,[5]

---

2. The term *yuanming* has a long history, beginning with the *Shujing*, "Duoshi" chapter, wherein it is used to refer to the mandate of Heaven to rule China, which Shang has forfeited. See *Shangshu zhengyi* 16/3a.

3. Following DZ in reading *dongnan* 東南, "south-east," for *dongxi* 東西, "east-west." Phosphors are luminous bodies, particularly "spectacular sky-lights," and here refer to the two asterisms mentioned in the second chapter. See Schafer 1977: 75–78, 182.

4. The Great Monad 太一 is a complex figure with a long history. Here it seems close to its early conception as a cosmogonic force or stage. The *Lüshi chunqiu* (5/5a) tells us, "When the myriad things were produced, they were created by the Great Monad and transformed by yin and yang."

5. The term Twin Maidens 雙女 is not well known. Morohashi identifies the constellation as the Closeted Maiden(s) 室女, to be equated with the four stars of the Attentive Woman 須女 lunar lodging (ε, μ, 2, and 3 Aquarii). Schafer (1977: 140–43) translates a tenth-century tale of an encounter with the Weaving Maiden, who was attended by the Attentive Woman and the Minx Woman 婺女, then remarks that dictionaries often equate the Attentive Woman and the Minx Woman. It would seem the constellation was conceived of as a pair of women. Perhaps Attentive Woman was used by synecdoche for the pair. This constellation governed marriage, textiles, and tailoring. See Ho Peng Yoke 1966: 99.

Governing the Fire Virtue, the quintessence of the Five
   activities.[6]
Abruptly tired of dwelling in this desolate region,
I shed my slough and end my term, the fruit of the Tao
   achieved.

I was originally a man of the Wu-Gui 吳會 region.[7] I was born in
the early years of the Zhou dynasty, and up until now [1181?] have
experienced seventy-three transformations.

COMMENTARY

In this introductory chapter the Divine Lord of Zitong reveals his cosmological origins. He was present at the first division of primordial
chaos, *hundun* 混沌, and observed the formation of the solid and ethereal substances which make up the world.[8] During this time he was
lodged among the stars in the southeast quadrant of the sky, and par-
took of their fiery nature. When his sojourn had reached the end of a
cycle, he left these stellar precincts to roam the world of man. In the
profane world it was the beginning of the Zhou dynasty, a time when
the pattern of Chinese civilization was being set, and when, according
to tradition, sage rulers were aided by a host of divine figures.[9]
   Whereas the poem describes the god's personal cultivation in the
astral reaches, the narrative recounts his incarnation as a mortal man.
The god's primordial power and divine nature make him a man-god
in transformation, passing from identity to identity, now incarnate, now
ethereal, but always serving in some bureaucratic position. With his
seventy-third transformation the god reached a plateau and was awarded
his highest and apparently permanent position as master of the Wen-

---

6. Following DZ in reading *qing* 情 for *jing* 精.
   7. Zang (1936: 372) lists two referents for this term. The first is the ancient Wu county, seat of
Guiji commandery, located west of modern Kunshan county in Jiangsu. The second is a broader term
referring to the Guiji commandery of Qin time, which in the Latter Han was split into the two
commanderies of Wu and Guiji.
   8. On the term hundun and its place in Chinese religious thought, see Girardot 1983.
   9. Several of the most common exemplars of proper conduct are from this time, like King Wen,
King Wu, and the Duke of Zhou. This era was also a favorite setting for tales about the gods, as in the
late sixteenth-century novel *Fengshen yanyi*.

chang Palace 文昌宮 and keeper of the Cinnamon Record 桂籍 (see below, ch. 73). He is careful to qualify that he has undergone seventy-three transformations "up until now," and in this he is prescient, as all current versions of the *Book of Transformations* include ninety-seven transformations.

The transforming power of gods is a near universal theme, but Buddhist doctrines of the "body of transformation" or *nirmana-kaya* 應身 certainly are one source of this Chinese conception. Transformational bodies are manifestations of the god in corporeal or quasi-material form, intended to respond to the needs of the unenlightened as expressed in the doctrine of "skill in means." There is also a strong Daoist element in the teleological nature of these transformations, aimed at an ultimate accomplishment of the Dao.

2.   *Flowing Form*   流形

I hid my tracks beneath the sacred cliff for uncounted autumns.
Waking and sleeping I turned hard and soft with the cycle of
    yin and yang.
Filling my belly with auroral vapors, I knew no hunger or thirst.
Cultivating my breath and submerging into my true nature, I let
    things come and go.
In the fullness of time my form was recycled and I returned to
    infancy.
When the time came I followed my destiny and served the
    rulers of this world.
In the majestic region of Guiji I deigned to manifest my
    transformation,
And was born into the Zhang 張 clan, the age was that of the
    Zhou.

I had just begun my sojourn among men when I found myself in the shadow of Guiji 會稽.[10] There I saw a recluse in his fifties, who, with incense and a lamp, raised his face to Heaven and prayed. It was the evening of a bing 丙 day (the third day of the ten-day week), the Middle of Spring, and the stars in the sky sparkled. The two asterisms Zhang 張 and Yi 翼 shone above.[11] I glanced down and listened. The recluse's surname was Zhang, in perfect accord with the arrayed asterism. I was thereupon born to him.

COMMENTARY

After many of years of practicing the Tao in the mountains, the god attained the ultimate stage of personal cultivation, the return to the purity and naturalness of infancy that had been advocated by Laozi.[12] When he was ready to manifest himself in the physical world, he happened upon a pious gentleman near the sacred mountain of Guiji. There were numerous auspicious signs, including the surname of the man, Zhang, which was the same as an asterism visible in the corresponding quadrant of the sky, and the time, the Middle of Spring, when yang forces had just reached dominance. The god descended and was born as the old man's son.

---

10. The "shadow" of a mountain indicates the northern slopes.

11. These asterisms, two of a system of twenty-eight lunar lodgings, are translated "Spread" and "Wing" by Schafer. They correspond to the Jupiter stations Quail Fire and Quail Tail, and form part of the great bird constellation of the South. Although the classical referent of Yi is the southern state of Chu, that of Zhang is the central Zhou domain. See Schafer 1977: 76–77.

12. See *Laozi* 10. This passage is strongly reminiscent of the internal alchemy so popular during the Song.

3. *Born as a Commoner*   生民

One night my mother[13] dreamed she had swallowed a pearl,
The quickening, hidden deep within her bosom, was an august
   beginning,
Then that month the birth drew near, leading to the auspicious
   morning,
A sacred radiance filled with light the rough-woven bamboo
   hut.
Serious and thoughtful, I did not play with all the children,
I loved study, and lost myself in contemplation,
Whenever I met elders they would talk amongst themselves,
Saying that I would one day be a great literati.

The Zhang clan was descended from a son of the Yellow Thearch,
named Hui 揮. He was the first to make bows and arrows, and the first
to set (*zhang* 張) a net. The position was passed down hereditarily,
and his descendents took Zhang as their surname. They are prominent in Wu 吳.

COMMENTARY

The family the Divine Lord chooses has an illustrious patrimony.
They are direct descendants of the Yellow Thearch or Huangdi, the
ancestor of the Chinese people and the patron of Daoism.[14] By Han
times Huangdi had been adopted as spokesman by schools as diverse
as those of administrative theory and sexual techniques. The Celestial
Masters, the first family of Daoism, shared the surname Zhang, and
hailed from the same region of Wu, which perhaps explains the
comment that the family was prominent there.

---

13. The text reads *beitang* 北堂 or "northern hall." According to classical ritual texts the northern
hall was the proper station of the principal wife during ritual observances, and came to be used as
another term for the primary wife, and then to one's own mother. See *Yili zhushu*, "Shihunli," 6/7b.
14. See *Fengsu tongjian*, p. 135, where the Zhang clan is listed as a descendant of Huangdi, and one
of the examples cited is Zhang Zhong, the Divine Lord's second incarnation.

The Divine Lord had been conceived miraculously, when his mother dreamed she swallowed a pearl. There are numerous parallels in the accounts of the births of other saints. Yu the Great, legendary founder of the Xia dynasty, was conceived after his mother had seen a comet, dreamed of conceiving, and swallowed the "sacred pearl," adlay.[15] This recalls the tale of Jiandi 簡狄, ancestress of the Shang, who conceived after swallowing the egg of a black bird.[16] An eleventh-century biography of Laozi relates that he was conceived when his mother, later Jade Woman of Arcane Marvels, "while taking a nap during the day, swallowed a five-color flowing jewel."[17] The god was a precocious youngster, wise beyond his years. This also is a standard topos in Chinese biographies of great men and in tales of heroes the world over.

4. *Changing Customs*   移俗

After the residual influence of Taibo[18] waned, the Wu region
Completely changed, the people's feelings became like those of
   island barbarians.
Cutting their hair, they endeavored to pacify a swampy land.
They tattooed their bodies in order to ward off dragons.
My nature was such I did not wish to follow the current
   customs,
Donning cap and shoes I thought only to practice ritual
   deportment.

---

15. *Shiji* 2/49, Zhengyi commentary quoting a *Diwang ji* 帝王紀. The grain of the adlay looked enough like a pearl that after Ma Yuan's death he was slandered by those who claimed the cartload of them he had brought back from Vietnam for medical purposes were in fact pearls. See *Hou Hanshu* 24/846.

16. *Shiji* 3/91.

17. See *774 Yulong zhuan* 3/1b.

18. Taibo 太伯 was the eldest son of King Tai 周太王 of the Zhou house. Knowing that his father wished to pass the throne to his younger brother, Jili 季歷, and thus allow Jili's son, the future King Wen 文, to come to the throne, Taibo and another brother fled to the barbarian regions of the south, where they adopted local custom by chopping their hair off and tattooing their bodies. See *Shiji* 4/115, 31/1445.

At first relatives and friends thought it overweening
ornamentation.[19]
In the end all in the region followed my example.

In my native region they cut their hair and tattooed their bodies.
No doubt because it is convenient for swimming, it had become the
custom of the barbarians.[20] When I reached adolescence, this dis-
tressed me. So I sought out a cap and shoes, and practiced the arts of
civilization by myself. Everyone both inside and outside my family
thought me strange. But after I continued this for a time, seventy to
eighty percent of them were converted by following me.

COMMENTARY

Although the god was born an aborigine in the southeast, he was
dissatisfied with native customs and was naturally drawn to those
of the Han people. The state of China had grown over the centuries
through a process of assimilation and absorption of neighboring
peoples. This process of Sinification had been founded on a myth of
the cultural superiority of Chinese civilization, a superiority that en-
compassed even minor items of apparel and decoration.[21] Witness
the horror with which Confucius contemplated the prospect that, but
for Guan Zhong 管仲, the Chinese might have been reduced to
letting their hair hang down free and buttoning their clothing on the
left, rather than the right.[22] In his divine sagacity, the Divine Lord of
Zitong also realizes the inappropriateness of his native attire and
adopts distinctive items of Han dress, the cap and shoes.

---

19. Following DZ in reading *shi* 飾, "ornament," for *jie* 節, "bamboo segment, principle."

20. The "Jijie" commentary to *Shiji* 4/115 quotes the late Han scholar Ying Shao 應劭: "Since they
are often in the water, they chop off their hair and tattoo their bodies in order to resemble dragons, so that
they will not be harmed."

21. Western scholars, like Wolfram Eberhard, have emphasized the contributions of these cultures
to the Chinese world. See Eberhard 1942. Archaeological discoveries also continue to reveal that the level
of development of these neighboring cultures was not necessarily inferior to that of the Central Plain.

22. The exact comment was, "Had it not been for Guan Zhong, we might well be wearing our hair
down and folding our garments to the left" (*Lunyu* 28/14/17). Translation from Lau 1979: 126–7
(romanization modified).

5.　*Investigating Antiquity*　　稽古

The Three Wu[23] are in a remote land at the fringes of the
　heavens,
The arts of civilization[24] were not esteemed; things of beauty
　were few.
The canons of the emperors were never transmitted to their
　distant descendants,
How could the imperial documents have reached a peasant
　household?
Fortunately a worthy emissary transmitted (documents) on
　double-thread silk.[25]
Awaking to our lowly state, we learned to make hemp cloth.[26]
From this time on throughout the region the chants and music
　were beautiful,
And our insignificant culture already merited praise.

My home was very far from the Zhou capital, and there was no
esteem for the arts of civilization. One day an aged gentleman called
upon my father and recited several chapters of the Great Admonish-
ments of Tang 唐 and Yu 虞 (i.e. the *Shujing*),[27] saying, "An emissary of the Central States transmitted this." I liked them, and went to

---

23. There are many definitions of the Three Wu 三吳. Perhaps what is meant here is the trio of
Wuxing 吳興, Wu commandery 吳郡 (modern Suzhou), and Guiji (modern Shaoxing), which is
referred to in *Wangshi hejiao Shuijing zhu* 40/15b. See Zang 1936: 29.4.

24. The "arts of civilization" (*wenwu* 文物) here refers to the abstract institutions like laws,
government, religion, and the arts that define and identify a culture.

25. Fine silk woven with a double thread (*jian* 縑) was often used as a medium for writing and
painting and came to be used as a synecdoche for the documents and paintings themselves. Here, as the
next line makes clear, what was transmitted was not merely a given document but the concept of writing on such materials itself. Note, however, that Kuhn (1988: 310) cites a Han passage wherein *jian*
refers to a different type of silk fiber.

26. Following the 1645 ed. and DZ in reading *wu* 悟, "to become aware of," for *ling* 令, "to
command, to cause."

27. Tang and Yu are the reign names of the two legendary emperors Yao 堯 and Shun 舜. The
modern Shujing contains a "Canon of Yao" and a "Canon of Shun."

study with him. I learned everything he could recite. Then anyone in
the village who wanted to study came to me to learn them and all
took me as teacher.

COMMENTARY

The god's Sinicization continues. Having mastered the rudiments
of Chinese dress, he now comes into contact with classical literature in
the form of the *Scripture of Documents* (Shujing 書經), which he learns
by rote from a teacher. The poem implies that he also came into contact with written Chinese at this time. Having mastered these works
easily, it is natural that he should himself become the teacher of others,
and continue to spread Chinese culture. We see here a traditional
Confucian conception of culture as defined by the rites, music and
classical learning.

---

6. *Worshipping the Perfected*   奉眞

Silent the thatched hut; during the day the door is shut.
Travelers seldom come to this village by the water.
Plowing deeply I happened to find a golden statue,
Long interred, it was still wrapped in purple vine roots.
I could not bear to split and melt it, diminishing its natural
    value,
Rather I would pass my days burning incense and making
    offerings.
From atop a seaside peak I sent it back to exorcise disastrous
    influences.
All the souls of the entire region depend on its grace.

One day I was at work on the irrigation ditches when suddenly
beneath my hoe I found a metal statue of a man. The hat on his head

was like lofty mountains towering one upon the other; he wore a robe of auroral-patterned silk, flowing and beautiful; his eyebrows were indigo, his face moon-shaped; he looked stern yet compassionate; he perched precariously, leaning on a table; a lotus blossom formed a pedestal. The statue was over a foot high, and weighed more than a catty (approx. 600 g). At first I did not know what god this was, but I inquired of the elders, and someone said, "It is the Primordial Heavenly Worthy (Yuanshi Tianzun 元始天尊).[28] Of old, when Yu 禹 of Xia was ordering the waters, he melted metal and made gods, using them to quell the marchmounts of the regions. They must have been like this statue." My family had always been poor, but even though we were pressed for food and clothing, I did not dare to think of splitting it into pieces and melting it down. One day a wind from the ocean churned up the waves, and far and near fled in fright. It was not something that a man's might could withstand. I spoke to the crowd, saying, "In my home we have a metal statue that I happened to find. Now I will cast it away for your sake, so that the Sovereign of the Seas might be appeased." I then led the multitude to a high spot and threw the statue into the madly dashing breakers. Suddenly the wind stopped, the tide retreated, and the whole area was saved. The people of the village were grateful for this. For all of this I was[29] thanked with dried rice and cloth, and I was not permitted to refuse them. From this time on my family's finances were fairly stable. Some time later I retraced my steps to where I remembered throwing the statue. Something gleamed on a sandbar, and I dug up the same statue. So I brought it home and built a hall where it could be installed and worshiped. The people of my land venerated the statue reverently.

COMMENTARY

This episode is the god's first encounter with the Chinese sacred world. He finds a golden statue of the supreme Daoist deity, the Pri-

---

28. Yuanshi Tianzun is one of the Three Pures, the three highest deities of Taoism. Technically the Three Pures are incorporeal breaths of the Tao, but in later times Yuanshi Tianzun was singled out for special worship. He was often identified with the Jade Emperor, Yuhuang Dadi 玉皇大帝, who presides over the divine bureaucracy.

29. Following the 1645 ed. and DZ in reading the passive marker *jian* 見 for *wei* 爲.

mordial Heavenly Worthy. The cap of this statue is described as a mountain, and Daoist caps were often conceived as representations of Mount Kunlun, the *axis mundi*. The Heavenly Worthy is seated on a lotus pad, a Buddhist image showing his miraculous origin in Nature. Yu the Great is known to have channeled the rivers and fixed the mountains, but I have found no reference to him casting golden images of gods and placing them on the marchmounts.[30]

Blessed beyond all his fellow villagers by his discovery of this precious image, the Divine Lord of Zitong is still willing to sacrifice it for the good of the community. He casts the statue into the sea as an offering to Hairuo, an ancient deity of the sea mentioned in *Zhuangzi* and the *Chuci*.[31] The practice of placing statues in rivers to control or quell them is an old one. Li Bing 李冰, the great hydraulic engineer who created the Guanxian waterworks in Sichuan, is said to have placed in the river three stone men and five stone rhinoceri.[32] Recently a statue of Li Bing made by a local prefect in A.D. 168 has been unearthed from the bed of the river.[33]

The Divine Lord's selfless, altruistic action has an unforeseen consequence: the gratitude of his fellow villagers establishes the fortune of his family, the first of many examples in this text of virtue rewarded and one that points out in particular the significance of individual sacrifice for the clan as a whole.

7. *Giving Repose to my Parents*   寧親

Many are the months that my mother toiled,
Long did the wind and cold, heat and humidity batter her.
Doctors and shamans examined her, all to no avail.

---

30. See *Shiji* 2/51, where it says that Yu fixed (*ding* 定) the high mountains and great rivers.

31. *Zhuangzi* 42/17/5ff., *Chuci* 5/10a; Hawkes 1985: 198. In *Zhuangzi* the deity is called Peihairuo or *ruo* (monarch?) of the Northern Sea. Cf. *Sanjiao yuanliu soushen daquan* 7/17b, p. 338.

32. Chang Qu, *Huayangguo zhi* 3/30–31.

33. See Sichuan Guanxian wenjiaoju 1974. The statue is now on display at the Sichuan Provincial Museum and a copy of it is displayed at the Lurking Dragon Belvedere 伏龍觀 at Guanxian.

Acupuncture and moxa were so frequent[34] it was almost
  unbearable.
I sliced the flesh of my thigh to make a soup, fulfilling a karmic
  vow.
Sucked the pus and drew out the blood, firm in my sincerity.
Clearly one night I heard the words of a heavenly spirit,
Her life was extended one cycle as a sign of my extreme
  integrity.

By the time I was capped my mother was in her sixties. When
young she had worked hard, weaving and sewing, and often missed
her meals. This had brought upon her a malady, which, in the autumn
of her life, was aggravated by an excess of the six breaths,[35] until it
became a grand affliction, an abscess forming on her back. At first we
tried the prayers of shamans, then the proddings[36] and drugs of physicians, but after more than a month none had proved effective. I did
not leave her bedroom, watching over her day and night. I never took
off my clothes to rest. When all my plans were exhausted, I sucked
the abscess, drawing out a great quantity of blood and pus. The malady relented somewhat. The doctor said, "The root of the abscess is
attached to the bones and cannot easily be removed." Three days
later I sucked it again. Suddenly I felt something filling my mouth.
When I spit it out and examined it, there was a membrane like silk
threads and a thick milk-like substance in grains the size of rice. My
mother gradually stabilized, but because she had lacked nutrition
during her illness, when she recovered a bit, it turned into prostra-
tion. The doctor said, "This is a chronic disease. To fortify humans
with human (flesh) is true fortification. The real thing might bring
her back to normal." So that night I sliced off the flesh of my thighs,
cooked it, and fed it to her. Suddenly I heard a voice in the sky saying,

34. Following the 1645 ed. and DZ in reading *pinreng* 頻仍 "frequently," for *gongji* 攻肌,
"attacked the flesh."

35. The six breaths have various definitions, the most appropriate being: heat, cold, aridity, humidity,
wind, and fire. See Morohashi 2/50.1, entry 1453.104.

36. *Bian* 砭 refers to jabbing the afflicted place with stone needles.

"Because of your pure filial piety, the Supreme Heaven extends your mother's life one cycle." The next day, with no medicine, she recovered, just as the spirit had said she would.

COMMENTARY

This is the first and most dramatic of a number of episodes that center on the virtue of filial piety. This theme of children giving of their own body for the health of the parent is a familiar trope in stories of filial piety. Wing-tsit Chan finds the earliest example in the Tang dynasty.[37] The closest parallel, and perhaps the direct inspiration for this episode, is found in the tale of Miaoshan, an incarnation of Guanyin. While Miaoshan is practicing austerities on Xiangshan her father, the king, comes down with jaundice. The king sends an envoy to Xiangshan to ask the aid of the hermit there, not knowing it is his daughter. In an inscription dating to 1104, some seventy years before this portion of the *Book of Transformations* was written, the story continues: "she gouged out both her eyes with a knife, then told the envoy to sever her two arms. At that moment the whole mountain shook, and from the sky came a voice commending her: 'Rare, how rare! She is able to save all beings, to do things impossible in this world.'"[38]

A preference for the parents' welfare over that of the child's was a continuing feature of the cult. In an undated tract probably from the late Ming or early Qing called the "Eight Inversions" (Bafan 八反) the Divine Lord chides those who give more consideration to their children than to their parents. The fifth inversion concerns medical care:[39]

> The medicine stands in the market only have baby-fattening pills; they have none to strengthen the parents. Why are the two treated so differently? Both the child and the parent suffer illness. It is not more urgent to heal the child than to heal the parent. Even if you slice off your thigh, the meat is still your parents'. I exhort you to immediately protect the lives of both your parents.

---

37. Chan 1967:107, citing *Xin Tang shu* 196: 5600. In this tale also a man shaves meat from his thigh to feed and cure an ailing mother.

38. Translation from Dudbridge 1982: 600.

39. *Wendi quanshu* 13/35a.

Filial piety is a cardinal virtue in almost every type of Chinese religious belief but it seems to hold special significance for the Wenchang cult with its emphasis on the family unit.

8. *Spirit Marriage*   幽婚

Finding a mate cannot be left to chance,

Meetings in this life are the result of karmic affinities.

Her mind and body did not decompose, as if waiting for me,

Reliving the events of a dream, how can it be coincidence?

Once there was an heir to carry on my enterprise

Suddenly her fragrant soul was sealed again within the deepest springs.[40]

Abruptly cut off in my prime from the relations of man and woman,

The sentiment of all was to praise me as a born transcendent.

As a youth I was by nature quiet and seldom hit it off with others. As I grew older, and passed the age of capping, I still had no spouse. It was not just that no worthy matchmaker appeared. I also was not really interested in pursuing a mate. Previously, when my mother was suffering her illness, she regretted never having seen her grandchildren, and it troubled me that I was acting unfilially. One night I dreamed that I came to a forest at the foot of a mountain, where a solitary tomb towered. Beside it there was a gate, and within a beautifully adorned young woman sat. She looked at me and said, "Are you not Zhang Shanxun 張善勳?" I was surprised to be referred to by my name,[41] and asked her reason for doing so. She said, "You and I live so close

---

40. These are the famous Yellow Springs, abode of the dead in archaic Chinese cosmology.

41. In ancient China it was taboo to use the name of one's direct ancestor, and impolite to use the name of someone living in general except in relations of the closest intimacy.

we can hear the other's chickens and dogs. I am from the Zhong 仲 family. Once my uncle met with your family to discuss your good qualities, because he considered that you were fond of learning and esteemed propriety, like a gentleman of old. He argued for giving me to you in marriage, but my father criticized this plan because of your unattractive appearance. I, however, had already come to admire you wholeheartedly. Later I was promised to Zhong Anru 鍾安孺.[42] Zhong was the son of a rich family, but had made no reputation for himself. I was humiliated, and for this reason became ill and died. It has been three years now. I have come here for your sake. Why do you not think of a way to deal with this situation?" I awoke with a start.

A month later I had the same dream again. So when I had a free day I went for a stroll with my friend Yi Jiancheng 儀堅成, seeking out secluded spots. Suddenly we found ourselves at a place identical to that in the dream. I had just told my friend this, and we were both wondering at the similarity, when someone emerged from the tomb and called me "husband" (lang 郎). It was the person I had seen in my dream. It turned out that Yi was a maternal uncle of the woman. He ran to tell her parents to bring her back home, and in the end we were married.

COMMENTARY

Zhang Shanxun's encounter with his deceased bride-to-be shows that the power of Fate transcends even death and offers a further proof of of Zhang's true divine identity. But the tale also reflects a custom of performing spirit marriages that was in existence in the Song and survives today both in China and in the Chinese diaspora.

When a daughter dies before marriage, this is considered a great tragedy, both because the girl will have no descendants to sustain her in the other world and because the force of her sexuality remains pent-up and unvented. The souls of dead virgins are credited with such power that sometimes they are able to climb the ladder of divinity,

---

42. The given name Anru here means "the content wimp." Several of the names in this story have meanings, perhaps reflecting the allegorical nature of the tale (see the Commentary). The family name of the young woman, Zhong, is the personal name of the god in a later incarnation. The surname and given name of his friend, Yi Jiancheng, might be translated "deportment steadfastly complete."

passing from frightening unquiet ghost to local goddess to national deity, as the patron saint of seafarers, Mazu 媽祖, did during the Song. To protect themselves from the rancor of these unfortunate spirits, families arrange a marriage for the girl, either with the dead son of a neighbor or with a living individual willing to take responsibility for her. The groom may be selected in a number of ways, but in at least one modern example, recorded by David Jordan, he was visited in a dream by the spirit of the dead girl, just as in this episode.[43] By accepting such a match the god encourages others to agree to such disagreeable but necessary arrangements.

Such beliefs were already prevalent during the Song. The Southern Song author Kang Yuzhi 康與之 (fl. 1131), in his recollections of life under the Northern Song titled *A Record of Yesterday's Dreams* (*Zuomenglu* 昨夢錄), records the custom of arranging ghost marriages between young men and women who had died before marriage.[44] A special "ghost matchmaker" was employed and divinations were performed on the appropriateness of the match; the bride was often supplied with a symbolic dowry. During the wedding ceremony the spectral bride and groom showed their approval by causing banners to shake. Sometimes a teacher who had passed on was also designated to continue the education of the young man, presumably in preparation for a career in the divine bureaucracy. It is said that after the ceremony the bride or groom would appear in the dreams of their new relatives. If all these procedures were not followed properly, one of the newlyweds might visit misfortune upon the living.

In this chapter the Divine Lord also goes out of his way to point out his lack of interest in sex. As a clan god of the Zhangs and as a provider of progeny the god of Zitong was expected to have a large and extended family. One structure found in his temple-complex, the Family Blessings Tower (Jiaqinglou 家慶樓), celebrated this aspect of his identity; there his image was surrounded by those of his parents, sons, grandsons, and great-grandsons. But fertility must not be confused with debauchery. The Divine Lord affirms his sacred nature, and sets a good example for the householder, by transcending sexual desire without rejecting the sexual relations necessary to maintain the family.

---

43. Jordan 1972: 140–55, esp. 143.
44. *Zuomeng lu* 11b–12b.

9. *Yuanshi* 淵石

The spring sunlight was soft, the brilliance prolonged,
Spring streams cascaded in torrents, shallow but rippling.
Silken garments by the shore shimmered in reflected image,
In this transcendent seed I awoke to my former knowledge.[45]
Finely carved white lines formed the character *yuan* 淵,
A green stone, round in shape, like a small turtle.
A son was born and given a name fitting the omen.
Best know it is a gift of Heaven and be not selfish about him.

Madame née Zhong had been married for three months. Local girls of good family who have already married, but have not yet conceived, go together to the edge of a sacred pool, where they try to grasp a stone. Those who grab hold of a stone are supposed to have a boy, while those who get a tile are supposed to have a girl. It is an old custom. My wife was in the midst of the company. My mother said to her, "The waters of the pool are quiet and deep, murky and fathomless. You should look for a stone at the shallow place near the top of the pool." My wife was just hesitating in the midst of the pool when suddenly frothy waves arose as if someone had blown them. She groped in them and caught hold of a stone the size of a chicken's egg. It was shaped like a turtle, with six projections, and was green with white lines that faintly formed the character *yuan*. She was moved by this and conceived. When a son was born to her we named him Yuanshi 淵石 ("yuan stone"). When he was just losing his baby teeth she suddenly announced to me, "My son is really just like you. Take good care of him. My karmic affinity with you in this world is exhausted." She died as soon as she had finished speaking. I never remarried.

---

45. This passage is difficult to construe. I have adopted the reading of the illustrated edition of 1771, which has *zhong* 種, "seed," for *zhong* 眾, "crowd." In this interpretation, the god recognizes his son, who was part of his celestial family before his incarnation.

COMMENTARY

This divinatory ritual for conceiving a child of a certain sex must reflect a local custom, perhaps of the Guiji region, but I have found no record of such a practice. Granet describes a ritual that bears some similarity, in which maidens would cross a flowing stream so that they could become impregnated by the ancestral spirits.[46] The turtle is a symbol of longevity in China, most recently studied by Allan (1991). The divine or spirit mother who stays with a mortal only long enough to rear a child to a certain age is a common theme in Chinese folktales. The Divine Lord of Zitong realizes that this is in the nature of things, and expresses no grief at her death. Still, he remains true to her by never remarrying. She makes the point that their karmic affinity in this world is at an end, implying that their relationship will continue in the next. The Divine Lord was renowned for his large divine family, each member of which received official titles during the Song.[47]

IO. *The Tame Pheasants*   馴稚

Heaven was shattered and the Earth rent, my feelings I leave to
   your imagination.
How bitter! There was no way I could save my parents.
I hauled dirt to form a tomb to repay their support.
Sleeping on a straw mat with a clod of earth for a pillow
   increased my sorrow.[48]
Cut off from the path to the Yellow Springs, alas, how could I
   reach them?
The white pheasants, their feelings grieved, tamed themselves.
The ritual dictates three years, but my grief knew no end.
I limited my mourning to lead the common people.

---

46. Granet 1975: 49. Granet gives no specific time or place for this practice.
47. See *Song huiyao jigao*, "Li" 禮, 20/56a–b; *169 Qinghe neizhuan* 2a–7a; *Mengliang lu* 14/6a.
48. See *Yili zhushu* 41/4a–b, from which the first four characters of this line is a direct quote.

When I was thirty-six years old, the Year Star was in *you* 酉.[49] An epidemic was abroad and no one escaped. The villages became empty and the roads were deserted. My father was eighty-five and my mother seventy-three. In full summer they both caught the disease, and they died on the same day. I took shovel and scoop in hand to dig their tomb. Then I built a lean-to beside the road and slept with a rock for a pillow until the three-year mourning period had ended. There was often a pair of white pheasants who perched in a tree above me, and each time I sacrificed they would fly down singing, and, nodding their heads, twitter as if they wanted to say something. When the term of mourning was completed they left.

COMMENTARY

Here the god provides a model for proper conduct upon the loss of one's parents. According to classical injunctions one is supposed to build a lean-to near the grave where the son sleeps with only a straw mat for a bed and a rock or clod of earth for a pillow. The straw and earth or rock symbolize the ground in which the parents now rest.[50] So pure is the Divine Lord's filial devotion, and so moving his grief, that the souls of his parents manifest as a pair of white pheasants, and descend each time to partake of the sacrifices he offers to them.

This chapter should be understood in the context of a move during the Song to revive Confucian funerary and mourning practices in the face of an increasing dominance of Buddhist ritual in this area. Ebrey (1993) details the actions of the state in regulating ritual activity of this type. The Divine Lord would have applauded the actions of Neo-Confucians in this regard.

---

49. Literally, "Jupiter was doing startling things" (*zuo e* 作噩). The Year Star (Taisui 太歲) is technically Counter-Jupiter, an imaginary planet whose orbit is a mirror image of Jupiter's and spends one year in each of twelve Jupiter stations, which are correlated with the earthly stems. During such years a variety of disasters were prone to occur, including epidemics. See *Erya zhushu* 6/6b.

50. The literature on mourning ritual and practices in China is quite extensive. The most comprehensive source in English remains de Groot 1892–1910. See also *Yili zhushu* 41.

II. *Diverting the Stream* 回流

I gave no thought to the toil when building their tomb,
How could I foresee that waves would arise on level ground?
The pines and catalpas were about to be swept away,[51]
I worried that even the coffin would not be spared.
But the Transcendent Scripture of the Great Grotto eliminated
  the danger.
The sacred statue of true gold restrained the whales and turtles.
When autumn storms had cleared and rushing torrents were
  stilled,
I was happy to see a level field, broad and high.

The tomb of my revered parents was only about a hundred paces south of the house. I relied too hurriedly on the divination's auspicious report, thinking this location would be convenient for me to keep watch. At first I had no time to think more about it. Five years after the burial a flood burst out thirty *li* west of the grave, turning level ground into streams. The grave was on the bank of one. The source of the water was inexhaustible, and the current quite powerful and swift. I was frightened by this and wanted to rebury my parents but it was too late. So I fasted and kept watch over the tomb day and night, ceaselessly chanting the *Scripture of the Great Grotto.* I also took out our family's golden statue and worshiped it fervently. Thus I was able to get through the crisis without incident. The next year the autumn rains were copious, and the tributaries swelled to overflowing, until several courses merged into one. I was even more afraid, but, when the waters subsided and I looked, the stream channel in front of the tomb had become a solid dike over one *li* wide. From this time on the pines and catalpas (of the tomb) were safe.

---

51. Pines and catalpas (*qiu* 楸, *catalpa bungei*) were commonly planted on top of tombs. See the commentary to a poem by Xie Tiao 謝朓 in *Wenxuan* 58/8b. Pine trees, being evergreens, are a symbol of longevity, and the qiu, containing the homophonous character for "autumn," is perhaps a symbol of old age.

COMMENTARY

Flooding was a constant danger in many parts of China, in part because the extensive use of irrigation led people to settle in low areas near water. Early awareness of changes in geological time led the Chinese to a concern for the future topography of their graves.[52] Divination prior to determining the site for a new city, residence, or grave is an ancient practice in China.[53] This story points out one rationale for this divination: it absolved the diviner of blame should something unforeseen happen to the grave in the future.

But even if one could escape public condemnation, the destruction of ancestral graves was a serious matter with significant consquences. Most important was the severance of communication, maintained through sacrifices at the tomb, and the consequent loss of the ancestors' supernatural support and aid. Thus for moral, emotional, and practical reasons, the Divine Lord took care to build a proper tomb, then bury his parents according to prescribed ritual and accepted custom. One custom was to plant trees, especially pines and catalpas with their auspicious associations, on top of the tomb. Preservation of these trees was then a sacred trust. Lu You 陸游 gives some idea of the importance of these trees when describing the dilapidated tomb of the famous Northern Sung statesman Zhang Shangying 張尚英 (1043–1121), which he encountered on a trip into the Sichuan region during 1170:[54]

> The trees of the tomb had been cut down and were lying across the road, so it was almost impossible to proceed. [Zhang Shangying]'s son Mao, who was (once) an Auxiliary Academician of the Lung-t'u Pavillion, is already dead. Of his two grandsons, one has an official post but is insane; the other has no post or rank.

If the Divine Lord permitted the tomb of his parents to suffer such a fate, he might also be judged insane or impotent. In the midst of this dilemma the Divine Lord again appeals for divine aid through the *Transcendent Scripture of the Great Grotto*, which exists in two editions

---

52. The eminent philologist-magician Guo Pu 郭璞 (276–324) is said to have located his mother's grave near a stream because his divination indicated that the area would become dry land. See *Jinshu* 72/1908.

53. Zhang Zhenglang has found evidence for the practice of divining the location of a city on the oracle bones. See Zhang Zhenglang 1980–81.

54. Translation from Chang and Smythe 1981: 145.

in the Daozang, both attributed to Wenchang.[55] The gods responded to his pious worship by constructing a dike. The second reference to pines and catalpas may be regarded as metonymy for the tomb as a whole.

12. *Subduing the Epidemic* 降瘟

The death of both my parents was due to an epidemic.
I suffered and grieved with a resentment at this injustice that cut
    to the bone.
As long as they lived their loving support never faltered,
On diverging paths in the worlds of light and darkness, I could
    not give vent to my fury.
Divine troops seized the fiends and appeared in a bright light,
The perfected being who transmitted the rite and register had
    come in a dream.
My brush alit and wrote a charm, saving the people from
    ailments.
How could I permit the five demons to tarry for even a
    moment?

When both my parents died from an epidemic, they caught this misery in summer, and suffered all the more. Every time I thought of the cruelty of the epidemic demons, my hatred for them cut to the bones. But the worlds of light and darkness are on different paths, and I could not revenge myself on them no matter how I tried. Once in desperation I compared this to the time I had diverted the stream at the banks of their grave; then I had in fact relied on the power of the

---

55. 5 *Taishang wuji zongzhen Wenchang dadong xianjing* and *103 Yuqing wuji zongzhen Wenchang dadong xianjing zhu.* On these scriptures and their relationship to the *Perfected Scripture of the Great Grotto,* see Robinet 1983.

Perfected Scripture of the Great Grotto and the golden statue. So I chanted the scripture and worshiped the statue even more fervently, until[56] I should receive supernatural aid in controlling the epidemic demons. After three years I suddenly dreamed that the golden statue I worshiped spoke to me, saying, "You have memorized the True Scripture of the Great Grotto thoroughly, but you have never seen the Rite and the Talisman of the Great Grotto. Now I will bestow these upon you, that you may master the evil devils. Thus not only may you achieve your original purpose, but also aid Heaven in promoting moral transformation and assist the state in saving the populace." He took from his sleeve two books. I bowed one hundred times and accepted them. When I awoke the books were before my pillow. One was titled *Register of the Great Grotto* 大洞籙, the other *Rite of the Great Grotto* 大洞法. I opened the register and began reading. When I reached the line "Ten thousand heavenly cavaliers and armored troops are placed under your command," suddenly there was wind and thunder and daylight turned to night. Countless figures in golden armor and vermillion sashes were arrayed before me. They bowed and asked[57] for my orders. Three[58] men holding red banners in the midst of the troops first addressed me, saying, "We wish to hear your commands." I was flustered, but found myself saying in a sharp voice, "I command you to subdue the epidemic demons. All the members of a certain[59] household in this village are suffering from the epidemic. Go there and drive them forth to me." When I had finished speaking one of the banner-bearers led a hundred-odd men into the house, and in a moment had captured the demons. He pushed five men forward. One wore a tiger skin, another a cock's crown, a third had the face of a dog,[60] a fourth the face of a crow[61], the fifth the head of a donkey. They held feathered placards, representing fire and water,

---

56. Following the 1645 ed. and DZ in reading *ji* 洎, "until," for *ji* 冀, "to hope for."
57. Following the 1645 ed. and DZ in reading *qing* 請, "to request," for *ting* 聽, "to hear, obey."
58. Following the 1645 ed. and DZ in reading *san* 三, "three," for *yi* 一, "one."
59. Following the 1645 ed. and DZ in reading *mou* 某, "a certain," for "Zhang Tunshi" 張屯使.
60. DZ's reading, "face of a man," must reflect a graphic error confusing *ren* 人, "man," with *quan* 犬, "dog."
61. DZ reads "head of a swan" (*hutou* 鵠頭) for "crow" (*wuya* 烏鴉)

axes[62] and chisels. I rebuked them angrily, and was about to destroy their forms, when they pleaded, "We, your disciples,[63] are born from the seasonal cycle and take form from seasonal breaths. There are certain districts in which we roam and certain people whom we afflict. Those who have a heavy accumulation of otherworldly offenses are visited with disaster; death comes to those whose heavenly lifespan is at an end. We certainly do not dare to act on our own initiative. If Your Perfected Honor would deign to treat us with indulgence, we will henceforth observe your restrictions. If when we are spreading epidemics we see your honor's charm, we shall not dare to enter there." I thereupon instructed them in accordance with the ritual and they left. Whenever anyone in the neighborhood came down with the epidemic I gave them a talisman and performed a ritual on their behalf. All recovered completely.

COMMENTARY

The rising population density and increasing inter-regional trade that were characteristic of the Song facilitated the spread of communicable diseases. By the twelfth century epidemics occurred on the average once every five years.[64] They must have been particularly severe in Sichuan, which was at the time among the most densely populated regions of China, and the phenomenal drop in population during the late Song and early Yuan has been attributed to the ravages of epidemics.[65]

In this episode the Divine Lord of Zitong confronts the demons thought to spread these epidemics. Since at least Han times epidemic diseases have been attributed to demonic influence, and the great *nuo* 儺 exorcism performed at the end of each year was intended to drive off such malefic spirits.[66] Early sources name three such spirits, sons of the legendary emperor Zhuanxu 顓頊.[67] The Ming dynasty *1476*

---

62. Following the 1645 ed. and DZ in reading *fu* 斧, "axe," for *fu* 釜, "kettle."
63. Following the 1645 ed. and DZ in omitting the name Yuanbo 元伯.
64. Elvin 1973: 175.
65. Hartwell 1982 and 1988. Hartwell (1988) finds a ninety-three percent drop in population in the Chengdu plain between 1200 and 1390, from 32.53 households per square kilometer to 2.21.
66. See Bodde 1975: 75–138 for a description of the *nuo* during the Han.
67. See, for example, *Lunheng jiaoshi* 22/934–5, 25/1038.

Soushen ji relates that the Five Emissaries of the Epidemic appeared to Emperor Wendi of the Sui (r. 581–604). The ensuing epidemic left many dead, and when Emperor Wendi was told that there was no way to control these spirits, he enfeoffed them as generals (*jiangjun* 將軍) and established a shrine to them.[68] A scripture from the Yuan or Ming, *209 Zhengyi wensi bidu shendeng yi*, consists of a ritual to propitiate five epidemic spirits in which each is named and associated with one of the cardinal directions. In modern Taiwan, epidemic gods are a prime focus of worship, though usually they are found in a group of twelve.[69]

Gods or demons of the epidemic have an important but ambiguous position in Daoism. They are originally evil demons who had to be subjugated or propitiated. But they are also powerful gods, who control the fates of many, and who have their function in the ordained workings of the world. The Divine Lord faces just this dilemma. Having acquired certain powers through the bestowal of two magic scriptures, he wants only to revenge himself upon the epidemic spirits for having caused the death of his parents. But the spirits point out that they only attack those who are destined to die, either due to moral transgressions or because they have reached the end of their natural lifespan. Demons also are agents of Heaven. The Divine Lord contents himself with an agreement by which they will defer to his authority, when such is made manifest through the posting of one of his talismans. No doubt the Zitong cult at this time was actively writing such talismans and bestowing them on adherents of the cult in return for donations. The passage from the *Register of the Great Grotto* cited in this episode probably is a paraphrase of a line in the *Precious Register*, which reads "Ten thousand cavaliers, armored troops and divine emissaries are placed under your command."[70]

We should note also the transformation the Divine Lord goes through when he begins to give orders to his divine soldiers. Although

---

68. *1476 Soushen ji* 6/10a–b. On the title "general" often given to malefic spirits, see Stein 1979: 65.

69. Liu Zhiwan (1984: 225–284) describes the modern belief in epidemic spirits and gives a certain amount of historical background. It is often said that there are 360 of these spirits, and by Liu's own count over one hundred are actively worshiped in Taiwan.

70. There are in fact three such cohorts bestowed upon the practitioner in this text, each led by a Great General, the Great General Establishing Principles, the Great General Supervising Merit, and the Great General of the Mounted Guard. *1214 Gaoshang dadong Wenchang silu ziyang baolu* 2/16a.

in his conscious waking mind he does not know how to address these divine figures, a deeper layer of his being asserts itself, and he naturally assumes the authority that is his in his true identity as a celestial deity. A similar awakening occurs in a later incarnation, in chapter 72. In Chinese legend and folklore divine beings who assume human form often are unaware of their true identity until some crisis or other event stimulates their memory.

13. *Loving the Living*   好生

Wind, cold, heat, and humidity change with the heavens;
Food and drink, rest and activity, these illnesses come from man.
The Meridian Scripture of Huangdi 黃帝脈經 is detailed about sons and mothers,
The characteristics of drugs expounded by Shennong 神農 differentiate ruler and subject.[71]
Using massage and acupuncture according to the severity,
Replenishers and purgatives move and shift, distinguishing old and new.[72]
If only Heaven's people[73] would not die before their time,
I would toil without regret; this is my sincere intention.

I saved many people with my charms. The people who came to me from far and near seeking healing were too numerous to count. Those who had been infected by an epidemic disease, come in contact with malefic curses, contracted malaria, encountered hapless souls, or been attacked by demons, vicious spirits, or evil breaths all recovered com-

---

71. On the significance of the distinction between "ruler" and "minister" drugs in early Chinese medicine, see Unschuld 1985: 115.

72. Cf. Unschuld 1985: 179, 183.

73. Following the 1645 ed. and DZ in reading *min* 民, "people," for *ming* 命, "mandate."

pletely. But as to those who suffered from imbalances of heat and cold or depletion and repletion of the viscera,[74] for whom eating and sleeping, activity and rest, toil and ease were not harmonized, or who were affected internally by the emotions of joy, anger, grief, and happiness, or who had caught something externally from wind, cold, heat, and humidity—these all belong to the domains of Shennong and Qi Bo 岐伯, and are not the affair of Daoist charms. When there was someone who came to me earnestly and I was unable to save him, I was truly mortified and felt inadequate. So I explored the principle of meridians and tested the nature of drugs, discussed the ascendance and return of the five activities, became familiar with the nine acupuncture techniques. After six years of toil I had mastered the fine points. From this time on, anyone whose Heavenly lifespan was not exhausted did not die before his time.

COMMENTARY

Finding that his Daoist arts are of limited effectiveness, the Divine Lord of Zitong sets out to learn Chinese medicine. It is interesting to see how the fields of competence of these two techniques are delimited. All illnesses except those he was unable to cure must have been thought to have a supernatural origin. In a recent work on Chinese magical practices Sawada Mizuho discusses malaria demons, and translates many tales about their activities.[75] Unschuld (1985) has pointed out the importance of demon-induced illness in Chinese medical thought from Shang on, and Harper (1982) has shown the major role this element played in a medical manual of the second century B.C.

Traditional medicine is here associated with two legendary figures. The first is Shennong, the Divine Husbandman. He is the inventor of agriculture and also the originator of Chinese pharmacology, having tasted all the plants of the world to determine the nutritive and/or medicinal properties of each. Qi Bo was a famous physician of high antiquity who answered the questions of the Yellow Thearch in China's earliest surviving medical treatise, the *Plain Questions* (*Suwen*) of the

---

74. On these causes of illness, see Unschuld 1985: 83.
75. Sawada 1984: 93–106.

Esoteric Scripture of the Yellow Thearch (*Huangdi neijing*).[76] Their theories are founded on naturalistic conceptions of channels called meridians that transported *qi* or breath through the body and its internal organs and the five elements that guide the body in all its functioning.

The Divine Lord of Zitong also acknowledges an ultimate limitation upon all healing arts: for some, their time is up, their fate (*ming*) decreed, and nothing can save them. Of course, for crass real-world physicians such a belief could explain many a botched treatment or inappropriate medication, but to the Divine Lord, and to all the aspiring and practicing physicians who read this tale through the ages, it expressed the frustration felt by one who, having assumed responsibility for the health of his patients, then discovers he is powerless in the face of the many illnesses, diseases, and injuries that afflict humankind.

14. *The Celestial Office*   天官[77]

Families who perform good works are only concerned for
  themselves,
They do not expect that their fame will be publicized.
But when one's name is heard in the royal kingdom, this is no
  cause for shame,
When one's position is among the Heavenly officials, it is due to
  karmic affinity.
The six breaths were harmonious and peaceful, clear and bright,
The pain and suffering of the myriad people was exchanged for
  safety and security.

---

76. The tenth-century encyclopedia of Daoism, *1032 Yunji qiqian* (100/12b), records that "A transcendent sire (*xianbo* 仙伯) emerged from the foot of Mount Qi and called himself Qi Bo (Sire of Qi). He was adept at explaining the medicinal qualities of plants and trees. He became the Grand Physician and the [Yellow] Thearch requested that he take charge of prescriptions and medicines."

77. DZ reads "The Celestial Palace." The two characters, *guan* 官 and *gong* 宮, are very similar in form and one is certainly a graphic error for the other. Both can be construed in this context, referring either to the god's position at court or the court itself, but I have followed DZJY because of the occurrence of the term *tianguan* in the following poem. Either way "celestial" is hyperbolic.

What power did I have that I should fulfill my duties then?
The ruler and ministers were enlightened, and this made it
   possible.

I had saved many people, and the ruler came to hear of this.
Engaged in healing by acupuncture and drugs, and having come to
the attention of the Zhou capital, I was summoned to the metropolis
by relaying couriers. Recommended by the ruler of my state, who had
repeatedly tested me, I was appointed Physician. I was in charge of the
ailments of the myriad people, and was subordinate to the Heavenly
officials. I was delighted at this. I thereupon instructed my apprentices,
ordering them to be diligent in their profession. It was the reign of
King Cheng 成. At that time the royal domain enjoyed bountiful
harvests, the six breaths were harmonious, and there were few fatal
diseases. This was due to the virtue of those above me, and I was
thereby able to fulfill the duties of my office.

COMMENTARY

In this episode the fame of the Divine Lord as a healer results in a
summons to the royal Zhou court and an official appointment as the
chief royal physician. The ruler at the time is King Cheng (r. 1042–
1005 B.C.), son of the founder and an exemplar of sagacity and
probity in his own right who was aided by the saintly Duke of Zhou
whom Confucius took as his model. Heaven responds to this worthy
leadership with auspicious signs. The Divine Lord modestly opines
that it was the influence of these men that made it possible for him to
successfully discharge his office. Thus a virtuous ruler and ministers
are shown to influence not only the efficiency of the government of
the whole, but also natural forces and the health of the populace.

15. *Recommending the Worthy*   薦賢

If someone else has a talent it is as if I had it myself,
Having attained a position I still thought of those who had not.
Great wisdom sinks deep into the heart, and is creative,
Marvelous prescriptions that cure illness can open a path to the
   gods.
I recommended the worthy eagerly, earnestly and openly.
That I should be replaced was trivial, my intent was sincere.
My memorial reached the ears of the king and received unusual
   commendation,[78]
Suddenly I was promoted to the ranks of remonstrators, a
   colleague of high officials.

Among my subordinates was a specialist in abscesses, Gongsun
Zhishu 公孫智叔. He was, by nature, compassionate and broad of
learning. He had a profound knowledge of the properties of the various drugs and could compound cinnabar, realgar, kalinite, magnetite,
and chalcanthite to make the medicine called the Five Poisons.
According to his theory, one used cinnabar to nurture the blood and
strengthen the heart, realgar to increase the flesh and fortify the
spleen, kalinite to regulate fat and aid the lungs, magnetite to circulate
the marrow and strengthen the kidneys, and chalcanthite to control
the muscles and dilate the liver. Externally this cured the five symp-
toms of boils and abscesses, internally it corresponded to the five
viscera. Containing them within an unglazed yellow vessel, he ripened
them with timed firings. When the medicine was done he would apply it to the abscess; it always worked marvelously. This method had
gained him renown in the world.[79] I considered myself inferior to
him, and yet he was my subordinate. I therefore recommended that

---

78. DZ reads "the monarch's commendation" (*shangshang* 上賞) for "unusual commendation"
(*yishang* 異賞).

79. Following DZ in reading "world" (*shi* 世) for "canons" (*dian* 典).

Zhishu replace me, and that he take over my duties in addition to his own. Soon the king himself suffered an unforeseen malady; an ulcer formed on his temple. One night it burst, and his situation turned critical. The drug mentioned above was applied to it and it healed immediately. From this time on Zhishu was appointed Physician. Because I had stated the truth with no omissions, and had recommended an appropriate person, it was judged that I should receive the highest honor, and I was promoted to the post of Controller of Remonstrances.[80]

COMMENTARY

This episode provides an example of proper conduct in office. Since the primary concern should be the well-being of the state, one must always recommend the worthy, even though it do harm to one's own career. But such commendable behavior always has its just reward, as in this case, in which the Divine Lord of Zitong received an even higher post than the one from which he had just excluded himself.

The Specialist in Abscesses is a classical post described in the *Zhouli*, where we read that the specialist treats abscesses with the Five Poisons.[81] Zheng Xuan's commentary provides a recipe very similar to that given here, except that it uses arsenolite rather than kalinite; as here the substances are compounded in a yellow earthenware vessel. Thus it seems likely that the author was familiar with this commentary.[82] The substances employed in this recipe are identified and discussed in Sivin 1968 (esp. pp. 277–94).

---

80. The Director of Remonstrances (*sijian* 司諫) is a classical office described in the *Rites of Zhou.* See *Zhouli zhushu* 14/8b–9a.

81. *Zhouli zhushu* 5/7a–b.

82. Even the difference in the formula may simply be a graphic error given the similarity of the characters for kalinite (*fan* 礬) and arsenolite (*yu* 礜).

16. *Correcting Errors* 格非[83]

A Great Physician cures the country, his contribution[84] is not
    slight,
But only when one pledges his loyalty in obscurity is the
    administration successful.
Traces of the act are forgotten, all think[85] the problem solved
    itself.
If the pivotal point is not hidden, disaster will arise from it.
If you permit pointed language to expose the ruler's failings,
What harm is there in erasing the draft and hiding your
    forthrightness?
If only the sainted dynasty would have no faults to point out,
I would not regret losing prestige and position, this is my true
    feeling.

The king thus proclaimed, "Praise to thee, Shanxun. You reveal
your true feelings and hide nothing. I am of the opinion that a worthy
physician saves people, but a great physician saves the state. Now I
place you on the line of communication (with me) to make manifest
your worthiness. Save me from my faults as if you were saving someone from illness. For good medicine is bitter to the mouth but re-
lieves the malady; loyal words are unpleasant to the ears but beneficial
to one's conduct. In the future reverently maintain your responsibilities." I declined three times, then accepted this appointment. I was
member of a group of seven who daily were close to the pure brilliance (of the king). Although the ruler and his ministers were enlightened and committed no great faults, my love for my lord and

---

83. This expression goes back to the *Shujing*, where we read, "Rectifying his excesses and untangling his mistakes, correct his erring thoughts." see *Shangshu Zhengyi* 19/14b. Cf. also *Mengzi* 29/4A/21: "A great man is one who can correct the errors in his ruler's thoughts."

84. Following DZ in reading *li* 利 ("contribution") for *li* 理 ("principle").

85. Following DZ in reading *yi* 疑 ("suspect") for the homophonous *yi* 宜 ("should").

concern for my country never allowed me a moment's peace of mind, whether walking or resting. When King Cheng was young he entrusted the administration to the Duke of Zhou, and it was a long time before he took personal control of the administration. There were some complaints of partiality. I feared that the king's attendants would seize upon this. Each time I would admonish him that one must serve his lord to the death, and that disaster and fortune are decided by minor affairs. But I often burnt my remonstrances, and no one saw them. Thus when the Duke campaigned in the east there were rifts caused by rumors in four states and the unhappiness of the Duke of Shao, but in the end the state survived intact, and I may have contributed slightly to that.

COMMENTARY

The Divine Lord, as Zhang Shanxun, now assumes the position won by his loyalty and self-sacrifice in recommending his subordinate for his own job. It is now his duty to remonstrate with the ruler and point out the mistakes in his policy. This perilous practice became a mainstay of the Confucian ethic during imperial times, and one of the most important limitations upon the powers of the emperor. It was the duty of every loyal minister to protest the improper decisions of the government, at whatever cost to himself. Although he might give up his life in doing so, he would hope that history would justify him, and praise him for putting the interests of the state before his own. Here the Divine Lord of Zitong is in a sense proposing a still higher goal. Although one must remonstrate, it need not be done openly, lest one damage the prestige of the ruler for the sake of one's own reputation. The Duke of Zhou's regency aroused dissent, as his siblings, who did not share equally in the new government, allied with remnants of the Shang state in rebellion (see the commentary to the next chapter). The god modestly claims a small part in putting down this rebellion.

17. *Returning Home in Glory* 榮歸

For ten years I abandoned my home for a high-paying post.
One day I went back to my village, returning in glory.
My son and children in pigtails[86] were surprised at my cap and
  robe,
In the pathways of the fields and orchards, startled by tales of
  mounds and ruins.
Like a roving transcendent awaking from a dream, I realized I
  had toiled and worried in vain.
Passing through this world aloofly, I sometimes hide, sometimes
  display my talents.
I relearned the pleasure of a spring sleep beneath the northern
  window;[87]
Let the cocks crow at four in the morning![88]

I had lived in the Zhou capital for ten years, and had been away
from the mulberry and catalpa trees of my native place a long time.
Like a bird with tired wings, I longed to go home. When [my parents
were alive and] I constantly worried about their health, I lived in the
backwoods. Only after I had lost my revered father did I receive a
glorious emolument. Though I ate rice and clothed myself in damask,

---

86. Chinese children traditionally wear their hair tied up into two knots on the left and right sides
of the head, toward the back.

87. Tao Qian's biography tells us that he once said, "In the idleness of the summer months I lie on
a high bed below the northern window, and as the cool breezes sigh, I think I am the august Fu Xi
伏犧 of antiquity." See *Jinshu* 94/2462–63.

88. The balmy spring nights lull one into a sleep so sound that dawn does not disturb it, as in the
famous poem "Spring daybreak" 春曉 by Meng Haoran 孟浩然 (689–740):

  In springtime slumber I did not notice the daybreak,
  Everywhere I hear the singing birds,
  During the night there was the sound of wind and rain,
  I do not know how many flowers have fallen.

See *Wenyuan yinghua* 157/5b.

what joy was there in it? One day I saw the Duke of Zhou's series of poems, "The Owl," and found them sadly moving. Then arose in me the desire to return home. I repeatedly submitted memorials asking to be dismissed due to my old age and finally this was granted. The high officials of state set forth a farewell banquet outside the Eastern Gate. When I got home, the people of my village had come out to wait for me. At the outskirts of the village I dismounted and walked. All the county was proud of me.

COMMENTARY

The high point of an official's career in imperial China was always retirement. As an official he was nearly always poorly paid, had to contribute to local charities and bestow "gifts" in a variety of situations, and was in constant danger of indictment, dismissal, and even imprisonment on a wide range of counts. Because of the rule of avoidance he was forever in a foreign land where he knew no one, had no base of support, and often could not understand the local dialect. But once he had retired, he was able to assume a secure place among the upper ranks of the local gentry. Moreover, the contacts made during his career could now serve him well as he acted as a representative of his clan and community in securing government services and support.

In this chapter the Divine Lord of Zitong does not openly point out these many advantages. Instead, he focuses on the emotional gratification of returning home after a long absence. He dreams of sleeping the long sleep of balmy spring nights with no duties that would force him to awake at the crack of dawn. He compares himself to a roving transcendent, who sojourns temporarily in this world, but will eventually awaken to his true celestial heritage.[89] In his retirement he adopts the exalted viewpoint of a Daoist recluse, which poets like Tao Qian have expressed so well. He now sees that his official concerns were superficial and ultimately unimportant when compared with the fundamental human joys of family life in his native place.

---

89. There was a genre of "Roving Transcendent" poems popular during the Six Dynasties and Tang periods. The early examples, most attributed to Guo Pu 郭璞, can be found in *Wenxuan* 21/22a ff. Edward Schafer has studied several Tang examples of the genre. See Schafer 1981–3. Schafer's interpretation of the term as verb-locative complement, "saunters in sylphdom," though attested in Tang usage, is not the original sense, nor is it appropriate in the present context.

The Divine Lord of Zitong mentions only his homesickness as his reason for retirement, but his real reason is concealed in his reference to the poem "Chixiao" 鴟鴞, "The Owl." The Shang practice had been for younger brother to succeed elder brother, rather than son succeed father. After King Wu's death several of his brothers, suspecting that the Duke of Zhou intended to claim the throne in place of the young King Cheng, rose in rebellion, and King Cheng believed their rumors. The "Jinteng" chapter of the *Shujing* tells us that after the Duke of Zhou's campaign in the east to suppress these rebels, he wrote the poem "The Owl" to enlighten King Cheng as to his true intentions.[90] The Tang subcommentary of Kong Yingda 孔穎達 (574–648) to the poem itself is more explicit.[91] Kong explains that when these rumors arose the Duke of Zhou moved to the eastern capital, and members of his clique also fled. The following year these associates of the Duke of Zhou were captured by King Cheng and accused of treason. It was to save these innocent men that the Duke of Zhou wrote the poem in question. Now in the previous chapter the Divine Lord has told us that he supported the Duke of Zhou when these rumors arose, and here it would seem he implies that he retired because of the danger to his person as a member of the Duke's party. Both the indirect mode of expression used here and familiarity with the classical commentarial tradition that it bespeaks indicate that the author of this section had a solid classical education.

The esteem in which his fellow officials hold the Divine Lord is shown by the farewell banquet attended by all the great officers. When he reaches his village they have heard he is coming, and all have come out to welcome him in his official's carriage. To show that he is still one of them, he gets out of his carriage and walks into the village with them. There his official dress and his tales of the ancient ruins in the traditional Chinese heartland astound his still un-Sinified peasant relatives.

---

90. *Shangshu zhengyi* 13/11a.
91. *Maoshi zhengyi* 8.2/1a–b.

18.   *Consideration for the Clan*   敦族

Members of a clan all come from the same root,
It is truly hard to judge their importance from their poverty or
    wealth.
Should I happen to receive an income, it is not worthy of
    hoarding,
At this point whether relatives or friends, it is a matter of
    sentiment.
For the newborn and the dead one arranges marriages and
    funerals.
Even outstanding youths still need someone to sponsor them.
When other clans heard of my actions they happily emulated
    them.
The Three Wus gradually came to be famous for charitable
    estates.

There were several lineages in the Zhang clan, and most were poor.
After I returned home I sought out and visited all of them. Those
who had been children when I left were all grown, and those who
had been mature had all become old. It was amazing to see the
changes that life brings. Those who had been so poor they could not
support themselves were just as before. I therefore established a
charity estate and put Yuanshi in charge of it. I aided those who were
impoverished, treated those who were ill, arranged marriages for
children of marriageable age, and provided education for promising
boys. When other lineages heard of this they all emulated me. Charitable estates proliferated and customs were improved.

COMMENTARY

In this chapter the Divine Lord of Zitong provides a model for the
proper conduct toward other members of one's clan. He advocates a

clan-centered charity that involves the establishment of charity estates (*yizhuang* 義莊). These are parcels of land the proceeds from which are distributed to needy members of the clan. Fan Zhongyan 范仲淹 (989–1052) established such an estate in his native village for other members of his lineage.[92] Such institutions probably have their origin in the charitable houses (*yishe* 義舍) established by the early Celestial Master movement, at which food was provided for travelers according to their needs.[93] Fan was a man of Wu county, one of the three Wus mentioned in the poem, so this practice may have begun in that part of China, though at a much later date than the Divine Lord suggests.

19. *Returning to Nirvana* 歸寂

I heard tales of the great sage of the western regions
Who taught sorrow, emptiness and extinction, and I believed them.
Singing as I walked, I became convinced that [ill-gotten worldly success] was like a floating cloud.
Sitting in meditation I realized that I labored in vain this dream illusion body.
Obtaining the secret, I effortlessly crossed to the other shore,
And forgot words in order to nurture my spirit.
From this time I awoke to the principle of returning to the root,
And let myself expand and contract throughout the four quarters.

When I was in court I had heard reports from beyond the borders about a land in the west where a great sage named the Ancient August

---

92. *Songshi* 314/10276. Fan's rules for the administration of his lineage's charitable estate have been translated by Ebrey (1981: 98–99) and the Fan estate has been the subject of two studies by Twitchett (1959 and 1960).
93. *Sanguozhi* 8/263.

Master (Guhuang xiansheng 古皇先生) lived. He engendered spontaneous transformation in one without speaking, caused understanding without action. His primary concern was compassion and he
made use of expedient means. He constantly practiced religious austerities and took joy in extinction. He viewed birth and death as
morning and night and equated grace and enmity with dreaming and
wakefulness. He knew neither worry nor anger. He must have
realized that this floating life is fleeting and sought a cessation of rebirth. I admired him. When I had resigned my illustrious position,
on the road home I met a recluse who was singing as he walked:

> The brilliance of the morning sun
> Strikes stone and gives birth to clouds.
> At first all is hazy,
> Then they scatter;
> They leave on the trail of the winds,
> Billowing with no limits.
> In a moment they transform and return to extinction,
> We know not where in the murky distance they survive.
> Now for a rich salary an official
> Races, forgetting the toil.
> Suddenly sunset presses upon him,
> And at the Ultimate Limit he recoils.
> He is about to set foot on the Shadowy Paths,
> And become another of the myriad species.

When I first heard him, I stopped my carriage and listened.
Shortly thereafter I was leaning against the railing and bowing. When
he finished I got down from my carriage and, crying, thanked him,
saying, "I have just heard[94] your wonderful truths, and they accord
perfectly with my innermost thoughts. I ask that you bestow upon
me your axioms in order to save these lasts few gasps of my life." I
then bowed one hundred times in the middle of the road and im-

---

94. Following the 1645 ed. and DZ in reading *ling* 聆, "to hear," for *ling* 領, "to receive."

plored him ardently. The singer looked up at Heaven and sighed, then pointing to me with the heart mudra, he conferred upon me the true mantra, saying, "This is the way of returning to extinction of the great sage of the West, the Ancient August Master. If you can memorize and recite it, then you can transcend life and death, die without perishing, confirm the fruit of limitless longevity, and finally on the other shore achieve the complete, true enlightenment of the Middle Way. If you do not carry on this far, then at least you will be able to choose the place of your existence and become a divine transcendent." I accepted his teaching. My ties to this dusty world came to an end, and my many troubles became as ashes. At the time of the midautumn meeting on a *dingchou* 丁丑 day[95] I assembled friends and relatives and, leaving them a poem, departed this life. The poem went:

> The autumn wind soughs,
> The autumn moon is white.
> I learned it from a Perfected:
> This body is but a guest.

COMMENTARY

In this episode the Divine Lord of Zitong first hears of the Ancient August Master, a figure clearly based on the Buddha. The terminology is a mélange of Buddhism and Daoism, recalling the earliest Chinese accounts of the Buddha, and bears a marked similarity to the *huahu,* or "converting the barbarians," literature, in which Daoists tried to prove that Daoism was supreme and the Buddha only a limited incarnation of Laozi.[96]

The name Ancient August Master (Guhuang xiansheng) is otherwise unknown; it resembles one designation of the historical Buddha, "the ancient Buddha" (*gufo* 古佛), but the deified Laozi is also referred to as "the ancient master" (*gu xiansheng* 古先生).[97] The doctrine of extinction is, of course, that of nirvana, the cessation of rebirth, and

---

95. Following the DZJY reading; the 1645 ed. and DZ both read *hao* 灝 for *chou* 丑.
96. On this topic, see Zürcher 1959: 288–320.
97. See *666 Xisheng jing* 1/1b, where we are told that this was Laozi's sobriquet (*hao*) when his head entered the "flowing sands" of the Central Asian deserts.

the Buddha stressed that life was essentially sorrowful (*ku* 苦, Sanskrit *duhkha*) and empty of true reality (*kong* 空, S. *sūnya*). He also advocated compassion (*cibei* 慈悲, S. *karunā*), and the use of expedient means (*fangbian* 方便, S. *upāya*) in propagating the doctrine.

Other elements of this description are Daoist in origin. Thus when the Divine Lord "forgets words," this is almost certainly a reference to the Daoist concept of "wordless teaching," and the use of *gu* 穀, "grain," in the sense of "nurture" is founded on the Heshanggong commentary to a line in *Laozi*, which would accordingly be translated, "Nourish one's spirit and one will not die."[98] The principle of returning to the root is stated in *Laozi* 16: "For there is a profusion of things, and each returns to its root." Spontaneous transformation and nonaction are well-known Daoist concepts, as in *Laozi* 20, where we read, "I perform no actions and they spontaneously transform." The equation of life and death with morning and night recalls the famous allegory in *Zhuangzi* of the man who dreams he is a butterfly, then wakes to wonder if he is not really a butterfly dreaming he is a man.[99]

The references to death and extinction display a similar mixture of Buddhist and Daoist doctrine. In his song the recluse refers to death as the Ultimate Limit, a Daoist conception of death as demarcating two distinct worlds, yet he goes on to mention the Shadowy Paths, the three lower paths of possible transmigration in Buddhist eschatology, being incarnation in purgatory, as a hungry ghost, or as an animal. The ultimate goal, as presented by the recluse, is "complete, true enlightenment," the sambodhi of a Buddha, and there are several other references to nirvana; to attain this, however, one must "die without perishing," a phrase taken from *Laozi* 33: "To die but not perish is longevity."[100] In *Laozi* the passage seems to mean that one identifies with the eternal Tao rather than one's individual identity. Moreover, the recluse offers a lesser goal if one cannot attain complete extinction. In such a case one will become a divine transcendent, or Daoist immortal. And the Divine Lord of Zitong later describes the recluse as a "Perfected" or Daoist saint.

All of this "confusion" is not the result of conscious syncretism, but rather reveals the popular conception of the divine world during the

---

98. *Laozi* 6.
99. *Zhuangzi* 7/2/94–6. *Zhuangzi* 40/15/12 says that to a saint death is like rest.
100. See Duyvendak 1953: 79.

Song. Buddhism had entered China a thousand years earlier, and its gods and terminology were firmly planted in the Chinese consciousness. Religious professionals, especially Buddhists, were careful to distinguish between Daoist and Buddhist elements, branding anything from the competing school myth and heresy. But the majority of the Chinese people patronized both monks and Daoist priests, and prayed at both their temples. Their conception of divine forces and the afterlife was perforce shaped by both the great religions. When Buddhism entered China it had done so "piggybacked" on Daoism, using similar but not completely identical Daoist terms to translate its own foreign technical vocabulary. As the centuries passed the doctrine was continuously refined and inexact equivalences were rejected for newly coined Chinese terms. It is usually considered that the last of these inexact equivalents were purged in the seventh-century translations of Xuanzang 玄奘.[101] It is interesting that this tale, which reflects lay conceptions of Buddhism, has retained many of these early, archaic identifications. Buddhist influence on Daoism was also considerable, and here we can see how Daoism has assimilated and accommodated itself to many Buddhist ideas.[102]

20. *Mount Monarch*   君山

The area of Mount Monarch is most pure and secluded,
Circling about on a crane, I pause briefly to take it in.
The lighting of the lake scene changes from day to night,[103]
The forest goes from dense to sparse according to the seasons.
With no body, no need to worry about a thousand year elixir,

---

101. On these early translations, see Link 1957 and for the early development of Chinese Buddhism in general, Zürcher 1959.

102. Buddhist influences on early religious Taoism have been studied by Zürcher, who concludes that the influence was substantial but superficial, and did not extend to fundamental conceptions. See Zürcher 1980.

103. Following the 1645 ed. and DZ in reading *hun* 昏 ("dark") for *fen* 分 ("delineated"). Both readings are possible but *hunming* provides a better parallel to the following *zhouye*, "day to night."

Possessing the Dao, who would lust after a hundred-li-square
    marquisate?
Billowing clouds as far as the eye can see are at my disposal.
Hearing to my heart's content a fisherman's song I linger on to
    watch.

When I had passed over [into the other world], I was about to
make my way to the West. I happened to find myself atop Mount
Monarch in Grotto-courtyard Lake 洞庭湖. I loved the magnificent
scenery, and so stayed there a while. I had no ruler or superior above
me observing and directing me, and no worries about familial responsibilities. Transcending the profane material world, I came and went
alone. The lights on the water and the colors of the mountains were
delightful all year round. Humming with the wind and whistling at
the moon, what limit was there to this joy? When I thought back to
previous events they seemed no more than a dream. I would go for
astral roves with excellent companions, returning the same day. I
heard nothing of the toiling life of the dusty world, and saw only the
true pleasure of the grotto-heaven. Much later two blue lads appeared
from Heaven and reverently announced the Thearch's proclamation
appointing me Sovereign of Mount Monarch and Director of the
Waters of Grotto-courtyard Lake.

COMMENTARY

Having rid himself of his mortal body, the Divine Lord prepares to
make the pilgrimage to the West in search of the Ancient August One.
But in the course of his astral flight he passes over the island of Mount
Monarch in the middle of Lake Dongting. As the name Dongting
("grotto courtyard") implies, this is the site of one of the major grotto-
heavens, paradaisical, microcosmic worlds secluded under the sacred
mountains of China.[104] The otherworldly beauty and divine pleasures
of that place ensnare the Divine Lord, who is still reeling from the
temporal concerns of his last life. His enjoyment here is totally Daoist,

---

104. Du Guangting lists Mount Monarch as one of seventy-two "places of bounty" (*fudi* 福地). See
599 Dongtian fudi yuedu mingshan ji (pref. dated 901), p. 9a.

delighting in nature with no troubling thoughts of the fate of man or the necesssity of his salvation. His meritorious actions in his last lifetime have earned him this interlude, and he is further rewarded with a divine post as ruler of the grotto-heaven.

This chapter reflects a degree of ambivalence with which aspirants have viewed the Daoist heavens from a very early time. Ascension to these heavens meant a post in the divine bureaucracy and such a post meant many responsibilities as well as much glory and power. Ge Hong, writing in the fourth century, already noted that some preferred to remain at the next lower level of Terrestrial Transcendent (*dixian* 地仙) "like Pengzu or Laozi, remaining among men for several hundred years so that they do not lose out on the pleasures appropriate to men."[105] Such individuals had only limited, though by human standards greatly extended, lifespans, but were free to pursue the lifestyle of a typical "Daoist" recluse, wandering the mountains and delighting in nature with not a care in the world.

---

21. *Moved to Be Born*   感生

I held a divine office on Mount Monarch through long months
    and years,
Deep in the recesses of Grotto-courtyard, cut off from the dust
    and noise of the world.
I happened to sigh at the cries that I heard coming from
    nowhere,
She already realized his forlorn soul could not be summoned
    back.
I "seized an abode"[106] and plunged into a fetus, my karma not
    yet resolved.
Mired in unresolved emotions, her grief could not be dispelled.

---

105. *Baopuzi* 14/62/2–3.
106. Following the DZ reading of *duoshe* 奪舍 for *huanshe* 換舍, which is otherwise unknown.

The jade jar was unwilling to bottle up spring.
As the harmonious yang breaths escaped I saw the willow
    branches.

I had been in Mount Monarch a long time. One day, when the spring waters had just begun to rise, a large boat pulled up to the shore at the mouth of the lake. Someone killed a sheep and poured out a libation of wine while crying aloud; the voice of the sacrificer was mournful and piercing. Hearing this voice I was unexpectedly moved. I approached and listened. A woman in her thirties, whose body was surrounded with a golden aura,[107] made three libations and prayed, "My husband unfortunately offended the ruler and fled afar to the southern wastelands, where he died of malarial miasmas. Now ten thousand li from our village, I must bring his sojourner's coffin home.[108] The sun and moon wait for no man, and as the limit for the cessation of weeping approaches, I consider anew that I have no mate to help support the family yet his parents reside in our home. I bear a child in my womb, but there has been no auspicious indication (of its sex). If the spirits of mountains and streams find that my husband was condemned for his loyalty, then take pity on my father- and mother-in-law, who will have no one to support them in the twilight of their lives. Now I am about to give birth. Send down on their behalf your supernatural aid and permit me to bear a male child to carry on the Zhang clan. Then though I may forfeit my own life I would have no regrets." Up on the cloudy paths I could not overcome my sadness and broke into tears. Suddenly I found myself falling into the woman's womb and abruptly I lost consciousness. Long afterward I heard someone saying, "It's a boy, it's a boy!" I opened my eyes to see that I was in a bathing basin. I had been born.

COMMENTARY

After a long respite as the ruler of the idyllic grotto-heaven at Mount Monarch, the Divine Lord of Zitong is reborn into the world.

---

107. Following DZ in reading *jinguang* 金光 for *tuguang* 塗光.

108. Following the 1645 ed. and DZ in reading *yan* 言, here a particle meaning something like "then," for *nan* 難, "difficult."

He compares his residence in Mount Monarch to the microcosm within a jade *hu* 壺-bottle. This jar and the *hu* 葫 gourd on which it is modeled were thought to sometimes contain sacred paradises into which Daoist adepts could gain entry through magical means. Like the miniature gardens discussed by Stein (1942), they are microcosms of vast size in what we might term a different dimension.

The Divine Lord is moved by the sincere prayer of a young widow, whose husband had died as a consequence of his loyal remonstrance to his ruler. She has voyaged far to the site of his banishment in the barbarian South, to bring his corpse home for proper burial, and now comes to the sacred lake to seek divine aid in her quest for a male heir to carry on her husband's line and support his parents in their old age. She first sacrifices a live sheep and wine, then offers up her own life in return for the birth of a healthy son. A son is necessary both economically, to care for her dead spouse's aging parents, and ritually, to care for them and provide sacrificial sustenance after their death.

The Divine Lord is touched by her sincerity, her spirit of self-sacrifice, and the commendable character of her request. His sympathy decides his fate, and suddenly he finds himself in the body of the newborn infant. He characterizes this act as "seizing an abode" (*duoshe* 奪舍), a magical practice by which one endowed with spiritual power can choose the body of his next incarnation. The Qing author Liang Gongchen 梁恭辰 (1814–?) relates a remarkably similar tale under the title "The eminent monk seizes an abode."[109] A virtuous man named Wang had no children late in life. His dead father appeared to him in a dream and told him to go to a local monastery and pray for offspring. The next year he was blessed with a son, who married, had children, and even passed the preliminary examination. Then suddenly one day he wrote a note to his father, explaining that he was actually a monk from the monastery where Mr. Wang had prayed. He had been moved by Wang's sincerity, and having some karma yet to work off before he could enter *nirvana*, he decided to be born as Wang's son. Now he must leave to be reborn yet again, but he was leaving Wang with a grandson to carry on his line. He died the next day. Both in Liang's tale and in the story here a virtuous individual is in danger of being left without descendants when a highly spiritually evolved being decides to incarnate as his son to save him

---

109. *Beidongyuan bilu quanji, Sanbian,* vol. 3b, pp. 20a–21b.

from this fate, and in both cases the incarnating being gives as one reason his own need to work off residual karma.[110]

The Divine Lord describes his birth as the escape of his yang essence into this profane world. The time of the year is spring, when the snow is melting, the streams are filling, and the willow branches turning are green. Everywhere there is new life.

22.   *Serving Forebears*   奉先

King Li "restricted calumny," and lost the hearts of the people,
With his loyal words my late father had walked the brink of disaster.
Fleeing to Zhi the king soon knew the throne would be transferred.
He of "barbed scales" regretted not heeding advice to forestall problems while still incipient.
Unstinting was the saintly grace (of King Xuan) who employed this orphan,
A fair posthumous title further embellished the valiant soul of my father.
Climbing directly into the cirle of remonstraters, I assumed my hereditary position.
People said, "He has a son who can assume his robes."

---

110. Another aspect of the *duoshe* practice is seen in a tale recounted by Yuan Mei (1716–97). There a monk animates a long dead horse and has it walk away on its own. Yuan goes on to explain that there is a "seizing of the living" (*duosheng* 奪生), in which the *hun* soul is changed but the *po* soul remains the same, and a "seizing of the dead" (*duosi* 奪死), in which case no *po* soul remains to be assumed. After seizing a dead person, religious austerities are necessary to nourish the *po*. Yuan states that the red-clothed Lamaist monks are conversant in this technique and that it is contained in the *Lankāvatāra Sūtra* under the title "the exterior method of casting oneself into ashes" (*touhui waidao* 投灰外道). See *Xu Zibuyu* 5/1a.

My revered father's name was Wuji 無忌, and he was laid to rest in Heshuo 河朔.[111] My mother, Madame née Huang 黃, was compassionate and discerning, and applied herself assiduously to my education. Whether nursing me, putting me to sleep or singing lullabies, she would guide me with the words of the *Shijing* (*Scripture of Poetry*) and *Shujing* (*Scripture of Documents*). When neighboring children played with me, she would make figures out of clay and wrap them in bits of silk, creating famous men of old about whom she would relate ancient affairs; sometimes it would be a ruler and his officials meeting at court, other times a father admonishing his son, or a teacher instructing his students, or friends receiving and entertaining each other. In each case she would direct me so that I could become practiced in the ways of the world. When I was ten, she sent me to a school, and she named me Zhongsi 忠嗣 ("Loyal Successor"), in accordance with my late father's wishes. When I had grown and was capped, Wangfu Pingzi 王父平子 gave me the cognomen Zhong 仲. My mother solemnly performed the ritual of the three bestowals and returned my bow by the western wall. Then, crying, she said to me, "Your father once served King Li as Protector, and was in charge[112] of remonstrating against the king's evil conduct. But the king was by nature suspicious and was ashamed to hear his own shortcomings. He would invariably execute those who remonstrated. After a while those who had died because of the restriction on calumny were many. People on the roads would communicate with their eyes. They could not withstand their fate and became estranged and wrathful. Your father then memorialized the king, asking that the king reform his behavior and rescind the law against calumny so that the opinions of the lower classes could be known. The king did not follow this advice. My father was thereupon banished to Panyu (modern Canton), where he died.[113] The whole empire thought this unjust. The current king practices benevolent government and has proclaimed that the descendants of those officials of the previous reign who had

---

111. Literally "north of the Yellow River," this term refers to an area in modern Hebei.

112. Following the 1645 ed. and DZ in reading *zhang* 掌 "to be in charge of," for the graphically similar *chang* 常, "often."

113. Near the modern city of Canton. See Zang 1936: 924.4.

died unjustly would all be employed. You should go." So I made my way to the capital and climbed atop the Lungstone to make known my case. A proclamation posthumously restored my father's office and gave him the appellation Xianfa 獻法 ("Bestower of the Law"), saying, "When the loyal must announce something to the king, this is called 'to bestow' (*xian* 獻)." I was further appointed Protector, continuing my father's office. This was during the reign of King Xuan 宣.

COMMENTARY

In this episode we see the Divine Lord of Zitong, in his second incarnation, as a youth. We are presented with a model for the proper raising and instruction of a child, and a fine example of a single parent.

In his new incarnation the Divine Lord is fortunate to be blessed with a sage mother, who instructs him according to the traditional Chinese ideal. In his impressionable infancy she often uses the classical formulations of the Confucian scriptures in his presence, so that he can internalize their teachings. When he is a bit older and plays with other children she makes of each game an instructive lesson, letting him role-play the various human relationships that he will encounter in his later life. In each case she uses exemplary models from former times as her subjects. The Chinese tradition has always seen history as above all else a collection of moral prototypes of good and bad conduct, and here we are given a good example of how these anecdotes were used to indoctrinate the young in standard values and to promote socialization.

At some point the playful instruction of childhood must give way to the serious study of young manhood. At the age of ten *sui* (probably nine years old in our terms), the young Divine Lord is sent to a school outside the home, where he will begin instruction in the classics. Up until this time he had been referred to at home by his "milkname" 奶名, which we are not told, but now he is given the formal name of Zhongsi ("loyal heir"), a name containing within it the hope that he will be a worthy descendant loyal to his deceased father's ideals.

The next major stage in a young man's life is capping, usually undertaken at the age of twenty *sui*. The *Record of Rites* tells us that, "Capping is the beginning of ritual."[114] The capping ritual consisted of three stages, in each of which a different type of headgear was bestowed. The first was a cap of black silk; this was followed by a leather hat, and then a "sparrow hat," a red silk hat with no tassels.[115] It was after capping that the individual received his cognomen, *zi* 字, the honorific name by which he would be referred except in the presence of his father or ruler. In the capping ceremony it is bestowed by the "Guest," who is supposed to be a colleague of the father of the lad to be capped.[116] Wangfu Pingzi, no doubt an esteemed friend of the family, here has the honor to name the child. It is uncertain why his mother officiates at the capping ceremony. Normally, if the father was deceased this role would be filled by a senior male relative, either an uncle or classificatory elder brother.[117] Perhaps there were no such figures living or in the vicinity.

The Divine Lord's mother goes on to explain about his father's death. His father had been Baoshi 保氏, or Protector, to King Li 厲 王. The *Zhouli* describes the duties of the Protector in the following terms: "He is in charge of remonstrating against the king's evil and and rearing 'the sons of state' (sons of the nobility and high officials) in accordance with the Dao."[118] He was in charge of instructing in the six arts and six deportments. But it was the Protector's responsibility to remonstrate with the king that had gotten Zhang Wuji into trouble. King Li was a rather inept king, and did not like to hear about his own failings. To stifle dissent he instituted a law against "calumny," which he then used to persecute anyone who spoke against him. The *Book of Transformations* here follows the *Shiji* account. There the Grand Officer Rui Liangfu 芮良夫, like the Divine Lord, remonstrated with the king over his overweening desires and his proposed employment of Duke Yi of Rong 榮夷公, but the king did not heed his counsels. The account continues, in Chavannes' translation:[119]

---

114. *Liji zhengyi* 61/1b.

115. See *Liji zhengyi* 61/3a; *Yili zhushu* 2/6b–7a; Steele 1917: Vol. 1, p. 10.

116. *Yili zhushu* 1/10a.

117. *Yili zhushu* 3/5b.

118. *Zhouli zhushu* 14/6b. Cf. Hucker 1985: 369, entry 4494.

119. Chavannes 1895: Vol. 1, p. 270ff.; *Shiji* 4/141–2. In the following passsage I have underlined phrases that closely parallel those in the *Book of Transformations*, and have provided in square brackets the pinyin transcription of Chinese words which Chavannes cites in French transcription.

Le roi eut une conduite cruelle et hautaine. Les gens du royaume
le blamèrent. Le duc de Chao [Shao] reprit (le roi) en lui disant:
«Le peuple ne peut supporter son sort.» Le roi se mit en colère et
chargea un devin du pays de Wei de *découvrir ceux qui le blâme-*
raient; ceux qu'il dènonçait étaient aussitôt mis à mort; les
critiques furent rares, mais les seigneurs ne vinrent plus à la cour
rendre leur homage. La trente-quatrième année, le roi redoubla
de sévérité; les gens du royaume n'osaient plus parler; *ils se*
jetaient seulement un regard en passant leur chemin. . . . Trois ans
plus tard, des gens se liguèrent pour faire une révolte et atta-
quèrent à l'improviste le roi Li. Le roi Li sortit (du royaume) et
se réfugia a Tche [Zhi].

What King Li failed to understand, according to the traditional
conception of government, was that it is only by listening earnestly to
loyal remonstrance that one can hope to govern successfully. Instead
he lost the allegiance of the people. The Protector, like Rui Liangfu in
the historical account, saw the potential danger for the kingdom in
this growing estrangement of the king from his subjects, and made a
formal announcement (*gao*) to the king, pointing out his errors and
asking that the ban on criticism be lifted. He was rewarded for his
loyalty with an ultimately fatal banishment to the southern extremity
of the empire. The poem makes reference to King Li's unhappy end.
An uprising of the people in 842 B.C. forced him to flee to Zhi (in
modern Shansi), where he died in exile some fourteen years later. We
are told that during this time he came to regret not listening to Zhang
Wuji's advice.

After an interregnum presided over by Earl He of Gong, King Li's
son, King Xuan came to the throne. He had learned from his father's
tragic history, and immediately sought to regain the support of the
hereditary retainers and the people.[120] One of his first acts is to summon the sons of those who had died unjustly during his father's reign,
and Zhang Wuji's son is told to go and claim his rightful position. He
proceeds to the capital and stands atop the Lungstone to make his
plaint. The *Zhouli* tells us that the Lungstone was a large red rock
upon which the common people could stand for three days and have
their complaints heard. The knights would hear what they had to say

---

120. The *Shiji* does not portray King Xuan in such a favorable light. See *Shiji* 4/144–45;
Chavannes 1895: Vol. 1, pp. 276–78.

and relay it to the ruler. The name refers to the red color, matching that of the lungs: the stone was red to insure that the plaintiff spoke with a "red" (i.e., sincere) heart.[121] The king appoints the Divine Lord to his father's previous post of Protector and further ennobles his father with a posthumous title.

---

23. *The Filial Friend* 孝友

My elder brother unfortunately left no descendants.
We came from the same breath, were of the same stock.
My mother's anguish touched my heart,
It was fitting that I made Maoyang his successor.
Once I had assuaged the worries of my mother, the
　　compassionate parent,
In the dark earth the departed came to know of this.
When I completed the rites of mourning for my grandfather
　　and grandmother,
My reputation as a filial friend was renowned in my time.

My elder brother, Yunsi 允思, unfortunately had died as a child, and I never got to see him. When I reached maturity, I had two sons, the elder named Ranming 然名, and the second named Maoyang 楙陽. Maoyang was a precocious child, and was the favorite of his great-grandfather. On the eve of the summer solstice we offered sacrifices in our ancestral temple. My mother cried forlornly, saying that my departed elder brother's line was cut off. I requested that Maoyang be accepted as his heir to continue the line, so that my mother's heart would be assuaged. My paternal grandmother, Madame née Zhao 趙 passed away at eighty. My paternal grandfather stopped eating out of grief, and soon he also went to his final rest. As a grandson I took the

---

121. *Zhouli zhushu* 34/16b–17a.

role of a son, donning unhemmed sackcloth mourning garments for three years, exhausting the ritual requirements for grief and self-deprivation. Those both within and without who heard of me praised me as "filial and amicable," referring to me by my *zi* 字 rather than my name.

COMMENTARY

In this episode the Divine Lord gives another demonstration of his filial behavior and his supreme regard for his family. He is confronted with a problem peculiar to the Chinese religious world. His elder brother died before siring a child, and hence was in that terrifying state of "lacking posterity" (*wuhou* 無後) that was always considered one of the worst of fates.[122] The fear of this state is based on the belief that only a direct male descendant can effectively offer sustenance to one's disembodied spirit through sacrifice, hence a person without descendants is condemned to eternal wandering in search of nourishment among the cohort of homeless spirits, called *li* 厲, who had died violently, had not received proper burial, whose body had been dismembered, or had not been blessed with male children. One possible solution to this dilemma was for the dead male to adopt the son of another, usually one of his relatives. Yuan Cai 袁采 (fl. 1140–95) considered it only natural that a brother with several male heirs would give one to a childless sibling.[123] This practice has survived to the present day. Jordan describes the case of a man named Guo Tongming, who had died without children at the age of thirty. One of his elder brothers "gave him one of his own sons, and they will have the duty of making sacrifices to their adopted father for the rest of their lives, although the adoption will have no effect on their legal status as sons of their biological father, nor on their residence or emotional attachments."[124] We cannot be certain how such arrangements worked at the time of the composition of the *Book of Transformations*, but it does seem that the Divine Lord, by permitting the adoption of his second son, Maoyang, did not relinquish his customary duties or authority

---

122. This is the fate that Confucius speculated had befallen the nefarious, unknown individual who had initiated the practice of burying human statues with the deceased, a practice which he believed (incorrectly) at the origin of human sacrifice in China. See *Mengzi* 2/1A/4.

123. Ebrey 1984: 106, 206.

124. Jordan 1972: 151.

with regard to the boy, because in the twenty-seventh chapter we find him arranging a marriage for Maoyang, and still speaking of him as his son. In modern China the search for an heir is most commonly instigated by a manifestation of the dead brother's ghost. This chapter, together with the earlier chapter (8), in which the Divine Lord marries a dead girl, shed interesting light on the early history of current practices for the pacification of souls of individuals who die childless.

The Divine Lord of Zitong resolves a second family crisis when his paternal grandfather and grandmother die. It would normally be the responsibility of his late father to observe mourning for them. Instead, the Divine Lord steps into his shoes, dons the unhemmed hemp garments, and for three years makes the proper display of his grief and the emaciation to which it is supposed to lead.[125] Through this he acquires a reputation, and comes to be referred to as "filial and amicable." People combine this sobriquet with his *zi* 字 or cognomen rather than his proper name or *ming* 名, showing even greater respect, and he is thus the "filial and amicable Zhang Zhong" (Zhang Zhong xiaoyou 張仲孝友), a figure mentioned as one of the worthy companions of Yin Jifu in the *Shijing* poem "Sixth Month."[126]

---

24. *The Mian River*   沔水

Oh, the soaring spirit of Jifu,

His achievements, prestige, talent, and intelligence outshone an
   enlightened court.

Weaving together martial valor and civil virtue, his heart was
   fair indeed.

Campaigning to the west, attacking the north, in distant regions.

---

125. For a description of these mourning garments see de Groot 1895: Vol. 2, pp. 491–99; Steele 1917: Vol. 2, pp. 9–13. As de Groot (pp. 498 and 500) explains, the "three years" actually entailed a period of twenty-five to twenty-seven months.

126. *Maoshi zhengyi* 10.2/8a. Zheng Xuan states that the man's surname was Zhang, his cognomen Zhong, and that he was a friend of Yin Jifu.

Unfounded rumors in the capital of Hao gave rise to calumny.

In the tones of "The Mian River" I lodged my reprimand.

The ruler and his minister were on good terms and magnificent
   deeds achieved,

Through my loyal remonstrance the evil words were laid to rest.

The king had a wise official, Yin Jifu 尹吉甫. Endowed with civil
and military prowess, he was admired by all the officials. In the course
of its history the state had fallen into evil and decadence, and the
barbarians of the four directions invaded one after another.[127] When
King Xuan ascended the throne, he campaigned to the north and attacked to the west in order to reestablish a region of civilization. Yin
Jifu was placed in sole charge of the armies. Only I remained with the
king. Jifu was full of grand plans but ignored details. Many of the officials attending the king were displeased and waves of slander arose.
The king could not avoid harboring some doubts. When Yin Jifu was
in Hao 鎬 there were unfounded rumors reported to the king. I
made all sorts of explanations, but still his doubts were not resolved. I
wrote the poem "The Mian River," and this the king heeded. When
Yin Jifu returned, his glorious deeds had been achieved, and ruler and
minister were reconciled. If the achievements of Shaokang 少康 and
Gaozong 高宗 in revitalizing the empire are examined, then those of
King Xuan will be found superior to them.

COMMENTARY

The Divine Lord of Zitong aids in the reestablishment of Zhou
power after the debacle of King Li's rule and the Gonghe interregnum. The state depends upon valorous military leaders to stave off
invasion and put down rebellion, but a general in the field is far from
the center of power and also subject to vagrant rumors and the calum-
nies of members of opposing factions, which could undercut the king's
support. Here the Divine Lord presents a model of responsible action
for an official at court in such a situation. Having recognized the

---

127. This phrase is taken from the Mao preface to the poem "Sixth Month" ("Liuyue"). See *Maoshi
zhengyi* 10.2/1b.

worthiness of the head of the military expedition, Yin Jifu, he strives to support him and protect him from factional strife so that he can accomplish his mission. When words are insufficient, he resorts to a tried method of political persuasion, lodging his thoughts in a poem, which by oblique and historical references reveals the true nature of the situation and the proper course of action.

Yin Jifu is known from the *Shijing* and the *Zhushu jinian* (*Bamboo Annals*). The *Zhushu jinian* does not seem to have been widely available during the Song,[128] hence the primary source concerning Yin for the author of the *Book of Transformations* was the *Shijing* and its commentaries. The poem "Liuyue" ("Sixth Month") praises the expedition of Yin Jifu against the Xianyun in the north.[129] When he returned in glory, this poem informs us, he was feted by the king, and among the company was his friend Zhang Zhong, here revealed to be the Divine Lord.

The Divine Lord defends him through the composition and presentation of the poem "The Mian River." This poem is traditionally interpreted as a criticism of King Xuan.[130] The final stanza of this poem (in Arthur Waley's translation) makes clear the author's message:[131]

Swift that flying kite
Makes for that middle mound.
The false words of the people
Why does no one stop them?
My friends be on your guard;
Slanderous words are on the rise.

The Divine Lord's support of Yin Jifu is justified by Yin's accomplishments. The resulting dynastic revival is compared to those of the preceding Xia and Shang dynasties, associated with Kings Shaokang and Gaozong, better known to history as King Wuding 武丁.[132]

---

128. It does not appear in any of the bibliographies assembled in *Songshi yiwenzhi guangbian.*

129. *Maoshi zhengyi* 10.2/1a–8a. See also d'Hormon 1985: 147–8, n. 2, and Prusek 1971: 119–25 for a discussion of the course of this expedition. They arrive at very different conclusions, as can be seen in the location of the Hao mentioned there and in our text. D'Hormon would put it in Gansu, while Prusek identifies it as the capital city of the Zhou in the Wei River valley. Our text would seem to agree with Prusek's interpretation, since it refers to "the capital Hao."

130. *Maoshi zhengyi* 11.1/6a–11a.

131. Waley 1937: 313.

132. See *Shiji* 2/86–87 and 3/102–3 for accounts of these two kings.

25. *The White Colt*   白駒

The royal mind fretted and strove at the beginning of the reign.
When the entire court was replete in virtue he stifled worthy
    plans.
Exceptional talents fled into hiding, alas for the lost elders.
In the form of a poem I sang the praises of a white colt.
From that time on bundles of silk were sent to the minor states,
The worthies soon returned, assembling in the eastern capital.
The monarch summoned the secluded, promoting the kingly
    transformation,
Truly this was due to my loyal words exhorting him to employ
    scholars.

When the great enterprise had been accomplished, the king widely
distributed exceptional favors, and promoted me to a great officer of
state. At the time the four quarters were free from threats, and the
king became a bit lax. One day the Master of Arms Wei Zhongjiang
韋仲將 remonstrated; as soon as the document was submitted the
royal anger was aroused and Wei was arrested. Thereupon the virtuous officials and experienced men began to leave. I was worried at
this and composed the poem, "The White Colt," to reprimand the
king. I exhorted him to pay attention to talented and worthy officials
and accept remonstrance gracefully, so that those in office would
have no thought of leaving, those who had already left might return,
and that recluses might be willing to serve. The poem was submitted
to the king, and he was moved by it. Thereupon he issued a proclamation in court, blaming himself and repenting for his faults. He
re-appointed Wei to his former position and there was not a day that
bundles of silk, bows and flags were not dispatched (to recruit men
for office). Before long the king's reputation was restored and the
spirit of the officials was re-established. The world again knew the
transforming influence of the times of King Cheng 成王 and King
Kang 康王.

COMMENTARY

King Xuan regained the throne through his virtue, sincerity, and openness to criticism, but soon began to take umbrage at righteous criticism. In this episode the Divine Lord of Zitong again uses the indirect criticism of a poem to show him the error of his ways.

The individual who remonstrates with the king is a Wei Zhongjiang, who is otherwise unknown. He is the Master of Arms (Shishi 師氏). The *Zhouli* tells us that the duties of this office were to counsel the king and to instruct the "sons of state,"that is, the sons of the high ministers and great officials, in morality.[133] The Kong Anguo commentary to the *Shujing* says, on the other hand, that he, at the head of a company of troops, guarded the entry to the palace.[134] This seems to agree more closely with the title, but the *Zhouli*'s explanation accords well with Wei's actions in this story and in the following chapter.

The poem the Divine Lord composes and presents to the king is "The White Colt" ("Baiju").[135] According to Mao Heng 毛亨, this poem is written by a great officer, who reprimands King Xuan, and the commentary says that at the end of his reign King Xuan did not employ talented officials. Such an official leaves the court riding on a white horse (symbolizing his purity), and the implied author expresses the hope that this fine horse (and its rider) will come to stay with him.

In response to this poem the king returns Wei to his former position and embarks on a policy of energetic recruitment of talented officials. We are told that not a day went by that he did not summon someone with the traditional gifts of silk, bows, and flags. Of these the gift of silk is the most traditional, and is mentioned in the *Yili*.[136] It involves a bundle of ten lengths (*duan* 段) rolled into five bolts (*pi* 匹). The recruitment of worthy officials was considered important enough that four chapters of the *Yili* are devoted to the ritual actions surrounding this process.[137]

King Xuan's reformed attitude and the aid of his newly acquired subordinates resulted in proper government and a consequent peace

---

133. *Zhouli zhushu* 14/2a–b.
134. *Shangshu zhengyi* 11/15b.
135. *Maoshi zhengyi* 11.1/12b–14a, Waley 1937: 194.
136. *Yili zhushu* 21/1a, 2a; 22/3b.
137. *Yili zhushu* 21–24.

and stability that had not been known since the times of Kings Cheng and Kang.[138] The *Shiji* tells us that during their reigns "the entire empire was at peace, and for over forty years penal punishments were not employed."[139]

26. *Recommending an Enemy for Promotion* 舉讎

My late father went down to the Yellow Springs choking on his hatred.

According to the Rituals an enemy must not walk the same earth.

I had no way of reaching Fengcheng, who was already dead,

But his descendant Wenshu was meritorious.

I focused only on today, and I could recommend only the talented,

How could I think back to that year when my father was slandered in his innocence?

The ruler also understood my feelings and the circumstances,

What does it matter if it is bruited about within and without the court?

My late father's death was caused by the calumny of Nan Fengcheng 南風成. All the court knew about this. I had not forgotten this eternal enmity. Fengcheng was long dead. He had a son named Wen-

---

138. According to Shaughnessy's chronology, these kings reigned 1049/45–1043 and 1005/3–978 (the second date for the beginning of the reign indicates the end of the mourning period). See Shaughnessy 1991: 241–45.

139. *Shiji* 4/134.

shu 溫叔 who was talented and meritorious. As a "son of state"[140] he was once under the tutelage of Master of Arms Wei. Wei said to me, "The son of Fengcheng has an unflagging love of learning. He is exemplary in both speech and conduct. There is no one like him among the aristocratic children of today. The Way of Heaven is difficult to know. I never thought Fengcheng, with his conduct like a bluebottle, would have a son like this. It is like Gu 瞽 and Gun 鯀 giving birth to Shun 舜 and Yu 禹. Someday he will certainly be an important officer." Although I had this rift with him which should not permit me to share the same earth, when I heard of his virtuous conduct, I was delighted. When I was promoted to Great Minister the post of Protector was vacant, and a royal command gave me permission to nominate someone I knew as my replacement. I recommended Wenshu, and the king permitted this. In the end he performed well in the post.

COMMENTARY

Chinese law was always limited in application, and many offenses were settled within the local community, often by clan vendetta.[141] As we see in this episode, even the classical canons sanctioned this approach. But the Divine Lord of Zitong sees a higher duty, that to the state; not only does he forego vengeance upon the family of the man who caused his father's death through slander, but he nominates the man's son for his own vacated position.

Nan Fengcheng had calumnated the Divine Lord's father, Zhang Wuji. This resulted in his banishment and eventual death, as we read in chapter 22. The Master of Arms, Wei Zhongjiang, compares his conduct to that of a bluebottle. This is a reference to the poem "Bluebottle" ("Qingying" 青蠅) in the *Shijing*. This poem is variously attributed to the reigns of Kings Li and You.[142] The import is evident in the first stanza:[143]

Buzz, buzz the bluebottles
That have settled on the hedge.

---

140. The son of a minister or great officer.
141. On the vendetta in China, see Dalby 1981.
142. *Maoshi zhengyi* 14.3/1a–b; Legge 1893: 394–95.
143. Waley 1937: 322.

Oh, my blessed lord,
Do not believe slanders that are said.

The sanction for vengeance occurs in the "Quli" chapter of the *Liji*, where it is stated that, "With the enemy of one's father one should not share the same earth" (literally, "be under the same heaven," *bu gong dai tian* 不共戴天).[144] The commentary explains that one who would allow the killer of one's father to live is unfilial, and that the son should not rest until the killer is dead.

Since Nan Fengcheng was already dead, this enmity could only be expressed toward his son, Nan Wenshu. But Wenshu was an exemplary young man, with a great love of learning. Wei Zhongjiang compares him to the legendary emperors Shun and Yu, who were both the offspring of rather unsavory characters. Shun's father, Gu, remarried after the death of Shun's mother and repeatedly conspired with this second wife and Xiang, his son by her, to kill Shun. Shun evaded all these dastardly plans yet continued to serve his father and step-mother filially.[145] Yu's father, Gun, is characterized as "disobeying orders and bringing destruction upon his colleagues." No details are recorded of his evil actions, but he was commissioned to subdue the flood waters, and after nine years was executed for his failure to do so. Yu then took up this task and accomplished it.[146]

This high praise from an esteemed colleague convinces the Divine Lord. He nominates Wenshu to fill his own post of Protector when he is promoted to Great Official, and his confidence is not misplaced, for Wenshu carries out his duties admirably.

---

144. *Liji zhengyi* 3/10b.

145. *Shiji* 1/32–34; Chavannes 1895: Vol. 1, pp. 71–76. There is disagreement as to whether the name Gu ("blind") refers to an actual physical condition (as the *Shiji* claims) or merely a moral blindness toward the distinction between good and evil, as we read in the Kong Anguo commentary to the *Shujing* (*Shangshu zhengyi* 2/24b).

146. See *Shiji* 2/50–51; Chavannes 1895: Vol. 1, p. 99; *Shangshu zhengyi* 2/20a.

27. *Taking Pity on Orphans* 恤孤

It is hard to know the future, longevity or premature death.
Zhongjiang was just fifty when suddenly his condition turned
    critical.
Now he is gone forever, I sigh for his lack of posterity,[147]
It is even sadder that his five daughters were all orphaned.
I accepted betrothal gifts and was asked their names just as if
    their father were present,
I was presented a kid and offered a goose, leading up to the
    marriage date.[148]
The day of discussing the exchange would be the same whether
    he were alive or dead,
Even his forlorn soul down in the Springs must have stopped
    frowning.

The Master of Arms Wei Zhongjiang had collaborated with me on
tasks, and we had known each other a long time. One day the royal
carriage departed early in the morning. As it emerged from the Tiger
Gate Zhongjiang wanted to set something before the king. He advanced, then retreated, and suddenly fell to the ground. The guards
helped him to his feet, but he was already gasping for breath. By the
time he reached home he was dead. There were no sons in his family,
only five daughters. The oldest had returned home after being
widowed. The second was at the age of pinning but had not been betrothed. The youngest was already fifteen. Because Wei had died
suddenly in the forbidden precincts of the palace while opposing
the king, he was awarded no posthumous office. Whom did the five
daughters have to rely on? I completed all the rituals and arranged

---

147. DZ reads "my sighs cannot reach him" (*jie wuji* 嗟無及).

148. It is possible that this line refers not to his role as a substitute for Wei in accepting these gifts,
but rather to his own presentation of these gifts when arranging the marriage of the two younger
daughters to his sons.

marriages for three of them. The two youngest were boarded with the Director of Remonstrances Gao Zhiliang 高之量 until they were grown. I then took them in as the wives of Ranming and Maoyang.

COMMENTARY

Having already saved his worthy colleague Wei Zhongjiang from royal wrath, the Divine Lord of Zitong now comes to his aid again, taking care of his daughters after his death. He thus provides an example of the duties to a friend and to orphans.

Wei was only middle-aged, having just turned fifty, and he cannot be faulted for not having made arrangements for his daughters. One, in fact, had already been married off, but unfortunately her husband died before she could bear him a child, and hence she was returned to her family of birth. Another daughter had reached the age of pinning, a rite of passage when a girl first begins to put up her hair with a hair pin, but was not betrothed. Although the Record of Rites (Liji) says that a girl is pinned at fifteen, the commentary explains that this is only a lower limit, for cases when a match has already been arranged, and that normally the age of pinning is twenty.[149] This is clearly the sense here, for Wei has three other daughters between the ages of fifteen and twenty.

Widow remarriage was a controversial topic throughout Chinese history, but especially during the Sung, when Neo-Confucian philosophers were emphasizing the role of agnatic kinship groups. Cheng Yi emphatically condemned the practice, even in the case of extreme poverty, saying, "To starve to death is a very small matter. To lose one's integrity, however, is a very serious manner."[150] The Divine Lord praises his own widowed mother in chapter 28 for upholding this virtue. But such lofty principles were often compromised in dealing with real life. Ch'ü T'ung-tsu (1972: 42–44) notes that even at the height of the filial piety craze in the Latter Han, there were many examples of prominent men marrying widows. Cheng Yi's father gave a widowed cousin in marriage and both Cheng Yi and Zhu Xi approved of this action.[151]

---

149. Liji zhengyi 28/21b.
150. Chan 1967: 177.
151. See Birge 1989: 340.

If Wei Zhongjiang had died in other circumstances, in the service of the state, the king might have granted him a posthumous office, assuring his family an income, and might even have taken it upon himself to arrange for the marriage of his daughters. But it seems that Wei died in the midst of making a remonstrance when the king passed his post at the gate to the inner palace. It was unfortunate, also, that he besmirched the sacred forbidden precincts of the palace with his death. He did not even leave behind a male descendant who could take care of his sisters. The Divine Lord was forced to step in and help his old friend.

As we might expect, the Divine Lord carried out all of the ritual requirements in Wei's place, just as if he were still alive. He was offered a goose as a betrothal gift. The goose is appropriate because it migrates with the seasons following the yang forces, just as a wife is supposed to follow her husband, who is also yang.[152] He also was given a kid, a standard gift between higher-level great officers when meeting.[153] This indicates that the matches he concluded were with young men of the same class. The two youngest daughters were barely of marriageable age. He entrusted them to another high official for safekeeping, and when they had fully matured, he betrothed and married them to his two sons, Ranming and Maoyang.

---

28. *Compassionate Instructions* 慈訓

She had maintained her resolve (not to remarry) though in the full bloom of youth,
Now at one hundred her eyes and ears were still sharp.
Her karmic affinity was deep and she was not confused by heterodox paths,
Her heart was fixed on the constant recitation of the Scripture of Inner Meditation.

---

152. *Yili zhushu* 4/1a; *Liji zhengyi* 61/4b–5a.
153. *Yili zhushu* 7/7a.

Flowers bloom and flowers fall, but the root is always there,
The moon waxes to fullness then wanes, the body is an empty
  vessel for the soul.
Approaching death she vigorously made known her
  compassionate instructions,
Then ascending to her position on the transcendent hierarchy,
  attained the realm of darkness.

My mother was widowed when young. Even reaching the exalted
age of one hundred, her sight and hearing had not deteriorated because she made a practice of frequently reciting the Scripture of Inner
Meditation. Slowly unraveling the meaning, in her later years she
came to understand. One day when I was on my way home from the
morning court I was hurrying past her courtyard when she called to
me to come sit with her. Her two grandsons waited upon her. Sigh-
ing contentedly, she said, "Our karmic paths crossed and we were
able to become mother and son. Now your hair is turning grey, and
from this you can see that I must be old. I am of the opinion that for
people in this world birth and death are uncertain; one comes for a
moment then returns, like the waxing and waning moon or the
blooming and withering of flowers. This lifetime's birth is the death
of the previous lifetime. If one never died before how could one be
born now? If one does not understand today's death, how can one
secure one's birth at a later date? If one knows that the body is an
illusion and that one must only preserve the True and Constant, that
all one can do is be resolute in one's nature and strong in the face of
fate, then this is what they call 'that which does not fail for countless
eons.' Those who possess meritorious deeds will rise up into the exalted
regions, and those with no evil karma will not lose their human
bodies. Persevere in the midst of this dream illusion; do not sow the
seeds of animosity.[154] I am about to go to my final rest. You need
not be too sad about this. But pay close attention to what I have said
as I am about to leave you." When she had finished speaking she

---

154. Following DZ in reading *mo* 莫, "do not," for *geng* 更, "further."

passed away leaning on a table. Later she was reborn and attained the Dao as a young girl. She was reborn into the Heavens where she is the Perfected of Wondrous Grace.

COMMENTARY

As she is about to die the mother of the Divine Lord of Zitong gives her final instructions to her son. Her life has itself been exemplary. Though widowed young she never remarried, and reared a child by herself.[155] Now in her old age she is rewarded by the grandchildren who surround her and wait on her.

Though she has reached the venerable age of one hundred, she has maintained her sight and hearing through the constant recitation of the Scripture of Inner Meditation. The Daoist canon contains a *Scripture of Inner Mediation of the Most High Lord Lao* (*641 Taishang Laojun neiguan jing*), which is probably to be identified with the scripture mentioned here. It focuses on meditation upon the guardian spirits that dwell within the body. This practice originates with the *Exoteric Scripture of the Yellow Court,* an ancient text that may date from the Latter Han, and was particularly well developed in the Shangqing school, as exemplified by its reworking of this text as the *Esoteric Scripture of the Yellow Court.*[156] The *Scripture of Inner Meditation of the Most High Lord Lao* would have been particularly appropriate for a female practitioner because it begins with an exposition on the spiritual development of the embryo during pregnancy.[157]

The Divine Lord's mother goes on to transmit to her son the lessons she has learned from the prolonged study of this scripture and the sum of her life experiences. Essentially, her message is that corporeal life is fleeting, but there is a greater, eternal reality. She calls this the True and Constant, originally a Buddhist description of the realm of nirvana. We find a similar thought expressed in the *Scripture of Inner Meditation of the Most High Lord Lao*:[158]

---

155. Jordan (1972:156–58) discusses the high value placed on a widow foregoing remarriage in both traditional and modern China. See Ebrey 1993:205–12 for an account of widow remarriage in the Song.

156. On the *Scripture of the Yellow Court,* see Homann 1971. The controversy over the dating of the two versions is reviewed and resolved in the "Introduction" to Schipper 1975.

157. *641 Taishang Laojun neiguan jing* 1b.

158. *641 Taishang Laojun neiguan jing* 5a.

In the Dao there is neither birth nor death, yet the physical form is born and dies. Those things about which one says that they are born and die are things that belong to the physical form, not things that belong to the Dao. The physical form is born because it obtains its Dao, and it dies because it loses its Dao. If a man can preserve his life and maintain the Dao then he will exist forever and never perish.

But the primary teaching that she has distilled from her long years of study is something never explicitly stated in the *Scripture of Inner Meditation of the Most High Lord Lao,* but a teaching that accords well with everything the Divine Lord of Zitong stands for: moral conduct is the key to salvation. Through good deeds one may be reborn on a higher plane, while the avoidance of evil actions will at least assure that one will not be reborn as a lower order of life. She specifically warns him against forming any ties of hatred that would have to be resolved in future incarnations. This is perhaps a prophetic reference to his involvement with the Lü clan and his punishment in Qiong Lake, in chapters 64 and 65 below.

Having said her piece, the mother of the Divine Lord departs this mortal realm. She is later reborn, and attains the Dao while still a pure undefiled young maiden. In the Heavens she is given the title of Perfected of Wondrous Grace (Miaohui zhenren 妙惠眞人), and becomes part of the Divine Lord's supernatural family, with whom he is finally reunited in the ultimate episode of the 1181 revelation, chapter 73.

29.　*Exhausting Loyalty*　　　盡忠

Bereft of my grief in a departure from ritual, I applied myself to
　the king's business.
Moved by my lord's grace, I longed for the old officials.
Earnestly I made sharp remonstrance, but was not heeded.
My loyal heart was evident, but in the end I spoke in vain.
The occupant of the Green Palace lacked great virtue;

In my old age I was too proud to become a sycophant.
Having fully upheld my principles, in the Nine Springs, I have
    no regrets.
Still I worry that the way of the Zhou house is slowly
    submerging.

In the midst of the sorrow of my mourning in hemmed sackcloth, the ruler issued a command that I be reft of my mourning sentiments and return to office. I declined three times, but then had no choice but to obey and attend to affairs. This was a departure from proper ritual conduct. The ruler had been on the throne a long time, and was weary of governing. One by one, the meritorious veteran officials like Yin Jifu, Duke Mu of Shao, and Nanzhong Fangshu had retired due to illness or died. I was the only old official left. When the ruler had first made Gongnie 宮涅 heir-apparent I strongly remonstrated against this, but I could not sway the king's favor, and in the end he was appointed. When the king abandoned the altars of grain and soil in death and the succeeding king came into personal control of the government, he was lascivious, cruel, and violent. I again remonstrated. Because I was relying on my old position in the former court, and because he bore a grudge over my previous memorial, the king displayed his anger. I begged to be allowed to retire and went to live at home. One day an emissary came with a gift of (poisoned) wine, which I accepted with a bow. When I had finished drinking, there was a second message, saying that I had "exhausted loyalty in service of the state." From the first I did not allow my single death to disrupt my perfect composure. But I still was worried that the way of the Zhou house was in decline and that the foundation of civil and martial virtue had been lost.

COMMENTARY

In this incarnation again the Divine Lord of Zitong is forced to taste the bitter fruits of loyalty. He was originally a member of a group of talented and virtuous officials who had helped King Xuan establish his rule. We have met Yin Jifu before (ch. 24). Nanzhong

Shufang took part in Yin's expedition to the north, then himself led an expedition against the non-Chinese people of the south that is celebrated in the *Shijing* poem "Caiji" ("Picking White Millet").[159] Duke Mu of Shao was responsible for hiding and protecting King Xuan after his father was driven out by an uprising and during the "regency" of Earl He of Gong.[160] Now all these other loyal retainers have passed away, and the Divine Lord alone of this company is left to counsel the king. So important is he to the court that even though he should retire from office for three years at the death of his mother, the king "reaves from him his grief," commanding that he serve in office in spite of his mourning. The hemmed sackcloth mourning dress is the second degree, normally appropriate for the death of a grandfather or grandmother, a wife, or a step-mother. Perhaps it is adopted here because the Divine Lord is not really the eldest son, his elder brother having died in infancy.

In his dotage King Xuan has come to fancy one of his sons above the others. The Divine Lord warns that the individual in question is unworthy. The heir-apparent in traditional China resided in the Eastern Palace, which because of the Chinese system of cosmological correspondences was also called the Green Palace or the Spring Palace. The *Shujing* records that when Yi Yin was instructing the future King Tai Jia 太甲 of the Shang he told him that, "When the one person possesses primordial virtue (*yuanliang* 元良), the entire world is rectified." The *Liji* made this line a standard reference to a worthy heir-apparent.[161] Gongnie did not measure up. But the king's resolve is unwavering, and eventually Gongnie comes to the throne as King You 幽.

Involving oneself in a succession struggle was an inherently dangerous enterprise, no matter how pure one's motives. When King You accedes to the throne he does not forget the Divine Lord's opposition to his appointment. Moreover, he is as lacking in kingly virtues as the Divine Lord foresaw. When the Divine Lord dares to oppose the king's policies he rouses the king's ire, and is forced to "beg for his

---

159. *Maoshi zhengyi* 10.2/8b–13a.
160. See *Shiji* 4/143–44. In fact the *Shiji* states that the Duke of Shao collaborated with the Duke of Zhou in this regency, and this may have been commonly believed during the Song; however, the *Bamboo Annals*, quoted in the Tang *Suoyin* commentary to this passage, correctly identifies the Duke of Gong as exercising this function.
161. *Shangshu zhengyi* 8/23b; *Liji zhengyi* 20/16a–b.

bones," that is, ask that he be released from his duties at court so that he can return home to die and be buried. The king takes him at his word, and lest he be forced to wait too long for his own demise, sends a messenger with a cup of poisoned wine, a non-too-subtle royal command to commit suicide. Loyal to the end, the Divine Lord downs the wine forthwith. In recognition of his long service to the court, the king has sent along a second command, to be delivered only after the first is followed, which praises the Divine Lord as "exhausting loyalty."

Amidst the Nine Springs, another term for the Yellow Springs of the land of the dead in the nine-layered earth, the Divine Lord does not regret the course of action that led to his death. At times loyalty calls for the supreme sacrifice. But he is saddened and frightened at the future of the Zhou house, which has lost its foundation and is in the process of sinking into oblivion. In fact, King You's reign marked the end of the Western Zhou, and after this time the Zhou ruler was largely symbolic, real power resting with the feudal nobility.

30. *A Perch in Perfection* 棲眞

Again I had risen to prominence; problems were even more
  numerous.
How many times had I laughed happily, how often sung sad
  songs?
As a loyal official[162] I worried for the state, but, alas, I was too
  late.
When my forthright words met with anger, what could I do?
Seeing in the distance the pines and catalpas of my grave,
  ashamed of my white hair,
I regretted my desire for an emolument, which led to a criminal
  record written in red.

---

162. DZ reads "loyal and earnest" (*zhongcheng* 忠誠) for "loyal official" (*zhongchen* 臣).

The realm of Snow Mountain is not of this dusty world,
I'll just come here and perch in perfection.

Though born into this world I had clung fast to the old way. Not
only were my words not heeded; I was punished for them. There was
no place for my soul to go, and my emotions would not be silenced. I
wailed in the inner compartments of the palace for three days. The
king, hearing it, thought I was a demon, and ordered the Forester to
lead his troops armed with bows and arrows and shoot at the sound. I
had no body. What did it matter if they shot me? Then, being too
ashamed to face my home, I took leave of the kingdom and went on a
long excursion, my only thoughts being of the West. I went past the
Min and Emei mountains, turned my back on the stars of the Well
Network. On the western edge of Shu there is a mountain named
Feiyue 飛越. Since in a previous life I had been born in Wu-Gui,
next to Yue 越, I dropped down to take a look. The name was the
same but the customs different. Again I looked to the far west. There
was a high mountain over a hundred li across. In the full heat of summer it was covered with frozen snow, not part of this dusty realm.
The god of the mountain, Bai Hui 白輝, said to me, "This place is
called Snow Mountain. In the past the Prabhūtaratnā Tathāgathā
practiced austerities here, attaining the Dao after eight years, and the
Perfected of the Western Bourne, after protracted residence, received
confirmation of the fruit of his enlightenment. Your transcendent
manner is imposing, Great Minister. Why do you not stay here?" I
heeded him and stayed. Before long there was a rescript from the
Thearch appointing me the Great Transcendent of Snow Mountain
雪山大僊.[163]

COMMENTARY

Having committed suicide at the command of his lord after pre-
senting righteous remonstrances, the Divine Lord is troubled by his
tarnished reputation. In ancient China crimes were recorded in red
cinnabar so that the record would never fade, cinnabar deriving its close

---

163. The DZ edition reads "Great King 王 of Snow Mountain."

association with eternity or longevity from its common use in elixirs of immortality.

Bitter resentment at his unjust fate leads the Divine Lord to manifest as a wailing specter.[164] The location of the haunting is the inner compartments, where the king's wife and concubines dwell. This was the most yin place in the palace, and the Divine Lord now belongs to the world of the dead, also yin. The king believes that the wailing comes from a demon, *yao* 妖. The word *yao* also can refer to an ominous portent, and the appearance of such a demon was viewed as a harbinger of greater evil to come.

The king responds by ordering his Forester (*tingshi* 庭氏) and the Forester's subordinates to try to shoot the creature with an arrow. The *Rites of Zhou* tell us the Forester was responsible for the shooting of ill-omened (*yao* 妖) birds within the state. He did so with the Sun-saving bow and Moon-saving arrows ordinarily used to dispel eclipses. When the apparition was truly a spirit rather than an inauspicious animal, he used the Great-*yin* bow and crooked arrows.[165]

As the Divine Lord points out, in his incorporeal state, even the Forester's arrows could not harm him, and perhaps because he was not truly a demon but rather a wronged ghost, the exorcistic archery magic was also ineffective against him. But after three days of haunting, the Divine Lord is ready to move on. Following his humiliating death he cannot face a return to his native home, so he resumes the journey to the West that he first began after his second incarnation.

The trip is a "distant excursion" (*yuanyou* 遠遊), the title of a poem in the *Elegies of Chu* describing an astral journey through the universe.[166] He passes over the Min and Emei mountain ranges of Sichuan, and thus leaves the region ruled by the asterism Well Network (*jingluo* 井絡). In his "Rhapsody on the Shu Capital," Zuo Si 左思 (250?–310) tells us that the quintessence of the Min mountains ascended into the heavens to form these two asterisms.[167]

---

164. Vengeful ghosts are an ancient theme in China and continue throughout Chinese literature and drama down to modern movies. On early examples, see Cohen 1979, which discusses pre-Han examples, and Cohen 1982, which translates a sixth-century collection of such tales.

156. *Zhouli zhushu* 37/7b–8a.

166. *Chuci buzhu* 5; Hawkes 1985: 191–203. This is in fact the chapter that mentions Wenchang (5/8a).

167. *Wenxuan* 4/26a; Knechtges 1982: 369. A similar statement is found in the Han dynasty apocryphal work, *Hetu Kuodixiang* 河圖括地象, quoted in the Li Shan commentary to this passage. Cf. *Huayangguo zhi* 3/27. Schafer (1977: 76) identifies Well as the first constellation in Quail Head, corresponding to stars in Gemini.

The god considers taking up residence on Feiyue Mountain, drawn to the similarity of the name to that of an area near his abode in his first incarnation, but finds the customs too alien. The mountain was and is surrounded by regions inhabited by Qiang tribesmen, and their seminomadic herding lifestyle must have been very different from the stream- and lake-centered life of the Yue peoples he had known.[168]

Finally he comes to Snow Mountain, probably referring here to the Himalayas or some specific Himalayan peak. There he is greeted by the local mountain god, Bai Hui ("white brilliance," suggesting the snow). Mountain gods here would seem to be relatively lowly local gods who administer their mountain and its inhabitants much as a city god administers his city. Bai Hui tells the Divine Lord of the illustrious history of Snow Mountain. It was the place where the buddha Prabhūtaratnā ("many-jeweled") pursued his austerities and eventually attained enlightenment. After entering nirvana his entire body became relics and he now appears whenever the Lotus Sūtra is recited to testify to its veracity.[169] Another, otherwise unknown figure is also associated with the mountain, the Perfected of the Western Bourne 西極眞人.

Recognizing the lofty spiritual attainments of the Divine Lord, the mountain spirit invites him to stay on the mountain as these illustrious predecessors had, for a period of reclusion and self-cultivation. The Divine Lord accepts, and soon his decision is confirmed by an official appointment from the Supreme Thearch, much as occurred when he decided to reside on Mount Monarch (ch. 20).

With this episode the Divine Lord finishes a cycle of incarnations in the classical period of the Western Zhou. He will now spend the next several centuries as a disembodied spirit, and concentrate on the western portion of China. The opening poem of this episode is considerably more colloquial than those preceding it, perhaps reflecting a change in the individual wielding the planchette.

---

168. *Dushi fangyu jiyao* 73/3121.
169. Set forth in chapter 4 of the *Lotus Sutra*. Cf. Mochizuki 1954–71: 3489–90.

31. *The Mountain King* 山王

Over a thousand li from the capital Hao to the north,
To the west, I look out over the myriad peaks of Min and Emei.
Having cast aside fame and disgrace I am outside the net.
Right and wrong do not extend to this place between the water
  and the clouds.
I strove to punish the white tiger, who left behind a starry stone,
Imprisoned the green dragon in the circle of the bright moon.
I faced south and proclaimed myself king; my court faced
  north.[170]
I must trouble the Thearch to reissue his rescript.

Not long after I had come to stay on Snow Mountain and been appointed Great Transcendent, there was a rescript ordering that I promote[171] moral transformation at the Gate of Shu. So I returned riding on a crane. In the northeast I saw myriad peaks of green and kingfisher, an adorable, unparalleled realm. After a while five mountain gods, led by Gong Yuanchang 公元長, came to greet me, saying, "We are assigned to this region. Recently we noticed that Your Perfection's abundant spirit is imposing,[172] that your eyes flash, and that the sound of your cough rumbles through the cliffs and valleys. We concluded you must surely be a heavenly being. It has been three hundred years since the time when King Wu led his expedition against King Zhou, and the ruler of Shu, supported by the leaders of the states of Wei, Lu, Peng, and Pu, passed through here headed north at the head of a great army. The road is remote and the population sparse. No distinguished figure has passed by. Fortunately the dazzling power of Your Perfection announced your arrival." I related

---

170. DZ reads "[all] paid court for a hundred *li*" (*chao baili* 朝百里) for "my court faced north" (*chao beimian* 朝北面).

171. DZ reads *wang* 旺, "to make flourish," for *xing* 行, "to promote."

172. Both DZJY and SG present variants on the wording and word order from that of the 1645 ed. and DZ. Here I follow DZJY and SG in reading *feng* 丰, "abundant," for *feng* 鋒, "spearpoint."

to them the circumstances of my arrival. The mountain gods said, "We also tired of the company of men and sojourned to this place. This mountain is under the rule of the Emperor of Shu, and is called Jianling ("swordridge" 劍嶺). To the north it abuts Zhongnan, to the west links up with the Min and Emei 岷峨 ranges, to the south it communicates with Mount Qionglai 邛徠, and to the east bows before Ba and Yong 庸.[173] It covers an area over one thousand li in circumference, and is in a strategic location. It has been almost a hundred years, since Peaklord Bai was born as the heir-apparent of Shu, that we have been without a king. Now Your Perfection is the descendant of a saint, is unsullied and resplendent in your person, has accumulated virtue and amassed good works, has maintained your principles of loyalty and filiality, and has come here on a spirit-journey. There are times proper to serving and to withdrawing. Why not rest here a bit? Further, near Swordridge there is a huge beast with a white forehead over a thousand years old. It lies in wait in the mountain crevices and feeds on people. Since Your Perfection was once the high officer of the Son of Heaven, all the spirits of the mountains and streams were once under your command. Further, a jade rescript has ordered you here. You can yourself summon the many spirits and, breathing forth transformation, dispatch nether forces to drive forth this tiger. This would both aid Heaven and show your love of sentient beings."

I was persuaded and counterfeited a divine rescript summoning forth all the ghosts and spirits of the mountains and streams within a thousand li. All came to hear my commands. I said, "The Thearch has sent a jade rescript noting that the white tiger is taking human life, and ordering me, as king of this mountain, to lead you many spirits in punishing and destroying it. Those who obey this command will enjoy bloody sacrifice for generation after generation; for those who do not, Heaven possesses terrible punishments." All said, "Yes, we reverently obey your commands." I then looked up and gazed all

---

173. DZ reads Shu 蜀 for Yong. Both are names of ancient people who participated in the Zhou conquest. Yong is traditionally place in Northeast Sichuan or Northwest Hubei; hence it is a better pairing with Ba, in eastern Sichuan.

about. Creating an image and transforming, I manifested a form as high as the mountain. Plucking out a lone bamboo I chanted a spell and transformed it into a long sword. Ping Yi summoned the Masters of Wind and Rain to clear the way. I waved my sword with a single shout and the echo rumbled through the valley. The tiger's angry breaths formed clouds and the light of his eyes shot forth lightning bolts. It leapt back and forth, but I blocked it with my body. All the blades advanced together, and it died under the knives. In the midst of the blood and gore I found a round stone shaped like a fallen star. Gong Yuanchang examined it and said, "This is a 'tiger's potency.'" When I wore it belted to my waist all the gods feared me. The deed completed, I memorialized the Thearch. First I confessed my crime in counterfeiting the summons, then touched upon my achievements. The Thearch consequently made me Mountain King of the Northern Gate of Shu.

COMMENTARY

Having just been installed in his new position as Great Transcendent of Snow Mountain, the Divine Lord is suddenly transferred. He is to promote conversion or moral tranformation (*xinghua* 行化) at the Gate of Shu 蜀門, a traditional term for the Sword Gate 劍門 or Sword Pavilion 劍閣 pass that separates the modern provinces of Shaanxi and Sichuan.[174]

There he is met by five of the local mountain gods, who have noticed the supernatural signs that accompany the presence of so highly developed a spirit as the Divine Lord, and address him as Your Perfection in recognition of his divine rank among the Perfected. They remark that their mountain has not seen such excitement since the time of the Zhou conquest of the Shang. At that time history records that King Wu was aided by the armies of eight non-Chinese states from

---

174. Cf. the "Inscription at Sword Pavilion" 劍閣銘 by Zhang Zai 張載 of the Jin dynasty, "The Gate of Shu; Make it solid, make it secure; This is Sword Pavilion; Its walls soar a thousand fathoms." *Quan Shanggu Sandai Qin Han Sanguo Liuchao wen* 85/5b, *Jinshu* 55/1516 (the poem is attributed to the beginning of the Taikang era, 280–289). In his "Rhapsody on the Shu Capital" Zuo Si also speaks of the Shu region as "Hemmed in by Sword Tower." Knechtges explains that the name refers to the way the two peaks drop off sharply. See Knechtges 1982: 347–48.

south of the Zhou domain, among them Shu 蜀, Wei 微, Lu 纑, Peng 彭, and Pu 濮.[175] The mountain spirits saw the ruler of Shu leading the others as they passed through Sword Pavilion Pass.

The mountain spirits also point out that their mountain has lacked a king since a time a hundred years ago when the former mountain king, surnamed Bai, was incarnated as the heir-apparent of the ruler of Shu. This no doubt refers to some local legend concerning early Sichuan history, but I have found no record of such a tale.[176] The mountain spirits propose that the Divine Lord accept this position because of his unique qualifications. He is the scion of a saint, perhaps referring to the founder of the Zhang clan, Hui, who was introduced in chapter 3, and he is "unsullied and resplendent in his person," a description applied by Confucius to the saint.[177]

The Divine Lord is also needed to rid the mountain of the predations of a giant white tiger of great age.[178] The tiger in China is divine, the symbol of the West, and the white tiger possesses special powers. When Linjun 廩君, the mythical founder of the Ba 巴 tribe that inhabited ancient Eastern Sichuan, died, his soul repeatedly came back as a white tiger, and the Ba people for this reason offered human sacrifice to it.[179] But more than this, any animal or plant that reaches such advanced age accumulates magical power that will eventually allow it to transform into a spirit.

The Divine Lord brings to his confrontation with this man-eating beast special powers by virtue of his recent tenure as a high official of the Son of Heaven, who has sovereignty over the gods and spirits of the mountains and rivers. The Divine Lord can use that authority to

---

175. *Shiji* 4/122. The commentaries to this passage discuss the location of these peoples and there has been speculation also in recent works on ethnological history concerning their proper location and identification, but results are inconclusive. Traditional commentaries do not place all of the peoples mentioned in the present passage in the Sichuan area, and it is uncertain why these four groups were chosen from the eight in *Shiji*.

176. According to the *Huayangguo zhi* the first king of Shu was Can Cong, who taught the people sericulture. His son, the first heir-apparent, was named Bo Guan (or Bo Huo). See *Huayangguo zhi* 3/27; *Huayangguo zhi jiaozhu* 3/181–82, esp. n. 3.

177. *Liji zhengyi* 51/6a.

178. Tigers were a very real threat in this part of northern Sichuan. One of the first records of the region is when the King of Qin offered a reward to anyone who could kill a marauding tiger that had already taken 1200 lives. The tiger was killed by tribesmen of the Banshun Man, who lived on the upper reaches of the Jialing River. See *Huayangguo zhi* 1/3; *Huayangguo zhi jiaozhu* 1/34–35. Sage (1992: 138–39) discusses this incident in some detail, giving a rather rationalized account of what was clearly a legendary event.

179. *Hou Han shu* 86/2840.

summon the local nature spirits to make common cause against the tiger not because of the statutory prerogative of an office he no longer holds, but because as an adjutant to the Son of Heaven in his divine governance he has become imbued with a spiritual power that survives loss of the physical form. The cohort of local spirits assembled to aid in the killing of the tiger derive their sustenance and supernatural power from offerings of blood sacrifice,[180] and he promises them, in return for their cooperation, rich offerings for generation after generation, while at the same time threatening any who would disobey with divine torture.

When he has gained their assent, the Divine Lord sets out on the hunt. He transforms himself into a giant, and makes of a bamboo a giant sword, then sends the heavenly messenger Ping Yi 屏翳 to summon forth the gods of wind and rain to lead the way for him.[181] The tiger also displays his supernatural powers, breathing out clouds and flashing bolts of lightning from his eyes, but the Divine Lord stands undaunted and the company of spirits converge to kill the beast. Afterwards they find an apotropaic gem of great power called a "tiger's potency" (*huwei* 虎威), here described as shaped like a fallen star (a meteorite?).[182] The reference in the poem to the chaining of a dragon is unclear. Usually a dragon is chained to prevent him from causing floods, as in the case of the dragon imprisoned by Li Bing at Fulongguan 伏龍觀 near Guanxian, Sichuan.

The Divine Lord must first explain to the Thearch his reasons for falsifying a divine rescript, before being confirmed in his new position as Mountain King of the Gate of Shu. This chapter could be understood to sanction a certain amount of independent action on the part of local officials in the real-world bureaucracy, where communications were slow and precipitous developments often made promulgated commands irrelevant.

---

180. Zhu Xi tells us that the god Erlang at Dujiangyan in Guanxian, Sichuan, lost his numinous efficacy because he had been promoted to the exalted realm of Taoist perfected deities, and hence denied his bloody nourishment. *Zhuzi yulei* 3/21a.

181. Ping Yi is himself sometimes identified as the god of the wind or the rain, but fulfills the same function as here in the "Rhapsody on the Great Man" 大人賦 of Sima Xiangru 司馬相如 (179–117 B.C.). See *Quan shanggu sandai Qin Han Sanguo Liuchao wen* 21/7b.

182. Duan Chengshi 段成式 (?–863) tells us that such an object looks like amber (*hupo* 琥珀), is formed when the light of the tiger's shining eyes enters the earth after his death, and can "dispel the hundred malefics." *Youyang zazu* 11/6a–b.

32. *Punishments and Rewards* 刑賞

Although administration is different in the worlds of shades and
  light,
The principle of maintaining justice and righteousness is the
  same.
Sun Di had a grievance, his disgrace had to be erased.
Yijian strove to be filial but had not yet been rewarded.
Strict punishments show no mercy, Yu's back was whipped.
My recommendation saying Yijian's time had come reached the
  Thearch's sharp ears.
Great and minor gods and spirits all revered and feared me,
The clear and bright Heaven and Earth were flushed clean by an
  august wind.

Once I had assumed my perfected position as king of the mountains,
I concerned myself with every flood, drought, good or bad harvest,
good or evil portent, achievement and fault within the mountains
and streams under my control. Whenever I heard of some problem I
would deal with it justly. Sun Di 孫滌 resided within the district of
Gao Yusheng 高魚生, the god of Mount Qingli 青黎山. On the night
of the marriage of Sun's daughter, Gao Yusheng, who took delight in
this maiden, seized her soul and despoiled her. This was discovered
and reported by the neighboring official, the dragon god of White
Pool. I looked into the matter, and questioned both Gao and the girl.
Gao admitted his guilt and returned the soul of the girl, who regained
consciousness. I had him whipped three hundred lashes on the back,
and dismissed him from his office. Below the mountain there was a
former filial son, Wu Yijian 吳宜肩, who had once drawn his own
blood to copy the four scrolls of the *Lankāvatāra Sūtra* in order to aid
his father, who was ill. Three years[183] after he died of natural causes,
he still had not received an official position. I memorialized on his

---

183. DZ reads "five years."

behalf, recommending him to replace Gao Yusheng. The Thearch replied, approving this recommendation. From this time on gods great and small all respected and feared me even more.[184]

COMMENTARY

Now secure in his new post as mountain king, the Divine Lord sets to rectifying the situation in the region under his control. We see here a good model of how local administration in both the temporal and sacred worlds was supposed to work. Any individual official might commit a fault. It was the responsibility of his colleagues to report any misconduct of which they might hear to their superior. Thus the dragon of White Pool acts properly in reporting to the Divine Lord what he has heard of the actions of a local mountain god, Gao Yusheng. Gao has let lust get the best of him, and has exercised a sort of supernatural *ius primus nocte* in stealing the soul of a new bride on her wedding night and raping her. Now the poor girl lies unconscious while the fiendish Gao sports with her soul. The Divine Lord investigates just as a secular magistrate would, and interrogates both Gao and the girl. He obtains a confession from Gao, as is proper in Chinese jurisprudence, then fixes his sentence, which includes a severe corporal punishment and the loss of Gao's official position. From an anthropological perspective, we can see in this tale a young girl faced with the prospect of marriage, a wrenching experience in which she leaves her home and family forever, entering into an unknown world in which she will occupy the lowest position. When she reacts with hysterical loss of consciousness this is attributed to soul-loss and a local deity is blamed.

An important official duty was to recruit other worthy candidates for office, though this was a perilous practice, because the recommender was held responsible for the future conduct of the one recommended.[185] The Divine Lord, while searching for a replacement for Gao, hears of the virtuous but as yet unrewarded virtue of Wu Yijian. It is unrecompensed good that creates the "hidden virtue" (*yinde*) that assures favorable treatment in the other world and an auspicious rebirth. That the virtuous act here was the copying in blood of an important

---

184. DZ reads "all knew to respect and honor me" (*zhi jingyang* 知敬仰).
185. On recommendation, see Kracke 1953: 6–7, 75.

Buddhist scripture again shows the ecumenical attitude of the Zitong sect toward the three religions.[186]

33. *Preserving Bao* 存褒

The Marquis of Bao used his daughter to captivate King You.

The king favored Bao Si, destroying the mainstays of the state.

He deposed his son and rejected his wife, an abomination to Heaven.

He persecuted the worthy and killed the good; their ghosts cursed him.

Although it was satisfying for the marchmount spirit to transfer his anger,

The common people of the state of Bao should be pitied.

My memorial reached the vault of heaven, and merited a positive response;

The lifespans of the remaining inhabitants were consequently extended.

In the beginning King You 幽王 (r. 781–771 B.C.) had made the daughter of the Marquis of Shen 申侯 his queen. She was worthy and had a son named Yijiu 宜臼, who was not only the son of the queen, but also the king's eldest son. His benevolent and filial manner was evident in his precocious youth. When the Marquis of Bao presented Si 姒 to the king, he favored her and became estranged from the queen. Soon thereafter, when Si had given birth to a son, he deposed the Queen née Shen and put Si in her place. The son that Si had born, the king named Bofu 伯服, meaning by *bo* ("eldest son") that there was no one senior to him, and by *fu* ("to submit") that all

---

186. On the *Lankāvatāra Sūtra*, see the translation and studies of D. T. Suzuki, esp. Suzuki 1930.

in the world would submit to him. Thereupon he drove out Yijiu and established Bofu as the heir-apparent. Nine of the great officers of state remonstrated against this, and all were put to death together with their entire clans. This vileness came to be known on high, and the Thearch permitted the Western Marchmount to create anomalies to warn the king. As a result, the gods of the mountains and streams were unsettled. The three streams all trembled, mountains toppled, and rivers ran dry, all things going against the proper course of events. The god of the marchmount was an avatar (*jiangling* 降靈) of the White Thearch, Biao Ju. Transferring his anger,[187] he sent a directive to the Han and Mian river gods and the mountain gods of Bao and Ye, ordering the inundation of the city of Bao. Bao was on the borders of Shu, and I was taken aback by his overreaction. So I submitted a memorial saying, "It is proper to punish the Marquis of Bao. He is not deserving of sympathy. But what crime have the people of Bao committed? Please pardon them." A proclamation stated, "The god of the Metal Heaven issued a directive on his own authority. His superior should discipline him lightly. The people of the city of Bao are pardoned from immersion." Later the Dog Rong invaded Zhou and it abandoned the region of the Han and Mian rivers and the city of Bao, which became subordinate to Shu, all in accordance with the will of the Thearch.

COMMENTARY

This episode stresses the importance of compassion in governing, at the same time reinforcing the responsibility of officials to oversee each other and warning against rash conduct in office.

King You is accused of falling under the influence of a woman, one of the most serious charges made against the evil last ruler of the Shang by the Zhou conquerors when trying to justify their rebellion.[188] Besides the obvious danger of undue influence from the relatives of the favored wife or concubine, such behavior offended Chinese cosmological ethics. Governing was an exclusively male, yang

---

187. Following the 1645 ed. and DZ in reading *qian* 遷, "to transfer," for *zhen* 震, "to quake, thunder."

188. See *Shangshu zhengyi* 11/12b.

endeavor, and it was considered immoral for the yin influence of a woman to gain precedence in this realm.[189]

Most of the incidents related here are well known from the standard historical sources like the *Shiji*. In the second year of King You's reign there was an earthquake in the region of the Three Rivers, which the commentaries to the *Shiji* identify as the Jing, Wei, and Luo, near the Western Zhou capital of Hao in modern Shaanxi; the Three Rivers dried up, and Mount Qi collapsed.[190] The following year the king deposed the queen and her son. In Chavannes' translation, the passage reads:[191]

> La troisème année de son règne (779 av. J.-C.), le roi Yeou [You] devint fort épris de Pao-se [Bao Si]. Pao-se enfanta un fils, Po-fou [Bofu], et le roi Yeou voulut dégrader l'héritier présomptif. La mère de l'héritier présomptif était fille de marquis de Chen [Shen] et était reine. Mais plus tard, lorsque le roi Yeou eut Pao-se et l'aima, il voulut dégrader la reine Chen, renvoyer en même temps l'héritier présomptif I-kieou [Yijiu] et nommer Pao-se reine et Po-fou héritier présomptif.

The *Shiji* goes on to relate the miraculous origin of Bao Si, which is not touched upon in our account. She was conceived by a young maiden impregnated by the spit of two divine dragons, which had been stored in the palace since the Xia dynasty.[192] The *Shiji* makes no mention of the nine loyal officials who, our text claims, remonstrated against the king's actions, and were executed along with their entire clans for this presumption. But the *Shiji* does mention the invasion of the Dog Rong, allied with the Marquis of Shen, which resulted in the death of King You and the eventual enthronement of the rightful heir-apparent, Yijiu, as King Ping 平王.[193]

When the temporal administration deviates so far from proper conduct it is expected that Heaven will make manifest its displeasure through

---

189. The *Shiji* records that after the natural disasters mentioned below Boyang Fu remonstrated that the cause was that "yang has lost its place and yin has filled it" and specifically compares the current situation of the Zhou rule to that of the Xia and Shang at the end of their dynasties. See *Shiji* 4/145–46; *Guoyu*, "Zhouyu" 1–10; d'Hormon 1985: 151–52.

190. *Shiji* 4/145–46.

191. Chavannes 1895: Vol. 1, pp. 280–81. The pinyin romanization of Chinese words has been supplied in brackets.

192. *Shiji* 4/147; Chavannes 1895: Vol. 1, p. 281–83.

193. *Shiji* 4/149.

omens, anomalies, and natural disasters. In this case the Supreme Thearch deputed this task to the Western Marchmount, who, our text explains, is an avatar of the White Thearch.[194] Being the regional representative of the West, he is associated with the element metal, and for this reason is sometimes called the God of the Metal Heaven. In mythology he is the emperor Shao Hao. The DZJY text gives his name as Biao Ju 標矩, but DZ reads Bai Tuoju 白拓矩, probably a mistake for Bai Zhaoju 白招矩, the name attributed to the White Thearch in the Han apocrypha and the *Jinshu* treatise on astronomy.[195]

The White Thearch, in his zeal to punish the source of the evil influence, Bao, sends about a directive ordering the local mountain spirits to plunge the entire capital city of the domain under water. Now Bao is situated on the border between the regions of Shu and Hanzhong, with Bao at the south and Ye at the north end of a valley in the Zhongnan Mountains, the mountains that the mountain gods in the previous chapter had noted as the northern limit of the Sword Ridge mountains over which the Divine Lord now has suzerainty. The Divine Lord hears of this directive and feels it is unjust. Like the dragon in the previous episode, he reports the action to his superior, in this case the Supreme Thearch himself. Thus here a member of the supernatural administration acted on his own initiative but made the incorrect decision. This is perhaps a warning to temporal officials lest they be overly inspired by the Divine Lord's example and act rashly. Since the White Thearch was acting out of a sense of moral outrage, his punishment is not severe, but the area in question is removed from his control and transferred to the stewardship of the Divine Lord.[196] A corresponding change in the temporal rulership of the region shows the parallel nature of sacred and profane administrative geography, and in this case, the primacy of sacred geography.

---

194. The cult to this member of the original five cardinal-direction deities was alive in Sichuan during the Song. Lu You visited a temple to the deity outside of Baidi cheng that displayed steles from the Five Dynasties and from the beginning of the twelfth century, attesting to the long-term popularity of this god. See Chang and Smythe 1981: 172. This shrine was associated with the name of a Han dynasty figure, Gongsun Shu. The reference to this god as an "avatar" of a yet higher deity is unusual. Perhaps in Taoist cosmology of the time a descent from the pure Taoist heavens to the profane heavens of the terrestrial administration of earth spirits (*diqi* 地祇) was considered equivalent to incarnating in human form.

195. *Chunqiu wei*, cited in the subcommentary to *Liji zhengyi* 14/20a; *Jinshu* 11/292.

196. That this region was in fact once under the control of the King of Shu is attested in the *Huayangguo zhi*, in a story about a chance meeting of the Shu monarch and King Hui of Qin in this valley. See *Huayangguo zhi* 3/28; *Huayangguo zhi jiaozhu* 3/187 and 188, n. 2.

34.   *The Whirlwind*   回風

When evil men practice evil they summon their own
   misfortune,
It is different when a filial son earnestly serves his parent.
If you become enemies over food, you have already let your
   emotions get carried away.
Only when I diverted the wind and blew the fire back did my
   power reach its height.
Even one full of valor can vomit,
Surprised when the mad whirlwind that scraped the cheeks
   turned to attack him.
He left his words as a warning to people of the world,
You must know that the intelligent and candid display divine
   powers.

Li Yuan 李轅, who lived south of Sword Ridge, was filial toward
his mother. At twilight a guest took refuge with him. Yuan had just
cooked a chicken and made a meal. The guest thought that Yuan
would feed him this,[197] and his pleasure showed in his appearance
and his words. Soon thereafter the food arrived, but it was only freshly
hulled, unpolished rice. The guest did not lift his spoon. Yuan said,
"My elderly mother has just gotten over an illness and wants meat.
There is not enough of the controller-of-the-morning (i.e., chicken)
to provide for you." Redfaced, the guest raised his sleeves and rose,
saying, "Do you think I have never eaten meat?" He then left without
bowing. Late that night he set a fire upwind to burn the house down.
It was just the coldest time of the year, and the grass and trees were
yellow and withered. The smoke and flames bellowed with an un-
faceable fury. Yuan ran out carrying his mother, then cried to Heaven.
I happened to be passing above the place, and thought the situation

---

197. DZ reads *guan* 館, "establishment, office," for *kui* 饋, "to feed."

very unfair. So I exhaled, creating a wind that made the cruel flames turn back on themselves. The guest still held the torch in his hand, and his sideburns and eyebrows were burnt off. He tried to flee but lost his direction and fell down in the midst of the fire, barely escaping alive.[198] When I interrogated him, he said, "I am the knight-errant Pu Guangdu 蒲光度. This summer when the gentlemen and ladies of the city were washing flowers and partying, a friend of mine got drunk and offended someone from a good family. He was brutalized by this person until he was on the point of death. In order to resolve the quarrel I threw the man into the water and he almost drowned. He filed a complaint against me with the local officials and I thereupon fled. After roaming for half a year I was really extremely hungry. I hated this son in my heart. Just as I set fire to the grass, it was as if someone cursed me. When the fire reached the son's house, it was blown by the wind.[199] Now I am going to die. I have told you this so that I do not become a nameless ghost." When he had finished speaking he died.

COMMENTARY

The Divine Lord comes to the aid of a filial son. There is an obligation to provide hospitality for travelers who seek refuge in one's home, but this duty is not as important as one's responsibilities toward one's parents. Here Li Yuan has only enough chicken to serve his mother, who is recovering from an illness. A wandering knight-errant who has sought lodging from him for the night takes offense at this and tries to burn the house and its inhabitants. The Divine Lord, on patrol, notices this, and using his powers over natural forces creates a great wind that saves the house and turns the fire back upon the knight.

As he lies dying the knight, Pu Guangdu, explains what brought an otherwise valorous figure to such depths. The previous summer he had been in the city during a celebration. This was undoubtedly the "Flower Washing Day" 浣花日 observed on the nineteenth day of the fourth month every year at the "Grass Hut" of Du Fu in Chengdu. Lu

---

198. Following the 1645 ed. and DZ in reading *tuo* 脫, "to escape," for *cun* 存, "to preserve."
199. DZ reads "was turned upon by the wind" (*wei feng suo chou* 爲風所讎).

You 陸游 (1125–1210) attended several of these celebrations on the banks of Flower Washing Creek during his stay there.[200] There one of Pu's friends overindulged in drinking and got into an argument with a member of the local gentry. He was set upon and nearly killed before Pu stepped in and threw his attacker into the creek. But the individual could not swim and was barely saved in time. In anger he sought to set the law upon Pu, who was forced to flee. Pu had been on the run for half a year when he was welcomed into Li Yuan's home, and this explains to a degree his overreaction to Li's filial behavior.

Pu makes this explanation because he does not want to become a "nameless ghost." Although it is unlikely that he would ever receive normal ancestral sacrifices, if his identity were known it is possible that the local populace would set up a shrine to his soul so that it would not wreak havoc on the region. Otherwise, he would be fated to become one of the hoard of li 厲, homeless spirits who must contest for the paltry offerings made at the local altar to such spirits, the litan 厲壇. The knight-errant is a romantic but ambiguous figure in Chinese literature. Sima Qian devoted a chapter of his Shiji to them, and characterized them in the following fashion:[201]

> Their words were always sincere and trustworthy, and their actions always quick and decisive. They were always true to what they promised, and without regard to their own persons, they would rush into dangers threatening others.

But Sima Qian was roundly criticized by later historians for his treatment of these independent, order-threatening individuals. Moreover, there was a fine line between antinomian, honor-based ethic of the true knight-errant and the cynical amorality of the brigand, and the common people must have seen enough would-be Robin Hoods who finally resorted to banditry. In this episode Pu reflects this mixed heritage. He is an evildoer and receives his just desserts, but he is ultimately also a tragic figure, who went wrong with the best of intentions. It is a story, in fact, well-crafted to inspire the sort of votive sacrifices that Pu implicitly requests with his comment about becoming a nameless ghost, and this implies an ultimate origin of the tale in some sort of a cult to Pu, but no record of such a group survives.

200. *Laoxueyan biji* 8.
201. Translation from Fung 1948: 50, cited in Yang Lien-sheng 1957: 294.

35. *Clarifying Injustice* 明冤

You must know that a man's life is as weighty as a mountain,
Never treat a doubtful case as a trifle.[202]
Madame née Mao lost her body and the crime had not yet been
  requited,
Liangneng was to die in error, how could I return (without
  resolving this)?
I attached the soaring soul to the body (of Niu Zi) to make clear
  the unjust verdict,
Seized the bandit and sought the truth concerning this great
  hidden villainy.
Ai Min with his one word produced great benefit,[203]
He could enjoy the people's bloody sacrifice without
  embarrassment.

Three hundred li to the north of Swordridge, at the foot of
Tortoise Mountain 龜山, there was a man named He Zhiqing 何志
清. He had a son named Wufang 無方 who married the daughter of
Hou Fu 侯釜 of Fish Mountain 魚山. The next year Hou Fu fell ill,
and his condition was grave. His daughter announced this fact to her
mother-in-law, and asked permission to return to her maternal home.
Her mother-in-law consented and she left with her husband. On the
way she remembered the two golden earrings in her dowry chest that
she had intended to bring in case her father had sudden need of

---

202. Following the 1645 edition and DZ in reading *yixing* 疑刑, "doubtful legal case," for DZJY
xingyi 形疑, "form is doubtful." The DZJY reading could be explained as a reference to the mysterious
headless body discovered in the following story, but the DZ reading is clearly superior in the context of
this poem.

203. DZ gives the name of this mountain god as Yi 義 Min rather than Ai Min. I follow DZJY in
reading *pu* 溥, "great, universal"; DZ has the synonym *bo* 博, "broad, great"; both are to be preferred
over the graphically similar *pu* 浦, "estuary," of the 1645 ed. It is uncertain whether the benefit here is
that received by Ai Min, which is referred to in the following line, or that of the unjustly convicted
man, who was freed, and his brother and sister-in-law, who were reunited.

them. Leaving so hurriedly she had forgotten them. She wanted to go back and get them, but the sun was already setting. Suddenly Wu-fang's younger brother Liangneng 良能 came up behind them, hol-lering and holding the golden earrings in his hand. When he reached them, he said, "Our mother has fallen ill. She sent me to tell you, elder brother, and give sister-in-law these things she had forgotten. When you have reached your in-laws' home, elder brother should re-turn home first. Mother is already anxiously[204] awaiting your return." Wufang said, "You go on with your sister-in-law. I am going to go home to look after Mother." A while after Wufang had left, Madame née Hou regretted this decision, and said, "My home is less than ten li from here. There is no need to trouble you, younger brother, to accompany me." Liangneng took her at her word, and hurriedly taking his leave, went back, but by then it was late at night.

The next day Hou Fu was surprised that his daughter had prom-ised to come home, yet was so late in arriving. He sent someone to meet her on the road, and this man found the beheaded corpse of a woman. Fu's condition took a turn for the worse and he died. His family made a complaint to the local authorities. The He family sent the younger son to be questioned. After more than a month the case was decided. Liangneng falsely confessed that after taking leave of his elder brother he had tried to force his attentions upon his sister-in-law, and when she did not comply, he had killed her, explaining that her missing head was probably eaten by a tiger or panther. When he was about to be executed, Liangneng cried indignantly.

The god of Tortoise Mountain, Ai Min 艾敏, came to report this. I investigated and discovered the truth. It seems that there was a rob-ber named Niu Zi 牛資 who had a falling out with his wife Madame née Mao 毛. Zi met née Hou on the road, robbed her, and forced his attentions on her. He then took Hou's clothes and changed them with Mao's. Mao and Hou were of about the same age. He chopped off Mao's head and led Hou off to stay with him.[205] I caught up with Mao's soul and attached it to Niu Zi's body, then used Zi's mouth to

---

204. Following the 1645 ed. and DZ in reading *yong* 顒 for *yu* 禺.
205. DZ reads "led Hou to his home."

speak Mao's words. From his confession the truth was revealed. Zi was prosecuted for the crime and the woman was returned to Hou. Liangneng was released.

COMMENTARY

A recurrent problem in Chinese jurisprudence was the forced confession. Local magistrates with no specialized training in jurisprudence were entrusted with the adjudication of all cases arising within their jurisdiction. A confession was considered the ultimate and indispensable proof of guilt, and torture was routinely employed to extract such a confession. In doubtful cases this often resulted in forced conessions from innocent individuals. Although there was some provision for appeal, in most cases such a wronged person could only hope for divine intervention, and a plea of injustice from an honest, upright man or woman was considered particularly moving to the gods.

Here He Liangneng has fallen victim to just such a situation. There is circumstantial evidence that he murdered his sister-in-law, a complaint is laid against him, and he is forced to confess. As he is about to suffer the ultimate punishment his plea for justice is heard by an attentive local spirit, the god of Tortoise Mountain. This again shows the role of the divine bureaucracy in overseeing and correcting the temporal administration. He reports Liangneng's plight to his superior, the Divine Lord of Zitong. We are told that for this attentive oversight he will be rewarded with nourishment in the form of bloody sacrifice as well as the relief of not having an injustice perpetrated in an area within his jurisdiction. Since the divine bureaucracy in the *Book of Transformations* is a model for the secular, this story, with its admonishment in the poem to adjudicate difficult cases carefully, can be seen as a warning to secular magistrates.

---

36.   *The Town of Ju*   苴邑

Of beings possessing a spirit none is more esteemed than man,
It is not easy to cultivate oneself in order to obtain this body.
Once a fetus is conceived it should be loved and treasured,
Yet some on the contrary let it perish for the sake of clothes and
     food.
Everyone cherishes children, how could they feel differently?
Heaven and Earth originally are impartial in giving birth to life.
After my actions the customs of the whole region were
     transformed.
The cruel rifts caused by cutting down orchids no longer
     wounded the soul.

One hundred li to the north of Sword(ridge) and veering sharply
to the east for something over two days' march is the town of Jurao
苴饒. The land there is infertile and the people poor. When the
common folks have one son, they rear him, but sometimes not the
second, and they abandon the third or fourth. They are stingy about
clothing and food in order to accommodate their present needs, and
give no thought to their posterity.

Zhang Qianshi 張千十 was from a rich family. Over eighty households rented land from him to grow food for their sustenance. On
the day when he bestowed land upon them he made a contract with
them that if they had one son strong enough to plow and harvest
they could keep him, but any others born after him absolutely could
not be kept, and this became the common practice.

Qianshi had two sons. The elder had a wasting disease, and could do
no work. The younger caught meningitis[206] at age three, and neither
physicians, diviners, shamans, nor exorcists were able to cure him.
Qianshi prayed to the god of the town, Gongsun Zhang 公孫掌,

---

206. Or perhaps epilepsy? *Xian* 癎.

continuously for ten days.[207] Zhang reported this to me, and asked that I save the boy. I acceded to this request.

When I looked into the reason why he had suffered this calamity, I found it was due to forty-odd children abandoned by the tenants and now dwelling in darkness with no home to which they could return; they were cursing him. I appeared in a dream to Qianshi's wife, Madame née Li 李, and told her the reason. Although Madame née Li spoke of this to Qianshi, he did not repent. I then sent the deputy Xun Ming 荀明 to transmit my words, having him speak through the younger son, saying, "To abandon someone else's child is like abandoning your own. Love your own child just as you love the children of others. You covet the labor of others, but despise freeloaders, who expend your grain. Now forty-odd lives are pressing upon those of your sons, and they are about to die." Qianshi castigated himself and changed his ways. Kowtowing until his blood flowed, he asked for my command. I admonished him for his actions, and told him to reform his conduct. Qianshi followed my advice, and his sons were saved. From this time on all the people of the town valued human life and the population gradually increased.

COMMENTARY

In this episode the Divine Lord of Zitong tackles an ethical question that still has relevance today and that has a special significance for China. In order to assure their survival and well-being, the people of Jurao practiced infanticide. The Divine Lord argues against this practice, pointing out that man is to be esteemed over all other creatures possessing souls. He justifies this claim in two ways. He first paraphrases the Kong Anguo commentary to the line in the "Taishi" chapter of the *Scripture of Documents*, "Man is the most spiritual of the ten thousand creatures."[208] He then goes on to make an argument based upon the Buddhist conception of reincarnation, in which one is reborn in a variety of levels from denizen of hell to celestial divinity. Within this cycle man ranks quite high. It is only through many lives

---

207. Following the DZ in reading *jie* 解, "to pause," for *su* 蘇, "to revive."

208. *Shangshu zhengyi* 11/4a. The commentary reads, "Of those things born of Heaven and Earth it is man that is to be esteemed."

of virtuous conduct that one can hope to be reborn in a human body, and misconduct can cause one to descend rapidly to less pleasant states. We recall that when the Divine Lord's mother in his previous incarnation was about to die (ch. 28), among the wisdom that she passed on to him was the statement that "those with no evil karma will not lose their human bodies."

This question of infanticide has a special significance for the Chinese because of the importance placed on providing bountiful progeny to carry on the family line. The need to provide continuing nourishment in the form of sacrifice for the family ancestors, and eventually oneself as well, made this a sacred duty. This ancient belief has presented many problems for modern China's planners in their efforts to restrict population growth. Further, the souls of children abandoned in youth are particularly pitiable. Since they were never accepted as members of the family, they will never have a place on the family ancestral altar. As the Divine Lord expresses it, they have no home.

There is a also an element of hypocrisy in the conduct of the rich landowner, Zhang Qianshi. He forces his tenants to abandon all children after their first son, but he himself has two sons who he hopes will grow to manhood. Unfortunately, they are cursed by the forlorn souls of the dead children of his tenants.[209] Zhang Qianshi tries all the traditional Chinese healing arts, and it is interesting to note that what we would term occult practitioners outnumber physicians three to one. Qianshi then turns to the local representative of the divine bureaucracy, and, through a display of great sincerity, praying continuously for ten days, convinces this individual to aid him. The god of the town then reports to his superior and asks for permission to intercede. The Divine Lord grants this permission, but also conducts his own investigation and turns up the source of the problems. He first tries to reform Qianshi by appearing in his wife's dream, and when this fails, speaks directly to him by possessing his younger son. Here we should note that the Divine Lord does not perform the possession himself. Rather, he sends an underling, who puts the words of the Divine Lord in the boy's mouth. In modern Chinese séances and

---

209. The exact term used is *sui* 祟, denoting a spirit-induced affliction. See Riegel 1982: p. 8 and p. 17, n. 52. For an example of the souls of children who died young of supernatural affliction in the context of Korean shamanism, see Grim 1984: 237.

spirit writing sessions there is also often a relatively low-level spirit who acts as the herald of a great god and conveys his message.

This message has the desired effect and Zhang Qianshi reforms his behavior. The execrable practice of abandoning the newborn, which the Divine Lord compares to mowing down orchids,[210] is discontinued and the population increases, an event that the secular administration always considered highly desirable.

37. *Saving the Drowning* 拯溺

The autumn rain came down in unceasing torrents,
The three rivers flowed together, combining the force of their currents.
Mirror Pool filled and overflowed, limitlessly deep.
The city parapets swayed and toppled, an emergency meriting worry.
The remaining inhabitants of White Horse truly maintain excellent customs,
Huang Gao practices benevolent administration, a worthy marquis.
As soon as Bai Jian rebuked them the waves were calmed,
Who says the alarming torrents would dare destroy his boat?

The town of White Horse (Baima) had a population of over eight hundred and was situated at the mouth of three rivers. The autumn rains fell in torrents, not stopping for three months. The streams in

---

210. Flowers are a well known symbol of children in China. Here there is perhaps a more explicit reference to the "flower fate" (*huaming* 花命). There is a divine garden in which each woman is represented by a flowering tree. Mediums will often travel to this garden and count the number of flowers to determine how many children a woman is fated to have. See Ahern 1974: 287; Potter 1974: 213–14; Topley 1974: 238.

the two valleys to the east and west[211] were swollen, as was the river. The mouth of Numinous Cliff Gorge (Lingyanxia 靈巖峽) choked their flow and they could not run off. The waves swelled and spread. The people were terrified of drowning and fearful of becoming food for the fish.

The god of the town, Bai Jian 柏堅, came to report this to me, saying, "The small town of White Horse used to belong to the Min 岷 area. Now it is appended to Shu. The marquis of the town, Huang Gao 黃高, is benevolent and loves the people. Recently Heaven has sent down torrential rains, harming the vessels of sacrificial millet. Three rivers surround the town, and the lives of the inhabitants are endangered." Since it was on the borders of the area under my control, I went with Jian.

When we arrived, the waters were blocked and overflowing, ten times their normal level. The people were in confusion, like ants moving to a new anthill. Only fifty to sixty percent of the parapets of the city wall were standing. The young were led about or carried but did not reach [safety];[212] the elderly had been abandoned and waited to die. I grieved for them in my heart. So I had Bai Jian transmit the Thearch's rescript, commanding the waters to soak down into the ground and to settle back into their old courses. This is what they refer to now as the "god who rebuked the river" (*heheshen* 喝河神). Because of this, the entire town of several thousand was saved from drowning.

COMMENTARY

Natural disasters could be divine portents visited upon the guilty, as was almost the case with Bao, but they sometimes occurred through carelessness or chance, requiring divine intervention. Here the people of the town of White Horse were threatened by a great flood. This was not a supernatural punishment; the people were good and were ruled by an able and benevolent individual who served the gods faithfully, as shown by the ritual vesssels of grain awaiting sacrifice that the

---

211. DZ reads "to the east and north" or "to the northeast" (*dongbei* 東北).
212. Following the 1645 ed. and DZ in reading *da* 達, "to reach," for *xi* 息, "to rest."

floods destroyed. The god of the town reports the situation to his superior, the Divine Lord of Zitong, who promptly goes to investigate the situation in person. Seeing the people's desperate plight, the Divine Lord authorizes the local deity to command the waters to recede in the name of the Thearch. In this story we see again a concern with administrative geography, and specifically with its use in justifying the intervention of the Divine Lord of Zitong in affairs remote from Zitong.

The epithet earned by the god in this episode, the River-rebuking god, recalls another term applied to him in one of the more famous of his feats. When Wang Renyu, in the tenth century, recorded the tale of how he sunk the entire town of Qiongdu beneath a deluge of water, he called the god "the god who inundated with a river" (*xianheshen* 陷河神). Perhaps this tale is meant to improve the god's image by providing him with a new, more salutary epithet and appropriately heroic explanation of its origins.

38. *Raining Grain*   雨穀

People ask how hidden virtue can be sown,
In all things first cultivate a concern for the masses.
Mister Xu aided the starving until his wealth was almost
    exhausted;
The Luo family refused to sell grain, their stocks so full not a
    pin could be added to them.
To be able to distribute that which you amass is the Way of
    Heaven;
When the prosperous become poor it is because they have been
    invaded by ghosts.
In this one death and one success there is truly a message:
How profound is the design of heavenly Creation.

In the great city of Baxi 巴西 only one or two out of a hundred are rich. The poor toil to pass their days. The Emperor of Shu had just been enthroned, and the harvest was very poor. Although the emperor was parsimonious in expenditures for his own support, and was sincerely devoted to the people, the fragrance of his virtue was not yet evident, and the residual misfortunes (of his ancestors) had not yet abated. The people of Baxi who died from the torments of starvation were especially numerous.

In the town there was a rich farmer, Luo Mi 羅密, who refused to sell his grain, and a man of principles, Xu Rong 許容, who exhausted his wealth in aiding the impoverished. There was no end to those who came to Xu for help. When he could no longer continue, no matter how he strove, he prayed to Heaven through the night with candles and incense, imploring divine help. The town spirit, He Laisun 和來孫, reported this. I memorialized the Supreme Thearch. A rescript commanded that five thousand pecks of the grain stored by Luo be seized and rained down on the town. I then ordered that the Master of the Winds be instructed to blow off Luo's roof. The grain was carried up in the swirling winds and rained down from the sky. It collected in piles according to the variety of grain, speading over all the suburban thoroughfares. There was no one in the town who did not eat his fill. Luo's entire store of grain was exhausted in one day. The people of the town were grateful to Xu for his compassion, and many returned what he had given them. Thanks to Luo's disaster Xu was content. The Emperor of Shu made Xu the Attendant of the town. Hearing this, Luo Mi cut his throat.[213]

COMMENTARY

The Divine Lord of Zitong rewards the good and punishes the evil. The first Emperor of Shu was Du Yu 杜宇.[214] He was a worthy ruler, concerned for his people, but he had yet to perform acts of great merit and bore the burden of the evil actions of his forebears. This concept

---

213. DZ reads *yi* 縊, "strangled or hanged himself."

214. The rulers of Shu traditionally styled themselves "king," thus placing themselves on equal footing with the ruler of the Zhou royal house. When the feudal lords within the Zhou domain began to claim the title of "king," Du Yu made himself emperor (*di* 帝). See *Huayangguo zhi* 3/27.

of inherited moral responsibility is first expressed in one of the appendixes to the *Yijing* (generally thought to be of late Warring States or Early Han date): "A family that accumulates good deeds will certainly have residual good fortune; a family that accumulates evil deeds will certainly have residual misfortune."[215] The result of this ethical indebtedness was natural disasters afflicting the citizens of the Shu state. The harvest was poor, resulting in a famine that struck the northeastern corner of his realm particularly severely.

In the town of Baxi (modern Mianyang, Sichuan), Luo Mi and Xu Rong present a diametric contrast in their response to the crisis. Luo greedily tries to hoard his grain while Xu freely gives of everything that he owns to help the starving. Their names also reflect their basic character, Luo Mi meaning "a fine-meshed net"[216] while Xu Rong means literally "to permit and accept."

When Xu's own resources are exhausted he piously implores Heaven to aid the town. The local god responds, transmitting his request to the Divine Lord, who in turn memorializes the supreme deity, all in proper bureaucratic fashion. When the Thearch, whom the poem refers to as the Creator, approves the distribution of Luo's hoarded grain, the task of implementing the order is delegated to the Master of the Wind, whom we have met previously in our encounter with the great white tiger (ch. 31). He performs magnificently, sorting the grain according to its various varieties and distributing it throughout the area.

The poem asks how one can accumulate hidden virtue (*yinde* 陰德). Hidden virtue is a store of merit (*de*) accumulated in the divine (*yin*) world through charitable or benevolent actions that do not receive immediate temporal recompense. At this point the hidden virtue that Xu Rong has accumulated through his acts of charity begins to manifest itself. All the people he has aided now seek to repay him from their newfound bounty, and the emperor also rewards him with an official post. Luo, on the other hand, is laid destitute, and seeing Xu, whom he no doubt once thought a fool, now rich and successful, commits suicide. All of this, we are told, has taken place according to the secret plan of the Supreme Thearch.

---

215. *Zhouyi zhengyi* 1/26a.

216. Nets are a common metaphor for the law, a loose net representing a lenient system and a fine-meshed net an exacting, unforgiving legal administration.

39. *Diverting the Rain*   曲雨

North of the outskirts of Ju, west of the river Ba,
There is Dragon Mountain, whose heights can be scaled.
Its people have always been completely filial and respectful,
Yet for many years the harvest has been barren, they long for
    clouds and rainbows.
I diverted some propitious moisture to mature the fruits of
    autumn
And save the remaining inhabitants from worry about their
    summer fields.
From this time on the immigrants came in throngs,
Supporting their old people and leading the young.

North of the town of Ju and west of the Ba River there is Dragon
Mountain. Some three hundred-odd households live below Dragon
Mountain. At the beginning of Emperor Wang's reign all of Shu suffered a great drought.[217] The town god, Su Gongchang 蘇公長,
could not bear to see the remaining inhabitants die from the ill-fated
harvests. He took the blame and castigated himself, saying, "Of the
people under my control, the young and mature work strenuously
while the elderly rest; they are not unfilial. The exactions of corvée
labor are not liberal, but they have never dared to complain; they are
not disloyal. When plowing in the spring and planting in the summer thay always sacrifice to Heaven and Earth; when they see a
beautiful field, they mark off square borders and set it aside for the
sacrificial vessels of millet; they are not disrespectful.[218] When they

217. DZ reads "Emperor Can" 蠶帝. Apparently the first Emperor of Shu, mentioned in the
previous chapter was misidentified by the editor of the DZ text as Can Cong, the first King of Shu.
Wang 望, "hope," was the name adopted by Du Yu when he claimed the title of emperor. See *Huayangguo zhi* 3/27. The 1645 ed. reads "the Qin emperor," which makes little sense.

218. DZ reads, "They plow in the spring, plant in the summer, and sacrifice to Heaven and Earth
in the winter; they are not disrespectful," then continues with the following phrase about the establishment of a sacrificial field as a comment on the people's obedience.

have harvested something, they do not venture to first taste it; they are not disobedient. When there is a people who is loyal, filial, respectful, and obedient like this, and yet they are plagued by a drought, they having never slighted me, this is my fault." I transmitted this message to Heaven. There was a command authorizing the terrestrial spirits (*diqi* 地祇) to take care of the matter themselves. I then combined this with my labors at the town of Ju.[219] Borrowing the waters of the Ba River, I diverted the rain and moisture for three days then stopped. The whole region had an autumn harvest. The townspeople named the area Propitious Moisture 嘉澤, and gradually more and more people from other regions came to live there.

COMMENTARY

A virtuous town is saved from an undeserved drought, another of the natural calamities at the beginning of the reign of Du Yu. Again we see that natural disasters are considered to be heavenly punishment for immorality or impiety, and when disasters do not correspond to moral behavior, it is considered anomolous. The people of Dragon Mountain are neither immoral or impious. They are hard-working and respectful of their elders, and acknowledge and carry out their responsibilities to the gods and their rulers. They offer sacrifices to Heaven and Earth at the proper times and set aside their best fields to provide the grain for the sacrifices. They also offer up the first products of their harvest to the ruler.

Confronted with the exemplary character of the people under his jurisdiction and their sad fate, the local god decides that the fault must be his. He criticizes himself (demonstrating the early origins of a practice still in vogue) and asks that the blame be shifted to him. The Divine Lord supports and relays this petition, and permission is granted to the local divine bureaucracy to deal with the matter as it sees fit. The Divine Lord diverts some of the excess moisture from the flooded town of Ju (ch. 37) to Dragon Mountain, the crops are saved, immigrants stream into this virtuous land, and the population booms.

---

219. The 1645 ed. and DZ gives the full name of the town, Jurao. See chapter 37.

---

40.   *Slaying the Bandit*   殂賊

The filial wife toiled to support her mother-in-law,
With a resolution as pure as ice she grieved for her former
   husband.[220]
She foresook cosmetics, others gaped at her.
She contented herself by making a living through needlework.
She buried her mother-in-law with ritual and great grief, had
   just re-sacrificed,
When a cretin in broad daylight suddenly broke in and stole.
It was not only because of her proper virtue that she received
   divine aid,
But also to show that avaricious cruelty is punished by demons.

On the shores[221] of the Han River, there was a filial wife named
Yang Jingzhong 楊靚中, who was the offspring of an official. She
married Yong Youzhang 雍有章, from a poor family, who died
young. She vowed to never remarry. Soon her purse and cupboard
were empty. She had no mate to share in the support of the family,
and her mother-in-law was aged and infirm. Matchmakers came every
day. Jingzhong thought, "People long for only beauty and wealth.
My family was always poor, and I have just met with this great
calamity, yet now there is no limit to the men who seek after me. I
think that it is because I am still in my prime, still have my vigor, and
am free from any evil disease. It is only this that they are seeking.
How could I bear to abandon my mother-in-law in her old age and,
forgetting the husband I married in my youth, change my countenance and serve another? I have never given up my minor skills in
needlework, and by sewing and washing for others I will be able to
provide for myself and my elderly mother-in-law somehow or other.

---

210. Following DZ in reading *nian yuanfu* 念元夫, thought of her original spouse for DZJY *wei
wufu* 爲無夫 because she had no spouse.
    221. The 1645 ed. and DZ consistently read *yuan* 源, "at the source" for *bin* 濱, "on the shore of."

If I have no choice, then it will not be too late if I wait until my mother-in-law has lived out her allotted hundred years (i.e., died) before divining another match." She then cut off her hair and put on a mournful face, forsaking cosmetics and supporting herself with wifely arts. After doing this for six years, her mother-in-law died. She buried her with proper ritual, and on the third day offered sacrifice again. Over a hundred of the people of her village attended. A bandit took advantage of her absence to climb over the wall of her house, pick the lock, and take everything therein. Jingzhong did not yet realize what had happened. The tutelary spirit of her house, Bai Zhiyi 白致一, together with the duly appointed god of the town, Kang Chaosheng 康潮生, wanted to take care of this fellow. I just happened to be in Bao, and they came to me to report.[222] I sent thirty otherworldly troops to capture the bandit. In the marketplace he lifted up all the things he had stolen one by one and announced, "This belongs to the virtuous wife Madam née Yang. It should be returned." When he had finished, he raised his hands, stuffed them in his mouth, and died swallowing all ten fingers.

COMMENTARY

This story has two purposes, as pointed out in the poem: to present an example of the proper conduct of a widow, and to dissuade potential bandits.

Yang Jingzhong is an exemplar of the perfect daughter-in-law and widow. She refuses to remarry in order to care for her ailing mother-in-law. There were both social and religious reasons for opposition to the remarriage of widows. Socially it presented problems concerning the care of the husband's parents, a primary function of the family that we see illustrated in this story. Religiously it presented anomalies in the pattern of ancestral sacrifices concerning the placement of the woman's spirit tablet and where she is to receive sacrifice.[223] Perhaps the closest parallel in the West is the question of which spouse a woman who has married more than once is eventually to be buried with.

These arguments would have had special force for a figure like

---

222. This is the same Bao that the Divine Lord saved in chapter 33.
223. See Jordan 1972: 156–59.

Yang Jingzhong. She was the daughter of an official, and grew up in the world of strictly observed ritual injunctions (*li* 禮). Further, she had married her husband when both had just reached maturity, underwent pinning and capping respectively, and first braided their hair (*jiefa* 結髮).[224] This must have formed a particularly strong bond. She speaks of remarriage contemptuously as "changing her countenance," a reference to the line from the *Yijing* describing a hypocritical sycophant: "The small man changes his countenance and follows obediently in serving his lord."[225] Finally, her husband died early, leaving to her the care of his ailing mother, and this stimulated Yang's filial nature.

Eberhard has argued that elite condemnation of the remarriage of widows began in the thirteenth century, under the influence of Neo-Confucianism, but concedes that the practice continued among the lower classes.[226] The reality of late twelfth-century elite society as reflected in the *Book of Transformations* would seem to have been somewhat more complex. The chaste widow was a praiseworthy exemplar of virtuous conduct and was rewarded with the special favor and protection of the gods, as in the present story. But a variety of pragmatic concerns were also acknowledged. If the widow's parents and parents-in-law were already dead, the woman faced a very real problem of survival. In such a case (ch. 27) the Divine Lord himself arranged a second marriage for the widowed daughter of a deceased colleague. In the present story as well the virtuous widow concedes that in the future she may be forced to remarry to survive.

In any case, Yang resolved to remain chaste at least as long as her mother-in-law remained alive. She supports both of them by sewing, mending, and washing for others, a great humiliation for one of her station, and purposely makes herself unattractive to dissuade suitors.

It is during the course of funeral ceremonies that Yang has arranged at considerable personal expense that her house is burgled. Her virtuous conduct has assured her the protection of the spirits, and before she even knows about the theft two local gods have reported it to the Divine Lord. The tutelary deity (*tudi* 土地) is the primary object of local worship in modern China, and Schipper has shown how a

---

224. At the age of nineteen (by Chinese reckoning) in the case of a woman and twenty in the case of a man.

225. *Yijing zhengyi* 5/20a.

226. Eberhard 1967: 85.

network of temples to these deities serves to define communities.[227] Here the tutelary deity has an even more restricted jurisdiction, being in charge of the household itself. We can assume that Yang has reverently made offerings at an altar to this deity over the years. He is joined in his petition by the deity of the village, who is described as "duly appointed" or "orthodox" (*zheng* 正). This is a significant distinction, and today in Taiwan local tutelary deities are most commonly referred to as the "Duly appointed God of Fortune and Virtue" (*Fude zhengshen* 福德正神). The joint petition is modeled on temporal bureaucratic practice.

In response the Divine Lord dispatches "otherworldly troops" (*yinbing* 陰兵), sometimes also called "divine troops" (*shenbing* 神兵). The poem refers to these nether soldiers as demons (*gui* 鬼), though they have been subjugated and now serve the cause of right. We have seen that the Divine Lord gained control of these fearsome legions as a mortal when he was combatting the epidemic demons (ch. 12), but here they play their more common role as lictors of the divine administration. They seize the miscreant, force him to confess in such a way that Yang will get back all of her possessions, then cause him to commit suicide in a gruesome fashion.

---

41. *The Northern Suburb*   北郭

A man's heir is not a trifling matter,
Only a tree planted in the heart will bear fruit.
If you fret, wanting it to grow fast, this results in clumsiness.
Summoning forth a mountain of worries, how can you be at
    peace?
Planting plants and trees can stand as a metaphor,
Aiding the orphaned and destitute forces one to use one's
    emotions.

---

227. Schipper 1977.

His precious son inherited the household, and was named
    Shenbao (Divinely Protected).
Then he knew that the rewards of virtue are themselves evident.

In the northern suburb of the capital of Shu there was a man
named Wang Shangzhong 王尙忠. He was rich, but had no son, and
had reached the age of forty. Worrying in his heart, he quickly laid
plans. He broadly sought concubines, but in the end they produced
nothing. He also took children of his own lineage as his heirs. But he
was by nature unfair and demanding. If one of his concubines did
some small thing he did not like, he would whip and beat her, or replace her. If one of his adopted sons went against his instructions, he
would drive him out. The more desperately he schemed, the more
careless his planning became. The months and seasons followed one
after the other, and soon he was approaching the half-century mark.
He thereupon set forth a great feast and invited all the notables. The
invocations and dances of male and female shamans continued for
more than a month. I transformed into a recluse and spoke to him,
saying, "When growing pears or plums, after having planting and
ringed the tree, you water it; before long you prune it hoping that it
will grow faster, then you transplant it and add fertilizer; before the
appointed time you pluck out its roots to see if it is healthy; seeing
that its leaves and branches flourish, you again take it out and, dis-
carding the old soil, again transplant it. Thus you are too attentive,
and in the end it will bear no fruit. Can this be said to be wise?" He
answered, "It cannot." I said, "In what way is your search for progeny
different from this? I now urge you to give your mind and body a
rest. Reform your former behavior. Be generous in dealing with the
labor of others, forgive their faults. Keep those maidservants and concubines whom you can support, and marry off those you cannot.
Once a child of your lineage has abandoned those who gave him
birth and called you father, make firm your initial resolve, ignore his
minor failings. When someone in your household has a child, do not
entertain thoughts of abandoning it. Help people avoid death, aid
them in their adversities, assist them when destitute, and take pity on
them when orphaned. Practice this wholeheartedly and listen to the

commands of Heaven. If you do so for three years, there will certainly be a good response." When I had finished speaking, I turned invisible and disappeared. Shangzhong believed my words, taking them as a divine warning. Afterwards he married off thirteen of his maidservants, took wives for his two adopted sons, then set them up in other professions so that they would have long-term prospects. He buried the parents of over fifty poor people and arranged for the marriage of over eighty poor couples. Within three years[228] he obtained his precious heir, whom he named Shenbao 神保 ("Divinely Protected"). When he reached adulthood, Shenbao succeeded to his father's business.

COMMENTARY

In this episode the Divine Lord teaches the proper way to seek progeny through good works.

Wang Shangzhong, living on the northern outskirts of the city of Chengdu, is blessed with wealth, but no son to carry on his line and offer sacrifice to him after his death. He tries a variety of methods to obtain an heir, establishing a large harem of concubines and adopting the sons of other members of his lineage in order to "lead in" a natural son. This practice of adopting a first child in order to facilitate the birth of natural children is still practiced in Taiwan.[229] These methods are all ineffective because of a basic moral failing on Wang's part: he is too severe and lacking in kindness. Finally he resorts to a grand religious festival replete with shamanic dances and rituals that lasts over a month, at what must have been prodigious expense, failing to see that the basic requirement for happiness in general and progeny in particular is moral in nature. The Divine Lord of Zitong appears at the festival in the guise of a sage from the mountains, and teaches him the proper approach through a homily based on agriculture that is rather Daoist in character: overattention can kill a tree rather than help it grow.[230] The solution is a program of charitable works starting with

---

228. Following the 1645 ed. and DZ in reading *nei* 內, "within," for *hou* 後, "after."

229. See Wolf 1972: 151–52.

230. This story recalls the tale of Hundun, the seamless amorphous mass of undifferentiated chaos, whom someone decided to aid by drilling orifices. When the seventh had been drilled Hundun died. See *Zhuangzi* 21/7/34–35.

Wang's own concubines and adopted sons and extending to disadvantaged members of the community. Wang proceeds to perform a
succession of good works, for which he is rewarded with a natural son
who grows up to succeed as head of the family and the family business.

This story reveals the Divine Lord in a new role: the provider of
progeny. It is not surprising that he should manifest this ability because he himself often incarnates as the child of worthy individuals,
both in the *Book of Transformations* and in later legends.[231] But the
primary reason for the attribution of this specialization to the Divine
Lord seems to be a merging with the cult to a local Chengdu god, Transcendent Zhang 張仙. The first reference to this god places his cult in
the Five Dynasties period.[232] Su Xun 蘇洵 (1009–1066), in an "appreciation" (*zan*), mentions that the god is called Master Zhang of the
Northern Ramparts.[233] This is the title used by the Divine Lord of
Zitong in this and the next several chapters. It is no doubt significant
that the events in this chapter, which center on the quest for progeny,
take place in just this suburb of Chengdu and that the chapter itself is
named for the area. Progeny was to remain a prominent feature of the
cult, and as late as the Qing a scripture was published linking Transcendent Zhang and the Divine Lord as a single god specializing in
the provision of sons.[234]

231. For example, his first two incarnations, recorded in chapters 2 and 21, above, fall into this
category, as does the story related by Liu Zhiwan of the man who is rewarded by the Divine Lord for
his parsimony with foodstuffs in a similar manner. See Liu 1984: 129.

232. It is said that Madame Flower Pistil (Huarui furen 花蕊夫人) took along a picture of her
former husband, the Latter Shu ruler Meng Chang, when she entered the Song harem. When the
picture was discovered she claimed it was Transcendent Zhang, a god of progeny. Zhao Yi rightly
discounts this legend, but other sources trace the cult back to a man who lived during the Five
Dynasties, and it seems that the cult is at least that old. See *Gaiyu congkao* 35/20b–22a.

233. I have been unable to find this appreciation in any collection of the writings of the Sus, but it
is quoted in a stele dated 1587, "Record of the Wenchang Shrine" ("Wenchangci ji" 文昌祠記), in the
1771 illustrated *Wenchang huashu* 1/9b.

234. See *Wenchang yinghua Zhang xian da zhenren shuo zhusheng yansi miaoying zhenjing*, preserved
in *Daozang jiyao*, sub *xing*.

42. *Turning Back the Fire*   反火

Siblings originally belong to the same branch,
How can they, from neighboring territories, spy on each other?
The Marquis of Ju desired profit, his emotions are hard to
    fathom.
The King of Shu esteemed his clan, had no doubts about
    himself.
Fierce flames reaching the sky were just at their most fearsome
When a strong wind blew across the earth, and (the arsonists)
    were themselves endangered.
From out of the sky a clear voice set out the true situation,
Only then did (the marquis) believe that the gods cannot be
    deceived.

The ruler of Shu, Yufu 魚鳧, had a younger brother, Jiameng 葭
萌, whom he enfeoffed at Ju 苴, becoming the Marquis of Ju. After
some time had passed, Ju sent an emissary seeking gifts. The ruler of
Shu did not respond. Thereupon the marquis sent men to burn the
Shu storehouse. Just when the fire was blazing I heard about this. I
ordered the Master of the Winds to turn back the fire, and clearly
proclaimed the immoral character of Ju. In an instant the emissaries
of Ju all died in the conflagration. After this, Ju and Shu fought for
three years but Ju was finally unable to overcome Shu.

COMMENTARY

Here the Divine Lord intercedes on the side of orthodox authority
and familial seniority. Siblings are supposed to act according to the
principle of *ti* 悌 or brotherly affection, whereby a younger brother
owes an elder brother respect and the elder owns the younger concern
and care. The King of Shu is mindful of these obligations, but his
younger brother, Jiameng, is not. When Jiameng sends a commando
unit of saboteurs, the Divine Lord foils their plans. Again he employs

the Master of Winds (as in ch. 38) to blow the fire back on the arsonists, in a manner very similar to that in chapter 34.

Standard histories present a somewhat different view of the conflict
between Shu and Ju. The *Huayangguo zhi* attributes the events to the
reign of King Wenhui 文惠 of Qin (r. 337–311 B.C.) and King Xian
顯 of Zhou (r. 368–321 B.C.). There the rift is traced to a personal
relationship between the Marquis of Ju and the ruler of Ba, traditional
enemy of Shu. It was this perhaps traitorous relationship that led the
King of Shu to attack Ju. Ju responded by asking for help from the
state of Qin, and Qin subsequently conquered and obliterated
Shu.[235] The events leading up to this eventual conquest are described
below, in later chapters of the *Book of Transformations.*

---

43. *Pacifying Ju*   平苴

The Marquis of Ju established a state called Jiameng,
He gave no thought to the fact that Yufu was his sibling.
He invaded with halberds and armor, the people died violently.
Though sharing a border, they contested in vain.
A reliable emissary was employed to discuss the situation,
I made divine troops appear to demonstrate the gravity of the
    situation.
The town of Jia in one morning submitted to righteousness,
I was able to spare the common people the mud and ash [of
    war].

Once ill-feeling had arisen between Ju and Shu, armed conflict continued a long time. The ruler of Shu wearied of this, and dispatched
an emissary, Zhuang Su 莊甦, to talk peace. The Marquis of Ju did
not listen. So Zhuang Su said, "The troops of Shu are numerous,"

---

235. See *Huayangguo zhi* 1/3 and 3/29; *Huayangguo zhi jiaozhu* 1/32 and 3/191–92.

and pointed to the western corner of the city. I then shocked the marquis by manifesting divine troops. The Marquis of Ju thought that the attack had already succeeded and pleaded for a conclave. The emissary related these events to the Shu king and he established a temple to me north of the capital.

COMMENTARY

The Divine Lord of Zitong acts to resolve a conflict between brothers and assure the triumph of the rightful ruler. As elder brother and king, Yufu clearly is owed obedience and loyalty, but the Marquis of Ju is oblivious to these ties of kinship and allegiance. The enmity between the two brothers is exacting a frightful cost from the populace, and the King of Shu, unable to bear the burden of this in good conscience, sues for peace. When the Marquis of Ju refuses this entreaty the Divine Lord is ready to step in, sending a cohort of the fell soldiers of the netherworld to frighten him into submission. The strategem works and the Divine Lord is rewarded with a sacred dwelling, a temple, and sacrifices. This is the first mention of a cult to the Divine Lord, and it is perhaps significant that it is associated with the northern suburbs of Chengdu, the site of the planchette sessions in which this book was revealed. This chapter is the second of a series related to the Transcendent Zhang cult, discussed in the commentary to the previous chapter.

44. *The Fei Stalwarts*   費丁

Though speaking forthrightly while alive may lead to disaster,
The spirit that survives the body will be shamed by keeping
   silent like a tied sack.[236]

---

236. An allusion to the fourth line of the Kun 坤 hexagram of the *Yijing*, which reads, "A tied sack. No reproach, no praise." The Kong Yingda (574–648) subcommentary notes, "It is like hiding knowledge in the heart. You shut up the knowledge and do not use it." Xunzi comments on the same passage that it refers to "a dissolute Confucian (*furu* 腐儒)." See *Yijing zhengyi* 1/24b; *Xunzi* 14/5/44.

The ruler favored the Five Stalwarts and forgot military
  preparedness;
Comparing them to the three Di barbarians, I protested in a
  sealed memorial.
Just because they transported earth to build up the concubine's
  tomb,
He did not believe that military discussions were more powerful
  in repelling the enemy.[237]
They said that my devilish words were unworthy of
  consideration.
When they then destroyed my temple, what harm did this do to
  me?

A sprite of Wudu Mountain 武都山精 transformed into a girl, whose beauty and allure were without parallel in Shu. This was reported to King Kaiming Shang 開明尚王, who granted her audience and, delighted with her, made her his concubine.[238] Before long she died. The king longed for her unceasingly. He built a tomb, making it high in order to show his resolve not to forget her. The Five Stalwarts of the Fei clan 費氏五丁, giants from Wudu, used this to captivate the king. With their great strength they hauled the earth of Wudu Mountain to build up the tumulus. Soon the tomb was as high as a mountain. The king named it Wudan Mountain (武擔山, "the mountain hauled from Wudu"),[239] saying that after her death the concubine longed for her native earth. Thereafter the king drew the five close to him and trusted them. They daily[240] waited on his person and never left his presence for an instant. The king was also physically strong and relied on his bravery. Having obtained the Five

237. Following DZ in reading *qiang* 彊, "strong," for *jiang* 彊, "border."
238. Following the 1645 ed., DZ, and SG. DZJY reads only King Kaiming 開明王. Kaiming Shang is one of a succession of kings surnamed Kaiming we find mentioned in some sources. He is variously reported to be the fifth or ninth in that line. See *Huayangguo zhi* 3/28; *Huayangguo zhi jiaozhu* 3/ 185–86, esp. n. 4.
239. For Wudu DZ has Wukai 武楷, which is otherwise unknown and perhaps a scribal error for Wudan.
240. Following the 1645 ed., DZ, and SG in reading *ri* 日, "daily," for *dan* 且, "morning."

Stalwarts, he said he could withstand halberds and spears with his bare hands and run faster than an enemy chariot or horseman. Afterwards he neglected border preparedness, even going so far as to withdraw the outposts and abandon the watchtowers. Since I was his god and enjoyed his bloody sacrifice, and because we shared a border with mighty Qin and I feared something unexpected might happen, I transformed into a scholar and, calling myself Master Zhang of the Northern Ramparts, knocked at the gate of the palace to present a memorial. It said, in essence, "Your servant has heard that those who rely solely on virtue flourish, while those who rely solely on might perish. We have a clear record of the names of officials at court when, of old, Yao, Shun, Yu, and Tang ruled the world, and there was not one who relied solely on physical might. Moreover,[241] the courage of a common fellow is insufficient to rely on and a skill surpassing all others is not enough to cow the enemy. Elai and Feilian could not save the Shang king Xin; Yi's archery and Ao's boat could not save them from unnatural deaths. More recently, the giants of the three Di tribes have been very powerful, but in the end they were exterminated. Now these five brothers from the Fei clan on the border were from the start lacking in virtue, and take physical strength as their occupation. You, King, think them worthy because of their imposing physical stature and neglect military preparedness. Your servant is of the opinion that the strength of a member of the Fei clan may perhaps be able to withstand that of ten other men, but when faced with a hundred would be useless. If you place them among the stewards of the pavilions or make of them grooms and charioteers so that they can drive and shoot with bared arms, running about to obey your commands, then this would be appropriate. If you use them to deflect the attacks of neighboring states, then this is impermissible. If forced to say who they may be compared to, it would be nothing greater than the three tribes of Di barbarians, Red, White, and Tall. Your servant would hope that you will apply yourself to the auspicious foundation of the former kings and strengthen the border precautions against mighty Qin. Do not for the sake of a common fellow's courage

---

241. DZ reads *dan* 但, "however," for *qie* 且, "moreover." Both readings are possible in context.

allow the command of the three armies to grow lax." The king was displeased, and said, "You remonstrate that I should apply myself to military preparedness yet reprimand me for nurturing talented knights. This is like wanting to hunt and doing without hawks, warning against bandits and dispensing with dogs." I argued forcefully for my position. At the time the Five Stalwarts were in front of me. Relying on the king's favor, they wanted to abuse me. I disappeared. The Five Stalwarts took me for a demon (*yao* 妖). They further said, "He must have been Zhang Zhongzi of the northern Ramparts." Thereupon they destroyed my temple image.[242] I did not try to stop them.

COMMENTARY

In this episode the Divine Lord displays his loyalty to the local temporal government under his supervision. He appears before the king to try to dissuade him from a disastrous course of action much as a civil official might. It would seem that the god's power is limited with regard to the legitimate temporal ruler. He can warn and counsel, but cannot impose his views on those at the pinnacle of this-worldly power.

With this chapter we enter into a section of the *Book of Transformations* which makes use of the legendary history of the ancient kingdom of Shu. The ruler is the king, Kaiming. Although no reference is made to it in this work, he is elsewhere identified with Bieling 鱉靈, around whom several legends revolve. It is said that after Bieling died in the Chu region, his corpse floated up the Yangzi River to Shu, where he revived and was made Chancellor by King Du Yu 杜宇. Bieling went on to subdue a great flood and cut channels for the rivers of Shu, like a local Yu the Great. Du Yu is then said to have yielded the throne to him.[243]

Another legend dealing with King Kaiming is that of the sprite (*jing* 精) from Wudu who entranced the king. The earliest version of this occurs in the *Annals of the Kings of Shu* (*Shuwang benji* 蜀王本記) of Yang Xiong 揚雄 (53 B.C.–A.D. 18):[244]

---

242. DZ reads, "destroyed my temple image."
243. See *Huayangguo zhi* 12/206; *Huayangguo zhi jiaozhu* 12/896, 898–99, n. 6; *Fengsu tongyi tongjian*, pp. 74 and 98.
244. Quoted in the Tang commentary to *Hou Hanshu* 82A/2708. Cf. Ngo 1976: 81.

A full-grown man of Wudu transformed into a girl whose features were beautiful beyond compare. It was a mountain sprite. The King of Shu took her in as his concubine. Before long she died. Soldiers were dispatched to Wudu to transport earth, and she was buried within the outer city walls of Chengdu. The place was called Wudan, and her grave was marked with a stone mirror.

Wudu Mountain is thirty li north of modern Mianzhu 綿竹. Wudan Mountain lies within the old city walls in the northwest corner of Chengdu, and is over twenty meters high, over one hundred meters long, and thirty to forty meters wide.[245] Its construction was thus a prodigious feat, expecially if, as all the legends agree, the earth was moved from so far away.

A later version of the legend, recorded in the fourth-century *Huayangguo zhi*, is the first to associate this feat with the Five Stalwarts.[246] They are said to have erected a large stone mirror on the top of the tumulus. Another legend says that they erected a huge stele thirty feet high and weighing thirty-thousand catties on the tomb of each ruler of Shu when he died.[247] We will see that in succeeding chapters two other legends concerning these five goliaths are adopted and adapted to express the Divine Lord's ethical teachings.

The Five Stalwarts may once have been heroes to the people of Shu, but in the *Book of Transformations* they are foolish, violent brutes, to be righteously opposed by upright officials. The Divine Lord is concerned because the king is so taken with these five that he thinks to defend the state solely through their might, ignoring the complex system of armed forces, reinforced outposts, and watchtowers that characterized military planning at this time.[248] In his memorial arguing against the employment of the Five Stalwarts the Divine Lord makes reference to several figures from antiquity. Fei Lian 蜚廉 and Elai 惡來 were a father and son team who aided King Zhou 紂王, the last Shang king also known as Xin 辛. Fei Lian was said to be adept at running and Elai was renowned for his strength.[249] King Zhou was

---

245. *Huayangguo zhi jiaozhu* 3/188–89.
246. *Huayangguo zhi* 3/28; *Huayangguo zhi jiaozhu* 3/188–89.
247. *Huayangguo zhi* 3/28; *Huayangguo zhi jiaozhu* 3/185.
248. This must have seemed particularly relevent in twelfth-century Sichuan, which was the the first line of defense against the Liao, Jin, and Mongol forces.
249. *Shiji* 5/174. Fei Lian was the ancestor of the state of Qin, making this a particularly apt example.

driven from the throne and killed despite their help. The example of Yi 羿 and Ao 奡 is taken from a comment made by Nangong Kua 南宮适 to Confucius: "Yi was adept at archery and Ao could beach a boat; neither died a natural death."[250] Yi is said to have killed the Xia king and usurped the throne; another myth has him shooting nine of the ten suns that were once scorched the earth. Yi was killed by his disciple Han Zhuo 寒浞. Ao was Han's son and was so powerful he could push a boat on land, but he was killed by the next Xia king, Shaokang 少康. The various Di 狄 tribes posed a constant problem for the Zhou state and were known for their imposing stature. The Tall Di, in particular, were variously said to tower thirty or one hundred feet in height.[251] Despite these examples of the inadequacy of physical prowess the King of Shu is not convinced and continues on his doomed path.

To the best of my knowledge, this episode is the sole source to attribute the surname Fei to the Five Stalwarts. This is particularly interesting because Fei was a traditional surname of the Qin ruling house. It was Great Fei 大費 who aided Yu in the great hydraulic enterprise and received in recognition the clan name Ying 嬴 by which the family was known in Eastern Zhou times. Great Fei's second son, Ruomu 若木, first bore the clan name Fei and his descendants are said to live both among the Chinese and non-Chinese. If this element of the story represents some ancient local tradition that escaped recording in surviving sources, we might wonder if these Fei Stalwarts do not in some sense represent the entry of Fei-surnamed immigrants from the north as a prelude to the eventual Qin invasion and colonization.

250. *Lunyu* 27/14/5; *Lunyu zhushu* 14/2a.
251. *Chunqiu Zuozhuan zhengyi*, Wen 11, 19B/2a–b.

45. *The Stone Oxen*   石牛

Ba and Shu attack each other; Shu is rich and strong.
The men of Qin desire Shu, craftily they plan.
It is not that Xiaohui was good at plotting,
From this time on Kaiming was careless in his thinking.
They ground stone to make oxen, set them below the
  mountain;
Then melted gold to make feces and hid them by the tails.
Craving wealth, the king did not heed loyal words of
  remonstrance;
Cutting through a road and dispatching troops, he brought
  about later disaster.

The Zhou house was gradually declining and the feudal lords fought among themselves. There was a rift in the relations between Ba and Shu. Shu shared a border with Qin. King Hui 惠王 adopted the scheme of Sima Cuo 司馬錯, plotting to swallow up Shu. But the road to Shu was extremely perilous, and there was no route by which to move troops. So he had boulders on the border between Qin and Shu carved into the shape of oxen of great size. They were placed among the bushes in five locations and gold was melted[252] into cakes and placed below the tails. Someone was assigned to covertly observe them. In something over a month men had taken them all away. Soon they were replaced, and men came frequently to collect them. When the King of Shu heard of this he sent a man to observe the place. In the course of several months the king collected over a thousand catties of gold. He then commanded the Five Stalwarts to cut a road through the passes and mobilized five thousand troops to bring the stone oxen back. The day that he dispatched the troops I again transformed into a scholar and, calling myself Zhonggong Zichang

---

252. Following the 1645 ed., DZ, and SG in reading *rong* 鎔, "to melt," for *zhu* 鑄, "to cast."

仲弓子長, went to the palace to request an audience, which the king granted.[253] I then submitted a memorial saying, "To open the road is not convenient; to obtain gold is not beneficial." The king, laughing, said to me, "Heaven does not love the Way; Earth does not love treasure. I am in charge of the spirits of the altars to soil and millet. The stone oxen that shit gold have come into my territory of themselves. Gold is the supreme treasure. It can enrich the state, strengthen the army, and ease the people's condition. You are truly worrying too much to think that it might be the plot of a neighboring state. Who would launch a plot by giving away several thousand catties of gold? Please wait a moment, sir. The stone oxen will soon be here." I turned my face to Heaven and screamed, then burst into tears. The king thought I was an inauspicious omen and had his attendants carry me out. I then disappeared.

COMMENTARY

The Divine Lord tries to save Shu from a cunning scheme of Qin. His loyal protests fail to move the King of Shu and the way is prepared for Shu's eventual subjugation and destruction at the hands of Qin.

The background for the decision of King Hui of Qin to invade Shu is found in the biography of Zhang Yi 張儀 in the *Shiji.* Shu and Ju were fighting and both requested aid from Qin. At the same time the state of Han 韓 invaded. The king was torn between two possible courses of action: an invasion of Shu to the south or an invasion of the state of Han and the royal Zhou kingdom to the east. Zhang Yi argued for the eastern expedition, maintaining that it was better for Qin to attack the Zhou heartland, seize the Son of Heaven and his imperial regalia, and thereby attain hegemony over the other states rather than waste its energies battling with a barbarian state on the western extremity of civilization. Sima Cuo took the opposite position. He pointed out that Shu could be easily taken and would supply

---

253. DZ omits the final phrase of this sentence. The name is a cipher for Zhang Zhongzi. "Chang" and "gong" combine to form the surname Zhang. The name of the messianic figure Li Hong 李弘 was often revealed in a similar fashion as Muzi Gongkou 木子弓口. See Seidel 1969–70, esp. pp. 237, 239. A more contemporary figure is Lü Dongbin 呂洞賓, who often reveals his identity in just such an enigmatic fashion. On Lü, see Baldrian 1986.

material wealth and valiant warriors, whereas an attack on the Zhou heartland would be sure to destroy the reputation of the Qin state and rouse the other states to common action against it. The king was convinced by Sima Cuo's arguments and invaded Shu, eventually demoting the King of Shu to marquis and installing a chancellor of Qin origin to control the region.[254]

One of King Hui's doubts about attacking Shu was the difficulty of moving troops through the mountain passes that separate the two regions. Through the stratagem of the gold-shitting oxen he was able to get Shu to open a road for him. The *Huayangguo zhi* contains an early version of this tale:[255]

> During the time of King Xian 顯 (r. 368–321 B.C.) of Zhou the King of Shu possessed the territory of Bao and Han. Once when he was hunting in a valley there[256] he encountered King Hui of Qin. King Hui presented the King of Shu with a scoop of gold and the king responded with some valuable trinkets. These turned into earth and King Hui was angry, but his company of officials congratulated him, saying, "Heaven is making a present to us. Your Highness will obtain the land of Shu." King Hui was pleased. He had five stone oxen made. Each morning gold was strewn behind them and they said, "The oxen shit gold." One hundred soldiers were assigned to attend to the oxen. The people of Shu took delight in them and sent an emissary to ask for the oxen. King Hui acceded to this request. They then sent the Five Stalwarts to bring the stone oxen back. When they did not shit gold, the people of Shu were angry, and sent them back. They derided the men of Qin, calling them "eastern calf herders." The men of Qin laughed at them, saying, "Though we herd calves, we will possess Shu."

Although this account in *Huayangguo zhi* would seem to be the ultimate source of this tale, there was probably a more directly related tale circulating orally in Sichuan during the Song.

---

254. *Shiji* 70/2281–84.
255. *Huayangguo zhi* 3/28; *Huayangguo zhi jiaozhu* 3/187–88. An earlier, shorter version was found in the now lost *Shuwang benji* of Yang Xiong, quoted in *Yiwen leiju* 94/1626.
256. No doubt Bao valley. See the commentary to chapter 33.

---

46.   *The Five Wives*   五婦

The people of Qin coveted Shu and wanted to annex it.
When the road through the passes was complete they could
    enter the Gate of Shu.
Still fearing that the stone oxen would reveal their treacherous
    plan,
They also sent women of the imperial clan, promising them in
    marriage.
[The king] did not consider that a great state makes a difficult
    mate,
Foolishly he thought that they possessed some sincerity.
I knew from the start[257] that my grating words would be
    wasted,
But to maintain my silence would have betrayed my lord's
    favor.

Once the stone oxen had been brought back, the King of Qin said,
"This was sufficient to open the road, but if once the oxen are brought
back to Shu there is no gold, my plan will fail." So he sent a man to
contract marriage with Shu, saying, "Qin and Shu are neighbors. To
draw close to the benevolent and treat neighbors well is a constant
principle of propriety. I have five women of the royal clan whom I
would like to marry to the King of Shu. Please, King, accept them."
The King of Shu was delighted. When I heard of this I sighed, saying, "Qin is a mighty state. How can it be right that we accept these
things." The king sent the Five Stalwarts to welcome the women at
the border. Every day[258] the king waited with a thousand chariots in
the northern suburb to hear their voices and see their faces. I appeared
among his guards in the form of a scholar and personally submitted a

---

257. Following the 1645 ed. and DZ in reading *gu* 固 for the homophonous *gu* 故.
258. Following the 1645 ed., DZ, and SG in reading *ri* 日, "daily," for *zi* 自, "personally."

memorial remonstrating against this. The king angrily said, "Are you not Zhang Zhongzi of the Northern Ramparts? With slanderous words you have insulted me three times." He ordered his attendants to put me to the sword. I manifested a wrathful appearance, the guards were startled and fled, and I escaped harm.

COMMENTARY

The Divine Lord continues his campaign to save the state of Shu from rash King Kaiming and his favorite musclemen. The King of Qin has succeeded in his plan to tempt Shu into building a road by which he could invade Shu. Now he fears that his ruse will be discovered and seeks to further distract the King of Shu by offering him five women from his own family, no doubt chosen for their beauty and allure. It is standard practice to portray the last ruler of a house as a dissolute sex fiend, the prototype being King Zhou of Shang, so care must be used in assessing the historicity of any such story.

The Divine Lord again appears to the king as a scholar in order to dissuade him from this benighted course of action. The king pays him no heed, and it is only through his transformation into a terrifying apparition that the Divine Lord is able to escape. For the historical antecedents of this tale, see the following chapter.

47. *Manifesting My Numinous Power*   顯靈

My loyal heart could not bear to see Qin invade Shu,
Forcefully I remonstrated my lord, but on the contrary was
   reviled.
At first I hoped that my angry appearance would frighten the
   neighboring enemies,
But suddenly Jade Tones ordered my huge form hidden.

The road curved[259] seven times before my journey was done,
The mountain crushed the several souls, their lives were all
   extinguished.
From this time the region knew to revere and respect me.
South of Swordridge my fame and power already blazed
   dazzlingly.

When the Five Stalwarts brought the Qin women back, they were greeted by a horde of thousands of the inhabitants of Shu, both young and old, all blind to the disastrous consequences. Mistaking right for wrong and disaster for success is a common failing of the masses. On the south side of Swordridge I transformed into a gigantic form and cut off the road, thinking to frighten the Qin women and cause them to turn their carriages around. The onlookers from Qin and Shu were terrified. In the midst of the clamor and commotion I heard the Jade Tones speak thus: "That which Heaven would cast down cannot be raised, such is the King of Shu; that which Heaven would raise up cannot be cast down, such is the King of Qin. You are truly sincere and loyal, but what can you do about the Mandate of Heaven?" I thereupon shrank my form. Soon the Five Stalwarts noticed me and said, "This must be the God of the Northern Ramparts, Zhang Zhongzi." I was about to pounce on them and eat them when the cries of the multitude shook the mountains and streams. The Five Stalwarts chased me. I moved through the mountain on my stomach, my path forming seven turns. As I was about to enter a cave the Stalwarts caught up to me and grabbed me. I was desperate, and having no other recourse, transformed my body until it was one hundred times its normal size. I let them pull and drag me. Soon my head broke through the peak of the mountain and my refulgent brilliance streamed back at them, shaking and knocking them over. The mountain moved with my body. The Five Stalwarts and the Qin women had all come to a place below a cliff and the mountain teetered above them. The Five Stalwarts and five women

---

259. Here the 1645 ed. reads *qian* 蹇, DZ reads *yu* 迂, and DZJY reads *huan* 還. All mean something like "to curve, to double back."

all sank into the earth. Afterwards, when Shu was annexed by Qin, I had no regrets.

COMMENTARY

The Divine Lord again tries to save Shu by foiling Qin's plan to bewitch the king and subvert the state. But ultimately the will of Heaven is revealed and he is forced to accept it. This episode demonstrates both the virtue of loyalty and the necessity to accept fate.

As the five beauties of the Qin royal clan are approaching the border, the Divine Lord makes one last valiant attempt to forestall disaster. He appears as a terrifying, huge snake that blocks their path.[260] This is the first attempt on the Divine Lord's part to use his supernatural powers to directly influence these events. He is stopped in his tracks by a voice from Heaven. This divine sound, as mellifluous as the tones of jade chimes, makes manifest to him Heaven's intention: Qin is fated to subjugate Shu and go on to unify the empire. The Divine Lord is commended for his admirable sentiments of loyalty to his temporal ruler and state, but it is pointed out that nothing he could do as a relatively low-level earth spirit could alter the course of events ordained by the Mandate of Heaven. It is this same Mandate of Heaven that was first employed to justify the Zhou conquest and was later used to legitimize each new ruling dynasty. Qin now possesses the Mandate.

Obediently, the Divine Lord shrinks to normal size and is about to slink away when he is spotted and recognized by the Five Stalwarts, who are anxious to revenge themselves upon him for his previous opposition to their rise to eminence. He thinks to attack them but is startled by the reaction of the crowd, and flees. They pursue him, and as he slithers along he cuts into the side of the mountain the serpentine path that will eventually give it its name, Sevenfold Mountain. As he is on the point of reaching safety, the Five Stalwarts catch up to him and seize his tail. He responds by swelling up to gigantic size again, until his form fills the entire mountain, and he brings it crashing down upon the heads of the Five Stalwarts and the prospective brides from Qin.

---

260. It is interesting that nowhere in this chapter is it explicitly stated that it is in the form of a snake that the deity reveals himself, though this is clear from the description of his actions, as well as from the original legend cited below.

The legend this section is based on is quite old, first recorded in the following passage from the fourth-century *Huayangguo zhi*:

In the twenty-second year of King Xian of Zhou (349 B.C.), the Marquis of Shu sent an envoy to pay court to Qin. King Hui of Qin (337–311 B.C.) had repeatedly presented the marquis with beautiful women, and it was because the King (*sic*) of Shu was grateful for this that he paid court to him.[261] King Hui knew that the King of Shu was enamored of the fairer sex, and gave five of his daughters in marriage to Shu. Shu sent the Five Stalwarts to meet and escort them back. Reaching Zitong they saw a large snake entering a cave. One man grasped its tail, but could not arrest it. Then all five combined their might, heaving on the snake with a great yell. The mountain collapsed, crushing to death the five men along with the five Qin women, a general and attendants. The mountain split into five ridges, and on the topmost peak there was a flat stone. The King of Shu grieved for them, and, climbing to the top of this stone, named the mountain the Burial Mound of the Five Wives Mountain. The top of the stone is Watching for Wives Lookout, and there he built a Longing for Spouses Tower. Now the mountain is sometimes called Burial Mound of the Five Stalwarts.[262]

Since this legend was already associated with the town of Zitong in the fourth century, and was probably already linked to the snake cult on Sevenfold Mountain outside Zitong, it is one of the earliest pieces of lore concerning the future Divine Lord of Zitong. In the *Book of Transformations* it is given a moralistic interpretation that may not have been part of the original legend. The Five Stalwarts seem to be local heroes, and are also known for having erected massive stele or gravemarkers for the former kings of Shu, but many of the projects they are involved in lead to the ruin of the state. The snake is a vio-

---

261. The two titles employed to refer to the ruler of the state of Shu reflect different standards of orthodoxy. In Chinese political theory the Zhou king was the only king and all local leaders received enfeoffments from him. In practice states outside the Central Plain, like Shu, probably always referred to their leaders as "kings," but Zhou sources sought to preserve the unique status of the Zhou king by assigning them feudal ranks subordinate to him. Within this system the ruler of Shu held the title of Marquis. But as Zhou power waned individual states within the heartland came to claim the title of "king" as well, and the kingly titles of the peripheral states became more acceptable.

262. *Huayangguo zhi* 3/29; *Huayangguo zhi jiaozhu* 3/190. For comments on this passage, see the Commentary to the translation of chapter 47 of the *Book of Transformations*.

lent, demonic killer, but his actions ultimately advance the interests of Shu. Here virtuous intent is explicitly attributed to the snake by an unimpeachable source, the Thearch, thus reinterpreting this fundamental element of cult lore so that it accords with the evolving identity of the god of Zitong.

48. *The Grand Elixir* 大丹

Master Lao wearied of the wars of the Central Plain.
Ascending into the West, he happily journeyed to convert the barbarians.[263]
Amidst the clouds the chariots and horsemen stretched a thousand li,
The local gods that he passed accompanied him ten days' journey.
When killing, my heart was fixed on the public good; the guilt dissolved of itself.
Swallowing the elixir with a focused mind, my body became light.
The Northwest is not my place to submerge into Perfection,
I will live in the southwest corner and comfort the masses.

Because Shu had been destroyed, the altars to soil and grain had changed, the sacrifices to the many spirits had been abandoned, and there was no place to turn for bloody sacrifice. I roamed in spirit to Kongtong 崆峒 to rest and relax. Suddenly on the cloudy pathways there was a procession of banners, pennants, carriages, and horsemen, which streamed past me for three days. The mountain spirits, speaking among themselves, concluded, "With a display like this there

---

263. Following the 1645 ed. and DZ in reading *hu* 胡, "barbarian," for *gu* 故 , "reason."

must be a holy sage passing by." Then Laozi 老子 passed, with two Perfected in attendance, traveling from east to west. I saluted him from my place among the ranks of earth spirits under the direction of the Western Marchmount. The Western Marchmount had commanded all the terrestrial spirits to pay obeisance to Laozi and accompany him for ten days' journey. I was among this group of attendants. One day I earnestly inquired of Master Lao. I set forth in detail all my former accomplishments and failings in Shu. Master Lao said, "'In the functioning of the Great Way all under Heaven works for the common good.' Since you had this common good in your heart, and three times remonstrated with the Shu king, this is your accomplishment. Although the Five Stalwarts and five wives died at your hands, your thoughts were for the common good, and this is not a failing. Since you have accomplished things for Shu, though now the state is called Qin, the wells and towns are still Shu, and you should enjoy the sacrifices of Shu forever in order to comfort its inhabitants." Then commanding Xu Jia 徐甲 to take from a satchel a pellet of elixir, he bestowed it upon me, saying, "This is the Great Elixir. Swallow it. The Great unites with the Dao. The true Elixir becomes one with the heart. From now on you will possess the five magic powers, and will be incomparably more powerful than your former self. The Central Plain is in disorder, and I am very weary of it. Now I am going to enter the Western Regions in order to carry on transformation (*xinghua* 行化). Three hundred years later, when the religion of the Western Regions is flourishing, it will come to China. You should believe in this religion." I reverently accepted his gift.

COMMENTARY

Following the Qin conquest of Shu (in 316 B.C.) the Divine Lord is dispossessed. Here again we see an interesting confirmation of the parallel character of the temporal and divine administrations. The heart and focus of an ancient Chinese state were its altars to the gods of soil and grain (*sheji* 社稷). When Qin annexed Shu, its first act was to destroy these altars. The state cult centered on but was not limited to these altars; it included every orthodox god within the realm. Hence when Shu was destroyed all of the gods within the Shu region were abandoned and their sacrificial nourishment ceased.

In his newfound leisure the Divine Lord roams to the sacred precincts of Mount Kongtong. Kongtong is to be identified with Mount Kunlun, the *axis mundi* and the center of primordial chaos. By returning there the Divine Lord symbolically returns to the undifferentiated mass from which he originally emerged. There he encounters a great procession of such length that it takes days for it to pass by his vantage point. The Divine Lord has happened upon Laozi and his retinue just as the master is prepared to leave China on his famous journey to the Western Regions. This theme is very ancient, and is first recorded in the *Shiji* biography of Laozi, which describes his passage through Hangu Barrier and his encounter there with Yinxi.[264] Later it was said that Laozi went into the Western Regions to convert the barbarians to Daoism (*huahu* 化胡), and it is this interpretation that is referred to in the poem. Zürcher has shown that originally this theory was meant to affirm the similarities between Daoism and Buddhism, but in the course of the Six dynasties it became a polemical tool by which the Daoists sought to prove that Daoism was antecedent to and indeed at the origins of Buddhism.[265]

In the *Book of Transformations* it seems that this polemical phase has ended and the theme, having come full circle, serves something like its original intentions. Laozi makes specific reference to the Buddhism that will enter China during the Han and instructs the Divine Lord to have faith in it. Further, in a previous episode (ch. 19) the Divine Lord had heard of a figure, the Ancient August Master, who strongly resembled the Buddha and taught certain Buddhist doctrines. He went in quest of this master and attained extinction through his teachings. There, as in the present chapter, the conflicts between Daoism and Buddhism were resolved and the teachings of both religions accepted as valid and worthy of belief.

When Laozi and his retinue pass his position, the Divine Lord pays his respects as one of a group of chthonous deities of the West who are subordinate to the Western Marchmount. These spirits are ordered to accompany Laozi on his journey for the distance of ten relay posts (*cheng* 程), a post being established at the end of what was considered

---

264. See *Shiji* 63/2141.
265. Zürcher 1959:288–320.

a full day's journey for an official courier or circulating official. One day while accompanying Laozi, the Divine Lord requests an audience and asks that his conduct in office be evaluated. Clearly he is concerned about the propriety of his actions in killing the Five Stalwarts and the five daughters of the Qin king. Using the famous line from the *Liji* that Sun Yatsen was to be so fond of,[266] Laozi reassures him that the most important thing is the public weal, and that insofar as he acted in pursuit of this commendable goal, his actions were justified and correct. He further notes that although Qin has conquered and exterminated the state of Shu, the region is still the same, and that in view of his contributions the Divine Lord should continue to receive sacrifice there. In recompense for his valiant deeds Laozi instructs his servant Xu Jia[267] to give the Divine Lord a pill of transformed cinnabar that will invest him with the five supernatural powers: super-sight, super-hearing, telepathy, knowledge of former existences, and omnipresence.

49. *Badu*   巴都

In approaching all situations harbor no thoughts of deceit.
Once the heart is beclouded disaster is sure to strike.
Craftily he planned to take the pearls,[268] proud of his
    instruments of torture,
Adjudicating cases in a sharp voice, he gave free rein to his
    inmost desires.
Being beaten two hundred lashes cannot be easily forgiven,
Suffering for thirty days, he was able to realize this for
    himself.

---

266. *Liji zhushu* 31/3a.
267. On the legends concerning Xu Jia see Schipper 1985a: 43.
268. Following the 1645 ed. and DZ in reading *zhu* 珠, "pearl," for *zhu* 誅, "punish, execute."

That they should burn incense[269] and make my temple image
    was not my intention,
Only that the correct path be reported to sympathetic friends.

When Qin had annexed Shu, it sent Zhang Yi to capture the King
of Ba and seize his territory, making Badu a commandery. Sometime
thereafter the Vice-Protector of Badu, Yi Tingyi 伊庭儀, assumed
the responsibilities of the Grand Protector,[270] who was ill. Wan Zhen
萬貞, the household slave of Zhang Wei 張威 of this commandery,
threw himself into a well and died. Wei was questioned for over a
month. Unable to withstand the beatings, he made a false confession,
saying that he had in fact killed Zhen and thrown him into the well.
Now Wan Zhen had previously committed an offense and Wei had
beaten him for it. Not three days later Zhen stole Wei's property.
Concluding that he could not get away with it, Zhen had taken his
own life, and it really was not the case that Wei had killed him.
When the verdict was reached, Wei's son heard of it and, taking one
hundred large pearls, sent someone to present them to Tingyi. Tingyi
said to the messenger, "You are a physician. Some other day just
bring them in a small box, pretending you have cold[271] medicine in
it. Even if there are guests present do not act flustered." Wei's family
was very happy. On the appointed day the messenger waited at his
door to present the pearls. Tingyi was in the midst of entertaining
ten-odd guests, and had just set out wine and victuals. When the
physician arrived he led him to a seat. After three rounds of toasts the
physician rose, saying that he had some medicine to present to Yi. Yi
Tingyi accepted the gift and had just taken it into the impluvium

---

269. Following DZ in reading *fen* 焚, "to burn (incense)," for *chong* 重, "again." The DZJY reading
would yield "My temple image was repaired," but the text does not suggest that a temple to the god
had existed in Badu prior to this story.

270. The Grand Protector (*taishou* 太守) was the civil and military head of a commandery. The
Vice-Protector (*cheng* 丞) mentioned here was presumably his second in command. See Hucker 1985:
482, entry 6221; 125, entry 457. In translating *taishou* here I deviate from Hucker, who differentiates
between a Governor of areas of direct central government rule and a Grand Protector among the tribes
of the south and southwest.

271. Following the 1645 ed. and DZ in reading *feng* 風, "the wind, a cold," for the homophonous
feng 封, "to seal."

when he regretted his actions, saying, "This matter looks suspicious and I fear it will give rise to criticism." He ordered that the box be taken out, sealed, and addressed just as before. Yi ordered the physician to open the box and take out the medicine then, fearing that the affair would be disclosed, and had him distribute the medicine to the assembled guests. The next day, in light of Wei's confession, he had him executed. Wei's son walked through the marketplace crying. He turned his face toward Heaven and proclaimed the injustice done him, saying, "Are there still gods to investigate this injustice?" I saw him. That night I summoned the souls of Tingyi, Wei and his son, and the physician, interrogated them, and discovered the truth. Tingyi said, "In truth I took the pearls. The medicine within the box was some that I had on hand. As soon as I got the pearls I exchanged them for the medicine. Having accepted the pearls I feared that the Grand Protector would find out about them, and therefore did not dare to alter the sentence." I ordered that Tingyi be whipped on the back two hundred lashes. The next day each of the people I had interrogated told the same story upon awaking, and everyone was amazed at this. Soon they heard that abscesses had formed on Tingyi's back. He screamed in agony for over a month before dying. Wei's family erected a temple on my behalf and all the inhabitants of the commandery showed their reverence.

COMMENTARY

As in chapter 35, the Chinese system of jurisprudence has failed. Its over-reliance on confessions extracted under torture has led an innocent individual to confess to a crime he did not commit. Here the man is Zhang Wei, a rich inhabitant of Badu. When one of his slaves commits suicide the local authorities suspect foul play, perhaps because Zhang had recently had the man beaten. They arrest Zhang Wei and after a month of continuous interrogation and unspecified physical tortures he makes a false confession.

What happens next reveals much about contemporary conceptions of justice. Zhang Wei's son attempts to get his father's conviction overturned by bribing the local official, Yi Tingyi. The intermediary is a physician, a figure on the lower reaches of polite society who is respectable enough to meet the acting administrator of the commandery yet low enough to be indebted to his rich patrons and willing to do their bidding. The corrupt Yi Tingyi desires the pearls offered him but cannot be seen accepting a precious gift from the condemned man's family. He uses the occupation of this intermediary to devise a secure way of transferring the pearls, accepting them openly at a gathering of local notables under the guise of medicine. Fearing that his deception will be uncovered, Tingyi refuses to commute the man's sentence. This leads his son to appeal for supernatural aid in righting the wrong. The Divine Lord of Zitong hears his plea and conducts his own investigation, summoning the souls of all living parties to the incident, together with the recently deceased Zhang Wei, before him for questioning. Having determined the facts, he condemns Yi Tingyi to severe corporal punishment. The next morning the participants in this supernatural tribunal all recall these events and Yi bears the marks of his beating as abscesses that lead to his death, all proofs of the supernatural efficacy of the god. It was commonly believed that the soul sometimes left the body during sleep, and one cause of illness was the soul going too far and not returning. Here we also see a possible supernatural explanation of abscesses as a divine punishment.

This chapter gives us several valuable insights into the nature of Chinese justice and public attitudes toward it. First is the matter-of-fact acceptance of the unreliability of forced confessions. They were a cornerstone of Chinese jurisprudence, and gave the adjudicating official solid justification for whatever sentence he passed, but often did not result in justice. In such a case one can turn to divine assistance as the son of Zhang Wei eventually did (and as we saw in ch. 35) but to those of sufficient wealth a second course of action was open. They could try to bribe the relevant officials in order to overturn the verdict. In Chinese society, because filial piety was esteemed over loyalty to the government, this was not as outrageous as it seems to modern Westerners. Even in a work promoting strict moral values like the *Book of Transformations* there is no condemnation of the actions of the son of Zhang Wei. Rather his deeds are implicitly sanctioned by the divine aid that he receives. This is no doubt in large part because of the true innocence of his father; nowhere in the *Book of Transformations* are we presented with the kind of moral dilemma that would arise if a filial son were to try to free a guilty father. Judging from Yi's trepidation when accepting the bribe, it seems that law and public opinion did strongly condemn the official who allowed himself to be influenced by such gifts. It is uncertain what the divine viewpoint was. Yi Tingyi is singled out for divine punishment not for his incompetence in incorrectly adjudicating the original case, but rather for his venality and duplicity in agreeing to help Zhang Wei, accepting payment for this help, then doing nothing. We can presume that had he really thought him innocent, Yi should have aided Zhang Wei without the encouragement of a bribe, but he is not specifically condemned for accepting the bribe because in doing so he was ultimately serving the purposes of justice.

The Divine Lord had been cut off from sacrifices by the Qin conquest of Shu. Now his cult is re-established by the family of Zhang Wei in gratitude for the Divine Lord's intervention in the matter of Zhang's death. This is perhaps to be seen as a fulfillment of the prophecy of Laozi in the preceding chapter that the Divine Lord will enjoy the bloody sacrifices of the people of Shu forever.

50. *Posuo*   婆娑

When born as a man's son, one should respect his parents.
They toiled since his youth to rear him.
Aware of the shame he would feel if others knew he had taken
    another surname
He would rather abandon in his penury the one who gave him
    life.
It was difficult for the father to endure being punished by
    officials,
The pain of being beaten in a dream was equal.
When one day the enemies became father and son
The local customs were restored to purity.

There is a mountain on the border between Ba and Shu called Posuo. The god of the mountain, Yuan Anxing 轅安行, came to the Yu

River 渝水 in Ba commandery to see me, and said, "The inhabitants
of the region I govern are hard-working and trustworthy. They are
filial in their worship at the temples of their ancestors and fathers and
respectful toward the gods. In all affairs, great or small, they first
divine with turtle and milfoil, and only when the prognostication is
favorable do they dare proceed. You, Mountain King, once controlled all the gods of Shu. Now the region has been divided into the
four commanderies of Ba, Shu, Qian(zhong) 黔中, and Han(zhong)
漢中, but the people of Qin tax[272] it all as Shu. Why not oversee the
region that I govern?" Since there was no official business I did not
dare to proceed, taking the matter lightly. One day Anxing came
again, saying, "There is a man in the territory I govern, Zhou Fu 周
符, who was originally a son of the Yuan family. He is of my clan. It
is the custom to abbreviate the surname by dropping the 'chariot'
(che 車, from yuan 轅) and using yuan 袁. Both the day and time of
Fu's birth were unlucky. His grandfather considered this inauspicious
and ordered that he not be nurtured. His father, Pingshu 平叔, could
not bear to abandon him and raised him outside the household. On
the morning of the first day of his third year of life he bowed to his
grandfather among the grandchildren. The old man got very angry
and rebuked his son, saying, 'Do you want to kill me with this ill-
fated child?' Pingshu led the boy out. Pingshu happened to run into
his friend Zhou Ningzhi 周寧之 on the road and told him the story.
Zhou said, 'I as yet have no descendant. Now I will reverently rear
him and if someday my family is blessed with another son then he
will return to your surname.' Pingshu gave the boy to him. From this
time on Zhou daily became more prosperous while Yuan, suffering a
series of family disasters, fell into abject poverty. By the time Zhou
had a son they talked no more about the previous agreement. After
Zhou Ningzhi died, Pingshu would often go to visit Fu and when on
occasion he would tell him he was in distress, Fu always aided him.
This happened several times. Pingshu thought to himself that Fu was
in fact his natural son and that he did have some concern for him, so
he found an opportunity to tell Fu the whole story. Just then Fu's

272. The 1645 ed. and DZ read shi 視, "to view as," for shui 稅, "to tax."

younger brother happened to come by and heard Pingshu's words. Fu ordered Pingshu to leave and the next day sent an indictment to the yamen accusing Pingshu of lying. Pingshu was beaten. He lit incense on the top of his head and made a plaint to me, saying that 'A son dares beat his father.' I know all the details and am concerned that this was not Fu's true intention, but I do not have a solution to this problem. Please, King, decide this for me."

I then went with Anxing. I appeared in a dream to Fu and showed him his birth as well as his grandfather's words that he not be brought up and his father's personal care for him. Before the dream was over, Fu awoke crying. He wanted to kill himself but his younger brother stopped him, because the matter had already been reported in an indictment. While he was secretly burdened with this I again appeared in a dream and castigated him for not immediately obeying me. I beat him one hundred strokes. Fu awoke immediately and slept no more that night. The next day he bowed at the door of the Yuan family and said to Pingshu, "I did not realize soon enough that I was your progeny. Now a god has come to castigate me and has beaten me almost to death. I repent. Further, the Zhou family has a son of its own that can continue the sacrifices. I already want no part of their fortune. I obey only you." The people of the neighborhood thought Fu was admirable. Zhou's son divined and divided the estate with Fu, permitting him to return to his original surname. The Yuans, husband and wife, had someone to depend on in their old age.[273]

COMMENTARY

This episode opens with the Divine Lord residing in his new temple in Badu, the construction of which was related in the previous chapter. There he is visited by a former subordinate, the god of Posuo Mountain,[274] Yuan Anxing. Yuan is disoriented because of the recent changes in the temporal sphere and the disorder they have brought to the divine world. Left without a superior to report to, he seeks out the

---

273. The 1645 ed. omits this last sentence.

274. This mountain is otherwise unknown. *Posuo* might be translated "dancing," "wandering," or "contented."

Divine Lord to ask that he resume these duties and come to inspect the region under Yuan's administration. The situation is confused because Qin has altered the administrative geography, establishing four commanderies in the territories of the ancient states of Ba and Shu.[275] Yuan points out that in spite of this formal division Qin still treats the entire region as a single entity, Shu, for tax purposes.[276] Since the Divine Lord formerly had jurisdiction over all the gods of Shu, this should justify his assuming responsibility for Yuan's area, on the Ba-Shu border. The Divine Lord recognizes the validity of his argument but demurs because there is no pressing need for him to act. When Yuan appears a second time with a problem requiring resolution the Divine Lord accepts this responsibility and sets out for Mount Posuo. This series of events is interesting for two reasons. First, it demonstrates again the close relationship and interaction between divine and temporal administrative geography. The jurisdiction of representatives of the divine administration depends upon the organization of the temporal government. Second, it provides a model for the conduct of temporal officials. The Southern Song dynasty was a chaotic time, when China was divided among several competing powers and often it was unclear who was the legitimate governing authority of a region. A local official might want to adhere to the orthodox Song administrative network but be unable for a variety of reasons to communicate with the Song government in Lin'an. It was important that there be standards by which a local official might accept responsibility for the administration of a region without explicit confirmation from the central government. This situation is completely analogous to that of the Divine Lord vis-à-vis the divine administration, and his actions serve to sanction such behavior as long as it promotes public order and can be rationalized according to accepted principles.

The immediate cause that spurs the Divine Lord into action is a certain Zhou Fu. He was born into the Yuan family, and thus was a distant descendant of the local mountain god, though the family had since simplified the orthographic representation of the surname. This Fu had been born at an inauspicious time. The eight cyclical charac-

---

275. On the establishment of these four commanderies, which took place over a number of years from 314 B.C. to 277 B.C., see *Huayangguo zhi* 1/3; *Huayangguo zhi jiaozhu* 1/32–34, esp. nn. 4 and 7.

276. This probably refers to the tax called *cong* 賨, variously explained as a type of local cloth or a tax of forty cash per head. See *Huayangguo zhi* 1/3; *Huayangguo zhi jiaozhu* 1/37 and 38, n. 7; *Hou Hanshu* 86/2831, 2842.

ters (*bazi* 八字) of his birth year, month, day, and time were in conflict, in terms of the system of mutual production and destruction of the five elements, with those of another member of the family, here no doubt his grandfather. The boy's father is unable to bring himself to let the child die, as his father demands. Instead he secretly rears the boy outside the family home. When he brings the boy back to wish his elders longevity (*bainian* 拜年) at the beginning of the new year the grandfather again drives him out, seeing his very presence as a direct threat to his existence. Marjorie Topley discusses modern beliefs in Hong Kong about such conflicts between the cosmological orientations of mother and child, and one possible solution practiced there is adoption.[277]

It is ultimately this option of adoption which the father, Yuan Pingshu, selects. He entrusts his son to an heirless friend, Zhou Ningzhi, who agrees to return the boy to the Yuan family if and when he should have a natural son. This is another example of the practice of adopting a son in order to "lead in" a natural heir, discussed in the commentary to chapter 41. But fortune estranges the two men as one becomes rich and the other poor. When a son is born to Zhou, it already seems inconceivable that Fu should be taken from this comfortable environment and returned to the now impoverished Yuan household. Although it is not explicitly stated, it is tempting to see in this change of fortunes a recompense for the evil actions of the Yuans in driving the boy out and the commendable behavior of the Zhous in taking him in. When the boy is grown he maintains an amicable relationship with Yuan Pingshu, though he knows him only as a friend of his father, and aids him when he is in distress.

Yuan Pingshu, however, is starting to face up to the harsh realities that have always encouraged Chinese to have large families. With no other sons, he has no one to support him in his old age and no one to sacrifice to him after his death. He decides to tell the boy about his true parentage in hopes that he will return to the Yuan lineage. His speech is overheard by Zhou Fu's younger brother, Zhou Ningzhi's natural son. Eager to maintain his place in the Zhou household and inheritance, and unsure of the truth of Yuan's claims, Fu has him thrown out, and further has him formally accused of a crime, for which he is beaten. Yuan is incensed and appeals for divine aid, dem-

---

277. Topley 1974, esp. pp. 238–45.

onstrating his sincerity and truthfulness by burning a cone of incense on his head.

It is this situation that has led Yuan Anxing, the local mountain god, to turn to the Divine Lord for guidance. The Divine Lord again uses a dream to communicate, revealing to Zhou Fu the circumstances of his birth and the sacrifices his natural father made on his behalf. Fu is mortified and seeks to avoid the shame of returning to this poor family by committing suicide, but his hand is stayed by his younger brother, who points out that the local officials are already involved and that the Zhou family would be endangered if it were discovered that they had misled the local yamen into incorrectly punishing a righteous father. It takes another nocturnal visit from the Divine Lord and a supernatural beating, like that administered to Yi Tingyi in the preceding chapter, to cause the lad to repent and accept his true father. All works out for the best as the locals are impressed by his willingness to forsake his rich patrimony and his younger brother decides to split the estate with him anyway. Most important from the viewpoint of the spirits, the vile example of a son who rejects and injures his father has been eliminated and the moral fiber of the community restored.

The tumult of frequent wars and natural disasters, the inexorable grind of social pressures like poverty, forced relocation, and migration, and the many ways in which men and women could fall into servitude often resulted in the involuntary dispersal of families. One dilemma resulting from this situation was the encounter with an unknown man or woman who claims to be the individual's true parent or child. Such incidents aroused particular suspicion when the claimant was not of the same class or economic level as the purported foundling or separated parent. The 10th c. *Jishen lu* tells of a Madame Ouyang who had been separated from her parents during a time of civil unrest, but had come to marry a clerk.[278] When a destitute man appeared claiming to be her father, she turned him away. The father ultimately accused her before the supernatural tribunal and she was struck down with lightning. The gods thus acted as a social force encouraging the acceptance of legitimate long-lost relatives and the extension of personal resources to them at the same that it warned potential abusers of the system.

---

278. *Jishen lu* (Siku quanshu ed.): 1/3b–4a.

51.   *Warning the Dragons*   戒龍

When Qin had succeeded Zhou and the Nine Tripods of State
    had been transferred,
All the dragons received commands before the God of the Sea.
They then vented their smoldering anger contesting for the way,
Not considering that if they distress the people severe
    punishment awaits.
Pointing at a stone they took an oath, their hearts sincere;
Looking to Heaven I established a vow, my words impartial.
From this time on the tillers and sericulturists on the banks,
Suffered no more from overflowing streams that destroyed their
    harvests.

The Qingyi 清衣 stream flows from the west and merges into the
Min River 岷江. When Qin had annexed Zhou the Nine Tripods
were transferred to the west. The gods of the mountains met before
the spirits of the marchmounts, and the dragons of the rivers attended
the court of the Sovereign of the Seas, there to hear the proclamation
of the change of Mandate and make manifest the divine blessings.
Two dragons, both traveling east, met in the midst of the confluence
of the two rivers. Vying for the lead, neither would concede to the
other. They fought in the depths of the river, causing both rivers to
back up and the waves to overflow. Over a thousand families lived
beside the river. Suddenly one day[279] the floodwaters burst through,
and they had no time to flee. Their wrathful, suffering voices pierced
the four directions. I happened to observe this. First I sent a myriad
of otherworldly troops to block the tempestuous waves, then entered
into the waters to break up the fight. I said to them, "This new
mandate has replaced our former virtue. You have not forgotten your

---

279. Following the 1645 ed. and DZ in reading *ri* 日, "day," for the graphically similar *dan* 旦,
"morning."

smoldering anger; in this the hundred spirits are all[280] the same. Why do only you two fight, contesting for the way? The disaster has reached to the inhabitants. If my troops had not just blocked the flow then no one from this town would be left. Moreover, the Supreme Thearch loves these mortals. What good would it do to regret later [should someone die]?" The two dragons said, "We reverently accept your instruction." I then sent them on their way together, agreeing that I would further admonish them upon their return. On the day of their return from the court, I officiated at their meeting. Turning my face to Heaven I established for them a vow. Then, pointing,[281] to two great rocks to the east and the west, I cast a spell on them, commanding them to stand. In a second they towered facing each other. I further admonished the dragons, saying, "The dragons of the two rivers say they will return to good. Heaven and Earth are their witnesses. Do not desecrate these words. If these two rocks join and become one then today's oath can be 'left grow cold' (i.e., repudiated)." I took my leave and returned home.

COMMENTARY

The process of adjustment to the new world order continues. The Mandate of Heaven has shifted from Zhou to Qin, symbolized by the transfer of the Nine Tripods 九鼎. These sacrificial vessels were cast by Yu the Great, legendary founder of the Xia dynasty, and followed the Mandate, shifting from Xia to Shang to Zhou until they came to symbolize the Chinese polity and the legitimacy of its rule.[282] When Zhang Yi counseled the Qin king to strike immediately at the Zhou royal domain (discussed in the commentary to chapter 47), his goal was to seize both the Zhou emperor and the tripods, thinking that possession of these two supreme tokens of Zhou rule would bring the empire under Qin control.

With the change of mandate, all of the members of the terrestrial divine bureaucracy must be confirmed in their offices. They assemble

---

280. Following the 1645 ed., DZ, and SG in reading *jie* 皆, "all," for *shang* 尚, "still."

281. Following the 1645 ed., DZ, and SG in inserting a *zhi* 指, "to point to."

282. See *Shiji* 28/1391. According to this passage the tripods vanished when the virtue of the Zhou declined, and hence all discussion of the Qin obtaining the tripods is to be understood metaphorically.

before the divine feudal lords under whose jurisdiction they serve. The mountain gods appear before the sovereign of the marchmount ruling their quarter of China. The dragons that govern each of China's rivers and streams all come to attend audience before the Sovereign of the Seas, Hairuo 海若 (introduced in ch. 6). All of the deities of China are in turmoil over the change of dynasties, the first in eight centuries, and the attendant political and social changes. The dragon lords of the Qingyi and Min rivers in Sichuan let this tension get the best of them when they meet on their way to the grand audience with the Sovereign of the Seas. The new temporal order raises the possibility of a new ordering of the divine world as well, and both rush to arrive first. Such dragon races are still ritually reenacted each year on the fifth day of the fifth moon on the Yangzi River and elsewhere; unfortunate racers who fall in and drown may be substituting for human sacrifices in an age-old ritual to avert just the sort of floods we see here. The Viper may once have accepted human sacrifice, but the Divine Lord of Zitong is appalled that his unruly subordinate officials should be causing pain and hardship to the people. He first dispatches a large cohort of his divine soldiers to divert the waters, then personally enters the fracas to separate the combatants.[283] He convinces the dragons to forget their argument by pointing out that the disaster they almost created would have incurred the wrath of the Supreme Thearch, and he would have undoubtedly punished them most harshly.

To bring a final resolution to this rivalry he agrees to meet with these dragons after the audience and lead them in a sacred oath. We see in this scene all of the elements of the classic Chinese vow. The Divine Lord is the neutral party who administers the oath. The divine natural forces of Heaven and Earth are invoked as witnesses to and guarantors of the oath. Finally, two giant boulders rise to stand on end as testimony to the contract. The oath may be disavowed only if these two monoliths should some day fuse into one. Much of the language here harkens back to antiquity. The reference to the oath "becoming cold" derives from an incident recorded in the *Zuozhuan*. When the ruler of Wu suggested to the Duke of Lu that they "rewarm" a former oath, affirming its validity, the duke sent Zigong 子貢 to refuse, arguing that to "rewarm" an oath which was made with the expectation

---

283. Li Bing is also said to have led a contingent of divine soldiers to move a weir one night when a town was threatened with flooding. See *327 Luyi ji* of Du Guangting (850–933), 4/3a–4a.

that it would be observed forever would imply that the oath could also be "chilled" or revoked.[284] The whole tale may originate in a local myth explaining the magical power of an unusual rock formation that was subsequently appropriated by the Zitong cult.

52. *Mount Pheonix*   鳳山

Within a thousand layers of flesh and meat she conceived an
　embryo.
Ten months of concern and trepidation could not have been
　easy.
One word of her true feelings contradicted her mistress's intent;
She suffered misfortune during twenty-four years of wandering.
It was not because he went soaring through the clouds[285] in a
　dream
That he fought his way through the rain to the mountainside.
That mother and son should be reunited is in accord with
　Heavenly principles,
In her later years she enjoyed sweet delicacies in his company.

In a corner of Fruit Mountain[286] there was a rich man named Wang Ji 王基, who was fifty but had no son. One day, after eating and drinking his fill, he looked askance at his wife, saying, "A man desires riches so that, while alive, he may have food and clothing, and, when dead, he may have the solace of sacrifices. Now I am rich but have no son. What good are all my riches?" His wife, Madame née An 安氏, was also from an important family. She had been unable to conceive

---

284. *Zuozhuan* 484/Ai 12/3; *Chunqiu Zuozhuan zhengyi* 59/3a.
285. DZ reads "his soaring soul" (*tenghun* 騰魂) for "soaring through the clouds" (*tengyun* 騰雲).
286. Fruit Mountain (*Guoshan* 果山) is located to the west of modern Nanchong in Sichuan. See Zang 1936: 501.2.

because of her harsh and jealous nature. Hearing these words, she was ashamed. With her dowry she bought a woman surnamed Liu 柳 to serve her husband. The next year Liu felt the quickening of pregnancy. A delighted An burnt incense and prayed to Heaven morning and night, asking that the child should be a male and heir to the Wang clan. When she found out that Liu was pregnant she gave her own clothing and jewelry to her. As for her care, there was no aspect of her eating, drinking, or sleeping with which An did not concern herself. When the month of birth approached, she arranged for a female physician to be ready and when the birth came, it was, as hoped, a boy. She was delighted, and personally washed the baby's nursing swaddling and diapers, treating the child as her own. Her husband was impressed. When the boy was one hundred days old, he was named Yishou 宜壽 ("should be long-lived"), and this was also An's idea. Soon thereafter she hired a nurse solely to take care of him. She said to Liu, "You and I are guest and host. It is only for the sake of my son that you eat, drink, and are treated the same as me in my house. Now my son is almost one year old. I am going to select a matchmaker and marry you off to someone." Liu wailed and cried, saying, "This is not my desire. I want to live with Yishou until my death." An was displeased, and said, "Do you want to replace me?" Soon thereafter she began to beat Liu, gave her different clothing, and fed her coarse grain. She treated her like a dog or pig, and always referred to her as an animal. Whenever a task was onerous, she demanded that Liu do it. One day when Yishou was three he ran and threw himself into Liu's arms. She faced him and, crying, said, "For you, my son, I endure hunger, cold, and toil with no regrets. It has been over a month since I last saw you. Do you miss your mother?" Yishou also cried and the sound was audible outside. An went to see what was the matter. She grabbed the boy and took him out. Then, seizing Liu, she beat her very cruelly with a cane. It was the coldest month of the year. She stripped off all of her clothing and threw her outside at night. The next morning she summoned the village headman and had her driven away. Wang Ji urged An to let her stay, fearing that her departure would seriously hurt Yishou's feelings. An said, "The situation is such that I and this creature cannot both remain. If you now want this creature for your concubine, then I will leave.[287] If you definitely want to keep me, then there is no room for this creature. If you have not decided in two hours I will seek my own death before your eyes." Ji could not resist her. He gave Liu the clothing and hairpin she was wearing to take along with her as a dowry, but An took them away. Liu had been starved and exhausted for a long time. Her bones protruded and her hair was falling out; her flesh was withered and black. No one would take her in marriage. She walked along the outskirts of the town, scrounging for food to feed herself. A member of the Wang clan happened to pass through the county[288] and took Liu along with him. After a year An found out about it and sent a letter castigating him. Liu was again driven out. Since she had no place to turn, she took to eking out a living by cooking and laboring for others. Two twelve-year Jupiter cycles passed. Yishou's parents had both died and he already had a son ten years of age, named Zhiwei 知微 ("know the subtle beginnings"). Suddenly[289] one day Yishou said to his wife, Madame née Kang 康氏, "Our family is quite prosperous and there is nothing that we lack. But I do not know if the mother who gave me birth is alive or dead. I worry about her day and night. This is the reason why my hair is already streaked with gray though I am only thirty." He then[290] entrusted the family affairs to his wife, saying, "Take good care of my son. I am going to search for my mother and will return only after I have seen her." He then departed, heading north. Every time he came to a village or hamlet he would tarry there, delaying his voyage. Soon a year had passed. Every time Yishou set out to travel he would cry forlornly and waste away. He ate only one meal of vegetables and grain each day. His sincerity moved the quick and the dead, and the feelings of the gods everywhere he went were aroused. At the confluence of the Ba 巴 and Qu 渠 rivers there is a mountain called Mount Pheonix. I was staying there. I saw an old woman carrying firewood,

---

287. Following the 1645 ed. and DZ in reading *chu* 出, "to leave," for *si* 死, "to die."

288. Following the 1645 ed. and DZ in reading *chuan* 川, "river" (here referring to Sichuan), for *zhou* 州, "province."

289. DZ reads *huo* 或, "once," for *hu* 忽, "suddenly."

290. Following DZ in reading *ji* 即, "then, thereupon," for *ji* 既, "since."

walking under the blazing sun and constantly wiping away her per-
spiration. Resting under a pine tree, she faced south and in a long cry
said, "Yishou, Yishou, are you healthy, my son?" Your mother is in
dire straits here. How can I get you to think about me?" I heard her
and could not stand it. I summoned the village (god) Dugu Zheng 獨
孤正 and asked him about it. Zheng said, "This is the natural mother
of Wang Yishou." At the time Yishou had been gone a long time and
his family was urging him to return. He had already gone halfway
back. I sent him a dream. Yishou with his own eyes saw all of the details of the happiness and sadness of his natural mother when she was
at home, as well as the places along the road upon which he would
meet her. The next day he was very happy, saying, "The gods have
communicated with me. There is a presage that mother and son will
meet." He then headed north again. The mountains, streams, paths,
and villages he crossed were all those he had seen in his dream. After
traveling three days he arrived at the foot of Mount Pheonix. He was
about to cook when a violent rainstorm suddenly came up. No traveler could go on. After a long while, a village woman came in carrying firewood. Seeing Yishou, she bowed to him. Yishou's heart leaped
and he asked her her identity. It was his mother. He brought her
back home. Liu died at the age of eighty.

COMMENTARY

In this episode the Divine Lord acts to reunite mother and son, at
the same time encouraging filial sons in their devotion to their mothers.

Here as in chapter 41 we see some of the problems engendered by
the emphasis placed on providing a male heir to carry on the family
line and provide sacrifice after death. Chinese society was mono-
gamous in the sense that only one woman could be formally acknowledged as the wife, *qi* 妻, but polygynous in structure because a man
could have any number of concubines (*ying* 媵 or *qie* 妾) as well as
female slaves who would serve him sexually and perhaps provide an
heir for the family.[291] Wives who did not produce male heirs were
subject to divorce and had no security once their mates were dead and

---

291. See the discussion of heirs in Ebrey 1984: 106–12.

the family was in the hands of someone else's son. Once Madame née An has secured an heir for the household, she immediately stakes her claim to his affection and seeks to drive out the birth mother. The child is also restrained by the dictates of filial piety. Only after Wang Yishou is fully grown and both his father and An dead can he go in search of his natural mother. His great sincerity and grief move the gods and lead to divine aid in reuniting the pair.

This story deals with a somewhat delicate topic: allegiance to one's natural parents. The poem stresses the emotional bonds of blood kinship, but in the highly hierarchical society of ancient China, peace within extended polygynous families demanded subservience and obedience to the senior woman within the household. Thus in this story An is within her rights in acting as she did and she suffers no supernatural punishment. But the loyal son has obligations to his natural mother that he should try to honor when it is possible. In this regard this story is similar to that in chapter 50, in which a son is led to recognize his natural father in part because he is no longer needed in his adoptive family. Yishou must respect An, his father's wife, while she is alive, but after her death he is free to follow the dictates of his heart and search out the woman who gave him birth.

---

53. *Yufu*   魚腹

Born a woman, one is already lowly and insignificant,
Not to mention being kidnapped and sold by a maniac.
Swallowing his tears, her father became a blind cripple;
Her mother, her worries accumulating, seemed to lose her
    reason.
Truly it is difficult to know the sorrows or joys of another land.
Even whether she was alive or dead could not be ascertained.
They had to wait for Zan Yuan to receive retribution for his
    actions,
Repenting only as death approached did him no good.

The people of Shu give birth to four daughters for every two sons. For this reason it is the custom to disdain girls. On the banks[292] of the Fu River 涪水 there lived a rich man named Ren Ying 任盈. He was old and had no heir, only a daughter of fifteen, on whom he doted, named Baozhu 寶珠 ("precious pearl"). She went for a stroll in the silkworm market with some neighborhood companions. Under the lamps, amidst the crowds, she lost her way and was abducted by an evil young man named Zan Yuan 昝元. Her father and mother offered a large reward and searched for her for over a month, but she had already been sold by Yuan to a man of Kui.[293] Her father cried for her until he lost his sight. Her mother, Madame née Ai 艾,[294] became senile. They passed ten years in this manner, searching in a hundred ways, but heard not a single word of her. Ying heard of the spirit on Sevenfold Mountain and came crying on hands and knees to see me. He requested that he be allowed to see Baozhu once more before he died. I took pity on him and ordered eight deputies to lead three hundred otherworldly troops to search an area of one thousand square li in all four directions for her. Someone saw Baozhu in Yufu, in Kui, forlornly porting water. I asked the dragon of the Rang River 瀼水 for the details of her story and sent a dream to Ying that very night, in which he traveled along the river south from Sevenfold Mountain until he reached Kui, where he saw his daughter and spoke with her. The girl also dreamed that she saw her father. When day broke, Ying paid his respects and set out. I sent someone along to assist him. Everything[295] along the way was as in the dream and finally he met her.

Baozhu had at first been a maidservant. Her mistress hated her and beat her too severely. She was sold to another household, her former master getting twice what he had paid for her.[296] Three years later she was again duped by a neighbor boy, who said, "Your father is searching for you and has told me to bring you to him." He again

---

292. The 1645 ed. and DZ consistently read *yuan* 源, "at the source," for *bin* 濱, "on the banks of."

293. Referring to Kueizhou 夔州, modern Fengjie, Sichuan. Following the 1645 ed. and DZ in reading *kuizi* 夔子, "a man of Kui," for the otherwise unattested *kuimen* 夔門, "gate of Kui."

294. DZ gives *yi* 義 for this surname.

295. DZ reads "in general" (*gai* 蓋) for "everything" (*jin* 盡).

296. Following the 1645 ed. and DZ in reading *yong* 傭, "wages," for *zhi* 值, "value."

sold her to another house, so that in all she had four owners. Baozhu was now in the home of Zhang Bai 張白. Her mistress was terrified of anyone in the household getting pregnant but Baozhu had conceived. Fearing punishment, she was about to throw herself into the river, when she seemed to hear a voice criticizing her.

When her father heard Baozhu's voice his vision was restored. They went together to her master to buy her freedom, and returned home. Her mother's illness also was cured. Zan Yuan had become an old man. I sent deputies to oversee and punish him. Each day they beat him three hundred strokes. After something more than a month he was holding his eyes in his hands and begging in the marketplace. He confessed, saying, "It was my fault that Baozhu lost her virginity. Now King Zhang[297] of Sevenfold Mountain is punishing me. I am in terrible pain and am about to die." He died the next year.

COMMENTARY

The Divine Lord punishes an evildoer and reunites a family.

This episode begins with a general comment on the mores of the Shu region. Because of an overabundance of females, girls are not valued. The primary focus of the story seems to be to encourage the people of Shu to regard female children more highly, and to this end a model family is presented, in which the parents dote on their daughter and are extremely distraught when she disappears. There is, however, no suggestion that girls should be valued as highly or treated the same as boys, the ritual and social realities of ancient China making such a position untenable. Girls could not support their parents, either in this life or, after their death, in the world of the spirits. Indeed, one wonders if Baozhu would have been so eagerly sought had she not been an only daughter.

The story opens with the adolescent Baozhu attending the silkworm market (*canshi* 蠶市) with some friends. These markets were gay, bustling festivals that combined the sale of the implements of sericulture (hence the name) with singing, dancing, and revelry. They took place on a rotating schedule at different places in Sichuan during the first three months of the lunar year, when the silkworms were about to

---

297. DZ reads "Lord Zhang" 張主.

emerge.[298] Unfortunately, amidst the commotion Baozhu is separated from her friends and comes under the influence of a young miscreant named Zan Yuan. After having his way with her, he sells her into slavery, sending her down the Yangzi to the city of Kuizhou, where her parents are unlikely to find her. There she passes through four different owners and suffers greatly at the hands of jealous and ill-tempered mistresses, who no doubt resent her youth and beauty. This passage gives us a rare glimpse into the life of female slaves during the Song.

Meanwhile her parents are racked with grief at losing their only child. During the course of a fruitless ten-year search, her father loses his sight and her mother, her mind. Finally the father decides to turn to the Divine Lord for aid. Making the long pilgrimage to northern Sichuan on his hands and knees in order to demonstrate his sincerity, he begs for one last meeting with his beloved daughter, so that he may go happily to his grave. The Divine Lord sends out his divine troops to scour the area for her and, once located, turns to the local representative of the divine bureaucracy for information on her. Here we see that dragons performed the same record-keeping and oversight functions as their more anthropomorphic colleagues.

Ren Ying had sought information through an incubatory dream, perhaps spending the night in the "Answering Dream Pavilion" (*Yingmengtai*) on Sevenfold Mountain. In twelfth-century anecdotes, the god most frequently communicates through dreams and the pavilion is described in a thirteenth century source.[299] The Divine Lord responds with a dream revealing his daughter's fate, and also communicates with the girl. When her father reaches her location, he finds his daughter, who has just been dissuaded from suicide by a supernatural voice (or perhaps the voice of the father?). He redeems her from bondage, he and his wife are healed of their ailments, and the evil Zan Yuan receives a painful punishment that results in his confession and eventual death.

---

298. Cf. *Suishi guangji* 1/12.

299. For early anecdotes in which the god reveals himself in a dream, see *Tieweishan congtan* 4/4b–5a; *Yijian zhi,* "*ding,*" 8/606, and "*jia,*" 18/158. For a description of the dream chamber, see above, pp. 00–00.

54.   *Verbal Karma*   口業

The recompense for verbal karma in this life is not light,
Do not make a study of evil words!
His reckless statements made facts out of empty lies,
Flowery phrases made a thousand names out of a hundred.
Blood flowed ceaselessly from the pricking stone,
His sins accumulated with the supernatural officials until his file
   was full.
No need to seek out the hells to see tongues plowed.
The case before your eyes is very clear.

Zhu Qisheng 祝期生, a man of Turtle Wall 龜城 (the main city wall of Chengdu), was eloquent but accustomed to disparaging others. When someone was congenitally crippled, he would make fun of him, and the beautiful he also derided and defamed. He insulted the stupid and also criticized the intelligent. He despised the poor and calumniated the rich as well. If the person was an official, he would broadcast his personal secrets; if a friend of similar status to himself, he would reveal what they hid and distorted. As for someone of good family whose talents exceeded his own and concerning whom nothing could be found to criticize, he would say that his grandfather was a commoner and his father was a country bumpkin, or that his mother's family were laborers and merchants and that his wife's were middlemen, or that his younger brother was unworthy and his sons lacking in virtue. None of Zhu's acquaintances could escape his defamatory barbs. And these were only the less serious examples. If someone committed a minor transgression, he would publicize and embellish it, making something out of nothing, turning one into ten, making certainties of doubts, deliberate offenses out of accidents, saying that someone took delight in doing something he did out of necessity or that a mistake represented his true desires. He even criticized the person to his face and abused him, and then reported him to the authorities. He did not just treat others like this, even members of his

own clan did not escape this treatment. He characterized his parents
as obdurate and treacherous and compared his brothers to Guan and
Cai.[300] Nor did he restrict himself to doing things personally.
Sometimes he would tell one person to sue another, then defend this
other's position; at other times, he would encourage someone to
insult another, then come to this person's defense. He had acted like
this for a long time and did not realize his error.

In his middle age he contracted "yellow tongue" (*shehuang* 舌黃).
When he had someone lance it, his tongue would bleed and his
condition would improve somewhat, but in a few days it would worsen
again. Soon thereafter he would have it treated again. In a year the illness would flare up five to seven times, and each time he would lose
no less than one or two pints of blood. This became a constant occurrence. One day he was discussing the gods and affairs of the worlds of
the living and the dead with his chums. From the unseasonality of
rain and sunshine and the varying fertility of the earth to the acceptance of sacrifice by the gods and the demands for offerings from the
ancestors, there was nothing that he did not revile. I happened to be
conversing with the gods of the rivers and streams and heard him
mouthing off. I was just snickering at him when the perfected official
of the locality, Yu Qishu 虞奇叔, said, "This is only one ten-
thousandth of it." He then gave the complete story in detail. I sent
the deputy Miao Zhen 繆眞[301] to seize him and make him grasp and
pull out his own tongue, then use his fingernails to "plow" his tongue.
The blood spurted out like a dog or a pig being butchered and flowed
onto the ground. Thousands looked on. Miao forced him to proclaim his faults, saying, "You must not create verbal karma." This
went on for over a month and his tongue withered. He was then unable to eat and died.

COMMENTARY

In this episode the Divine Lord presents a graphic warning of the
danger of speaking recklessly. Such speech creates "verbal karma," a

---

300. The rebellious younger brothers of the Duke of Zhou. See above, chapter 17.
301. DZ gives this name as Miao Qi 其.

category of evil moral debt that is often mentioned in lists of religious precepts and includes sins like reckless speech, flattery, disparagement, and duplicity. Zhu Qisheng commits a wide variety of offenses in his unrestrained rhetorical transports, but most can be subsumed under one of the foregoing rubrics. More serious, in the eyes of the *Book of Transformations*, are actions that threaten the harmony and order within the family, the foundation of Chinese society. Zhu disparages his parents with the terms used to describe the evil father and step-mother of Shun[302] and compares his brothers to the unworthy siblings of the Duke of Zhou, thus implying that he himself possesses the sterling virtue of a Shun or Duke of Zhou. He also trifles with public safety and the legal system, encouraging disputes and litigation so that he can play the big man in resolving the affairs.

Zhu's punishment is appropriate to his crime. There is a Buddhist hell called the "plow-tongue hell," where those whose have abused their verbal talents suffer by being forced to use their tongues as plows. The poem points out that Zhu suffers a parallel fate in this world. He contracts a disease involving swelling of the tongue that must be periodically leeched. This affliction arises spontaneously in recompense for his sadistic actions. When the Divine Lord hears of his many sins, he imposes a more severe, immediate punishment. Zhu is compelled to grasp his tongue and "plow" it with his fingernail, forcing the collected blood to spill out in what must have been an excruciatingly painful torrent. Zhu is also led to make a public confession of his sins so that his suffering will offer a clear, unambiguous lesson to others. Eventually his death results when the tongue that he has misused withers and he can no longer partake of nourishment.

55. *The Eastern Rampart*   東郭

Although labor is for the purpose of obtaining wealth,
You still must choose your methods and assess yourself.

---

302. See *Shangshu zhengyi* 2/24b and the commentary to chapter 26.

He reduced or increased the weights as his heart desired,
Pulling the back and pushing the front as he thought best.
When the karma was ripe both eyes became blind and useless,
His five fingers, so skilled in their craft, were all wounded and
    wasted.
His three years of public punishment provided a mirror for
    others.
Best to avoid the beatings of the soul and after-death disasters.

The soil of Shu commandery is thin and the water shallow. Most
of the people who live there are clever and cunning in the pursuit of
profit. The denizens of the marketplace will counterfeit a good
though it be worth only one cash. Li Yongzheng 黎永正, a man of
the eastern ramparts (of Chengdu), originally worked as a wheel-
wright and carriagemaker. Tired of the hard labor and poor market
for his goods, he changed occupations. He made peck (*dou* 斗) and
bushel (*hu* 斛) measures, and soon also began to make steelyards and
balances. The next year a man commissioned him to make a deep
peck measure and heavy weights. Yongzheng gave them to him at
twice the usual price. When someone wanted a pint (*sheng* 升)
measure that was short a spoon (*shao* 勺), a bushel measure that was
short a quart (*he* 合), an ounce (*liang* 兩) weight that was light a
dram (*zhu* 銖), or a catty (*jin* 斤) weight that was short an ounce, he
did the same. Yongzheng was also able to make a suspended, pulled-
string balance (*kongzhongjiesi zhi cheng* 空中接絲之秤) and a bent-
bottom, arched-seam peck measure (*zhedi longliang zhi dou* 折底隆
梁之斗).[303] Commoners who gave no thought to karmic retribution
found them convenient in daily use and repeatedly sought them. One
day an inspecting deity memorialized indicting him. A rescript pronounced that those who used such devices were basically wrong, but
those who made them were worse. The local deities were ordered to
openly warn him and secretly punish him. I thereupon sent the god

---

303. Following the 1645 ed. and DZ in reading *long* 隆, "arched," for the graphically similar *lu* 陸,
"land."

of the locality, Duan Yanmeng 段彥夢, to beat Yongzheng. Although he realized his mistake, he did not repent. Now that he was achieving a reputation, those who sought him out were even more numerous. Lusting after his wages, he worked day and night, causing his vision to weaken until he became blind. When he turned forty his wife deserted him for another man. His two sons were born blind. Still, he had worked long in this profession and did not want to suddenly abandon it. Since he was blind, and had no other way to earn a living, he used his hands for his eyes. Judging width by feel and guessing at length, he endangered himself using saw, axe, nails, and awl.[304] The five fingers of his left hand were wounded and crippled morning and night. The pus and blood had barely dried and the flesh had not yet healed before they were hurt again. The joints of the fingers deteriorated until he could hold nothing. He walked crying in the marketplace, but since everyone knew of him, no one pitied him. Hunger and cold pierced his body, and this continued for three years. Then I caused him to confess his transgressions and die. His two sons followed after him, dying of starvation. Due to this, there was a brief halt in the use of such devices.

COMMENTARY

In this episode a harmful commercial practice, the manufacture of inaccurate weights and measures, is condemned and an example of the divine retribution it calls forth is presented to all those who would pursue this dishonorable trade. The chapter begins with a sweeping indictment of the people of Shu for their crafty, avaricious ways, which should be understood as a general warning to those who think themselves safe because their own particular failing is not singled out for criticism.

The maintenance of honest, standard weights and measures has been a constant concern of Chinese governments from high antiquity. The "Yueling" 月令 ("Monthly Ordinances"), a calendar of appropriate seasonal activities dating from the Warring States period and found in the *Liji* and the *Lüshi chunqiu*, lists among the prescribed activities for

---

304. Following DZ in reading *zuan* 鑽, "awl," for *suo* 鎖, "lock."

the second month of autumn the correction and standardization of the weights and measures.[305] When Qin Shihuang first unified all of China, one of his first actions was to standardize the measures.[306]

There were officials who enforced the regulations concerning standard weights and measures, but the primary line of defense against dishonest traders was the measure-maker himself, and consumers, farmers, and merchants depended upon his integrity to assure that they were getting a fair deal. This is why the Supreme Thearch considers Yongzheng's conduct so reprehensible.

Yongzheng is first asked to make a "deep" (i.e., oversize) peck measure and a heavier than normal set of balance weights, presumably to be used when purchasing grain and other goods from their producers. He is then approached to make small measures and light weights, to be used in retailing the goods to consumers. In each case the article requested is one percent smaller or lighter than it should be.[307] He was also able to make specially rigged balances and peck measures, the exact nature of which we can only speculate upon. These devices made him wealthy, but he amassed a store of supernatural debt which would later take its toll.

One of the distinguishing features of the Chinese bureaucracy was an independent system of censorial officials who traveled about investigating local conditions and reporting directly to the emperor. In this story we encounter the divine counterpart of such an itinerant inspector. On a tour of the eastern suburbs of Chengdu he notices Li Yongzheng's dishonest behavior and reports him to the Supreme Thearch, who orders that he be punished in both this world and the next. The Divine Lord, receiving the divine pronouncement, immediately dispatches the local god to begin Li's punish with a supernatural beating. This does not, however, lead him to change his ways, and a succession of this-worldly disasters begins to plague him. First overwork causes him to lose his sight. Then his wife leaves him and his children, who were born blind. Still driven by his greed, he works blindly, doing grievous harm to his hands that eventually leads to his death, but only after making a public confession of his transgressions so that others will not follow his benighted course.

---

305. *Liji zhushu* 16/25a.
306. *Shiji* 6/245.
307. In Song times a pint (*sheng*) was approximately 664 ml and a peck (*dou*) hence about 6.64 l. An ounce (*liang*) was about 37.3 g and a catty (*jin*) 596.8 g. See Yang Diangui et. al. 1983: 286–89.

56.　*Ox Mountain*　　　牛山

Accumulated good acts will surely meet with a good, ripe fruit,
Evil men will still meet with an evil karmic fate.
Just and equitable Gou Xin received no harmful retribution,
Cruel and severe Su Zhen aroused a calamitous reproof.
Some only sow rice and sorghum until the field is full,
Then give no thought to briars that come to pierce the sky.
I ask you to take a look at the rain dripping from the eaves,
One drop follows another, showing no favoritism.

Ox Mountain is in Shu commandery, by the confluence of the Fu
涪 and Qi 郪 rivers. On the slopes of the mountain there is a town,
Fanyan 繁衍.[308] The dwellings of the town's two clerks, Gou Xin 苟
信 and Su Zhen 蘇珍, were adjacent, but the men were opposites in
every respect. Whereas Xin was just and forgiving, Zhen was extremely
harsh. Xin was honest and principled; Zhen, avaricious and corrupt.
Xin strove for individual excellence; Zhen resorted to secret plots. Xin
trusted others and hid nothing; Zhen hid his resentment deep within. Xin always kept his word and did not give it lightly; Zhen, squar-
ing his shoulders, flattered and fawned insincerely. Xin served his mother
filially and instructed his sons sternly; Zhen waited on his father dis-
respectfully and allowed his wife to offend those above her. Xin was
undemanding and economical; Zhen was extravagant and wasteful
and never saved anything. Xin got along with those above and below
him and never spoke resentfully; Zhen measured others by his own
standards and was unforgiving. Xin overlooked the faults of others
and seldom spoke of them; Zhen disclosed their secrets and published
them abroad. Both publicly and in private all the people of the community thought Xin was worthy and thought moreover that Xin was
incapable of opposing Zhen because Zhen would dare to do anything.

---

308. Following the 1645 ed. and DZ in reading Fanyan 繁衍 for DZJY's Xiyan 繫衍. Since the
town was too small to be recorded in geographical works, there is no basis upon which to choose
between these names, but Fanyan ("overflowing prosperity") seems more likely.

At the end of the year the people of the town gathered together in a great assembly. While drinking, a local elder, Zhou Tong 周同, raised his hand and pointed to the crowd, saying, "In Qin there are two rivers, the Wei 渭 and the Jing 涇. One is turbid, the other clear. Both empty into the Yellow River. They arise from different origins and flow down from there without turning back. A three-foot-high boy, seeing their color, can distinguish the Jing from the Wei, because he relies on their turbidity or clearness. It is the same with men." He had not yet finished speaking when Zhen, his face completely red,[309] rose with a flap of his sleeves, and said, "Master Gou is the (turbid) Wei and I am the Jing! I work together with Gou Xin and we live right next door to each other. Only Xin is completely familiar with my actions. Now Xin has bruited about my evil acts, having an elder make an analogy with rivers in front of this crowd. I will avenge myself upon Xin in order to make my feelings clear." Xin had actually never told anyone. From that day forward every time Zhen met Xin he would glare angrily at him. Though they interacted in a polite and cultured manner, in fact they were secretly enemies. Zhen also told his son, Mingneng 明能, to look for a chance to kill Xin's son, Yizhen 儀眞. The next year at the spring festivities for praying for the silkworms, Mingneng and Yizhen were walking together along the river, laughing and talking. Mingneng had evil intentions but Yizhen did not realize it. Mingneng pushed Yizhen into the water with all his might. Yizhen frantically grabbed Mingneng's robe and both fell in together, sinking and surfacing among the waves. The various dragon lords and I were in attendance in the seats provided for the gods. I ordered the dragons of the two rivers to go save them. The lords of the Qi and Fu rivers knew full well the details concerning the two boys. They led Yizhen close to the shore and swirled Mingneng out into the depths. Soon Su Zhen noticed this and, raising the hem of his robe, went in to grab Yizhen and push him away. Zhen was grabbed and dragged in by Yizhen. The observers were like a wall, their shouts and cries[310] boiling up. I thought this

---

309. DZ reads, "face and neck both red."
310. Following the 1645 ed. and DZ in reading *ku* 哭, "cry," for *xiao* 笑, "laugh."

was unfair and had the dragon of the Qi drag the foot of Zhen under. Yizhen escaped without injury, while Su Zhen and his son both drowned. The myriad people all said to each other, "Who says that the dragons and other heavenly creatures have favorites? The fortunes of Zhen and Xin were not to wait for another day. Surely Xin's good fruit was ripe and Zhen's bad karma was at a peak."

COMMENTARY

A good subofficial is rewarded and a bad one punished. This story presents us with both positive and negative models. Gou Xin is everything the ideal local clerk should be: liberal, just, honest, forgiving, and filial. Su Zhen represents the stereotypical evil clerk: greedy, dishonest, cruel, and vain.

The differences between the two men are obvious to themselves and to the townspeople, but no one dares mention it. An enraged subaltern can be a dangerous enemy. Then one day at a local festival one of the respected old men of the town, a bit inebriated, dares to broach the subject through an allegory that compares the two men to two rivers: one pure like Gou Xin, the other muddy and corrupt like Su Zhen. The comparison is taken from the *Shijing* where it is said that, "The Jing is made turbid by the Wei."[311] Su Zhen, of course, immediately divines the true intent of this statement and openly accuses Gou Xin of putting the old man up to it. He resolves to revenge himself upon Xin and instructs his own son to attack Xin's son. The chance comes at the annual prayer for an abundant silk crop the following spring. When Su Zhen's son tries to kill Gou Xin's by pushing him in the river, things do not go as planned, and Su Mingneng is pulled in as well. As in most religious festivals in China, a primary object of the festivities was to entertain the local gods, and the Divine Lord as well as the dragon rulers of the two rivers and no doubt other local deities have been installed in a good location to see the entertainments. They see what has happened and the Divine Lord decides to intervene. He dispatches the two dragons, who, knowing the nature of the two youths, decide to save Gou Yizhen and let Su Mingneng drown.

---

311. *Maoshi zhengyi* 2b/12a. There is dispute as to which stream is supposed to be clear and which muddy. Many, including Zhu Xi, would read, "The Jing is shown to be turbid by contrast with the Wei." However the statement by Su Zhen makes clear that the line is understood otherwise here.

When Su Zhen tries again to kill Yizhen he is himself pulled in, and this time it is the Divine Lord who orders that he be drowned.

The moral of this story is that the workings of karma are impartial and inexorable, punishing the evil and rewarding the good. The poem compares dispensation of this karma by Heaven to the water dripping from the eaves on a rainy day, constant and equally distributed. The story shows a fair amount of Buddhist influence, in both the emphasis on karma, and the reference to the dragons as members of the eight classes of supernatural creatures who guard the Buddhadharma. But the ethical ideals expressed, the religious festival portrayed, and the functioning of karma through the actions of official-like divine bureaucrats rather than an abstract cosmic principle are distinctively Chinese.

57. *The Daunting Power of Heaven*　　天威

A woman's nature is basically filled with predjudices.
How could it be easy to be perfect in filial reverence and earnest
　　diligence?
Though karma from a past life fated her to suffer the thunder axe,
In her present form she was favored by affinities from serving
　　her parents.
The cruel flames that span the heavens were stilled for a
　　moment;
The daunting wind that seemed to roll up the ground suddenly
　　shifted.
Madame née Ma's body was burned, the wife of Zhi was spared.
Thus we know that public opinion conforms to Heaven.

Zhi Zuyi 支祖宜 was an inhabitant of the town of Qi 郪. His wife, Madame née Yu 喻, was twenty-five years old. Her mother-in-law, Madame née Huang 黃, was eighty and had a malady of the eyes that rendered her blind. She was by nature narrow-minded and severe, fond of cleanliness, and difficult to serve. But Yu, in her youth, was diligent, economical, reverent, and obedient, and was able to please her for three years without criticism. Her husband, while drunk, mistakenly ran into someone and knocked him down, knocking out two teeth. He pleaded that he not be punished, offering to redeem himself by paying a portion of his wealth. He took Yu's dowry to pay this, but Yu had no regrets. One night the deity of the locality seized her and accused her, saying, "In your previous life you were the wife of a neighbor, Mou Rong 牟容. At the age of thirty you suffered recurring bouts of illness and for more than a year your mother-in-law, who was over seventy, cooked congee for you to eat. Because you got tired of eating this too often, you tearfully scolded her several times. The day before you were to die you called upon Heaven, facing your mother-in-law and saying, "This seventy-year-old does not die but I who am just thirty am caused to die. O Heaven, Heaven, why are you so unjust?" The Director of Fate of your household reported this to the Heavenly Thearch, who issued a command that your body be burned. But by then you had already died. The punishment having never been carried out, the documents are still there. Thirty years is one generation. Now the account should be resolved and it is your karma to die from a thunder axe. You can expect this in the coming days. Because you have been filial in this present life, I have come to inform you of this in advance." Yu started awake. In the middle of the night she sat up and cried. Her husband was away from home on family business and had not returned. Her mother-in-law said, "Do you think that because my son has destroyed your dowry that he will never be able to repay you?" Yu said, "No." Early the next morning she bathed, washed her hair, and put on new clothes, then bowing to her mother-in-law, said, "This bride has served you for three years without complaint. Now I ask for leave to return to my home briefly. I fear that I may unexpectedly die and never return. Please take good care of yourself." Her mother-in-law was startled by these unusual words. When Yu was taking leave of her parents she said the same thing. She then lit incense and, standing under a great tree south of the house, prayed, "This bride's death accords with karma and cannot be rejected. I worry much about the following: First, my husband is poor and my mother-in-law old. If they lose a wife at this late date who will serve them? Second, my mother and father taught and instructed me since my youth. If I am executed by Heaven, it will humiliate them. Third, I am now already seven months pregnant. If by some remote chance I should have a boy, this will provide a descendant for the Zhi family. Now the first two problems cannot be avoided. My only worry is that the Zhi family will be left without descendants. I ask a slight extension of three months, so that I might die after giving birth." At the time it was the middle of the hot season; clouds darkened the days and winds and thunder followed one after the other. The god of the locality mentioned this affair to me. When I understood her intentions, I submitted a memorial on her behalf. A rescript ordered that an evil member of the community be taken in her place. Madame née Ma 馬, the wife of the rich man Zhang Shi 張實, was lascivious and rebellious. She was impolite in serving her mother-in-law[312] and ordered her husband about like a slave. I sent the local god and the God of Thunder Fire to punish her. Soon Yu had no problems and Zhang Shi's wife had been incinerated.

COMMENTARY

The god adjusts karmically ordained fates in response to recent virtue. Madame née Yu had in a previously lifetime served her mother-in-law poorly. Although her aged mother-in-law had waited on her during a protracted illness, she rebuked her and wished her death. Her actions were reported by the Director of Fates assigned to her home, the lowest ranking of a hierarchy of like-named officials culminating in the astral deity whose stellar abode is located within the constellation Wenchang. The Supreme Thearch pronounces sentence, ordering that her body be consumed by the divine fire of a bolt of lightning. It was thought that such lightning was caused by a god hurling down a "thunder axe" or "thunder stone." The god that became the Divine

---

312. DZ reads "mother- and father-in-law."

Lord was originally a thunder god, and his projectiles were called "thunder shuttles" 雷杼.[313] In this story, however, the Divine Lord is already too exalted a figure to perform a common execution himself; instead he delegates the task to another deity with special talents, the God of Thunder Fire 雷火神, who is otherwise unknown.

In this story Madame née Yu is granted a reprieve from her karmically ordained fate for several reasons. First, she has served her mother-in-law in this present life with special diligence and respect, in spite of the fact that the woman is more than a little difficult to get along with. She is also devoted to her parents and her husband, and her unselfishness is revealed by her reaction when she is forced to give up her only possession, her dowry, in order to ransom her husband from the clutches of the law. Second, she makes a pious petition to the gods, not asking for her own life, but explaining why she should be granted a few more months so that she may bear a child for the Zhi family, and also pointing out how great a loss her death would be to the Zhis and how great an embarrassment to her parents. Her selfless attitude convinces the Divine Lord, who intercedes on her behalf. It is decided that the punishment be shifted to some other, more blameworthy individual.

The *Book of Transformations* teaches a doctrine of karma that entails retribution for good and evil actions in this life, in the afterlife, or in a subsequent incarnation. In the great majority of cases, however, the rewards and punishments come immediately, during this life, so that they can serve as a warning to others. This is the first case in the *Book of Transformations* in which a residual punishment awaits from a previous life, and it was only through an accident of fate that the implementation of supernatural punishment was delayed so long. Further, the reason why the punishment must now go forward is quite bureaucratic in nature: the documents are all made out and are awaiting execution. Thus we see in this episode a Chinese formulation of the Indian doctrine of karmic retribution, one that is more immediate, more bureaucratic, and more focused on the function of retribution as a warning to others than in the original Indian conception.

---

313. See Kleeman 1988: 10–12 for a discussion of thunder shuttles and thunder axes.

58. *Esteeming Righteousness*   尚義

Brothers[314] are born from the same father.
The closest of relatives; how can they lack emotion?
Li Hua's treatment of Wei was truly admirable,
Yong Di's cheating Yuan was too unjust.
When he broke his arm popular opinion recognized the
   immediate retribution,
On the community gates was published the public estimation of
   their fine reputation.
Thus niggardly customs were made rich and pure,
Siblings were harmonious like geese in flight, and strife was
   avoided.

On the banks of the Dang River[315] a town clerk, Yong Di 雍滌,
had a younger brother, Yuan 源, who also held a position in the bureaucracy. He was constantly mistreated by Di, but served him with
equanimity as an elder. Di and Yuan married two daughters of the
Liang 梁 family. The brothers fought for every little bit of the family
property; after a while Di and Yuan became sworn enemies, and the
sisters-in-law twins in enmity. The Yong father and mother were unable to control them and so suggested living separately. They wanted
to let Yuan keep his room but Di would not permit it and drove him
out with nothing. He also charged Yuan and his wife to contribute
regularly (to their parents). Soon thereafter Di met Yuan on the road
and, accusing Yuan of not bowing to him, beat him. Having already
injured him, he further lodged a complaint against him with the district administration. The District Grand Master 鄉大夫 investigated
his statement and punished Di for perjury. Di's wife went to Yuan's

---

314. DZ reads "sibling responsibilities" (*kunyi* 昆義). The 1645 ed. has *ji* 季, which can mean the
youngest in a group of brothers, for *di* 弟, "younger brother."

315. Following DZ in reading *dang* 瀁 for *tang* 儻. The Dang River, in southern Shaanxi province,
is mentioned in the *Shuijing zhu* 27/11a.

gate and, dragging her younger sister out, also beat her, saying, "According to the law there are distinctions of senior and junior. You cannot grant precedence to[316] the junior and whip the senior!" Local opinion did not support her.

The father of Li Hua李華 had a son by a scullery maid late in life. As he lay dying, he entrusted him to Hua, saying, "Take him as your son." Hua tearfully replied, "Although this child's mother was mean, he partakes of the same vital energy as I. When someday I have reared him and made him into something, he will have his due place in the ancestral hall, as Heaven is my witness!" Later he named the child Wei 蔚, and doted on him. When the boy was grown and had become a famous scholar, Hua arranged a marriage for him. Hua had a son named Miming 彌明 who was ten years older than Wei. As soon as Wei could talk, Hua had Miming bow to him. When he was grown, Miming accorded Wei a ritual respect one degree less than that accorded his father. Hua, his son, and Wei were all recommended by the men of the district. Their names reached the Grand Protector of the commandery who submitted them to the Spring Office. There the discussion resulted in an official position for Miming. Miming spoke improperly to Wei and Hua beat him. Miming accepted the correctness of this punishment. Shortly thereafter Hua gave all of the family possessions to Wei, saying, "Take charge of this, my younger brother. Miming has his own salary to support himself." His fellow villagers considered this excellent.

At the time of the autumn gathering at the altar to the god of the soil, I participated in the sacrifice. The people of the village compared Li and Yong to sweet basil 薰 and potamegeton 蕕.[317] Di, hearing this, castigated the assembly. Again he dragged Yuan forth and struck him. I thought this unfair and had the watchman on duty twist his arm, breaking it. An abscess soon appeared on the hand of Di's wife. His misfortune continued for three years until he had lost everything, both publicly and privately, and his life was in shambles. His father

---

316. DZ reads *li* 立, "establish," for *zhu* 主, "control, grant precedence to."

317. For the identification of these two plants, see Stuart 1911: 262 and 348. They are commonly cited as exemplars of fragrant and foul-smelling plants, based on a passage in the *Zuozhuan*. See *Chunqiu Zuozhuan zhengyi* 12/15a.

and mother passed away in succession, and Di and his wife died as beggars. People of the village thought it was the retribution for un-righteousness. The Grand Protector gave a banner to Hua's community, proclaiming it "Esteeming Righteousness."

The topic of this chapter is sibling relations. The Chinese ideal with regard to the relationship between siblings is expressed in the term *ti* 悌. It is a mutual relationship, within which the younger sibling owes the older respect and the older owes the younger consideration. An image often referred to is the v-shaped formation of a flock of geese in flight, each goose showing due deference to the one in front by flying behind him. As in chapter 56, we are presented with two conflicting models of behavior, one bad and one good, and the divine response that each occasions.

The first case presents an evil Yong Di who mistreats and persecutes his younger brother while this brother responds with perfect fraternal submission and respect. When the parents suggest that the younger brother establish a separate household, meaning an independent set of rooms with its own hearth within the family compound,[318] Yong Di seizes on the suggestion to force the brother out of the compound altogether, then continues to bully and mistreat him at every opportunity.

Li Hua's case exemplifies another tension within China's polygamous extended families. Since the patriarch had legitimate sexual access to a number of females and all offspring were considered potential heirs, sons of concubines and maidservants were often the cause of devastating intrafamilial conflicts, particularly upon the death of the patriarch. Li Hua presents an ideal model for treatment of a disadvantaged half-brother that would resolve such conflicts in favor of ethical standards rather than self-interest, but this altruism is rewarded when Li's neighbors recommend his son for an official post.[319]

To a certain degree the normal workings of the temporal government have already rewarded the good and punished the evil in this

---

318. This type of lineage fission is still practiced in Taiwan. See Wang Sung-hsing 1974: 184–86.

319. Such recommendation was a responsibility of the District Elders (*xianglao* 鄉老) and the District Grand Master during the Zhou dynasty. See *Zhouli zhushu* 12/2a–3a; Hucker 1985: 2338, 2353.

case, through the official position granted Li Hua's son and through the punishment imposed upon Yong Di for making unfounded accusations concerning his younger brother. Yong Di's intransigent ill-will leads the Divine Lord to intervene at the autumn convocation to thank the local god of the soil for that year's harvest (*qiushe* 秋社). The Divine Lord is among the deities receiving sacrifice at this festival, and hence he is in attendance. One of the social functions of these gatherings was to permit the entire community to gather together and discuss local problems and events.[320] It is during such gatherings and discussions that the public opinion that has been cited repeatedly in the last few chapters took form. Here the locals comment on the disparity between the conduct of the Yongs and the Lis. When Yong Di takes umbrage at this and again attacks his younger brother, the Divine Lord has his arm broken, though it is unclear whether his emissary here is a supernatural or temporal functionary. This is followed by several years of divinely ordained misfortune that lead to a pauper's death for Di and his wife. Li Hua's virtuous conduct results in official recognition of the entire community for its sterling moral character, demonstrating how individuals were thought to influence all those about them and to make a direct contribution to the community through their personal behavior.

59. *Recognizing a Recluse*   旌隱

Worldly realities and customs most influence men.
Through the dust and toil of daily life one loses one's original
   perfection.
Master Mou, maintaining the Dao, was aided by Heaven.
Rash Mister Su still suffers the wrath of demons.
Through transmission and recitation my supreme words became
   a model;

---

320. In this sense they are similar to the community compact meetings promoted by Neo-Confucian reformers in the Song. See Übelhör 1989.

Temple offerings and popular worship brought me a vast and
magnificent abode.[321]
The men of Shu for the first time respected the teachings of the
central states,
Common scholars in one day became real and pure.

Following the Qin annexation of Shu, men gradually appeared
who studied the flourishing Chinese culture and the transforming influence of the great Way of the former kings. But the winds of pure
sincerity had not yet made themselves felt and self-satisfied, frivolous
fellows vied for eminence. I feared that they would harm social mores
and decided I wanted to morally transform (*hua* 化) them. One day I
came across a man of Dangqu 宕渠, in Ba commandery, named Mou
Lin 牟麟. He was unflagging in his love of learning and enjoyed
teaching others. In his preservation of the Dao he was scrupulous and
unassuming. Unless there was some important reason for doing so he
would not leave his home, and during the seasonal activities he would
receive visitors but would not go out to visit others. He was very poor
but never complained resentfully about it. The Protector of the commandery, Wen Yu 溫瑀, invited him to take a position as his retainer
(*congshi* 從事). When he did not respond to this summons, Wen's
aide Yu Yi 于辰 went to call on him. They chatted for over two
hours, talking about how to find repose[322] in the times and adjust to
changes, how to take care of one's self and avoid the world. Yi wanted
to convey the words of the Protector, but did not get a chance to
speak of it. He finally gave up. When he reported this incident to
Wen Yu, Wen was impressed with Lin's integrity.

Su Shanggong 蘇尙功 had once studied with Lin. He had quit
before finishing his studies and opened his own school in which he

---

321. The term *huanlun* 奐輪 derives from a passage in the *Record of Rites*, in which the two words
are used independently to describe a residence just completed by Baron Wen of Zhao: "Sire Zhang said,
'How beautiful its vastness; how beautiful its extensiveness'" (*Meizai, huanyan. Meizai, lunyan* 美哉奐
焉美哉輪焉). It is possible the author intended a reference to this elderly Zhang in selecting this term
to describe the god's great success in winning devotees and the spacious quarters of his "palaces" (*gong*
宮), as the larger temples of Daoism and the popular cults were often dubbed. See *Liji zhengyi* 10/23b,
Legge, *Li Ki*, Vol. 1, p. 196.

322. Following the 1645 ed. and DZ in reading *an* 安, "repose," for *yin* 因, "rely upon."

accepted[323] disciples, declaring himself a teacher. But he was by nature competitive and never rested for a moment, making requests and paying calls with a slave's face and maidservant's knees. Lin held him in contempt. When someone told him about Lin's intention (to reject the appointment), Shanggong went to his home and argued with him. Lin, considering that he had once instructed Shanggong, still spoke to him as his mentor, saying, "'Fate controls life and death; prosperity and fame rest with Heaven'; these are the words of Zixia 子夏.[324] 'In seeking for things there is the Dao; in obtaining them there is fate. This means that seeking does not help in obtaining'; these are the words of Mengzi.[325] I am really ashamed of the things you do." Shanggong, relying on the physical prowess and courage of his youth, struck Lin.

I happened to observe this. I transformed into a scholar and interceded in the fight. Looking at the crowd I addressed them, saying, "Man's longevity and success are controlled by fate. They are not decided by men's actions. One who competes shamelessly does not know his fate. What good does it do to seek that which is not in one's fate? You should not seek for it.[326] If you should happen to get something and think that you got it because you sought for it and that seeking leads to obtaining, then you do not know the Dao. If one does not know one's fate and does not know the Dao, he has lost that which he seeks to preserve. Owing to this he will become self-indulgent, boorish, deviant, and extravagant, and will end up unrighteous, disloyal, and unfilial. What makes these two as different as ice and coal is the distinction between the superior man and the small man." The onlookers were packed shoulder to shoulder. One asked me, "Who are you?" I said, "I am the one they call Zhang Zhongzi." The crowd was startled, and while they were looking at each other I disappeared. Afterwards all near and far came to hear of this affair. Those who had been Shanggong's disciples reformed their

---

323. Following the 1645 ed. and DZ in reading *shou*受, "accepted," for *shou* 授, "instructed."

324. *Lunyu zhushu* 12/2b.

325. *Mengzi zhushu* 13a/4a. DZ refers to Mengzi by his sobriquet, Ziyu 子輿, rather than his surname.

326. DZ reads, "If you should constantly seek for it . . ." 以常求之.

behavior, and pure customs appeared. The people of Qu erected a temple to me.

COMMENTARY

The Divine Lord in this episode supports the role of the recluse and teaches a Confucian conception of fate.

A constant feature of Chinese society since at least the Warring States period has been the presence of individuals who preferred to withdraw from the intrigues and tribulations of an official career to a life of semi-retirement.[327] They did not go off into the wilds and practice the ascetic eremitism of the Christian hermit or Indian *sunnyasin*. Rather, they lived within the confines of rural Chinese society, often not far from major urban centers. Their distinguishing feature was that they refused to be drawn into a life of official service, with its constant pressures and dangers, and did not fully participate in the annual cycle of ritual visits, meetings, and exchanges of gifts through which a network of local alliances and hence a local power base was formed. They were not, however, completely estranged from their communities. Even a recluse must support himself, and many did so by accepting students, as is the case with Mou Lin in our current story. But the recluse should not engage in the shameless acts attributed to Lin's failed student, Su Shanggong, who rushes about currying favor with every local notable, displaying a sycophantic servility that is described as "a slave's face and a maidservant's knees."

Such a recluse might justify his refusal of official service in several ways. The ruler might be unenlightened, making the fulfillment of the duties of a highly principled official impossible, even dangerous. There might be no one in power perceptive enough to recognize the recluse's sterling qualities and offer him a position the recluse deemed suitable to his talents. Or the recluse might simply be be born at the wrong time, star-crossed, cosmologically restrained from achieving his potential. All three explanations distance the recluse personally from the potentially disloyal decision to refuse an offer of government service and all rationalize the recluse's lack of worldly success, but only the third accomplishes these tasks without arousing righteous anger at the willfully evil or simply incompetent representatives of the state.

---

327. On reclusion in China, see Berkowitz 1989 and Vervoorn 1990.

Such righteous anger was a threat to tranquility and religious development just as it was a potential threat to the state and its local representatives. Thus when the local official, Wen Yu, offers Ling the
position of Retainer, an unranked aide-de-camp who oversaw the
clerical staff,[328] it may be that Lin rejected this position because he
felt it inappropriate for a man of his abilities, but he formulates his
rejection as an acceptance of his fate (*ming* 命).

It is often assumed that the inspiration for a life of seclusion was
primarily Daoist, perhaps because the Daoists often seem negative and
world-rejecting when contrasted with the positivist Confucian ideal of
service to the state. In fact there seems to be little correlation between
recluses and specific philosophical schools. Confucius himself achieved
no great success career-wise, and it is not surprising, therefore, that we
find Confucian authors espousing a doctrine of fate that both relieved
them of the necessity to face their own failure and at the same time
avoided explicit condemnation of temporal rulers who were at once
perilous potential enemies and preferred potential employers. In rejecting Su Shanggong's impertinent advice, Mou Lin quotes one of
Confucius's disciples, Zixia, and Confucius's primary ideological heir,
Mengzi. When Su tries to silence Mou Lin with violence, the Divine
Lord appears and confirms the correctness of this essentially fatalistic
view of life. His dramatic appearance and subjugation of the bullying
Su lead the common people to revere him even more and establish a
temple in which to worship him.

This story is set within the context of the ongoing Sinicization of
the Shu region. It thus parallels the opening chapters (especially 4 and
5), in which the Divine Lord promotes the customs, culture, and
mores of the Central Plain culture among the aborigines of the
Southeast.

---

328. See Hucker 1985: 535, entry 7176.

60. *Aiding the Upright*   祐正

Scheming to obtain the wealth of others is already wrong,
How much more so when one conceives the intention to cruelly
  molest.
One word from an upright daughter prayed for a resounding
  response,
An entire room of fortunate people escaped imminent peril.
Suddenly they were startled to find the ropes fall from their
  bodies,
Soon the vicious robbers were all dismembered corpses.
Blessing the good and visiting disaster upon the evil is a
  Heavenly principle.
I did not act privately on their behalf because I had received
  their offerings.

Zhi Quanli 智全禮, of a rich family from the northern ramparts
(of Chengdu) offered sacrifice on the day of Mid-Spring. Everyone in
the house was drunk. The bandit Wang Cai 王才, summoning three
of his confederates, planned to rob them. Before the night was over
they burst through the door and bound everyone in Quanli's family,
including nine people of gentle and mean status and seven maidservants and concubines. Only Quanli's wife and two daughters had
not yet been bound. Having taken the family's possessions, the in-
truders meant to rape them. Quanli's wife frantically begged for mercy.
His younger daughter Shunhua 舜華, who was fifteen, and her elder
sister Shunying 舜英 embraced their mother, crying. Just as Cai was
about to force his intentions on them, Shunhua rebuked them saying, "You hungry villains invade our home. The Sacred Lord Zhang
張神君 does not know about you yet!" When she had finished
speaking, the Director of Fates of her house, Cui Xuan 崔瑄, and the
ancestral spirits of the Zhis reported the emergency to me. I immediately sent a deputy, Fu Xing 輔興, at the head of a hundred

supernatural troops to subdue them. All of the bound people, from Quanli on down, were released and all of the villains were captured. The next day these events were reported to the village headman, who memorialized them to the commandery. All were executed.

COMMENTARY

The theme in this episode is that the righteous receive the special protection of the gods. In this case it is the innocent adolescent daughter of the Zhi family who pleads for divine assistance.

The occasion is the fifteenth day of the second lunar month. There is little record of the Mid-Spring festival and we are not sure to whom sacrifices are offered on this occasion. The third day of the second month is the birthday of the Divine Lord of Zitong, and this would fit in nicely with the story. Today the festival at Zitong extends until the fifteenth day of the second month. The first *ding* day in the month is set aside for Confucius. But it is likely that reference is made to more general sacrifices to the god of the soil and to the ancestors. Sacrifices to the god of the soil occur twice a year, generally in the second and eighth months, although the date of the first day of the festival varies from community to community, ranging from the end of the first month to the beginning of the third.[329] Similarly, rituals to those gods on the official calendar of sacrifices are generally performed in the spring and fall, during the second and eighth months.

When the Zhi home is invaded by bandits, the household Director of Fates and the family's ancestral spirits report this to the Divine Lord, both because he is their superior in the divine hierarchy and because he has been specifically invoked by the daughter. We have seen the household tutelary god play a similar role in chapter 44. The ancestors are also thought to be constantly looking after their descendants, but they may have been especially attentive at this time because they were to receive sacrifice.

The Zhi family, living in the northern suburbs of Chengdu, no doubt would have had a special relationship with the Divine Lord, who was still known as Zhang Zhongzi of the Northern Ramparts, and would have regularly offered him sacrifice. But in the poem he insists that this is not why he came to their aid. Rather it was a natural

---

329. *Suishi guangji* 14/141.

response to the virtue and commendable moral character of the individuals in distress. Heaven protects the good and proper gods do not accept bribes.

61. *Killing Living Creatures*   殺生

All creatures that move and have spirits possess a life force.
They desire life and fear death just like man.
Because men long for the taste of their fat and marrow,
They consign them to chopping blocks, knives, cauldrons, and
  woks.
Giving no thought to the wrathful souls that will follow their
  shadows and echoes,
They only know the succulent flavors that moisten[330] their
  palates.
Du Zhang fully enjoyed good fortune in his early life,
When the karmic fruit was ripe, the retribution was not trivial.

In Qiong there was a man named Du Zhang 杜章, who was a distant relative of Emperor Wang.[331] He was born into a rich and distinguished family. His ancestors were fond of feasting and this had become a habit.[332] Zhang personally attended to all cooking and butchering. When he was grown he had his own household, and there was not a day that the kitchen was quiet. No sooner were the minced and roasted meats in his mouth than the knife and cudgel were in his hand. Later, through a succession of disasters, the family fortunes declined and he was left with nothing on which to live. He

---

330. DZ reads *mei* 美, "pleases."
331. Following DZ in reading *zhi* 支, "different branch of the same clan," for *you* 友, "friend." The DZJY reading is a copyist's error based on graphic similarity.
332. DZ reads "his father and mother were fond of feasting, entertaining, and gatherings and this had become a habit" (*fumu hao yanle jihui yiwei chang* 父母宴樂集會以為常).

butchered for others in order to feed himself. The money he got from others he called "life-passing cash." Further, he ate as much as two people and this gluttony became a disorder. As soon as he was full he was hungry again. Yet he was by nature fond of meat and could never get enough. He even took to catching fish with a net and shooting sparrows with tethered arrows. Whenever he saw a bird or animal he wanted to kill it.

In his middle-age he had five sons, all of whom were born without fingers. Pressed to feed so many mouths, his "life-passing" funds were insufficient to get by on. He was frantic, with no place to turn. Soon he developed leprosy. His skin split and blood and pus oozed forth. Those who saw him covered their noses. From this time on he suffered terribly from the burning fire of hunger. He tried to commit suicide by throwing himself down a well but was stopped by others and cursed them violently. Then he turned his face to the Heavens and proclaimed the injustice of his plight.

I happened to see him. Surprised, I inquired of the local administrator, Sun Hongshu 孫洪叔, who told me the details. He further said that this man's fortune was exhausted, but that his allotted lifespan was long, with five years still remaining. Once I knew how he had created this karma, I took pity on the bitterness of his suffering. Moreover his appointed time was still far off and I could not stand his reviling the Heavenly Thearch day and night. So I sent a deputy to change his heart, making him peel off the scabs of his abscesses with his fingers and eat them, dip fingers in the blood and pus and suck them to taste it, and to proclaim to others, "Do not create the karma of killing living creatures. Let me be your warning." He passed the years like this until the allotted number were all spent. When his lifespan[333] was exhausted he died. His sons all starved to death.

COMMENTARY

A prohibition on killing animals is not native to the Chinese religious tradition. The archaic religion of the Shang and Zhou centered

---

333. The 1645 ed., DZ, and SG all read *nian* 念, "thought, idea," for the graphically similar *ming* 命, "lifespan," but this reading makes no sense in context.

on elaborate sacrifices of a variety of animals, and, at least in the Shang period, large-scale human sacrifice. Bloody sacrifice of domestic animals and fowl remained a constant feature of the state cult throughout imperial times. Local gods and demons of the popular pantheon subsisted on bloody sacrifice, as did the terrestrial component of the divine bureaucracy, to which the Divine Lord belonged.

The origin of this prohibition is found in India, in the concept of *ahimsa*, no harm to living beings. Buddhism adopted this principle, designating as the first of the five precepts to be observed by all laymen abstention from destruction of life (*prānātipāta*, Chinese *shasheng* 殺生). Buddhism first entered China during the Latter Han dynasty and this principle soon began to influence Chinese religious concepts. One of the two great elements of the Pure Covenant enunciated by the Celestial Master sect at the end of the Han was that the gods (meaning the exalted celestial gods of Daoism in contrast to those of the popular or state cults) do not eat or drink.[334] Formulations of Daoist precepts sometimes included a general proscription on eating meat, although more common were restrictions on eating the domestic animals, the animals of the Chinese zodiac, or that particular animal of the zodiac under whose influence one was born. By Song times vegetarianism was increasing in popularity, especially among popular sectarian movements, the forerunners of the White Lotus organizations that were to form an important current in Chinese religious life throughout Ming and Qing.[335]

In this story it is a member of the aristocracy of the ancient state of Shu who ignores the restrictions against killing living beings. Du Zhang's family has a tradition of sumptuous feasts and, reared in this environment, he comes to undertake the tasks of slaughtering, dressing, and preparing the meat for these dinners himself. This is not as improbable as it seems. In ancient China the preparation of food was considered an extremely important task. The word used most commonly to designate the senior administrator of the government, *zai* 宰, originally referred to a butcher. When Du's family falls on hard times, no doubt because of their inhumane ways, he goes to work as a butcher. His own passion for meat becomes an obsession, to the point

---

334. *1127 Lu Xiansheng daomen kelüe* 1b, 8a.

335. On these groups, see Overmyer 1976. Modern sects like the Way of Former Heaven and the Unity sect are direct descendants of these groups. They are often referred to simply as "vegetarian hall religion" (*zhaitang jiao* 齋堂教).

where he cannot see a living animal without wanting to kill it and devour it on the spot.

These evil deeds soon begin to catch up with him. His five sons are all born without fingers, presumably to keep them from following in his bloody footsteps. In his reduced state he is unable to support his own gluttonous appetite and his large family. He is then afflicted with leprosy. Unaware of his own sins, he blames Heaven for his wretched fate. This draws the attention of the Divine Lord, who inquires into the matter. He finds that the man has used up all of the good fortune (*lu* 祿) which he has been allotted for this lifetime, but that several years still remain of his allotted lifespan (*ming* 命). Rather than have him spend these years uttering blasphemies against the gods, the Divine Lord sends a deputy to show him the error of his ways, so that in his remaining time he may dissuade others from making the same mistake.

62. *Cruel Mistreatment*   酷虐

Gongsun Wuzhong had an honest heart,
His fault lay in whipping and beating his staff too severely.
Lai En of Zishui, by contrast, gave his clerks free rein;
They oppressed the people, no end to their exactions.
My warnings in transformed identity were really the same:
Reform your behavior, be liberal and just and the benefits of
    both can be had.
I trimmed the excesses and augmented the insufficient.
The clerks and people of the two towns both received the
    blessings.

The prefect of the town of Niubei 牛鞞,[336] Gongsun Wuzhong 公孫武仲, administered the town honestly but was unforgiving in

---

336. During the Song this county was located northeast of Neijiang in Sichuan. See Zang 1936: 170.4.

his treatment of others. If one of his aides made some minor error, he beat him one or two hundred strokes. By the time he had been at the post for over a year, there was not a member of his staff of clerks with unmarked flesh. The clerks hated him. The prefect of the town of Zishui 資水, Lai En 賴恩, was by nature avaricious and miserly. It was his habit to accept bribes. He demanded that his clerks provide his daily expenses, his meals, and his seasonal clothing. Those who appeared in his court on civil matters (*minshi* 民事) he uniformly consigned to jail, regardless of whether the complaint was true or false. There he permitted the clerks to make exactions of the imprisoned to their hearts' content. If they were not satisfied, he would delay for months, the case set aside unresolved. The people hated this. Because the clerks and people of the two towns were suffering, I transformed my identity, becoming the Attendant of Shu commandery, Zhangsun Yi 長孫義, on a tour of the towns of the region to observe their customs. I indicted Wuzhong for abusing his staff and Lai En for his oppression of the people. The two prefects kowtowed and begged for forgiveness. I admonished them. Then I disappeared. Later they discovered that the commandery attendant had never gone on a tour of towns and all, taking me for a god, reverently believed in me. Wuzhong reformed himself, becoming loyal and forgiving. En also changed, becoming honest and pure.

COMMENTARY

In this episode the Divine Lord of Zitong addresses the problems of local government. In imperial China the local administrator coming to a new post was confronted by a staff of unknown background and uncertain loyalties upon whom he was forced to rely for almost all interaction with the local community. Since he seldom knew the local dialect, communications with all but the upper elite trained in official speech (*guanhua* 官話) were carried out through the mediation of the staff. How the local official was to gain effective control over this staff and oversee their conduct was a constant problem.

In this story we are presented with two extreme methods of dealing with subordinates. Gongsun Wuzhong is himself highly principled, and he demands the same sort of correct, efficient conduct on the part of his staff. When they fail to live up to his expectations he resorts to severe physical punishments. Lai En, less scrupulous in his own behavior, takes an opposite tack. He lets his staff run wild, manipulating all but the most serious violent crimes so as to maximize their own dishonest income in bribes and extorted payments. If the accused is not sufficiently forthcoming, they leave him to languish in jail for months. In return for this benign neglect, Lai En demands that his staff defray all of his living costs, including the ceremonial vestments required for the different seasons and their festivals and functions.

The Divine Lord condemns the behavior of both these men, the first for his offenses against his staff, the second for the depredations he permits his staff to visit upon the people. The Divine Lord himself set a different standard. The opening line of his *Writing on the Hidden Administration* 陰騭文 proclaims, "For seventeen incarnations I have been a scholar-official, and I have never mistreated the people or oppressed my staff."[337] He decides to manifest in human form and admonish them in person, and to do so he temporarily adopts the form of a real-world official, the second-highest official in the commandery of Shu. The god's previous human manifestations had been as poor, upright scholars, figures outside of the administrative order and, to some degree, in opposition to it. By now taking on the form of a high official, he brings the sacred into the power structure. The local magistrate now shares with Daoist hermits and mad monks the possibility of divinity. When Gongsun Wuzhong and Lai En discover that it was in fact a god who had visited them, they are shocked and change their ways.

63. *Commiserating with the World* 憫世

The Zhou house slid into decadence, became unbenevolent;
In a single morning the flourishing Jis gave way to the Yings of Qin.

---

337. On this text, see Sakai 1957, 1960.

Their cruel punishments and vicious officials[338] were devoid of
   harmonious breaths,
How many more springs will their sly schemes exhaust the
   army?
I could not bear to see the Central Plain suffer this disaster;
I wanted to open my heart to save the people.
Heaven Above issued a rescript, bestowing its approval,
After the rain the cosmic forces of yin and yang were renewed.

I had once served the Zhou and loyally gave up my life for them. It
was not long after I began to receive bloody sacrifice in Shu that Shu
was incorporated into Qin. Then the Zhou lost the empire and it all
belonged to the Ying clan. Qin employed punishments and laws,
treating the people as no more than weeds. When Qin declined, conflict arose again and the Central Plain was reduced to mud and ash. It
was like this for a long time. Because I had long resided in a peaceful
realm, I wanted to relieve the people's suffering. So I sent up a "flying"
(i.e., urgent) memorial, and the Thearch acceded to my request,
speaking thus: "The son of the White Thearch has been abroad
among men a long time, and has acted violently, killing and attacking others. I have already sent the son of the Red Thearch to replace
him. Since you were originally in charge of the virtue of fire you
should now be born into the world as a descendant of the son of the
Red Thearch." I accepted his command.

COMMENTARY

   The temporal order continues to change, and the Divine Lord,
moved by the plight of the common people, chooses to incarnate in
order to ameliorate their condition. The state of Qin completed its
unification of China in 221 B.C. and immediately initiated a series of
reforms that standardized weights and measures, the script, communication, currency, and the legal system, but enforced these reforms

---

338. Following DZ in reading *li* 吏 "official," for *li* 戾 "violent." The two words are similar both
graphically and phonetically.

with unprecedented severity. The dynasty was consistently faulted by later thinkers for its adoption of the unforgiving, manipulative administrative methods of the Legalist school, and the same criticism is made here. According to traditional opinion it was largely this ideological error that led to Qin's rapid demise. But the Divine Lord's criticism takes a Daoist turn, claiming that the Qin administration lacked "harmonious breaths" (*heqi* 和氣). These are the breaths of the Central Harmony that forms a triad with yin and yang and represents humankind in the triad with Heaven and Earth, a doctrine first espoused in the *Scripture of Great Peace* 太平經.[339] Through its lack of concern for the populace, Qin had lost possession of one of the three cosmic forces essential for continued existence, one of the Three Daos.

The Qin state disintegrated on the death of the First Emperor in 210 B.C., and local leaders arose in different regions of the country, many hoping to revive the feudal kingdoms of the Warring States era. Strife continued until 202, when Liu Bang 劉邦 succeeded in reunifying the country, establishing the Han dynasty. Many tales were told of the auspicious portents that presaged his illustrious role in history. One centered on an incident that occurred when he was still a local prefect. One night Liu Bang found a large snake blocking his path. He drew his knife and clove the serpent in two. Later an old woman was found there, who cried for her dead son, saying, "My son is the son of the White Thearch, who had transformed into a serpent and was blocking the road. Now he has been beheaded by the son of the Red Thearch."[340] White corresponds to the direction west; the White Thearch, one of a group of five deities associated with the five directions, ruled over the Western Marchmount and was the patron of the state of Qin.[341] His "son," who had been "roaming the world for a long time" was the First Emperor of Qin. Red corresponds to the south and was considered the ruling color of the Han dynasty during most of its reign; the son of the Red Thearch was, of course, Liu Bang. With his victory Harmony returns and the balance between yin and yang is restored. The Divine Lord is commanded to be born into the Liu house and help secure their rule.

---

339. Kaltenmark 1979: 26ff.
340. *Shiji* 8/347. Cf. Chavannes 1895: Vol. 2, p. 331.
341. On the White Thearch see above, chapter 33.

64. *Xianyang* 咸陽

When protecting all of Shu, I had enjoyed my leisure;
Now responding to the pulls of the world, I struggled to stand out.
Though praised, I did not succeed in assuming the succession;
I lost my life and vainly formed ties of enmity and vengeance.
In the end, what good did my ill-fated enfeoffment as king do?
Thoughts of avenging my mother torment me ceaselessly.
How could I possibly appear happy?
Only after all the Lüs have been swallowed up will my dark
    distress be dispelled.

Being sincere in my relationship to Heaven above, I wanted to use a transformational body (*huashen* 化身) to rescue the world from the midst of mud and ash and raise the people up to a peaceful, happy realm. What was I to do? The Thearch ordered me to be born as a descendant of the son of the Red Thearch 赤帝. His Jade Tones are awe-inspiring, and I did not dare protest, but when I quietly reflected upon it, it was not what I desired. Suddenly the Great Divinity of the Nine Heavens Supervising Births forced me to accept birth. From amidst the clouds I saw Xianyang below me. After the fiery demise of Qin, the palaces had been rebuilt. The Han emperor was just engaged in a conversation with Consort Qi 戚姬. The Supervisor of Births said to me, "This is the one referred to as the son of the Red Thearch. He is now the emperor of the Han." In a blink of the eye the Great Divinity Supervising Births 監生大神 pushed me and I plunged into the breast of Consort Qi, by the emperor's side. Confusedly I awoke. Because at birth I resembled him in build and appearance, and because my conduct was pleasing, the emperor named me Ruyi 如意 ("according to my wishes"). When I was still at the age of cooing and being held, my intentions were firm and my speech restrained. I especially pleased the emperor, who favored me before others. He would always criticize my elder brother for not resembling him. In his later years he wanted to make me heir-apparent, but this did not come about. After the emperor had passed away, I was finally killed by Madame née Lü 呂. My mother's death was especially cruel and sadistic. I deeply resented it. As I, having just entered the realm of darkness, watched my mother suffer, I would smile when I thought of obtaining vengeance. I would not stop until I had swallowed up all of the Lüs.

COMMENTARY

Having resolved to descend yet again into the mortal plane in order to aid suffering humanity, the Divine Lord is commanded to be born as a son of the founder of the Han dynasty, Liu Bang. He has forebodings about this decision, which foreshadow its tragic result, but does not dare to challenge the command of the Supreme Thearch. He is escorted to the place of his birth by a divine being in charge of the oversight of births.

As an infant the Divine Lord again demonstrates the precocious intelligence and noble demeanor that he has displayed in previous incarnations,[342] and this together with a physical resemblance so endears him to his father that Liu Bang considers naming the Divine Lord to succeed him.

This tale is based closely on accounts in standard historical sources. Sima Qian relates the tale in the following terms:[343]

When Gaozu (i.e., Liu Bang) was King of Han he got Consort Qi of Dingtao, whom he loved and favored. She gave birth to King Ruyi of Zhao. [The future emperor] Xiaohui 孝惠 (i.e., Liu Ying 劉盈, the son of Empress Lü and Heir Apparent) was kind and weak and Gaozu thought that he did not resemble himself. He often thought to depose the Heir Apparent and establish the son of Consort Qi, Ruyi, in that position, [saying], "Ruyi resembles me." Consort Qi had his favor and often accompanied the emperor on trips east of the passes. She would sob and cry day and night, wanting her son to be appointed in place of the Heir Apparent. Empress Lü was older and often

342. See above, chapter 22.
343. *Shiji* 9/395. Cf. Chavannes 1895: Vol. 2, pp. 406–7.

stayed behind to watch over the palace. She seldom saw the emperor and they grew more estranged. After Ruyi was appointed King of Zhao there were several occasions on which he almost replaced the Heir Apparent, and it was only through the opposition of the great officials and the schemes of the Marquis of Liu (Zhang Liang 張良) that the Heir Apparent was not deposed.

These repeated threats to the position of the son of Empress Lü, and hence to the empress herself and her family, greatly angered her. When her son finally acceded to the throne in 194 B.C. as Emperor Xiaohui, she lost no time in taking her vengeance upon Consort Qi and her son. The Divine Lord has, if anything, understated their sufferings, as recorded by Sima Qian:[344]

> Empress Lü most resented Lady Qi and her son, the King of Zhao. She ordered that Lady Qi be imprisoned in Yongxiang 永巷,[345] and summoned the King of Zhao. Three times her emissaries returned. The Chancellor of Zhao, Zhou Chang, Marquis of Jianping 趙相建平侯周昌, sent a messenger, saying, "Emperor Gaozu entrusted the King of Zhao to me, and he is still young. I have heard that Your Imperial Highness resents the Lady Qi and wants to summon the King of Zhao and execute him. I do not dare to send the king. Further, the king is ill, and cannot respond to your command."[346] This response enraged the Empress Lü and she dispatched an emissary to summon the Chancellor of Zhao to court. When the Chancellor of Zhao had been brought to Chang'an, she sent an emissary to again summon the King of Zhao. The king came. Before he had arrived, Emperor Xiaohui, who was compassionate and benevolent, heard of the Empress Dowager's anger. He personally welcomed the King of Zhao at the Ba River and entered the palace together with him. Keeping him by his side, he acted and rested, ate and drank with the King of Zhao. The Empress Dowager wanted to kill him but could find no opportunity. In the twelfth month of the first year of Xiaohui's reign (194–93 B.C.), Xiaohui went out

---

344. *Shiji* 9/397.

345. According to the commentaries, Yongxiang was a building within the palace compound later called Yeting 掖庭.

346. Zhou Chang had been appointed to this post by Gaozu specifically to protect Ruyi from the vengeance of the Empress Lü. See *Shiji* 96/2677–79.

shooting in the morning. The King of Zhao was young and could not rise early. The Empress Dowager heard that he was alone and sent someone to poison him. When Xiaohui returned that morning the King of Zhao was already dead. . . . The Empress Dowager subsequently cut off the hands and feet of Lady Qi, plucked out her eyes, burnt off her ears, fed her a drug that made her mute, and made her live in the toilet. She called her the "human pig." After she had been in there several days, the Empress Dowager summoned Emperor Xiaohui to see the "human pig." When Xiaohui saw her, he asked who she was, and learning that it was Lady Qi, burst into tears. This led to an illness, and he was bed-ridden for over a year.[347]

It is no wonder that these events left a psychic scar on Ruyi. Empress Lü feared his vengeance herself, and it is recorded that some time after his death, in 180, he appeared to her as a blue dog and, seizing her by the armpit, left a wound that led to an illness.[348]

The Divine Lord, brooding in the netherworld about the fate of his mother, vows vengeance. In doing so, he forgets the warning of his dying mother in his previous life (ch. 28) to avoid entanglements of revenge.

65. *Qiong Pool*   邛池

Relying on one's position to oppress others is impermissible.
An innocent mother and son were exterminated.
Bearing this injustice I entered the depths of the earth,
Though I "should not share the same heaven" (with an enemy),
    this continued so long.[349]
The Lüs were all reincarnated in the same town,

---

347. *Shiji* 9/397. Cf. Chavannes 1895: Vol. 2, pp. 409–10.
348. *Shiji* 9/405. Cf. Chavannes 1895: Vol. 2, p. 425.
349. DZ reads *shi* 是, "to affirm," for *jiu* 久, "a long time," yielding "I came to affirm strongly that I 'should not share the same Heaven' [with my enemies]." Both readings are plausible.

At the same time my own parents were begging for their lives.
The ocean waves flattened and inundated forty square li,
To repay the hundred miseries I had suffered back then.

After encountering the disaster wrought by the Lüs, my spirit wandered in darkness, and I held no official position. I nursed my pentup anger and longed for revenge, giving no thought to all my former accomplishments. Though the Lüs had died, they were imprisoned in the netherworld. The karma they had created was heavy and many years passed. Much later, they were finally reborn. I then visited a town on the shores of the Western Sea called Qiong Pool (Qiongchi).[350] The town prefect, Lü Mou 吕牟, was the reincarnation of Empress Lü, and many of the townspeople were originally members of the Lü clan. Those with karmic affinities from previous lives seek each other out and the karmic group of the Lüs was reassembled in this desolate wasteland.

My mother had also been born there and again belonged to the Qi 戚 clan. Because in her previous life she had enjoyed too much good fortune, now she was poor and emaciated. She was married to a man named Zhang. They were aged and without issue; man and wife made a living cutting hay. One day out in the fields they looked at each other and said, "We are really in distress. We toil to support ourselves, but when our strength fails in our waning years, we will not avoid dying in a ditch. Now we are sixty and have no son. Does Heaven intend to kill us?" They then agreed to cut their arms and let the blood drip into a depression in a rock, then covered this with a stone. They bowed to Heaven and prayed, saying, "All men have sons, only we have none. Now our blood and energy are thin and sparse, and we cannot reproduce. We vow that should some living thing appear beneath this stone, we will accept it as our offspring." When I recognized my mother, my heart warmed. I was moved and decided to stay.

---

350. Traditional Chinese cosmology placed a sea in each direction. Qiongchi, on the western periphery of Chinese civilization (southeast of modern Xichang, Sichuan, Zang 1936: 362.2), was therefore close to the sea of the west. Following the 1645 ed., DZ, and SG in reading *xihai* 西海, "Western Sea," for *xihu* 西湖, "Western Lake."

The next day the two old people returned and, removing the stone, examined the depression. Their blood had transformed into a golden snake an inch long. This was me. My mother brought me back and nurtured me. After a year, horns appeared on my head and legs appeared beneath my belly. I could transform, and each day when it was about to rain, I would assist. My body grew large and my appetite expanded. When I saw a goat, pig, dog, or horse, I would eat it. The town prefect had a spirited horse of good color, which he pastured by the river. Its hoof injured my foot[351] and I seized and bit[352] it. This horse was the retributive incarnation (*baoshen* 報身) of Lü Chan 呂產. The people of the town all knew about me and came looking for me at my house, but did not capture me. My father and mother were put in prison, and told that if within three days time there were no success in finding me, they would be killed.

The next day I transformed into a scholar and called upon the prefect to resolve the matter. The prefect said, "The old couple named Zhang raised a demonic snake in their home which has preyed on people's domestic animals for a long time. Now it has also eaten my horse. I am going to kill it, thereby eliminating a danger to the public. Since the Zhangs do not cooperate, then they are demons. Now I must execute them." I said, "When the life of a being is taken in repayment, this is brought about by karma from a previous incarnation. Nor was it accidental that your horse encountered and was eaten by that creature. If you, sir, should kill a man for the sake of a beast, how can this be considered proper conduct for a prefect?" The prefect rebuked me and forced me to leave. I advised him again, saying, "There is an aura of death floating about your visage. You should take good care of yourself, so that another day you will have no regrets." When I had finished speaking I disappeared. The aides of the prefect all considered me a demon.

I then memorialized Heaven. Proclaiming my injustice and setting forth the innocent death of mother and son in a previous life at the hands of the Lüs, I reported that I had now encountered them and

---

351. For *zu* 足, "foot," the 1645 ed. reads *zhua* 爪, "claw," DZ reads *mo* 末, "end," and SG reads *he* 禾, "rice." SG is clearly a graphic error.

352. For *shi* 嚙, "to bite," DZ reads *dan* 啖, "swallow."

wished to settle accounts. My words were sent up but no response was forthcoming. So I transformed into wind and thunder, breathing forth clouds and fog. Broad daylight turned to darkness and all of the inhabitants of the town looked at each other and said, "How is it that your head has become that of a fish." Crying, they felt each other's heads and faces. One night I raised up the waters of the ocean to become rain, which I poured into the town. Everything for forty li was inundated. I left carrying my mother and father on my body. The time was during the age of Emperor Xiaoxuan 孝宣 (r. 74–49 B.C.). This was what the people nowadays call "The Inundation Forming the River" (xianhe 陷河).

COMMENTARY

The hatred the Divine Lord has nursed for over a century finally manifests itself as he obtains vengeance on those who killed his mother and himself.

His death at age ten and the traumatic experience of watching his mother's gruesome fate so disorient the Divine Lord that he loses track of his own true identity, roaming the murky passages of the netherworld obsessed with obtaining vengeance on the Lüs.[353] During this rare period of inactivity the Lüs, forming a karmic group that will share a succession of incarnations while they work out the entanglements created during their incarnation at the beginning of the Han, suffer long in the infernal realm and are finally reborn, more than a hundred years later, in a town on the western extremity of Chinese civilization. The Lady Qi, the mother of Ruyi, is also a member of this karmic group and is reborn at the same place and time.

The Divine Lord in his aimless wandering happens upon this town, perhaps drawn by the same karmic affinities, and finds his former mother and her present husband, surnamed Zhang, as was the Divine Lord's father in his first two incarnations, in the midst of a magical rite in supplication of progeny. The Divine Lord manifests in the form of a small golden snake that grows into a horned dragon, assuming its appropriate role in the production of rain for the com-

---

353. The fortunes of the various members of the Lü family are chronicled in chapter 9 of the *Shiji*, the "Annals of the Empress Dowager Lü."

munity. Dragons, though supernatural, are creatures of the earth and subsist on a diet of flesh; the dragon preys on the domestic animals of his neighbors and eventually he eats the horse of the town prefect. Since the prefect is the reincarnation of Empress Lü and the horse is the transmigration of her nephew, Lü Chan,[354] this act is one of vengeance, but the Divine Lord is careful to give a justification for his killing of the horse, saying that it trod on him. He further distances himself from responsibility by giving the Empress Lü another chance to repent, but ultimately resorts to his rain-making powers to flood the entire town, thus obtaining his revenge on the Lüs.

This story is derived from a legend concerning Qiong Pool first recorded in the Latter Han. It partakes of a body of legends of submerged cities and old women who become lacustrine deities. Several elements of the original story have been changed in the course of its adoption by the cult in Zitong. Originally there was only a woman, with no husband, and she was assigned no surname. The snake simply appears in her home.[355] In a study of this and related tales of submerged villages Max Kaltenmark has paraphrased the story in the following terms:

A Qiongdu vivait une vielle femme, pauvre et solitaire. Chaque fois qu'elle mangeait, un petit serpent cornu venait près de sa couche. La vielle, le prenant en pitié, lui donnait à manger. Le serpent grandit et vint à mesurer plus d'un *zhang*. Il arriva qu'il tua, en suçant son sang, le cheval du préfet. Celui-ci, furieux, força la vielle à lui indiquer où se cachait le serpent. Elle lui dit qu'il était sous le lit, mais on eut beau creuser profondément, on ne trouva rien. Le prefet tua alors la vielle femme. Le serpent s'exprima par l'intermediaire d'un medium et annonça qu'il allait venger sa mère. A partir de ce moment, durant 40 jours, chaque nuit des bruits de tonnerre et de tempête se firent entendre. Puis les habitants de lieu eurent soudain des têtes de poisson, après quoi le pays alentour s'effondrèrent et devinrent un lac. Seule la maison de la vielle femme resta intacte et sert encore de refuge aux pêcheurs car elle n'est jamais atteinte par la

---

354. Lü Chan, second son of Empress Lu's eldest brother, was named Marquis of Jiao, then King of Liang and Imperial Tutor. Upon the death of the Empress Dowager he was made chancellor but was killed shortly thereafter in an attempt to take over the empire. See *Shiji* 9/403–10.
355. *Hou Hanshu* 86/2852.

tempête. Par temps calme, on aperçoit au fond de l'eau les murs
et les édifices de la ville engloutie.[356]

Kaltenmark has collected a number of similar stories. In each case a
city is submerged below the waters of a lake or river for having
offended a local god. Kaltenmark stresses that the fault is not moral in
nature, but rather a personal affront against the spirit.[357]

By the tenth century there was already a couple named Zhang, and
the snake takes form from some blood spilled by the old man, but
without the conscious intention to produce progeny. The snake is
explicitly identified as Zhang Ezi. The tale is recorded in the *Jianwen
ji* 見聞記 of Wang Renyu 王仁裕 (880–942):[358]

The god who inundated forming a river. In Sui county of Sui
province there was an elderly couple surnamed Zhang.[359] They
were old and had no children. The old man went into the river
gorges to search for firewood to support himself and his mate.
Suddenly one day in a cliffside cave he accidentally cut his finger
with a knife and the blood spurted out. It dripped into a depression in a rock. He covered it with some tree leaves and went
home. Another day he returned to the place, and took away the
leaves to see what was there. The blood had transformed into a
little snake. The old man took it in his palm and played with it
for a while. The creature was affectionate, as if it loved him. He
cut a section of bamboo to put it in and placed it inside the
breast (of his robe). When he got it home he fed it some scraps
of meat and it became very domesticated. In the course of time
it grew. One year later it stole chickens and dogs at night to eat.
After two years it was stealing goats and pigs. The neighbors all
remarked at their loss of livestock. The old man and woman said
nothing about the snake. Later the county magistrate lost a Shu
horse. Following its tracks he entered the old man's home. When

---

356. Kaltenmark 1985: 4–5. The romanization has been changed to conform to that used in this
book.
357. Kaltenmark 1985: 1. We must note that the story cited above fits Kaltenmark's model, as
detailed in this article, rather inexactly. Missing, in particular, is any mention of the woman being
warned of the coming disaster, of her surviving it, and of her turning into stone when she looks back at
the submerged town.
358. This work by Wang Renyu is lost, and reconstructed versions of the text do not include this
tale, but the story is recorded in *Taiping guangji* 312.2, pp. 2466–67.
359. Modern Xichang county in Sichuan. See Zang 1936: 1336.1.

he questioned them, he found that the horse had already been swallowed by the snake. The magistrate was astounded, and berated the old man for raising this evil creature. The old man was convicted of a crime and was about to be executed. Suddenly one night lightning flashed and thunder roared. The whole county was submerged, becoming a huge pond, so large one could not see the shores. Only the old Zhang couple survived. Later both they and the snake disappeared. The area was therefore renamed Xianhe county. The snake was called Zhang Ezi.

All of the material in this chapter dealing with the Lü family and the previous incarnation of the Divine Lord is new to the legend, appearing for the first time in the *Book of Transformations*. Further, some elements of the Han legend not recorded in the Five Dynasties version resurface here: the inhabitants develop piscine features and forty days of storm become forty *li* of destruction. It is uncertain when this story entered cult lore and through what process of development the story came to take on its present form. By the Five Dynasties period it was associated with the cult at Sevenfold Mountain and the person who raised the snake was already identified as being surnamed Zhang. Thus we see the cult expanding, assimilating related snake cults and their lore and incorporating it into a consistent body of hagiographical material concerning the Divine Lord of Zitong.

By setting this episode in the context of vengeance upon the Lüs for the injustices visited upon himself and his mother during a previous incarnation, the tale has been ethicized. In the *Book of Transformations* the god of Zitong is no longer a puissant, morally neutral nature god, but rather a bastion of morality and an exemplar of proper conduct. An episode like this had to be adjusted to fit this new context, and although the god's actions in this new version are not exactly proper they are at least understandable in the context of his great filial love for his mother.

66. *Liberation*   解脫

Do not lightly create thoughts of anger,
These thoughts are born in ignorance.
Knowing only that correct principles can be stated with
    equanimity,
I took direct action, not waiting for the Jade Tones.[360]
Condemned to a huge body I suffered the torments of heat,
Repaid my debts to the innocents, assuaging all their feelings.
With one word the World-honored One dissolved my karma,
And brought to completion the visage that I was to sport in the
    future.

I had previously memorialized concerning the injustice I suffered
at the hands of Empress Lü but acted on my own authority before
receiving the Thearch's response. Although this was satisfying at the
time and dispelled in an instant my pent-up anger, when I calmed
down I deeply regretted it. The next day the Jade Tones repeatedly descended. The God of the Seas, Zhao Hong 海神晁閎, had indicted
me for using, on my own authority, the waters of the seas to inundate
and drown over five hundred households, amounting to over two
thousand lives. Except for the eighty-odd enemies from my former
existence specified by the god of the locality, half of whom lived
within the city walls and half in the suburbs, all these people were
unjustly killed before their time had come. The Thearch ordered that
I be condemned, making me the dragon of Qiong Pool and stripping
me of my divine office. He also assigned officers of heaven 天吏 to
watch me and see that I did not interfere with the rain. I was imprisoned below the waters, which after successive years of drought
turned to mud. Since my body was so huge, there was no hole I could
hide in and when the blistering sun shone down from above I burned

---

360. Following the 1645 ed. and DZ in reading *dai* 待, "to wait," for *de* 得, "to obtain."

both inside and outside. Small bugs grew under my 84,000 scales and gnawed on me incessantly. I squirmed under this torture for countless years. One day the morning was cool and the heavens suddenly opened. Five-colored clouds floated past in the sky. In the midst of them was an auspicious figure with coiled dark blue hair and a golden face that gleamed like the moon. He manifested marvels that shone faintly. The mountain spirits, the Earl of the River, and the myriad creatures all bowed. They praised him joyfully, the sound shaking heaven and earth. There was also a heavenly fragrance that suffused everything, heavenly flowers fell in profusion, and everywhere spring burst out. My eyes and ears sharpened and my nostrils cleared. My heart was purified and my mouth became moist; my voice ascended. I raised my head and cried forlornly, pleading[361] for salvation. The myriad spirits and saints who guarded the front and rear all said to me, "This is the Great Sage of the West, the World-honored One of True Enlightenment, Sakyamuni Buddha 西方大聖正覺世尊釋加文佛. Now he is propagating his teaching in the eastern regions, transforming his form in accordance with his teachings. He is about to go to China. Since you have encountered him, your past-life karma can be escaped."[362] I therefore repented of my acts and produced compassionate thoughts. My body of itself vaulted up into the midst of the heavenly brilliance and I set forth all my previous acts and their retribution. The World-honored One replied, saying, "Excellent, Oh emperor's son. In the past you have been filial toward your family and loyal toward your country, making great contributions. You also have commiserated with the world and thought to protect it. Because your karma was not yet complete, you strove with your enemies. Due to your false belief[363] in an individual personality, you allowed cruelty to arise, transferring your anger to others. The karmic debt had to be repaid. Now you have yourself repented and desire liberation. Do you at this time still possess thoughts of the injustice done to your parent in your previous life or deluded thoughts of anger?" On hearing this supreme doctrine my heart was enlightened and everything

---

361. Following the 1645 ed., DZ, and SG in reading qi 乞, "to entreat," for qi 迄, "until."
362. The 1645 ed. and SG read gai 改, "to change," for tuo脫, "to shed, escape from."
363. Following DZ in reading xiang 想, "thoughts," for xiang 相, "aspect."

internal and external suddenly seemed empty (*rukong* 如空). I attained a state in which there was no distinction of self and other, and all my thoughts suddenly ceased. Looking at my body, it disappeared at my thought and I again became a man. Listening to the preaching of the Buddha I obtained the wisdom of anointment, great eloquence, divine powers, and complete perfection. All the eight classes of heavenly beings were delighted. I took refuge [in the Buddha].

COMMENTARY

In this strongly Buddhist-oriented episode the Divine Lord obtains liberation from the karma he had created by flooding the town of Qiongchi.

When the Divine Lord, without waiting for permission from the Supreme Thearch, makes use of his control, as a dragon, over the element water to drown the entire town, this is immediately reported to Heaven. The Divine Lord is ordered imprisoned in the depths of the lake he has just created, a common means of dealing with misbehaving dragons. It is said that Li Bing 李冰 chained a dragon who had caused flooding of the Min River at the site of the Fulongguan 伏龍觀 near Guanxian 灌縣, Sichuan (Kleeman 1992–93).

Salvation comes when the Buddha happens to pass by on his way to China to spread the Dharma. This is the event prophesied by Laozi in chapter 48, an episode that shares the theme of happening upon the procession of a passing deity. Otherwise, there is little evidence of residual Daoist influence in this section and the scene unfolds as in a classic Buddhist scripture. The Buddha instructs the supplicant, who is then enlightened to the empty, nondual nature of reality and the illusory character of individual existence. This enlightenment together with the renunciation of the residual emotional attachments of previous lives allows the Divine Lord to escape from the imprisonment imposed upon him by the Supreme Thearch.

This episode raises questions about the relationship of Daoism and Buddhism. It is strongly pro-Buddhist, as is the related chapter 48, where Laozi charges the Divine Lord to look for his return in foreign garb and to accept him in this new identity. Just how were the positions of these divine beings reconciled within the popular conception, which viewed them all as members of a single sacred realm? There is no clear hierarchical relationship placing the Buddha above the Supreme Thearch, yet the Buddha is able to undo the actions of the Thearch. Perhaps it is best to envision an overall structure to the world, which some might term the Dao, which shapes the actions of all the gods, permitting each to function according to his own principles within certain constraints. In any case, within the narrative this chapter, again like chapter 48, serves to reaffirm the god's divinity after a morally questionable act.

67. *Benevolent Administration* 仁政

The karma of anger burns,[364] it is the deepest obstacle.
Maintain steadfastly your armor of forbearance,[365] permit no invasion.
When a wound is inflicted on another's body, it is like my own body,
The pain that cuts another's heart seems to cut my own.
Since my staff did not cheat I could fulfill my tasks,
The people knew to love each other and delighted in my governance.
Thus it was that I obtained the insignificant praise of Qinghe.
When they sing of me who will accompany on the lute of Shun?

Having left the evil paths of rebirth, I obtained a good birth, being born into the princedom of Zhao as Xun 勛, the son of Zhang Yu 張禹. When grown I was recommended by the Impartial and Upright to be prefect of Qinghe 清河. My official duties were conducted with enlightened liberality and the people could not bear to cheat. I

---

364. DZ reads "burns up harmony" (*fenhe* 焚和) for "burns" (*fenru* 焚如).
365. Following the 1645 ed. and DZ in reading *ren kai* 忍鎧, "armor of forbearance," for *kaijia* 鎧甲, "armor."

treated my staff like colleagues and friends, viewed the populace as members of my own family. If a member of my staff made an error, I would correct him. If he were lax in his duties, I would exhort him. If he were negligent, I would instruct him. If he were avaricious, I would carefully observe him. If he were crafty, I would interrogate him. If he ignored proclamations and rescripts, I would dismiss him. If, however, he perverted the law in order to kill the people, turning white into black and endangering the lives of the populace, I would first let him defend himself, and when his words were exhausted I would turn him over to the legal system. If his original situation merited pity I would still pardon him. Any punishments for improperly releasing prisoners I myself shouldered with no protests. When the people quarreled over possessions, I would reconcile them justly. When they quarreled over ritual matters, I appealed to their emotions. If a person became a bandit, I would make him replace the objects stolen. If he injured someone, I would make him bow to his enemy in court. If the crime went as far as murder, I would turn him over to the legal system. But if his true intentions were forgivable, I would still release him. Though someone might disparage me for permitting evil, I would not protest this.

In this way throughout the region rain and sunshine came at the proper times, locust infestations did not occur, thieves and bandits warned each other to leave the area, and evildoers repented and reformed their behavior. After five years of my administration resentments were unheard of, and the people made a song that went:

I have a teacher,
The teacher is stern and uncompassionate,
Teach me kindness?
Master Zhang can do it.
I have a friend,
My friend is trustworthy but does not warn me,
To draw close to me and correct me
I rely on Master Zhang.
I have my mother

Whose grace is clothed in righteousness.
Master Zhang resembles her,
Flexible but with rules.
I have my elder brother
Who is truly rich in affection.[366]
Master Zhang resembles him,
Harmonious and not quarrelsome.

Later I was reprimanded by the Grand Protector for running as I entered his presence. I untied my sash of office. The time was the end of the Yuanhe 元和 reign period (A.D. 84–86) of Emperor Zhang 章帝.

COMMENTARY

Having regained human form through the divine intercession of the Buddha, the Divine Lord now resumes the course of his human incarnations. He chooses again to be reborn into a family surnamed Zhang, and again takes up a life of civil service. This incarnation is a model for the local government official. The Divine Lord shows how, through a policy of benevolence, forgiveness, and liberality, crime and corruption can be eliminated, interpersonal relationships improved, and the cosmological balance restored. The extremely indulgent attitude adopted in this episode toward evil-doers contrasts with the unrelenting justice which the Divine Lord had applied while a supernatural official in Shu, but may have antecedents in the portent-based protests against violent rule associated with wonder-working figures like Guo Pu 郭璞 (276–324).[367] It seems that this sort of punishment is in most cases to be left to divine forces while the civil administration concentrates on fostering humaneness through example.

It is unclear whether there is a historical model for this incarnation. The *Book of the Han* records a Confucian scholar named Zhang Yu who hailed from Qinghe.[368] This Zhang was trained in the *Tradition of Master Zuo*, served as Censor at the same time as Xiao Wangzhi

---

366. The 1645 ed. reads *jing* 敬, "respectful," for *yin* 殷, "rich." DZ reads, "who demands respect through his affection" (*zejing yuqing* 責敬於情).

367. *Jinshu* 72.

368. *Hanshu* 88/3620.

蕭望之 (106–47 B.C.), and died during the reign of Emperor Xuan
宣 (74–49 B.C.). The connection to Qinghe is intriguing, but the
dates are too early for his son to be alive at the end of Zhangdi's reign.
Another Zhang Yu was tutor to the future emperor Cheng 成 (r. 33–7
B.C.), probably still too early to sire the Divine Lord in this incarnation.[369] A third comes from Xiangguo 襄國 in Zhao and held high
court positions in a long career A.D. 64–111, but two sons are recorded for this Zhang Yu, neither named Xun.[370]

68. *The Quick and the Dead*   幽明

Wholeheartedly committed to the Dao, it is the Dao that I
   practice.
Seeking benevolence with earnest intent my benevolence
   became complete of itself.
Only after my nature was fixed could I pierce day and night;
Only after my spirit was complete could I govern the quick and
   the dead.
Guo Linzong in praising and selecting took cognizance of
   public opinion,
The Thearch's rescript transmitted words with nothing hidden.
After three Jupiter cycles of toiling endeavor many were my
   bountiful achievements,
No harm in aiding all the forms of life through the hidden
   administration.

Because I succeeded in governing well in my last incarnation, my
basic endeavor (*genye* 根業)[371] expanded and flourished. As soon as I

---

369. *Hanshu* 81/3347–48.
370. *Hou Hanshu* 44/1496–99.
371. DZ reads *fuye* 福業, "fortunate endeavor," for *genye.*

had lived out my allotted years I again took human form. I was born into this world during the Yonghe 永和 reign period (A.D. 136–141) of Emperor Shun 順 of Han (r. 126–144) as Zhang Xiaozhong 張孝仲, not forsaking my former name. I was evaluated favorably by Guo Yudao 郭有道 (i.e., Guo Tai 泰), and though I did not rise to illustrious office, I rose and sank with the times in my local community. The Supreme Thearch issued a rescript ordering me to attend to worldly affairs during the day and govern the quick and the dead at night. I was aware of and recorded every action, every injustice, every hidden merit, and every secret plot of each person, and even ghosts, spirits, malefics, and demons (*gui ling xie sui* 鬼靈邪祟) did not escape my charge. After I had worked thus for three Jupiter cycles (i.e., thirty-six years) both the quick and the dead were saved and men and ghosts had benefited. I contributed to this achievement.

COMMENTARY

The Divine Lord again incarnates into the human world to perform good works and aid the people. His virtuous actions in the immediately preceding life as Zhang Xun lead to his immediate rebirth into the body of a scholar-official. Again he chooses a family surnamed Zhang, and his personal name is Xiaozhong, recalling his previous life at the court of the Western Zhou, when he was named Zhong 仲 and styled Xiaoyou 孝友.

The Divine Lord's exemplary qualities bring him to the attention of Guo Tai (128–169), styled Linzong 林宗, a famous teacher and scholar of the Latter Han.[372] Guo refused to serve in office because he thought the Han doomed, but exerted an enormous influence over the educated elite of his day through his intellectual and moral accomplishments. After retiring to his native place to teach privately, he attracted thousands of students, and became a rallying point for the literati, who were persecuted during the suppression of cliques (*danggu* 黨錮). He was famous above all for his ability to evaluate men, and he is credited with being one of the founders of the practice of "pure criticism" (*qingyi* 清議). It was said that, "Those whom he praised

---

372. Guo's biography is found in chapter 68 of the *Hou Hanshu*.

and selected all turned out just as he foresaw."[373] Among the many people whom he evaluated his biography mentions the figure claimed by the Divine Lord in this incarnation, saying, "He recognized Zhang Xiaozhong among the grass-cutters and the shepherds."[374]

In this incarnation the Divine Lord does not achieve spectacular successes in the temporal world. He is content to fill a minor local position and accommodate himself to changes in the world surrounding him. But the Supreme Thearch entrusts him with a much more important role, as a keeper of the divine records. He performs this function, which seems a presage of his eventual position as custodian of the Cinnamon Record and arbiter of human fates, while asleep. He observes the conduct of all the beings of the terrestrial sphere, both human and supernatural, and notes their good and evil actions. In the poem his task is described as the "hidden administration" (*yinzhi* 陰騭), and this term comes to play a key role in the cult to the Divine Lord of Zitong, with one of his later moralistic tracts called the *Writing on the Hidden Administration* (*Yinzhiwen* 文).[375]

69. *Planning*   籌帷

Martial ardor within my breast, I also possessed civil virtues,
In the square inch of my heart the myriad images are distinct.
The jeweled fortunes were about to arrive for the Simas,
With military planning I aided General Deng.
Making a surprise attack from the backroads, he followed my plan,
Completely exhausted on the sandy fields I was commended for
  aiding the Emperor (Thearch?).
The documents of the historians lack any mention,
What harm in planning? No one will hear of it.

---

373. *Hou Hanshu* 68/2227.
374. *Hou Hanshu* 68/2231.
375. On this work, see Sakai 1957; 1960.

Because of my worthy achievements in successive lives I was gradually restored to my divine office, but the debt for taking lives had not been repaid, and it gave me no peace. I was reborn in He-shuo.[376] When young I was fervent and principled. I saw the world change before my eyes and came to expect that I would achieve merit and fame. I came to the notice of the Great General Deng Ai 鄧艾 (197–264), and he invited me to become his Retainer. I participated in the formulation of all of his strategic planning. The year when he invaded Sichuan I became Marshal of the Field Army.[377] I urged Deng to make a surprise attack using backroads in order to avoid battle losses. Having penetrated deep into Shu, we encountered Zhuge Zhan 諸葛瞻. He was offered an enfeoffment as King of Langye, but refused. The [first] confrontation ended in a mutual withdrawal. I went up against the elite troops of Zhan's central column. Once[378] a cloud of arrows flew forth, converging on my body. Zhan had just been captured and I wanted to save him, but my wounds were severe. This was no doubt the unrequited retribution for Qiong Pool. Be warned!

COMMENTARY

In this incarnation the Divine Lord is born into the troubled world of third-century China. After the fall of the Han, China was divided into three kingdoms, Wei, Shu, and Wu. The Cao 曹 family soon lost real control over the Wei state to the Sima 司馬 family, which went on to found the Jin in 265. Deng Ai was a protegé of Sima Yi 懿 (179–251), Great General of Wei and de facto ruler after the coup of 249.[379] Deng held a succession of important military offices, and was instrumental in fending off an invasion from Shu. In 263 he secretly invaded Shu through the perilous Yinping Road 陰平道[380] and was able to carry his attack directly to Chengdu, where he extinguished the state of Shu. A key battle occurred near Mianzhu, when he de-

---

376. For Heshuo, see above, p. 133, n. 111.
377. On this position, see Hucker 1985: 244, entry 2567. I have not adopted Hucker's translation of "Adjutant" for *sima* 司馬.
378. Following the 1645 ed. and DZ in reading *huo* 或, "once," for *hu* 忽, "suddenly."
379. Deng Ai's biography can be found in the *Wei Shu* of the *Sanguo zhi*, 28/775–83.
380. Northwest of modern Wenxian, Gansu.

feated the forces under the command of Zhuge Zhan, son of the famous strategist Zhuge Liang. Zhan, having refused an offer of the kingship of Langye, was captured in this battle and beheaded.[381]

These events occurred in the northern region of Shu, the area previously under the suzerainty of the Divine Lord in his office of Mountain King of the Gate of Shu. This familiarity with the region allows the Divine Lord to suggest a little used route, no doubt the same Yinping Road, by which Deng Ai might bring his forces into Sichuan undetected.

In view of the historical attachment of the Divine Lord to the Shu region in previous incarnations and of the actual prominence of this region in the cult at the time the *Book of Transformations* was written, it is strange that the Divine Lord should side with Wei against Shu at this time. The question of which state during the Three Kingdoms period deserved to be considered "legitimate" (*zhengtong* 正統) has occasioned much debate over the centuries, and was still a matter of contention during the Song. It was first assumed that Wei was legitimate because it had formally received the abdication of the last Han ruler in 220, because it occupied central China, and because it was the direct predecessor of the Jin dynasty (265–420), whose legitimacy is unquestioned. As early as the third century this position was challenged by those who maintained that the Shu state of Liu Bei was legitimate because of his descent from the Han royal house. We might expect that a cult centered in Sichuan would promote the position of the Shu Han state but this is not the case.[382] Still, it may be this sort of regional loyalty that prompts the Divine Lord to try to save the life of Zhuge Zhan at a critical moment.[383] Note also that in 1164 a shrine was erected to Deng Ai in the same prefecture as Zitong.[384]

The Divine Lord's violent death after a life that was meritorious but not distinguished enough to have left a mark in history is attributed to an unresolved karmic debt. The Buddha was able to liberate him from his imprisonment in Qiong Pool, but the mechanistic

---

381. The details of this campaign are recorded in *Sanguo zhi* 28/779; 35/932.

382. Deng Ai was, however, well thought of in Shu because of his refusal to allow his troops to loot Chengdu and his liberal treatment of the members of the Shu royal house and administration who surrendered. It was, in part, a dispute over this issue that led to his execution. See *Sanguo zhi* 28/780–81.

383. We should also note that the father of Zhuge Zhan, Zhuge Liang, was the subject of a major cult in the Sichuan region. See Zhuge Liang yu Wu Hou ci bianxiezu 1982.

384. *Songhuiyao jigao* 20/29b.

workings of this system of retribution are inexorable, and sooner or later the debt incurred in inflicting violence on others had to be repaid.

---

70.   *The Ruyi Scepter*   如意

How many years did the Thearch hold it in his own hand?
One day the Jade Capital bestowed it upon me.[385]
When I directed the field columns, supernatural troops
   appeared,
A look and a wave at my enemies and they were dissuaded from
   their evil intent.
Exceptional vessels were my common companions,
My former name was from time to time pronounced by me.
From this time on everything I encountered went as I wished,
What deity of the Three Realms would dare to deceive me?

Since my former karmic debt had been resolved, an imperial rescript summoned me to the Jade Capital 玉京 to wash clean my karmic record and renew my divine office, permitting me eternal blessing in the region of the Kun 坤 mainstay (i.e., the Southwest).[386] The Thearch also bestowed upon me the ruyi sceptre that he held. The Thearch's rescript read thus: "Praised be you, Xiaozhong. You are the hero of the myriad spirits. You are complete in your virtues of loyalty and filiality and the world is enriched by your achievements. I present to you this scepter, which is omnipotent." He further said, "This is a ruyi scepter." Because this scepter accorded with my name in a previous incarnation, I was delighted to receive it.

---

385. DZ reads *tai* 台, "terrace," for *yu* 余, "I."

386. Kun is one of the eight trigrams of the *Yijing*, each of which is correlated with a direction, in this case the southwest. The mainstays are massive cables that suspend the earth from the heavens. *Wenxuan* (29/24b) quotes the *Huainanzi*, "The Kun mainstay is in the southwest."

COMMENTARY

The Divine Lord is rewarded for his meritorious deeds in his past three incarnations. His karmic slate is wiped clean and his position in the divine bureaucracy is restored, as well as his special place in the southwestern corner of the empire. As a mark of his favor, the Thearch presents the Divine Lord with one of his own personal possessions, a magical ruyi or "as-you-like-it" scepter, which will give him unlimited powers. It permits him to direct divine soldiers and the inhabitants of all Three Realms (*sanjie* 三界, here referring to heavenly and terrestrial spirits in addition to men).

The presentation of this scepter serves to connect several disparate themes in the *Book of Transformations*. It is this same scepter that the Divine Lord bestows upon Yao Chang 姚萇 in chapter 75. That chapter was not a part of the original revelation, but the episode was perhaps the best-known element of cult lore and had been referred to by Li Shangyin 李商隱 some centuries earlier.[387] Further, this incident closely resembles the action of Tang Emperor Xizong in bestowing upon the Divine Lord his own sword during Xizong's sojourn in Shu.[388]

---

71. *Dingwei*   丁未

On the western edge of Yueshang, gold is the color of the
  mountains,
The southern border of Yuesui is close to the sea coast.
Drunken eyes awoke to see a new sun and moon,
My leisurely heart still[389] loved my former smoke and mist.
As Director of Fates of the Primordial Morning I was in charge
  of Dingwei,

---

387. *Quan Tang shi* 539/6171; *Taiping huanyu ji* 84/7a.

388. *Taiping huanyu ji* 84/7a; *Quan Tang shi* 557/6461 records a poem by Wang Duo 王鐸 commemorating the event.

389. Following DZ in reading *xian* 閒, "leisurely," for the graphically similar and sometimes interchangeable *jian* 間. DZ reads *mang* 忙, "is caught up in," for *you* 猶, "still."

The Zhao state experienced a revival, making prominent my old
   home.
Fire virtue aids the king for one hundred thousand years;
From this day on I was appointed to the ranks of the Perfected
   Worthies.

With the precious scepter in my possession there was no place I
could not go. Because I longed for my former home by the Western
Sea[390] I went by there again. West of Yueshang 越裳, south of Yuesui 越巂, between the two Yues, there is Golden Horse Mountain
金馬山. This marvelous place is pure and isolated. The old couple
surnamed Zhang there had been my father and mother in many successive lives. I was born to them.[391] The time was the eighth year of
Taikang 太康 reign period (287) during the reign of Emperor Wu
武 of Jin (r. 265–290), that year being a *dingwei* year in the sexagesimal cycle. It was the night of the third day of the second lunar
month, during the *zi* 子 hour (11 P.M.–1 A.M.), thus the day was actually already *xinhai* 辛亥. The Thearch commanded me to become
a this-worldly official of Dingwei with my fatestar being Yuanchen
元辰.

COMMENTARY

   The Divine Lord is reborn again in the far southwestern corner of
the Chinese world. Yueshang was an ancient state located to the south
of Annam. Yuesui was a commandery administered from Qiongdu 邛
都, southwest of modern Xichang, Sichuan. Golden Horse Mountain
is one of a pair of mountains flanking the Dian Pool 滇池 near Kunming, Yunnan. The Divine Lord had held official posts in this vast
region, and also had been incarnated as a snake and a dragon here.
Now with the freedom he has obtained through his new ruyi scepter
he decides to go visit his former home, and describes his return as like
waking from a drunken stupor. There he spies the two individuals
who had been his father and mother in many previous lives, and with

---

390. Following the 1645 ed., DZ, and SG in reading *hai* 海, "sea," for *hu* 湖, "lake."
391. At this point SG adds, "This was my seventy-first transformation."

whom he clearly forms a karmic group. Again they have taken the surname of Zhang. The Divine Lord is born as their son on the third day of the second lunar month of the eighth year of Taikang, that is, March 4, 287.[392] This date remains the officially celebrated birthday of the Divine Lord to this day.

72.   *The Water Bureau*   水漕

In my dreams I was a dragon, was a potentate.
The habituated attitudes of many lives I could not yet forget.
I laughed at worshipers of licentious cults with offerings of wine
    and food,
Writing my official rank, I memorialized the watery realm.
A donkey dashed amidst the clamor of wind and rain,
A Shangyang danced in the shade of mulberry and hemp.
Responsible for affairs of the quick and the dead for all of Shu,
The road is long to my new residence on Sevenfold Mountain.

I was fully grown and had both wife and son, but my filial revrence did not waver. I saw the men of my district during a drought pray to wooden and clay images for rain. I laughed at them, for I had already reported the situation in a dream. One day at the edge of a stream I wrote my own official position and submitted the document to the God of the Sea. I then saw an emissary who recounted to me all of

---

392. The comment about this being a *xinhai* day (48 in the sexagesimal system) would seem to be an error. March 4 was a *gengchen* day (17), and if in the *zi* hour this had carried over to next day, it would be *xinsi* (18). This probably reflects an error in calculation, since the fourth day of the first lunar month of 287 was indeed *xinhai*. The day of the Divine Lord's birth had been fixed as *xinhai* in the *Esoteric Biography of Qinghe*. It was no doubt discovered in the intervening years that this did not accord with the calendar and the passage here should be seen as an attempt to reconcile the earlier account with more exact, though still erroneous, calendrical calculations.

the seventy-three[393] transformations I had manifested since I had first taken human form during the Zhou dynasty. He then called me to be Judge of Fate (*yunpan* 運判). He urged me to mount a white donkey and in the midst of the clamor of wind and rain I suddenly was no longer in my native district. Entering into a great cave, I saw a palace, luminous and vast. All my relatives, from my father and mother on down, were there. The whole night it rained heavily throughout the Shu region. Soon there was a rescript entrusting me with the general custody of all of the affairs of the quick and the dead within Shu.

COMMENTARY

Having reached maturity, the Divine Lord slowly becomes cognizant of his true identity through dreams in which he recalls his incarnations as the Qiong Pool dragon and as a mountain king. The direct stimulus for his revelation is a drought, to which his neighbors respond with prayers and offerings to the wooden and clay images of heterodox deities. Here "licentious cults" (*yinsi* 淫祀) seems to refer to worship offered to deities not belonging to the divine hierarchy of celestial and terrestrial god-officials. The Divine Lord is amused by these actions because he knows that they are ultimately ineffective, and he recalls that in a dream he had already announced the region's meteorological problems to the appropriate officials. One day he is led to perform the same rite in a waking state. He writes a memorial to the God of the Seas, including his own true official title in the divine bureaucracy. This harbinger of a greater awakening leads Heaven to dispatch an emissary who stimulates the suppressed memories. This otherworldly messenger further summons the Divine Lord to a celestial office where he will sit in judgment on men and determine their futures. This office of Judge of Fates is otherwise unknown.

Mounting on a magical white donkey, the Divine Lord ascends into the heavens and is transported to a huge grotto-heaven, where he is reunited with his celestial family. His divine departure from this world coincides with a storm that brings much needed moisture to the parched land. The poem tells us that this is accompanied by the

---

393. SG reads "seventy-two."

dance of the mythical Shangyang bird, a one-legged bird whose dance presages rain.[394] In the grotto-heaven he is appointed to an illustrious office having overall control of both the divine and profane realms of the Sichuan region.

In its theme of the revelation of his true identity to the Divine Lord while he is in human form, this chapter bears a strong resemblance to chapter 12.

Chapters 72 and 73 are based upon the *Esoteric Biography of Qinghe*, which was revealed to the same medium. The exposition there is considerably more explicit and detailed, although somewhat confused. We find, for example, an explanation of the title of this chapter. Among the images the Divine Lord sees in his dreams is a celestial talisman announcing his office in the bureau of the Water Office (Shuifucao 水府漕).[395] The grotto in which the Divine Lord is reunited with his family is located, in the *Esoteric Biography*, on Mount Pheonix, in the Kniferidge mountain range.[396]

73. *The Cinnamon Record*   桂籍

The Cinnamon Record of scholars is administered by the
    Heavenly Bureau,
Success or failure, glory or decline, none escape their fate.
Dreams reveal the examination topic according to the degree of
    one's sincerity,
Hidden merit determines one's position on the placard of
    successful candidates.
A man of humble heritage may bring his wife enfeoffment and
    his son an assured office;

---

394. See *Lunheng jiaoshi* 15/650.
395. The *Secret Biography*, DZ, and DZJY all agree in reading *cao* 漕, "transport by canal," for *cao* 曹, "bureau."
396. *169 Qinghe neizhuan* 2a.

An official trailing purple, a golden seal at his waist, begins as a white-robed candidate.
To repay the student who works sleepless nights in the study
I have strived in literary and moral refinement, not recoiling at toil!

Because of my unstinting devotion to the classics through many incarnations as a scholar, the Thearch commanded me to take charge of the Cinnamon Record in the Heavenly Bureau. All local and national examinations, rankings, colors of clothing, salaries, and enfeoffments were memorialized to me and even promotions and demotions within the civil and military bureaucracies were under my supervision.

COMMENTARY

In this climactic chapter, which marked the end of the first revelation of the *Book of Transformations* in 1181, the Divine Lord of Zitong is appointed to the divine post for which he is most famous, that of master of the fates of the literati and overseer of the civil service examinations. Given into his charge is the Cinnamon Record, which records the good and evil deeds of literati and the official posts to which their conduct entitles them. This register of moral worth, the prototype for the ledgers of merit and demerit that record the actions and fate of all men, but confined to a distinct segment of society and a certain aspect of their lives, is maintained in the Heavenly Bureau (*tiancao* 天曹). There the Divine Lord receives memorials from all levels of the divine bureaucracy concerning the examinations and the subsequent careers of officials. He consults the record of hidden merit that each individual has accumulated and decides whether he should pass the exam and with what ranking, when he will be promoted and to what office, and what honors and titles he and his relatives should receive, including ritual privileges regarding the color of ceremonial vestments and posthumous ennoblements of the individual's ancestors.

The statement that if an aspiring examination candidate is judged worthy and sincere, the Divine Lord might aid him by revealing in a dream the questions to be asked on the examination reflects an abiding concern of cult adherents. This was an important feature of the cult from at least Song times on, when candidates would make a pilgrimage to the temple on Sevenfold Mountain to pray for revelatory dreams, and remained a key to the cult's popularity throughout imperial times.

Thus the god boldly claims authority over all the literati and officials in the empire. Through the centuries Chinese society would affirm this role as students and scholars prayed to him and sought to emulate his example.

Appendix:
Extant Editions of the Book of Transformations

All extant editions of the *Book of Transformations* except for DZ are of the Southern Song recension.

1645 edition

Title: *Wenchang huashu* 文昌化書

Four *juan*. Preface by Liu Yixiu 劉以脩 of Langzhong (Sichuan). Postface (*ba*) by Xu Zhongzhen 徐鍾震, dated first year of the Longwu period of the Southern Ming (1645).

A copy of this edition in the Naikaku Bunko, with a preface by Liu Yixiu, is cited in Ozaki 1986: 106. Another copy is held by Harvard University. The text begins with a ritual manual (*keyi* 科儀), followed by an imperial rescript dated 1477, ordering the construction of a new temple to the Divine Lord of Zitong in the capital. The appendix includes a postface attributed to Yang Xing 楊興, who is associated with the 1194 revelation.

1747 edition

Title: *Wenchang huashu* 文昌化書

Four *juan* in four volumes. First edition 1665. Edited by Cheng Jiupeng 程九鵬. Illustrated.

Unseen. Cited in van Gulik (1941: 35). Van Gulik comments (based on the preface?) that Cheng used records dating from the Ming. He further mentions a description of the sacrifices to Wenchang by the Ming playwright Wang Daokun 王道昆 (ca. 1561), author of two inscriptions in the 1645 ed.

293

1751 edition

Title: *Wenchang dijun huashu* 文昌帝君化書

Two *juan*. Bound together with the *Wenchang dijun da dong jing* 文昌帝君大洞經, an edition of the *Scripture of the Great Grotto*. Appended to the end of the work is a collection of fortune slips based on Tang poetry. Edited by He Guangdan 何光旦.

Preserved in the Bayerische Staatsbibliothek, Munich.

1771 illustrated edition

Title: *Chuxiang Wenchang huashu* 出像文昌化書*

Four *juan*. Edited by Xie Wen 謝雯. Prefaces by Li Zhongjian 李中簡, Wang Yongli 王永禮, and Xie Wen, all dated 1771. Editions of this version are preserved in the collection of the Projet Tao-tsang in Paris and in the library of Tsukuba University (the former Nihon Kyōiku Daigaku) in Japan.

Wendi quanshu 文帝全書 edition

Title: *Wendi huashu* 文帝化書

One *juan*. First published in 1743 by Liu Tishu 劉體恕. The initial thirty-two *juan* edition of this collectanea was expanded to fifty *juan* in 1774, and this fifty *juan* edition was subsequently reprinted in 1845. The original thirty-two *juan* work was reprinted in 1876.

This version of the *Book of Transformations* is a conflation of two earlier editions, a 1695 reprinting of an edition published by Liu Liangzhen 劉梁楨 of Guangling 廣陵 (modern Jiangdu, Jiangsu) and another annotated edition dated 1665 by Cheng Jiupeng, hence essentially the same as 1747 edition described above. This edition forms the basis for DZJY and includes all of the prefatory materials in DZJY. An 1876 reprint of the thirty-two *juan* edition is preserved in the Gest Memorial Library, Princeton University. The 1843 printing of the fifty *juan* edition can be found in the Bibliotheque Nationale and the British Library.

DZJY edition

Title: *Wendi huashu* 文帝化書

One *juan*. No prefaces. Under the character *xing* 星 in the Daozang jiyao 道藏輯要. Printed at Erxian'an 二仙庵 in Chengdu, 1906. The woodblocks are now kept in Qingyanggong 青羊宮.

The early printing history of the Daozang jiyao is unclear. This text

---

* This is the title given at the end of each chapter. The table of contents gives the title as *Wenchang dijun huashu* and at the center of each folded page the title reads simply *Wenchang huashu*.

seems to be based upon the *Wendi quanshu* edition, as noted above. This is the most readily available edition of the Southern Song recension.

DZ edition

Title: *Zitong dijun huashu* 梓潼帝君化書

Four *juan.* Unsigned preface (attributed to the god) dated 1316. Included in the original printing of the Ming canon, ca. 1444-45. Harvard-Yenching Index no. 170, Schipper (1975), no. 170.

The only surviving edition of the Yuan recension. It is unclear to what extent this edition ever circulated.

Bibliography

Primary Works in Chinese

Baopuzi 抱朴子. By Ge Hong 葛洪 (283–343). Ed. by Sun Xingyan 孫星衍. Zhuzi jicheng ed. Taipei: Shijie shuju, 1969.

Beidongyuan bilu san bian 北東園筆錄三編. By Liang Gongchen 梁恭辰 (fl. 1845). In *Beidongyuan bilu quanji* 全集. Beijing, 1895.

Biwu wanfang ji 碧梧玩芳集. By Ma Tingluan 馬廷鸞 (1222–89). Siku quanshu ed.

Chuci buzhu 楚辭補註. Annotated by Hong Xingzu 洪興祖 (1090–1155). Sibu beiyao ed. Taipei: Zhonghua shuju.

Chunqiu Zuozhuan zhengyi 春秋左傳正義. *Shisanjing zhushu* ed. Taipei: Yeewen Publishing Co., 1976 photo-reprint of 1816 carving.

Chunzai tang zawen 春在堂雜文. By Yu Yue 俞樾 (1821–1906). In *Chunzai tang quanshu*, vol. 70.

Daozang tiyao 道藏題要. Ed. by Ren Jiyu 任繼愈. Peking: Zhongguo shehui kexue chubanshe, 1991.

Dongpo zhilin, Chouchi biji 東坡志林, 仇池筆記. By Su Shi 蘇軾 (1036–1101). Ed. by Donghua shifan daxue guji yanjiusuo. Suzhou: Huadong shifan daxue chubanshe, 1983.

Dushi fangyu jiyao 讀史方輿紀要. By Gu Zuyu 顧祖禹. Guoxue jiben congshu ed. Taipei: Commercial Press, 1968.

Erya zhushu 爾雅注疏. *Shisanjing zhushu* ed. Taipei: Yeewen Publishing Co., 1976 photo-reprint of 1816 carving.

Fan tian lu conglu 凡天廬叢錄. By Chai E 柴萼. N.p. Preface dated 1925.

Fangzhou ji 方舟集. By Li Shi 李石 (d. ca. 1182). Siku quanshu ed.

Fengshi wenjian ji jiaozheng 封氏聞見記校正. By Feng Yan 封演 (fl. ca. 800). Harvard-Yenching Institute Index Series, Supplement 7. Peking, 1933.

Fengsu tongyi tongjian 風俗通義通檢. By Ying Shao 應劭 (fl. ca. 190). *Index du Fong sou t'ong yi.* Centre franco-chinois d'études Sinologiques. Publication 3. Taipei: Ch'eng-wen Publishing Co., 1968 reprint of Peking, 1943.

Gaiyu congkao 陔餘叢考. By Zhao Yi 趙翼 (1727–1814). Shanghai: Commercial Press, 1957.

Gengsi bian 庚巳編. By Lu Can 陸粲 (1494–1551). Congshu jicheng ed. Shanghai: Commercial Press, 1937.

Guixin zazhi 癸辛雜識. By Zhou Mi 周密 (1232–1308). Beijing: Zhonghua shuju, 1988.

Gujin tushu jicheng 古今圖書集成. Ed. by Chen Menglei 陳夢類 (?–1741) et al. Shanghai: 1934 reproduction of 1725 ed.

Guo Zizhang ji 郭子章集. By Guo Zizhang (1542–1618). 1571.

Guoshi Xuanzhongji 郭氏玄中記. Ed. by Ye Dehui 葉德輝 (?–1927). N.p., n.d.

Hanmen zhuixue xubian 韓門綴學續集. By Wang Shihan 王師韓 (1707–?). N.p., n.d.

Hanshu 漢書. By Ban Gu 班固 (32–92). Beijing, Zhonghua shuju, 1962.

Heshan xiansheng daquanji 鶴山先生大全集. By Wei Liaoweng 魏了翁 (1178–1237). Sibu congkan photo-reprint of Song ed. Preface dated 1249.

Hou Hanshu 後漢書. By Fan Ye 范曄 (398–445). Beijing: Zhonghua shuju, 1971.

Huayangguo zhi 華陽國志. By Chang Qu 常璩 (fl. 350). Basic Sinological Series ed. Shanghai: Commercial Press.

Huayangguo zhi jiaobu tuzhu 華陽國志校補圖注. By Chang Qu. Ed. by Ren Naiqiang 任乃強. Shanghai: Guji chubanshe, 1987.

Huayangguo zhi jiaozhu 華陽國志校注. By Chang Qu. Ed. by Liu Lin 劉琳. Chengdu: Ba Shu shushe, 1984.

Jingding Yanzhou xuzhi 景定嚴州續志. By Qian Keze 錢可則. Song Yuan difangzhi congshu edition. 1262.

Jingwen ji 景文集. By Song Qi 宋祁 (998–1061). Congshu jicheng chubian ed. Shanghai: Commercial Press, 1936.

Jishen lu 稽神錄. By Xu Xuan 徐鉉 (917–992). Siku quanshu ed.

Jinshu 晉書. By Fang Xuanling 房玄齡 (578–648). Beijing: Zhonghua shuju, 1974.

Kechuang xianhua 客窗閒話. By Wu Chichang 吳熾昌 (b. 1870). Biji xiao-shuo daguan ed. Biji xiaoshuo daguan gives the author's name as Wu Xianghan 吳薌厂. Preface dated 1908.

Laoxueyan biji 老學庵筆記. By Lu You 陸游 (1125–1210). Congshu ji-cheng ed.

Laozi 老子. Zhuzi jicheng ed.

Liang-Zhe jinshi zhi 兩浙金石志. Ed. by Ruan Yuan 阮元 (1764–1849). Reprinted in *Shike shiliao xinbian* 石刻史料新編 (Taipei: Hsin-wen-feng), vol. 14.

Liaohuazhou xianlu 蓼花州閒錄. By Gao Wenhu 高文虎 (1134–1212). Congshu jicheng reprint of *Gujin xiaoshuo* ed. Shanghai: Commercial Press, 1936.

Libu zhigao 禮部志稿. Ed. by Yu Ruji 俞汝輯. Siku quanshu ed.

Liji zhengyi 禮記正義. *Shisanjing zhushu* ed. Taipei: Yeewen Publishing Co., 1976 photo-reprint of 1816 carving.

Lunheng jiaoshi 論衡校釋. By Wang Chong 王充 (27–ca. 100). Ed. by Huang Hui 黃暉. Taipei: Commercial Press, 1975.

Lunyu 論語. Harvard-Yenching Index Series ed.

Lunyu zhushu 論語注疏. *Shisanjing zhushu* ed. Taipei: Yeewen Publishing Co., 1976 photo-reprint of 1816 carving.

Lüshi chunqiu jishi 呂氏春秋集釋. Ed. by Xu Weiyu 許維遹. Shanghai: Commercial Press, 1935.

Maoshi zhengyi 毛氏正義. *Shisanjing zhushu* ed. Taipei: Yeewen Publishing Co., 1976 photo-reprint of 1816 carving.

Mengliang lu 夢梁錄. By Wu Zimu 吳自牧 (fl. ca. 1270). Biji xiaoshuo daguan ed.

Mengzi 孟子. By Meng Ke 孟柯. Harvard-Yenching Index Series ed.

Mengzi zhushu 孟子注疏. *Shisanjing zhushu* ed. Taipei: Yeewen Publishing Co., 1976 photo-reprint of 1816 carving.

Mianyangxian zhi 綿陽縣志. Ed. by Cui Yingtang 崔映棠. Mianyang, 1932.

Mingshan ji 名山記. Anonymous. N.p., n.d.

Mingshi 明史. Ed. by Zhang Tingyu 張廷玉 (1672–1755). Beijing: Zhonghua shuju, 1974.

Ming yitongzhi 明一統志. By Li Xian 李賢 (1408–66) et al. Siku quanshu ed.

Moyu lu 墨餘錄. By Mao Xianglin 毛祥麟 (b. ca. 1815). Ed. by Bi Wan-chen 畢萬忱. Mingqing biji congshu. Shanghai: Guji chubanshe, 1985.

Nenggaizhai manlu 能改齋漫錄. By Wu Ceng 吳曾 (fl. 1155). Biji xiao-shuo daguan xubian vol. 31.

Qingchao xu wenxian tongkao 清朝續文獻通考. Ed. by Liu Jinzao 劉錦藻. *Shitong* 十通 ed. Shanghai: Commercial Press, 1936 reprint of 1921 original.

Qingjia lu 清嘉錄. By Gu Lu 顧祿 (ca. 1796–?). Renren wenku, *te*, no. 437. Taipei: Commercial Press, 1976 reprint of 1830 ed.

———. Ed. by Wang Mai 王邁. Jiangsu difang wenxian congshu. Jiangsu: Jiangsu Guji chubanshe, 1986.

Qingshan ji 青山集. By Zhao Wen 趙文 (1239–1315). Siku quanshu ed.

Quan shanggu sandai Qin Han Sanguo Liuchao wen 全上古三代秦漢三國六朝文. By Yan Kejun 嚴可鈞 (1762–1843). Guangzhou: Guangya shuju, 1887–93.

Quan Tang shi 全唐詩. Ed. by Peng Dingqiu 彭定求 (1645–1719). Peking: Zhonghua shuju, 1960

Quan Tang wen 全唐文. Ed. by Dong Gao 董誥 (1740–1818) et al. Peking: Zhonghua shuju, 1983.

Rongzhi suibi 容齋隨筆. By Hong Mai 洪邁 (1123–1202). Siku quanshu ed.

Sanguozhi 三國志. By Chen Shou 陳壽 (233–97). Beijing: Zhonghua shuju, 1963.

Sanjiao yuanliu soushen daquan 三敎源流搜神大全. Ye Dehui 葉德輝 Lilou congshu ed. of Xuantong 1909, reprinted together with *Soushen ji* (1926 Hanfenlou ed.). Taipei: Lianjing, 1980.

Shanyou shike congbian 山右石刻叢編. Ed. by Hu Pinzhi 胡聘之. 1899–1901.

Shangshu zhengyi 尚書正義. By Lu Deming 陸德明 (?–ca. 628). *Shisanjing zhushu* ed. Taipei: Yeewen Publishing Co., 1976 photo-reprint of 1816 carving.

Shiji 史記. By Sima Qian 司馬遷. Beijing: Zhonghua shuju, 1962.

Shiki kōchū kōshō 史記校注考證. Ed. by Takigawa Kametarō 瀧川龜太郎. Tokyo: Tōhō Bunka Gakuin Tōkyō Kenkyūjo, 1932–34.

Shiliu guo chunqiu jibu 十六國春秋輯補. By Cui Hong 崔鴻 (?–ca. 525). Ed. by Tang Qiu 湯球. Basic Sinological Series ed. Peking: Commercial Press, 1958.

Shiwu jiyuan 事物紀原. By Gao Cheng 高承 (fl. 1080). Congshu jicheng ed. Shanghai: Commercial Press, 1937.

Shu bi 蜀碧. By Peng Zunsi 彭遵泗 (1737 *jinshi*). Congshu jicheng chubian ed.

Shuijing zhu. See *Wangshi hejiao Shuijing zhu*.

Shuzhong guangji 蜀中廣記. By Cao Xuequan 曹學全 (1574–1647). Shanghai: Commercial Press, 1935.

Sichuan tongzhi 四川通志. Ed. by Yang Fangcan 楊芳燦 (1753–1815) et al. Chengdu: Ba Shu shushe, 1984 reprint of 1816 carving.

Songben Sun Kezhi wenji 宋本孫可之文集. By Sun Qiao 孫樵 (fl. 867). Xu Guyi congshu reprint of Song ed. Shanghai, 1922.

Songben Wenzhongzi Zhongshuo 宋本文中子中說. By Wang Tong 王通 (584–618). Xu Guyi congshu reprint of Song ed. Shanghai, 1923.

Songhuiyao jigao 宋會要輯稿. Ed. by Xu Song 徐松 (1781–1848). Beijing: Datong shuju, 1936.

Songshi 宋史. By Tuo Tuo 脫脫 (1313–55). Beijing: Zhonghua shuju, 1977.

Songshi yiwenzhi guangbian 宋使藝文志廣編. Ed. by Yang Jialuo 楊家駱. Taipei: Shijie shuju, 1975.

Suishi guangji 歲時廣記. By Chen Yuanjing 陳元靚 (fl. 1080). Taipei: Xinwenfeng, 1984 reprint of Commercial Press, 1939 edition.

Suishu 隋書. By Wei Zheng (580–643). Beijing: Zhonghua shuju, 1974.

Taiping huanyu ji 太平寰宇記. Ed. by Yue Shi 樂史 (930–1007). Taipei: Wenhai chubanshe, 1963.

Taiping guangji 太平廣記. Ed. by Li Fang 李昉 (925–996) et al. Peking: Zhonghua shuju, 1961.

Taiping yulan 太平御覽. Ed. by Li Fang et al. Peking: Renmin wenxue chubanshe, 1959.

Tang shi jishi 唐詩記事. Ed. by Ji Yougong 計有功 (fl. 1126). Shanghai: Zhonghua shuju, 1965.

Tieweishan congtan 鐵圍山叢談. By Cai Tao 蔡條 (?–1126). Siku quanshu ed., vol. 1037.

Tingshi 桯史. By Yue Ke 岳珂 (1173–1240). Biji xiaoshuo daguan ed.

Wangshi hejiao Shuijing zhu 王氏合校水經注. By Li Daoyuan 酈道元 (d. 527). Ed. by Wang Xianqian 王先謙. Sibu beiyao ed.

Wanzhai ji 萬齋記. By Gong Shitai 貢師泰 (1298–1362). Siku quanshu ed.

Wendi quanshu 文帝全書. Ed. by Liu Tishu 劉體恕. Preface dated 1775.

Wenxuan 文選. Ed. by Xiao Tong 蕭統 (501–31). Taipei: Yeewen Publishing, 1974 reprint of 1809 ed.

Wenyuan yinghua 文苑英華. Ed. by Li Fang 李昉. Peking: Zhonghua shuju, 1966.

Xihu youlan zhi 西湖遊覽志. Tian Rucheng 田汝成 (1526 *jinshi*). Taipei: Shijie shuju, 1963.

Xu Zi buyu 續子不語. By Yuan Mei 袁枚 (1716–90). Biji xiaoshuo daguan ed.

Xuegu lu 學古錄. By Yu Ji 虞集 (1272–1348). Ed. by Yu Wenggui 虞翁歸. Blocks engraved 1723–35.

Yanyou Siming zhi 延祐四明志. By Ma Ze 馬澤. Song Yuan difangzhi edition. 1320.

Yijian zhi 夷堅志. By Hong Mai 洪邁 (1123–1202). Peking: Zhonghua shuju, 1981.

Yili zhushu 儀禮注疏. *Shisanjing zhushu* ed. Taipei: Yeewen Publishing Co., 1976 photo-reprint of 1816 carving.

Yishi jishi 壹是記始. By Wei Song 魏崧 (1823 *jinshi*). 1891 recarving.

Yiwen leiju 藝文類聚. Ed. by Ouyang Xun 歐陽詢 (577–641). 2 vols. Shanghai: Zhonghua shuju, 1965.

Yongxian zhai biji 庸閒齋筆記. By Chen Qiyuan 陳其元 (1811–81). Biji xiaoshuo daguan ed.

Youyang zazu 酉陽雜俎. By Duan Chengshi 段成式 (?–863). Sibu congkan reprint of Ming ed.

Yuezhong jinshi ji 越中金石記. By Du Chunsheng 杜春生 (fl. 1835). N.p., n.d.

Yuzhi tang tanhui 玉芝堂談會. By Xu Yingqiu 徐應秋 (1616 *jinshi*). Siku quanshu zhenben ed.

Zangwai daoshu 藏外道書. 1992. Ed. by Chen Dali 陳大利. 20 vol. Chengdu: Ba Shu shushe.

Zhongguo lishi dacidian: Songshi 中國歷史大辭:宋史. Shanghai: Shanghai Cishu chubanshe, 1984.

Zhouli zhushu 周禮注疏. *Shisanjing zhushu* ed. Taipei: Yeewen Publishing Co., 1976 photo-reprint of 1816 carving.

Zhouyi zhengyi 周易正義. *Shisanjing zhushu* ed. Taipei: Yeewen Publishing Co., 1976 photo-reprint of 1816 carving.

Zhuangzi 莊子. Harvard-Yenching Institute Sinological Index Series.

Zhuzi yulei 朱子語類. By Zhu Xi 朱熹 (1130–1200). Zhuzi daquan ed.

Zitongxian zhi 梓潼縣志. Zhang Xianghai 張香海, ed. Zitong, Sichuan, 1867. Reprinted by Ch'eng-wen Publishing Co., 1976.

Zi buyu 子不語. By Yuan Mei 袁枚 (1716–90). *Biji xiaoshuo daguan* ed.

Zuomeng lu 昨夢錄. By Kang Yuzhi 康與之 (fl. 1131). Siku quanshu ed.

Zuozhuan 左傳. Harvard-Yenching Index Series ed.

Secondary Works

Ahern, Emily H. 1974. "Affines and the Ritual of Kinship." In *Religion and Ritual in Chinese Society*, ed. by Arthur P. Wolf, 279–308. Stanford: Stanford University Press.

Akizuki Kan'ei 秋月觀映. 1978. *Chūgoku kinsei Dōkyō no keisei: Jōmeidō no kisoteki kenkyū* 中國近世道教の形成淨明道の基處的研究 [*The Formation of Pre-modern Daoism: A Basic Study of the Way of Pure Illumination*]. Tokyo: Sōbunsha.

Allan, Sarah. 1991. *The Shape of the Turtle: Myth, Art, and Cosmos in Early China.* Albany: State University of New York Press.

Allan, Sarah, and Alvin P. Cohen. 1979. *Legend, Lore and Religion in China: Essays in Honor of Wolfram Eberhard on His Seventieth Birthday.* San Francisco: Chinese Materials Center.

An Pingqiu 安平秋 and Zhang Peiheng 章培恆. 1990. *Zhongguo jinshu daguan* 中國禁書大觀 [*A Survey of China's Banned Books*]. Shanghai: Shanghai wenhua chubanshe.

Araki Toshikazu 荒木敏一. 1969. *Sōdai kakyo seido kenkyū* 宋代科舉制度研究 [*A Study of the Song Dynasty Examination System*]. Oriental Research Series, 22. Kyoto: Dobosha Press.

Baity, Philip Chesley. 1975. *Religion in a Chinese Town.* Taipei: The Orient Cultural Service.

Baldrian, Farzeen. 1986. "Lü Tung-pin in Northern Sung Literature." *Cahiers d'Extrême-Asie* 2: 133–69.

Banck, Werner. 1976. *Das chinesische Tempelorakel.* Taipei: Guting shuju.

Berkowitz, Alan. 1989. "Patterns of Reclusion in Early and Medieval China: A Study of the Formulation of the Practice of Reclusion in China and Its Portrayal." Ph.D. dissertation, University of Washington.

Berling, Judith. 1980. *The Syncretic Religion of Lin Chao-en.* New York: Columbia University Press.

Birge, Bettine. 1989. "Chu Hsi and Women's Education." In *Neo-Confucian Education: The Formative Stage,* ed. by Wm. Theodore de Bary and John W. Chaffee. Berkeley: University of California Press.

Bishop, Mrs. J. F. (Bird, Isabella L.). 1900. *The Yangtze Valley and Beyond; An Account of Journeys in China, Chiefly in the Province of Sze Chuan and among the Man-tze of the Somo Territory.* New York: G.P. Putnam's.

Bodde, Derk. 1975. *Festivals in Classical China: New Year and Other Annual Observances during the Han Dynasty, 206 B.C.–A.D. 220.* Princeton: Princeton University Press.

Bodde, Derk, and Clarence Morris. 1967. *Law in Imperial China: Exemplified by 190 Ch'ing Dynasty Cases.* Cambridge, Mass.: Harvard University Press.

Bokenkamp, Stephen R. "The Peach Flower Font and the Grotto Passage." *Journal of the American Oriental Society* 106.1 (Winter): 65–77.

Boltz, Judy. 1987. *A Survey of Taoist Literature: Tenth to Seventeenth Cen-*

turies. Berkeley: Institute of East Asian Studies, University of California.

Brokaw, Cynthia. 1991. *The Ledgers of Merit and Demerit: Social Change and Moral Order in Late Imperial China.* Princeton: Princeton University Press.

Chaffee, John W. 1985. *The Thorny Gates of Learning In Sung China: A social history of the examinations.* Cambridge: Cambridge University Press.

Chan, Wing-tsit, tr. 1967. *Reflections on Things at Hand, the Neo-Confucian Anthology.* By Zhu Xi 朱熹. New York: Columbia University Press.

Chang Cheng-lang. 1980–81. "An Interpretation of the Divinatory Inscriptions on Early Zhou Bronzes." Tr. by H. Huber, R. Yates et al. *Early China* 6: 80–96.

Chang, Chun-shu and Joan Smythe. 1981. *South China in the Twelfth Century: A Translation of Lu Yu's Travel Diaries July 3–December 6, 1170.* Hong Kong: The Chinese University Press.

Chao, Wei-pang. 1942. "The origin and growth of the *fu chi* 扶乩." *Folklore Studies* 1: 9–27.

————. 1946. "The Chinese Science of Fate-Calculation." *Folklore Studies* 5: 279–315.

Chavannes, Edouard. 1895–1905. *Les Mémoires historiques de Se-Ma Ts'ien.* 5 vols. Paris: E. Leroux. Reprinted Paris: Maisonneuve, 1967.

————. 1910–11, 1934. *Cinq Cents Contes et Apologues: extraits du Tripitaka chinois.* 4 vols. Paris: Ernest Leroux.

Cheng Yizhong 程毅中. 1981. *Guxiaoshuo jianmu* 古小說簡目 [*A Select Bibliography of Ancient Anecdotal Literature*]. Beijing: Zhonghua shuju.

Ching, Julia, tr. 1987. *The Records of Ming Scholars.* By Huang Zongxi 黃宗羲. Honolulu: University of Hawaii Press.

Ch'ü, T'ung-tsu. 1961. *Law and Society in Traditional China.* Paris: Mouton.

————. 1972. *Han Social Structure.* Seattle: University of Washington Press.

Cohen, Alvin P. 1978. "Coercing the Rain Deities in Ancient China." *History of Religions* 17.3/4 (Feb–May): 244–265.

————. 1979. "Avenging Ghosts and Moral Judgement in Ancient Chinese Historiography: Three Examples from *Shih-chi*." In *Legend, Lore, and Religion in China: Essays in Honor of Wolfram Eberhard on His Seventieth Birthday,* ed. by Sarah Allan and Alvin P. Cohen, 97–108. San Francisco: Chinese Materials Center.

————. 1982. *Tales of Vengeful Souls: A Sixth Century Collection of Avenging Ghost Stories.* Taipei: Variétés Sinologiques.

Davis, Edward L. 1985. "Arms and the Tao: Hero Cult and Empire in Traditional China." In *Sōdai no shakai to shūkyō* 宋代の社會と宗教.

Sōdaishi kenkyūkai hōkoku 2: 1–56.

De Groot, J. 1880. J. M. "Two Gods of Literature and a God of Barbers." *China Review* 9.3, 188–90.

———. 1892–1910. *The Religious System of China.* 6 vols. Leiden: E.J. Brill.

———. 1886. *Les Fêtes annuellement célébrées à Emoui (Amoy): Étude concernant la religion populaire des Chinois.* Tr. by C. G. Chavannes. Annales de Musée Guimet, vols. 11 and 12. Paris: Ernest Leroux.

———. 1903. *Sectarianism and Religious Persecution in China.* Two volumes. Amsterdam: Johannes Muller.

De Harlez, Ch. 1894. *La Religion et les Cérémonies de la Chine moderne d'apres le Cérémonial et les Décrets officiels.* Mémoires de l'Academie royale des sciences des lettres et des beaux arts de Belgique, vol. 52. Brussels.

DeWoskin, Kenneth J. 1983. *Doctors, Diviners, and Magicians of Ancient China: Biographies of Fang-shih.* New York: Columbia University Press.

d'Hormon, André, tr. 1985. *Guoyu: Propos sur les Principautés, I — Zhouyu.* Complément par Rémi Mathieu. Mémoires de l'Institut des Hautes Études chinoises, XXV-1. Paris: Collège de France.

Ding Fubao 丁福保, ed. 1959. *Shuowen jiezi gulin* 說文解字詁林 [A Forest of Glosses on *Explaining Ideograms and Analyzing Phonograms*]. Taipei: Commercial Press.

Doolittle, Justus. 1865. *Social life of the Chinese, with Some Account of Their Religious, Governmental, Educational and Business Customs and Opinions. With Special But Not Exclusive Reference to Fuhchau.* Two vols. New York.

Doré, Henry. 1920. *Researches into Chinese Superstitions.* 13 vols. Tr. by M. Kennelly. Shanghai: T'usewei Printing Press.

Dudbridge, Glen. 1978. *The Legend of Miao-shan.* Oxford Oriental Monographs, 1. London: Ithaca Press.

———. 1982. "Miao-shan on Stone: Two Early Inscriptions." *Harvard Journal of Asian Studies* 42.2: 589–614.

Dull, Jack L. 1966. "A Historical Introduction to the Apocryphal (*ch'an-wei*) Texts of the Han Dynasty." Ph.D. dissertation, University of Washington.

Duyvendak, J.-J.-L. 1953. *Tao To King: Le Livre de la Voie et de la Vertu.* Paris: Maisonneuve.

Eberhard, Wolfram. 1942. *Lokalkulturen im alten China.* 2 vols. Leiden: E.J. Brill.

———. 1964. "Temple-building Activities in Medieval and Modern

China." *Monumenta Serica* 23: 264–318.

———. 1967. *Guilt and Sin in Traditional China.* Berkeley: University of California Press.

Ebrey, Patricia Buckley, ed. 1981. *Chinese Civilization and Society: A Sourcebook.* New York: Free Press-Macmillan.

———. 1984. *Family and Property in Sung China: Yüan Ts'ai's Precepts for Social Life.* Princeton: Princeton University Press.

———. 1991. *Chu Hsi's Family Rituals: A Twelfth-Century Chinese Manual for the Performance of Cappings, Weddings, Funerals, and Ancestral Rites.* Princeton Library of Asian Translations. Princeton: Princeton University Press.

———. 1993a. "The Response of the Sung State to Popular Funeral Practices." In *Religion and Society in T'ang-Sung China,* ed. by Patricia Buckley Ebrey and Peter Gregory, 209–40. Honolulu: Hawaii University Press.

———. 1993b. *The Inner Quarters: Marriage and the Lives of Chinese Women in the Sung Period.* Berkeley: University of California Press.

Egan, Ronald. 1977. "Narratives in *Tso-chuan.*" Harvard Journal of Asiatic Studies 37.2: 323–52.

Eichhorn, Werner. 1976. "Some Notes on Population Control during the Sung Dynasty." In *Études d'Historie et de Littérature Chinoises offertes au Professeur Jaroslav Prusek.* Bibliotheque de l'Institut des Hautes Études Chinoises, vol. 24. Paris.

Elliot, Alan. 1955. *Chinese Spirit-Medium Cults in Singapore.* London: University of London Press.

Elvin, Mark. 1973. *The Pattern of the Chinese Past.* Stanford: Stanford University Press.

Feer, Léon. 1891. *L'Avadāna-Cataka: cent légendes bouddhiques.* Annales du Musée Guimet, 18. Paris: Ernest Leroux.

Forke, Alfred. 1911. *Lun Heng.* 2 vol. New York: Paragon Book Gallery reprint of 1972.

Gernet, Jacques. 1962. *Daily Life in China on the Eve of the Mongol Invasion, 1250–1276.* Tr. by H. M. Wright. New York: Macmillan.

Giles, Herbert A. 1914. "Infanticide in China." In *Adversaria sinica:* 411–22.

Girardot, N. J. 1983. *Myth and Meaning in Early Taoism: The Theme of Chaos (Hun-tun).* Berkeley: University of California Press,.

Gjertson, Donald E. 1981. "The Early Chinese Buddhist Miracle Tale: A Preliminary Survey." *Journal of the American Oriental Society* 101.3 (July–Sept.): 287–301.

————. 1989. *Miraculous Retribution: A Study and Translation of T'ang Ling's* Ming-pao Chi. University of California, Center for South and Southeast Asia Studies.

Goidsenhoven, Jacques van. 1971. *Heros et Divinités de la Chine*. Brussels: DeTijdstroom-Lochem.

Goodrich, L. Carrington and Chaoying Fang, eds. 1976. *Dictionary of Ming Biography, 1368–1644*. 2 vol. New York: Columbia University Press.

Graham, David Crockett. 1930. "The Temples of Suifu." *Chinese Recorder* 61: 108–20.

Granet, Marcel. 1975. *The Religion of the Chinese People*. Tr. and forward by Maurice Freedman. Oxford: Basil Blackwell. Orig. published as *La Religion des Chinois*, 1922.

Gray, John Henry. 1878. *China: A History of the Laws, Manners and Customs of the People*. 2 vols. London: Macmillan.

Grim, John A. 1984. "*Chaesu Kut*: A Korean Shamanistic Performance." *Asian Folklore Studies* 43.2: 235–60.

Grootaers, Willem A., Li Shih-yu, and Chang Chi-wen. 1948. "Temples and History of Wanch'uan: The Geographical Method Applied to Folklore." *Monumenta Serica* 13: 209–316.

————. 1952. "The Hagiography of the Chinese God Chen-wu." *Folklore Studies* 12.2: 139–82.

Gulik, R. H. van. 1941. "On the Seal Representing the God of Literature on the Title Page of Old Chinese and Japanese Popular Editions." *Monumenta Nipponica* 4: 33–52.

————. 1956. T'ang-yin-pi-shih. *Parallel cases from under the pear-tree; a 13th century manual of jurisprudence and detection*. Leiden, E. J. Brill.

Haeger, John Winthrop, ed. 1975. *Crisis and Prosperity in Sung China*. Tucson, Ariz.: University of Arizona Press.

Hammond, Charles E. 1990. "T'ang Legends: Myth and Hearsay." *Tamkang Review* 20.4 (Summer): 359–82.

Hansen, Valerie Lynn. 1990. *Changing Gods in Medieval China, 1127–1276*. Princeton: Princeton University Press.

Harper, Donald. 1982. The *Wu-shih-erh ping fang*. Translation and Prolegomena. Ph.D. dissertation, University of California at Berkeley.

Hart, Rev. V.-C. 1879. "The Heavenly Teachers." *The Chinese Recorder* 10.6: 445–53.

Hartwell, Robert M. 1982. "Demographic, Political and Social Transformations of China, 750–1550." *Harvard Journal of Asian Studies* 42.2: 365–442.

————. 1987. "Societal Organization and Demographic Change: Catastrophe, Agrarian Technology and Interregional Population Trends in Traditional China." Paper presented at the "Deuxième Congrès International de Demographie Historique," Paris, France, June 4–5.

Hawkes, David. 1985. *The Songs of the South: An Anthology of Ancient Chinese Poems by Qu Yuan and Other Poets.* Middlesex: Penguin Books.

He Cijun 何次君. 1936. "Wenchang dijun kao" 文昌帝君考 ["A Study of the Divine Lord Wenchang"]. *Yijing* 9: 23–25.

Hervouet, Yves. 1964. *Un Poète de cour sous les Han: Sseu-ma Siang-jou.* Paris: Presses Universitaires de France.

————. 1972. *Le Chapitre 117 du Che-ki (Biographie de Sseu-ma Siang-jou).* Paris: Presses Universitaires de France.

————, ed. 1978. *A Sung Bibliography.* Initiated by Etienne Balazs. Hong Kong: Chinese University Press.

Ho, Peng Yoke. 1966. *The Astronomical Chapters of the Chin Shu.* Paris and The Hague: Mouton.

Hodous, Lewis. 1929. *Folkways in China.* London.

Holtzman, Donald. 1957. "Les débuts du Système Médiéval des Choix et de Classement: Les neuf catégories de l'Impartial et juste." In *Mélanges* (Institut des Hautes Études Chinoise): 387–414.

Homann, Rolf. 1971. *Die wichtigsten Körpergottheiten im Huang-t'ing ching.* Göppingen: Alfred Kümmerle.

Houn, Franklin W. 1956–69. "The Civil Service Recruitment System of the Han Dynasty." *Qinghua xuebao* n.s. 1: 138–64.

Hsiao, Kung-ch'üan. 1960. *Rural China: Imperial Control in the Nineteenth Century.* Seattle: University of Washington Press.

Hsü, Dau-lin. 1970–71. "The Myth of the 'Five Human Relations' of Confucius." *Monumenta Serica* 29: 27–37.

Hu Fuchen 胡孚琛. 1989. *Wei Jin shenxian daojiao* 魏晉神仙道教 [*The Taoism of the Divine Transcendents of the Wei and Jin Periods*]. Beijing: Renmin chubanshe.

Hucker, Charles O. 1985. *A Dictionary of Official Titles in Imperial China.* Stanford: Stanford University Press.

Hymes, Robert P. 1986. *Statesmen and Gentlemen: The Elite of Fu-chou, Chiang-Hsi, in Northern and Southern Sung.* Cambridge: Cambridge University Press.

————. 1987. "Not Quite Gentlemen? Doctors in Sung and in Yuan." *Chinese Science* 8: 9–76.

Inahata, Koichirō 稲畑小一郎. 1979. "Shimei shinsō no tenkai" 司命信想

の展開 ["The Development of Faith in the Controller of Destinies"]. *Chūgoku bungaku kenkyū* 5: 1–17.

Johnson, David. 1977. *The Medieval Chinese Oligarchy.* Boulder, Colo.: Westview Press.

———. 1985. "The City-God Cults of T'ang and Sung China." *Harvard Journal of Asiatic Studies* 45.2: 363–457.

Jordan, David K. 1972. *Gods, Ghosts and Ancestors: Folk Religion in a Taiwanese Village.* Berkeley: University of California Press.

Jordan, David K., and Daniel Overmyer. 1986. *The Flying Pheonix: Aspects of Chinese Sectarianism in Taiwan.* Princeton: Princeton University Press.

Ju Qingyuan 鞠清遠. 1936. "Tang Song shidai Sichuan de canshi" 唐宋時代四川的蠶市 ["The Silkworm Market in Sichuan during the Tang and Song"]. *Shihuo banyuekan* 3.6: 28–34.

Kaltenmark, Max. 1979. "The Ideology of the T'ai-p'ing ching." In *Facets of Taoism: Essays in Chinese Religion,* ed. by Holmes Welch and Anna Seidel, 19–52. New Haven: Yale University Press.

———. 1985. "Le Légende de la Ville immergée en Chine." *Cahiers d'Extrême-Asie* 1: 1–10.

Kanai, Noriyuki 金井德幸. 1979. "Sōdai no sonsha to shashin" 宋代の村社と社神 ["The Village *she* and the God of the *she* in the Song Dynasty"]. *Tōyōshi kenkyū* 38.2: 61–87.

Karlgren, Bernhard, trans. 1960. *The Book of Documents.* Stockholm: Museum of Far Eastern Antiquities.

Kawahara, Yoshirō 河原由郎. 1980. *Sōdai shakai keizaishi kenkyū* 宋代社會經濟史研究 [*A Study of Song Social and Economic History*]. Tokyo: Keisō shobō.

Kleeman, Terry. 1984. "Land Contracts and Related Documents." In *Makio Ryōkai Hakase Shōju Kinen Ronshū: Chūgoku no Shūkyō, Shisō to Kagaku,* 1–34. Tokyo: Kokusho Kankōkai.

———. 1988. "Wenchang and the Viper: The Creation of a Chinese National God." Ph.D. dissertation, University of California at Berkeley.

———. 1991. "Taoist Ethics." In *A Bibliographic Guide to the Comparative Study of Ethics,* ed. by John Carman and Mark Juergensmayer, 162–95. Cambridge: Cambridge University Press.

———. 1992–93. "Senshu: Seitōteki na chihō shinkō" 川主: 政統的な地方信仰 [The Lord(s) of Sichuan: An Orthodox Local Cult]. Tr. by Yamada Toshiaki and Yusa Noboru. *Tōhō shūkyō* 80 (1992): 33–50; 81 (1993): 43–50.

———. 1993. "The Expansion of the Wen-ch'ang Cult." In *Religion and*

Society in T'ang-Sung China, ed. by Patricia Buckley Ebrey and Peter Gregory, 45–73. Honolulu: Hawaii University Press.

————. 1994. "Mountain Deities in China: The Domestication of the Mountain God and the Subjugation of the Margins." To appear in *Journal of the American Oriental Society* 114.1 (Jan.–Mar. 1994).

Knechtges, David R. 1982. *Wenxuan or Selections of Refined Literature*, Volume 1: *Rhapsodies on Metropolises and Capitals*. Princeton: Princeton University Press.

Kracke, E. A., Jr. 1953. *Civil Service in Early Sung China: 960–1067*. Cambridge, Mass.: Harvard-Yenching Institute.

————. 1957. "Region, Family and Individual in the Chinese Examination System." In *Chinese Thought and Institutions*, ed. by John K. Fairbank, 251–68. . Chicago: University of Chicago Press.

Kubo Noritada 窪德忠. 1986. *Dōkyō no kamigami* 道教の神々 [*The Gods of Daoism*]. Tokyo: Hirakawa shuppansha.

————. 1992. *Mongoruchō no Dōkyo to Bukkyō* モンゴル朝道教と佛教 [*Daoism and Buddhism in the Mongol Dynasty*]. Tokyo: Hirakawa shuppansha.

Kuhn, Dieter. 1988. *Science and Civilization in China*, Volume Five, *Chemistry and Chemical Technology*, Part 9, *Textile Technology: Spinning and Reeling*. Ed. by Joseph Needham. Cambridge: Cambridge University Press.

Lagerwey, John. 1981. *Wu-shang pi-yao, somme taoïste de VIe siècle*. Publications de l'École française d'Extrême-Orient, vol. 124. Paris: École française d'Extrême-Orient.

————. 1992. "The Pilgrimage to Wu-tang Shan." In *Pilgrims and Sacred Sites in China*, ed. by Susan Naquin and Chün-fang Yü, 293–332. Berkeley, University of California Press.

Langlois, John D., and Sun K'o-k'uan. 1982. "Three Teachings Syncretism and the Thought of Ming T'ai-tsu." *Harvard Journal of Asian Studies* 42.1: 97–139.

Lau, D. C. 1979. *Confucius: The Analects*. Middlesex: Penguin Books.

Lee, Thomas H. C. 1985. *Government Education and Examinations in Sung China*. Hong Kong: Chinese University Press.

Legge, James. 1885. *Li Ki*. Oxford: Oxford University Press, reprinted New Hyde Park, N.Y.: University Books, 1967.

Lemoine, Jacques. 1982. *Yao Ceremonial Paintings*. Bangkok: White Lotus Col., Ltd.

Lévi, Jean. 1986. "Les fonctionnaires et le divin." *Cahiers d'Extrême-Asie* 2: 81–110.

Li Fengmao 李豐楙. 1990. "Songchao shuishen Xu Xun chuanshuo zhi yanjiu" 宋朝水神許遜傳說之研究 [A Study of the Song Dynasty River God Xu Xun Legend]. *Hanxue yanjiu* 8.1: 363–400.

Li Zhiqin 李志勤, Yan Shoucheng 閻守誠, and Hu Ji 胡戟. 1986. *Shudao hua gu* 蜀道話古 [*Tales of the Ancient Road to Shu*]. Xi'an: Xibei daxue chubanshe.

Link, Arthur E. 1957. "Shyh Daw-an's Preface to Sangharaksa's Yogācarabhūmisūtra and the Problem of Buddho-Taoist Terminology in Early Chinese Buddhism." *Journal of the American Oriental Society* 77: 1–14.

Liu, James J. Y. 1967. *The Chinese Knight-errant.* Chicago: University of Chicago Press.

Liu, James T. C. 1957. "An Early Sung Reformer: Fan Chung-yen." In *Chinese Thought and Institutions,* ed. by John K. Fairbank, 105–131. Chicago: University of Chicago Press.

Liu, Ts'un-yan. 1975. "The Compilation and Historical Volume of the Taotsang." In *Essays on the Sources for Chinese History,* ed. by Donald D. Leslie, 104–119. Columbia, S.C.: University of South Carolina Press.

Liu, Zhiwan 劉枝萬. 1984. *Chūgoku Dōkyō no matsuri to shinkō* 中國道教 の祭りと信仰 [*The Festivals and Beliefs of Chinese Taoism*). 2 vols. Tokyo: Eifūsha.

Lo, Winston. 1982. *Szechwan in Sung China.* Taipei: Chinese Culture University.

———. 1987. *An Introduction to the Civil Service of Sung China: With Emphasis on Its Personnel Administration.* Honolulu: University of Hawaii Press.

Loon, Piet van der. 1984. *Taoist Books in the Libraries of the Sung Period: A Critical Study and Index.* Oxford Oriental Institute Monographs 7, London: Ithaca Press.

Lyon, D. N. 1889. "Life and Writings of the God of Literature." *Chinese Recorder* 20.9: 411–420; 20.10; 439–49.

Mair, Victor. 1981. "Lay Students and the Making of Written Vernacular Narrative: An Inventory of Tun-huang Manuscripts." *CHINOPERL Papers* 10: 5–96.

———. 1983. "The Narrative Revolution in Chinese Literature: Ontological Presuppositions." *Chinese Literature: Essays, Articles, Reviews* 5.1: 1–27.

———. 1989. *T'ang Transformation Texts: A Study of the Buddhist Contribution to the Rise of Vernacular Fiction and Drama in China.* Cambridge, Mass.: Council on East Asian Studies, Harvard University.

Mair, Victor and Tsu-lin Mei. 1991. "The Sanskrit Origins of Recent Style Prosody." *Harvard Journal of Asiatic Studies* 51.2: 375–470.

Maspero, Henri. N.d. "The Mythology of Modern China." In *Asiatic Mythology*, ed. by J. Hackin et al, 254–384. New York: Crescent Books.

Maruyama, Hiroshi 丸山宏. 1986. "Shōitsu dōkyō no jōshō girei ni tsuite—'chōshōshō' o chūshin to shite" 正一道敎の上章儀禮について ——冢訟章のを中心として ["On the Rite of the Presentation of the Memorial in Zhengyi Taoism—Centering on the "Sepulchral Plaint Petition" *Tōhō shūkyō* 68 (Nov.): 44–64.

Maspero, Henri. N.d. "The Mythology of Modern China." In *Asiatic Mythology: A Detailed Description and Explanation of the Mythologies of All the Great Nations of Asia*, ed. by J. Hackin et al, 252–384. New York: Crescent Books.

———. 1981. *Taoism and Chinese Religion.* Tr. by Frank A. Kierman, Jr. Amherst: Univ. of Massachusetts Press.

Mather, Richard B. 1976. *Shih-shuo Hsin-yü: A New Account of Tales of the World.* By Liu I-ch'ing. Minneapolis: University of Minnesota Press.

Mayers, William Frederick. 1869–70. "On Wen-ch'ang, the God of Literature, His History and Worship." *Journal of the North China Branch of the Royal Asiatic Society*, new series, 6: 31–44.

McCreery, John L. 1973. "The Symbolism of Popular Taoist Magic." Ph.D. dissertation, Cornell University.

McKnight, Brian. 1971. *Village and Bureaucracy in Sung China.* Chicago: University of Chicago Press.

Miyakawa Hisayuki. 1960. "The Confucianization of South China." In *The Confucian Persuasion*, ed. by Arthur F. Wright, 21–46. Stanford: Stanford University Press.

Miyazaki Ichisada 宮崎市定. 1977. *Kyūhin kanjin hō no kenkyū* 九品官人法の研究 [*A Study of the Nine Grade Official Method*]. Tokyo: Dōhōsha.

Mochizuki Shinkō 望月信亨. 1954–71. *Bukkyō daijiten* 佛敎大辭典 [*Dictionary of Buddhism*] 3d ed. 10 vols. Kyoto: Sekai seiten kankō kyōkai.

Morita Kenji 森田憲司. 1984. "Bunshō teikun no seiritsu—chihōshin kara kakyo no kami e 文昌帝君の成立——地方神のから科擧の神へ ["The Establishment of the Divine Lord Wenchang: From Local God to God of the Examinations"]. In *Chūgoku kinsei no toshi to bunka*, ed.

by Umehara Kaoru, 389–418. Kyoto: Kyoto University Institute for Humanistic Studies.

Morohashi Tetsuji 諸橋轍次. 1955–60. *Dai Kanwa jiten* 大漢和辭典 [*Great Chinese-Japanese Dictionary*]. Tokyo: Taishūkan.

Mote, Frederick. 1961. "The Growth of Chinese Despotism." *Oriens Extremis* 8.1 (Aug.): 1–41.

Nakamura Hajime. 1980. *Indian Buddhism: A Survey with Bibliographical Notes*. Intercultural Research Institute Monograph, 9. Kirakata, Japan: Kufs Publications.

Ngo Van Xuyet. 1976. *Divination, magie, et politique dans la Chine ancienne*. Paris: Presses Universitaires de France.

Nivison, David S. 1983. "Western Chou History Reconstructed from Bronze Inscriptions." In *The Great Bronze Age of China: A Symposium*, ed. by George Kuwayama, 44–55. Seattle: Los Angeles County Museum of Art.

Overmyer, Daniel L. 1976. *Folk Buddhist Religion: Dissenting Sects in Late Traditional China*. Cambridge: Harvard University Press.

———. 1982. "The White Cloud Sect in Sung and Yüan China." *Harvard Journal of Asian Studies* 42.1: 615–42.

Ozaki Masaharu 尾崎正治. 1986. "Dōzō no seiritsu to sono shūhen" 道藏 の成立とその周邊 [The Formation of the Daoist Canon and its Circumstances]. In *Dōkyō kenkyū no susume*, ed. by Akizuki Kan'ei, 79–110. Tokyo: Hirakawa shuppansha.

Parsons, James B. 1956. "Overtones of Religion and Superstition in the Rebellion of Chang Hsien-chung." *Sinologica* 4: 170–76.

———. 1957. "The Culmination of a Chinese Peasant Rebellion: Chang Hsien-chung in Szechwan, 1644–46." *Journal of Asian Studies* 16: 387–99.

———. 1970. *The Peasant Rebellions of the Late Ming Dynasty*. Tucson: University of Arizona Press.

Potter, Jack M. 1974. "Cantonese Shamanism." In *Religion and Ritual in Chinese Society*, ed. by Arthur P. Wolf, 207–32. Stanford: Stanford University Press.

Prusek, Jaroslav. 1971. *Chinese Statelets and the Northern Barbarians, 1400– 300 B.C.* Dordrecht, Holland: Riedel.

Rees, Helen. 1993. "Music in *Dongjing* Ritual as an Expression of Power." Paper presented at the conference on "Music in Chinese Ritual: Expressions of Authority and Power," University of Pittsburgh, May 5–9.

Ren Jiyu 任繼愈. 1990. *Zhongguo Daojiao shi* 中國道敎史. Shanghai: Renmin chubanshe.

Riegel, Jeffrey K. 1982. "Early Chinese Target Magic. *Journal of Chinese Religion* 10: 1–18.

Robinet, Isabelle. 1983. "Le *Ta-tung chen-ching*—son authenticité et sa place dans les textes du *Shang-ch'ing ching*." In *Tantric and Taoist Studies in Honor of R.A. Stein*, ed. by Michel Strickmann, vol. 2, 394–433. *Mélanges Chinois et Bouddhiques* XXI, Brussels.

———. 1984. *La révélation du Shangqing dans l'histoire du taoïsme.* 2 vols. Publications de l'École Française d'Extrême-Orient 137. Paris.

———. 1985. "L'unité transcendante des trois enseignements selon les taoïstes des Sung et des Yüan." In *Religion und Philosophie in Ostasien*, ed. by G. Naundorf, K.H. Pohl, and H.H. Schmidt, 103–26. Würzburg: Königshausen & Neumann.

Rogers, Michael C. 1968. *The Chronicle of Fu Chien: A Case of Exemplar History.* Berkeley: University of California Press.

Sage, Steven F. 1992. *Ancient Sichuan and the Unification of China.* SUNY Series in Chinese Local Studies. Albany: State University of New York Press.

Sakai, Tadao 酒井忠夫. 1937. "Taizan shinkō no kenkyū" 泰山信仰の研究 ["A Study of the Faith in Mount Tai"]. *Shichō* 7.2: 70–118.

———. 1953. "Kōkakaku no kenkyū" 功過格の研究 ["A Study of the *Ledger of Merits and Demerits*"]. *Tōhō shūkyō* 1.3 (July): 32–49.

———. 1957. "Yinshitsubun no seiritsu ni tsuite" 陰騭文の成立について ["On the Composition of the *Yinzhiwen*"]. *Tōhō Shūkyō* 12: 1–14.

———. 1960. *Chūgoku zensho no kenkyū* 中國善書の研究 [*A Study of Chinese Morality Books*]. Tokyo: Kokusho kankōkai.

———. 1970. "Confucianism and Popular Educational Works." In *Self and Society in Ming Thought*, ed. by Wm. Theodore de Bary, 331–366. New York: Columbia University Press.

Sakai Tadao, Imai Usaburō 今井宇三郎, and Yoshimoto Shōji 吉元昭治. 1992. *Chūgoku no reisen, yakusen shūsei* 中國の靈籤藥籤集成 [*A Collection of Chinese Oracle Slips and Medical Slips*]. Tokyo: Fūkyōsha.

Sasaki, Hirosuke 佐佐木宏幹. 1991. "Hyōrei to dōri: Marēshia no Kōrō senshi jikyō sairon" 憑靈と道理 ── マレーシアの黃老仙師慈教再論 ["Possession and principles: A re-examination of Malaysia's Compassionate Teaching of the Transcendent Teacher Huanglao"]. In *Dentō shūkyō to chishiki* 傳統宗教と知識 [*Traditional Religion and Knowledge*], ed. by Sugimoto Yoshio 杉本良男, 249–76. Nanzan Studies in Cultural Anthropology, 4, Nagoya: Nanzan Anthropological Institute.

Sawada Mizuho 澤田瑞穗. 1984. *Chūgoku no juhō* 中國の咒法. Tokyo: Hirakawa shuppan.

Schafer, Edward H. 1977. *Pacing the Void: T'ang Approaches to the Stars.* Berkeley: University of California Press.

———. 1981–83. "Wu Yun's Stanzas on 'Saunters in Sylphdom.'" *Monumenta Serica* 35: 1–37.

———. 1981–84. *Schafer Sinological Papers.* Privately published.

Schipper, Kristofer Marinus. 1965. *L'Empereur Wou des Han dans la légende taoiste.* Publications de l'École Française d'Extrême-Orient, vol. 58. Paris: École Française d'Extrême-Orient.

———. 1966. "The Divine Jester: Some Remarks on the Gods of the Chinese Marionette Theater." *Bulletin of the Institute of Ethnology, Academia Sinica* 21: 81–95.

———. 1971. "Démonologie chinoise." In *Génies, anges et démons.* Sources orientales, vol. 8. Paris: Editions du Seuil, pp. 405–26.

———. 1975. *Concordance du Tao-tsang, titres des ouvrages.* Publications de l'École Française d'Extrême-Orient, vol. 102. Paris: École Française d'Extrême-Orient.

———. 1977. "Neighborhood cult associations in traditional Tainan." In *The City in Late Imperial China,* ed. by G. William Skinner, 651–76. Stanford: Stanford University Press.

———. 1978. "The Taoist Body." *History of Religions* 17.3/4 (Feb.–May): 355–86.

———. 1980. "Note on the Origin of Taoist 'Registers'." *Tōhō Shūkyō* 56 (Oct.): 31–47.

———. 1981. "Taoist Ritual and Local Cults of the T'ang Dynasty." *Proceedings of the International Conference on Sinology: Section on Folklore and Culture, Academia Sinica, Nankang, August 1980* (Taipei): 101–115.

———. 1985a. "Vernacular and Classical Ritual in Taoism." *Journal of Asian Studies* 45: 21–57.

———. 1985b. "Taoist Ordination Ranks in Tun-huang Manuscripts." In *Religion und Philosophie in Ostasien,* ed. by G. Naundorf, K. H. Pohl, and H. H. Schmidt, 127–48. Würzburg: Königshausen & Neumann.

Schurmann, H. F. 1957. "On Social Themes in Sung Tales." *Harvard Journal of Asian Studies* 20: 239–61.

Seaman, Gary. 1986. "The Divine Authorship of *Pei-yu chi* [Journey to the North]." *Journal of Asian Studies* 45.3: 483–97.

———. 1987. *Journey to the North: An Ethnohistorical Analysis and Annotated Translation of the Chinese Folk Novel* Pei-yu chi. Berkeley: University of California Press.

Seidel, Anna K. 1969. *La divinisation de Lao Tseu dans le taoïsme des Han.*

Publications de l' École Française d'Extrême-Orient, vol. 71. Paris: École Française d'Extrême-Orient.

———. 1969–70. "The Image of the Perfect Ruler in Early Taoist Messianism: Lao-tzu and Li Hung." *History of Religions* 9.2–3: 216–47.

———. 1984. "Le sutra merveilleux du Ling-pao Suprême." In *Contributions aux études de Toeun-houang*, ed. by Michel Soymié, vol. 3, 305–52. Publications de l'École Française d'Extrême-Orient 135, Paris.

———. 1987. "Traces of Han Religion in Funeral Texts Found in Tombs." In *Dōkyō to shūkyō bunka*, ed. by Akizuki Kan'ei, 714–678. Tokyo: Hirakawa shuppansha.

Shaughnessy, Edward L. 1991. *Sources of Western Zhou History: Inscribed Bronze Vessels.* Berkeley: University of California Press.

Shryock, John. 1931. *The Temples of Anking and Their Cults: A Study of Modern Chinese Religion.* Paris: Guenther.

Sichuansheng Guanxian wenjiaoju 四川省灌縣文教局. 1974. "Dujiangyan chutu Dong Han Li Bing shixiang" 都江堰出土東漢李冰石像. *Wen Wu* 7: 27–8.

Sivin, Nathan. 1968. *Chinese Alchemy: Preliminary Studies.* Cambridge: Harvard University Press.

———. 1978. "On the Word 'Taoist' as a Source of Perplexity. With Special Reference to the Relations of Science and Religion in Traditional China." *History of Religions* 17.3/4: 303–330.

Smith, Paul J. 1992. "Family, *Landsmann*, and Status-Group Affinity in Refugee Mobility Strategies: The Mongol Invasions and the Diaspora of Sichuanese Elites, 1230–1330." *Harvard Journal of Asiatic Studies* 52.2 (Dec.): 665–708.

Song Enchang.宋恩常. 1985. "Dali he Lijiang daojiao gaikuang" 大里和麗江道教概況 ["An Outline of Daoism in Dali and Lijiang"]. In *Yunnan minzu minsu he zongjiao diaocha*, ed. by Yunnan sheng bianjizu, 119–24. Kunming: Yunnan minzu chubanshe.

Speyer, J. S., ed. 1909. *Avadānaçataka: A Century of Edifying Tales Belonging to the Hīnayāna.* Reprinted, The Hague: Mouton, 1958.

Steele, John. 1917. *The I-li.* London: Probsthain.

Stein, Rolf A. 1942. "Jardins en miniature d'Extrême-Orient." *Bulletin de l'École-Française d'Extrême-Orient* 42: 1–104.

———. 1979. "Religious Taoism and Popular Religion from the Second to Seventh Centuries." In *Facets of Taoism: Essays in Chinese Religion*, ed. by Holmes Welch and Anna Seidel, 53–82. New Haven: Yale University Press.

Strickmann, Michel. 1978. "The Longest Taoist Scripture." *History of Religions* 17: 331–54.

―――. 1981. *Le taoïsme du Mao Chan: chronique d'une révélation.* Mémoires de l'Institut des Hautes Études chinoises, vol. 17. Paris: Collège de France.

―――. 1982. "The Tao among the Yao." In *Rekishi ni okeru minshū to bunka*, ed. by Sakai Tadao Sensei koki shukuga kinen no kai, 23–30. Tokyo: Kokusho kankōkai.

―――. 1983. "Chinese Oracles in Buddhist Vestments: Paper to the Berkeley Conference on Chinese Divination and Portent-lore." Typescript.

Strong, John. 1983. *The Legend of King Asoka: A Study and Translation of the "Asokāvadāna."* Princeton: Princeton University Press.

Stuart, Rev. G. A. 1911. *Chinese Materia Medica: Vegetable Kingdom.* Shanghai: American Presbyterian Mission Press.

Suzuki, D. T. 1930. *Studies in the Lankāvatāra Sūtra.* London: Rutledge and Kegan Paul.

Suzuki Seiichiro 鈴木清一郎. 1934. *Taiwan kyūkan kankonsōsai to nenchū gyōji* 臺灣舊慣冠婚葬祭と年中行事 [*Old Taiwanese Customs of Capping, Marriage, Burial, and Sacrifice and Seasonal Observances*]. Tr. by Gao Xianzhi 高賢治 and Feng Zuomin 馮作民 as *Taiwan jiuguan xisu xinyang* 臺灣舊慣習俗信仰 (Taipei: Zhongwen tushu gongsi, 1984).

Teiser, Stephen F. 1988. *The Ghost Festival in Medieval China.* Princeton: Princeton University Press.

Thompson, Laurence G. 1982. "The Moving Finger Writes: A Note on Revelation and Renewal in Chinese Religion." *Journal of Chinese Religions* 10 (Fall): 92–147.

Topley, Marjorie. 1974. "Cosmic antagonisms: A Mother-Child Syndrome." In *Religion and Ritual in Chinese Society*, ed. by Arthur P. Wolf, 233–50. Stanford: Stanford University Press.

Twitchett, Denis. 1959. "The Fan Clan's Charitable Estate, 1050–1760." In *Confucianism in Action*, ed. by David Nivison and Arthur Wright, 97–133. Stanford: Stanford University Press.

―――. 1960. "Documents on Clan Administration: I. The Rules of Administration of the Charitable Estate of the Fan Clan." *Asia Major* n.s. 8: 1–35.

Übelhör, Monika. 1989. "The Community Compact (Hsiang-yüeh) of the Sung and Its Educational Significance." In *Neo-Confucian Education: The Formative Stage*, ed. by Wm. Theodore deBary and John W. Chaffee, 371–88. Berkeley: University of California Press.

Umehara, Kaoru 梅原郁. 1985. *Sōdai kanryō seido kenkyū* 宋代官僚制度研究 [*A Study of the Bureaucratic System of the Song Dynasty*]. Kyoto: Dōhōsha.

Unschuld, Paul U. 1985. *Medicine in China: A History of Ideas.* Berkeley: University of California Press.

Verellen, Franciscus. 1989. *Du Guangting (850–933): Taoïste de Cour à la Fin de la Chine Médiévale.* Mémoires de l'Institut des Hautes Études Chinoises, 30. Paris: Collège de France.

Vervoorn, Aat. 1990. *Men of the Cliffs and Caves: The Development of the Chinese Eremetic Tradition to the End of the Han Dynasty.* Hong Kong: Chinese University Press.

Waley, Arthur. 1931. *The Travels of an Alchemist.* London: George Routledge.

——. 1937. *The Book of Songs.* London: George Allen and Unwin.

Wang, Daisheng 王代生. 1985. "Zhang Xianzhong yu Zitong Damiao" 張獻忠與梓潼大廟 ("Zhang Xianzhong and the Damiao Temple at Zitong"). *Sichuan wenwu* 1985.4: 51–53.

Wang, Sung-hsing. 1974. "Taiwanese Architecture and the Supernatural." In *Religion and Ritual in Chinese Society,* ed. by Arthur P. Wolf, 183–92. Stanford: Stanford University Press.

Wang Guoliang 王國良. 1984. *Wei, Jin, Nanbeichao zhiguai xiaoshuo yen-jiu* 魏晉南北朝志怪小說研究 [*A Study of Fiction Recording Anomalies of the Wei, Jin and Northern and Southern Dynasties Period*]. Taipei: Wenshizhe chubanshe.

Wang Yucheng 王育成. 1991. "Wuchang Nan-Qi Liu Ji diquan kefu chu-shi" 武昌南齊劉覬地券刻符初釋 ["A Preliminary Explication of the Engraved Charm on the Land Contract of Liu Ji of the Northern Qi dynasty Found in Wuchang"]. *Jiang-Han kaogu* 1991.2: 82–88.

Wang, Yü-ch'üan. 1949. "An Outline of the Central Government of the Former Han Dynasty." *Harvard Journal of Asian Studies* 12: 134–87.

Watt, John R. 1972. *The District Magistrate in Late Imperial China.* New York: Columbia University Press.

Ware, James. 1966. *Alchemy, Medicine, and Religion in the China of A.D. 320.* Cambridge: The M.I.T. Press.

Weng Tu-chien. 1935. *Combined Indices to the Authors and Titles of Books in Two Collections of Taoist Literature.* Harvard-Yenching Institute Sinological Index Series, 25. Beijing: Yenching Institute.

The White Cloud Daoist Temple. 1983. Peking: Chinese Daoist Association.

Winternitz, Maurice. 1927. *A History of Indian Literature.* Tr. by S. Ketkar and H. Kohn. 2 vols. Calcutta: University of Calcutta. Reprinted by Oriental Books Reprint Corporation, New Delhi, India, 1977.

Wolf, Margery. 1972. *Women and the Family in Rural Taiwan.* Stanford: Stanford University Press.

Worthy, Edmund H. 1975. "Regional Control in the Southern Salt Administration." In *Crisis and Prosperity in Sung China,* ed. by John Winthrop Haeger, 101–41. Tucson: University of Arizona Press.

Wu, Pei-yi. 1990. *The Confucian's Progress: Autobiographical Writings in Traditional China.* Princeton: Princeton University Press.

Yamada Toshiaki 山田利明. 1975. "Chūgoku no gakumonshin shinkō shotan" 中國の學問神信仰出探 ["A Preliminary Investigation of the Cult to China's God of Learning"]. *Tōyō gakujutsu kenkyū* 14.4: 141–57.

Yamaori Tetsuo 山折哲雄. 1989. "Kami to wa nani ka?" 神とは何か ["What Is a *kami*?"]. In *Nihon no kami* 日本の神, ed. by Yamaori Tetsuo. *Bessatsu Taiyō,* Winter.

Yang Cenglie 楊曾烈. 1990. "Lijiang Dongjing yinyue diaocha" 麗江洞經音樂調查 ["A Survey of the Dongjing Music of Lijiang"]. *Lijiang wenshi ziliao,* vol. 9 (Lijiang, Yunnan: Lijiangxian zhengxie wenshi ziliao weiyuanhui): 114–38.

Yang Diankui 楊殿奎. 1983. *Gudai wenhua changshi* 古代文化常識. Jinan, Shandong: Shandong jiaoyu chubanshe.

Yang, Lien-sheng. 1957. "The Concept of 'Pao' as a Basis for Social Relations in China." In *Chinese Thought and Institutions,* ed. by John K. Fairbank, 269–90. Chicago: University of Chicago Press.

Yao, Tao-chung. 1980. "Ch'üan-chen: A New Taoist Sect in North China during the Twelfth and Thirteenth Centuries." Ph.D. dissertation, University of Arizona.

Yi Shitong 伊世同. 1981. *Hengxing tubiao* 恆星圖表 [*Star Charts and Tables*]. Beijing: Kexue chubanshe.

Yoshioka Yoshitoyo. 1952. *Dōkyō no kenkyū* 道教の研究 [*A Study of Daoism*]. Kyoto: Hōzōkan.

———. 1959. *Dōkyō to Bukkyō* 道教と佛教 [*Daoism and Buddhism*]. Vol. 1. Tokyo: Kokusho kankōkai, 1970 reprint of 1959 original.

———. 1970. *Dōkyō to Bukkyō.* Vol. 2. Tokyo: Toshima shobō.

———. 1979. "Taoist Monastic Life." In *Facets of Taoism,* ed. by Holmes Welch and Anna Seidel, 229–52. New Haven: Yale University Press.

Yu, Anthony C. 1987. "Religion and Literature in China: The 'Obscure Way' of *The Journey to the West.* In *Tradition and Creativity: Essays on*

East Asian Civilization, ed. by Ching-I Tu, 109–54. New Brunswick, N.J.: Rutgers University Publications.

Yu Jiaxi 余嘉錫. 1980. *Siku tiyao bianzheng* 四庫提要辨證 [*On the Authenticity of Works in the Essentials of the Four Repositories*]. 4 vols. Beijing: Zhonghua shuju.

Zang Lihe 臧勵龢. 1936. *Zhongguo gujin diming da cidian* 中國古今地名大辭典 [*A Dicitionary of Ancient and Modern Chinese Place Names*]. Shanghai: Commercial Press.

Zhong Huacao 鍾華操. 1979. *Taiwan diqu shenming de youlai* 臺灣地區神明的由來 [*The Origins of Gods of the Taiwan Region*]. Taichung: Taiwansheng wenxian weiyuanhui.

Zürcher, Erik. 1959. *The Buddhist Conquest of China*. Leiden: Brill.

———. 1980. "Buddhist Influence on Early Taoism." *T'oung Pao* 66: 84–147.

Index

prefecture (*fu* 府): oversight of Zitong temple, 17
Primordial Heavenly King 元始天王, 20
Primordial Heavenly Worthy 元始天尊, 20, 95–96; statue of, 31
progeny, 190, 225; prayer for, 244, 268; sent by Wenchang, xi, 25, 34, 52, 192
Propitious Moisture 嘉澤, 185
prosimetric format, 60
Pu Guangdu 蒲光度, knight-errant, 171
punishment, corporal: of clerks, 260–61
Pure Covenant 清約, 258
pure criticism (*qingyi* 清議), 281
Purple Lady 紫姑, 9–10

qi 妻, primary wife, 228
Qi 戚: clan, 268, Lady Qi, consort of Liu Bang, 37, 43
Qi Bo 岐伯, legendary physician, 112
Qi 郪, 242
Qi 郪 River, 239
Qiang 羌 tribesmen, 158
Qin 秦 (state), 3, 194, 197, 201–8, 222; annexation of Shu, 250
Qin Shihuang 秦始皇, First Emperor of Qin, 238, 263
Qinghe 清河: as choronym of Zhang clan, 30; Wenchang as prefect of, 37, 277
Qingli 青黎山, Mount: god of, 164
Qionglai 邛徠, Mount, 160
Qingyi 清衣 stream, 222
Qiong Pool 邛池, 256, 267–68, 283
Qiongdu 邛都, 287
qiushe 秋社, autumn sacrifice to soil, 247–48
Qu 渠 River, 227

rain, 36, 269
Rang River 瀼水, 230
Ranming 然名: son of Wenchang, 137, 148
rape, 164, 254
realgar, 115
recitation: of *Transcendent Scripture of the Great Grotto*, 20
reclusion, 251–52
recommendation for office, 115, 165

Record of Investigations of the Divine (*Jishen lu* 稽神錄), 8
Record of Rites (*Liji* 禮記), 4, 32, 134, 146, 212, 237, 250n
Record of the Beginning and End of Lord Lao (*Laojun shizhong ji* 老君始終記), 61–62
Record of the Eighty-Five Transformations of the Perfected Lord Xu of West Mountain (*448 Xishan Xu Zhenjun bashiwu hua lu* 許眞君八十五化錄), 66
Record of the Land of Huayang (*Huayangguo zhi* 華陽國志), 1, 58, 194, 199, 203, 208
Record of the Revealed Sacred of the Supreme Thearch of the Mysterious Heaven (*958 Xuantian shangdi qisheng lu*), 64
Records of Clear Retribution (*Mingbao ji* 明報記), 60
Records of the Historian (*Shiji* 史記), 58, 168, 172, 202, 211
records: of individual conduct, 44
Red Thearch, 262–63
Register of the Great Grotto 大洞籙, 31, 108, 110
Register of the Transcendent Scripture of the Great Grotto 大洞仙經籙: revelation of, 18
Esoteric Biography of Qinghe (*Qinghe neizhuan* 清河內傳): revelation of, 18
registers, spirit 籙: produced through spirit writing, 12
reincarnation, 131, 177; of karmic groups, 37, 268
remonstrances: hidden, 118; result in death, 131, 133
retainer (*congshi* 從事), 250
retirement, 119–20
"Rhapsody on the Great Man" 大人賦, 163n
"Rhapsody on the Shu Capital" 蜀都賦, 157
Rite of the Great Grotto 大洞法, 18, 31, 108
rites (*li* 禮): as ethical principles, 51
Rites of Zhou (*Zhouli* 周禮), 157
ritual (*yi* 儀): revealed, 72, 293
Ruan Ji 阮籍 (210–63), 51
Rui Liangfu 芮良夫, 135

Zhang 張: clan, 88, 90, 122, 130; constellation, 29, 88; surname, 4, 29–30, 268, 281, 287

Zhang 章, Emperor of Han (r. 76–88), 279

Zhang Ezi 張噩子: identity of Wenchang, 3, 36, 272–73

Zhang Guang張光 (1062–1131): Song temple controller, 30

Zhang Jiugong 張九功 (1478 jinshi), 78–79

Zhang Jixian 張紀先 (1092–1126), 30th Celestial Master, 22

Zhang Jun 張浚 (1097–1164), 69

Zhang Liang 張良 (?–189 B.C.), 266

Zhang Shangying 張尚英 (1043–1121), 106

Zhang Shanxun 張善勳: incarnation of Wenchang, 29, 99–100

Zhang Wuji 張無忌: father, 133

Zhang Xianzhong 張獻忠 (1606–46), 39, 80

Zhang Xiaoyou 張孝友: alternate name of Wenchang, 23

Zhang Xiaozhong 張孝仲: incarnation of Wenchang, 37, 281

Zhang Xun 張勳: incarnation of Wenchang, 37, 277

Zhang Yi 張儀 (4th c. B.C.), 202, 223

Zhang Yu 張禹, 277–78

Zhang Yuchu 張宇初 (1361–1410), 43rd Celestial Master, 22n

Zhang Yuqing 張宇清 (1364–1427), 44th Celestial Master, 22n

Zhang Zai 張載 (1020–77), 161n

Zhang Zhengchang 張正常 (1335–77), 42nd Celestial Master, 22n

Zhang Zhongsi 忠嗣 (zi Zhong 仲): incarnation of Wenchang, 31, 133

Zhang Zhongzi 張仲子, transformation of Wenchang, 34, 198, 205–6, 251, 255

Zhang Zongyan 張宗演 (1244–1291), 36th Celestial Master, 22n

Zhao Hong, God of the Seas 海神晁閎, 274

Zhao Wen 趙文 (1239–1315), 72

Zhao 趙, princedom of, 277

Zheng Xuan 鄭玄 (127–200), 116

zhiguai. See accounts of anomalies

Zhongnan Mountains 終南山, 169

Zhou 紂, King of Shang, 199

Zhou Chang, Chancellor of Zhao and Marquis of Jianping 趙相建平侯周昌, 266

Zhou dynasty, 87

Zhou Hongmo 周洪謨 (1419–91), 78–79

Zhou Mi 周密 (1232–1308), 10

Zhou, Duke of 周公, 23, 118, 120, 121, 235

Zhou 紂, King of Shang, 159, 205

Zhu Xi 朱熹 (1130–1200), 148

Zhuang Su 莊甦, 194–95

Zhuangzi, 126

Zhuanxu顓頊: father of epidemic gods, 109

Zhuge Zhan 諸葛瞻 (227–63), 283–84

Zigong 子貢, disciple of Confucius, 224

Zishui 資水, 260

Zitong 梓潼: site of cult, 1

Zixia 子夏, 251

zodiac, Chinese, 258

Zuo Si 左思 (250?–310), 157

Zuozhuan. See Traditions of Zuo

Zürcher, Erik, 211